COLLEGE
BASKETBALL'S 25 GREATEST
TEAMS

COLLEGE
BASKETBALL'S 25 GREATEST
TEAMS

BILLY PACKER
& ROLAND LAZENBY

The Sporting News

BOOK PUBLISHING

Published in the United States by THE SPORTING NEWS
Publishing Co., 1212 North Lindbergh Boulevard,
St. Louis, Missouri 63132.

Library of Congress Catalog Card Number: 89-63063

ISBN: 0-89204-314-8
10 9 8 7 6 5 4 3 2 1

First Edition

Contents

College Basketball's 25 Greatest Teams

Number 1   UCLA, 1966-67, 1967-68, 1968-69............................Page 11

Number 2   Indiana, 1975-76............................Page 23

Number 3   UCLA, 1971-72, 1972-73............................Page 33

Number 4   San Francisco, 1954-55, 1955-56............................Page 43

Number 5   Kentucky, 1953-54............................Page 53

Number 6   Ohio State, 1959-60, 1960-61, 1961-62 ....Page 61

Number 7   Kentucky, 1947-48, 1948-49............................Page 71

Number 8   Cincinnati, 1960-61, 1961-62............................Page 81

Number 9   North Carolina State, 1973-74 ....Page 91

Number 10   Michigan State, 1978-79............................Page 101

Number 11   Houston, 1967-68............................Page 111

Number 12   UCLA, 1963-64............................Page 121

Number 13   Oklahoma, 1987-88............................Page 131

Number 14   North Carolina, 1956-57............................Page 141

Number 15   City College of New York, 1949-50............................Page 149

Number 16   Cincinnati, 1959-60............................Page 159

Number 17   Georgetown, 1983-84, 1984-85............................Page 167

Number 18   North Carolina, 1981-82............................Page 177

Number 19   Indiana, 1952-53............................Page 187

Number 20   Louisville, 1985-86............................Page 195

Number 21   Kansas, 1956-57............................Page 205

Number 22   Oklahoma A&M, 1944-45, 1945-46............................Page 213

Number 23   Houston, 1982-83............................Page 221

Number 24   Seton Hall, 1952-53............................Page 231

Number 25   Maryland, 1973-74............................Page 239

Acknowledgments

The authors would like to thank Greg Wiley, Book Publisher of The Sporting News, for the opportunity to do this book. We also would like to thank Ron Smith, Editorial Director of Books and Periodicals, as well as TSN editors Joe Hoppel and Steve Zesch for their long hours of shaping and directing the material.

In addition, we would like to recognize the editorial assistance and research work of Karen Lazenby, Ricky Lovegrove, Bob Hartman and Happy Chandler.

The authors also benefited greatly from the work of Jim Van Valkenburg, the NCAA's director of statistics, and the helpful assistance of the various sports information departments of the schools represented in this book.

Most of all, we would like to thank the many people who consented to be interviewed for this effort. They gave us one of their most valuable possessions—their memories.

Photographs

Some of the photographs appearing in this book came from the extensive basketball files of Malcolm Emmons. Many others were provided courtesy of the following schools: Indiana, Kentucky, Cincinnati, North Carolina State, Houston, Oklahoma, North Carolina, City College of New York, Kansas, Oklahoma State, Seton Hall and Maryland.

Special contributions were made by the Lawrence (Kan.) Journal-World, which provided a photo of Wilt Chamberlain during his playing days at Kansas, and author John Russell, who provided two photos of his father, former Seton Hall Coach Honey Russell, which appeared in a 1986 biography, "Honey Russell, Between Games, Between Halves," printed by Dryad Press.

Introduction

By Billy Packer

Lee Rose, a man who has taken two schools to the Final Four in the course of a varied and colorful coaching career, was once accused of saying that basketball was a life-and-death situation. He denied ever making such a comment.

"I feel it's much more important than that," said Rose, who directed UNC Charlotte and Purdue to Final Four berths in 1977 and 1980, respectively.

People have often said I take the same attitude toward college hoops. It's true. There are some nights when I think there's nothing in the world more important than a basketball game.

This may sound odd, but the reason I take basketball so seriously is that I find it so much fun. It's been that way from the time I was a grade-school gym rat hanging around the college team (Lehigh) my father coached in Bethlehem, Pa. It remains that way with each college game I broadcast for CBS Sports.

Roland Lazenby, the editors of The Sporting News and I are hoping that fans will take the same approach with our selection of "College Basketball's 25 Greatest Teams." Take the rankings as seriously as you want, but have fun with them.

Most important, remember the selections aren't set in stone. A book like this should create debate.

After all, there have been innumerable great teams in the history of the game—including many that easily could have made our list, but didn't. College basketball is the sport of the underdog, the Cinderella. It always seems that as soon as a team reaches the top, it's destined to fall. Picking a Top 20 each year seems to drive the pollsters crazy. Imagine how wacky it becomes when you attempt to pick 'em for the ages.

Heck, even I don't agree with a team or two on the final list of 25. Maybe that's because we were aided by a computer in making our selections, and while I won some of the arguments, the computer clearly won some, too.

Computer expert Jeff Sagarin, a serious basketball junkie, contributed analysis based on such factors as available statistics, won-lost records and strength of schedules. As he explained, the older a team is, the more difficult it is to evaluate. Statistics simply weren't as complete in the 1940s, '50s and '60s as they are today. For example, because of the lack of data, two of the old-time teams on our Top 25—Oklahoma A&M from the mid-1940s and Seton Hall, 1952-53—didn't receive computer rankings.

In fairness to the computer, we should acknowledge that when it did have all the necessary "tools," it acted with considerable impact. On a preliminary list of teams drawn up when this book was in its formative stage, high rankings were assigned to North Carolina, 1971-72, 1983-84 and 1986-87; Arizona, 1987-88; Jacksonville, 1969-70; Notre Dame, 1973-74, and St. Bonaventure, 1969-70. Fed with all the relevant information, the computer coughed out its decision: These teams, while highly talented, fell short of being Top 25 material.

The lowest-ranked computer teams to make our select list were Louisville, 1985-86, and Georgetown, 1983-84 and 1984-85. That Louisville team, you probably recall, won the NCAA championship, while Georgetown captured the national crown in '84 and wound up a one-point loser in the '85 title game.

The winning of championships was a factor in our thinking. But our list includes more than a few schools with no NCAA titles to their credit and even contains one team, Maryland, 1973-74, that failed to win a conference championship. The computer, by the way, ranked Maryland among the best 15 teams of all time. We modified that a bit—titles really have to be some kind of yardstick—and listed the Terrapins at No. 25.

For practical purposes, we did not include teams from schools that already were well-represented. For example, the UCLA team of 1969-70 fell from the list because the Bruins' run of great teams tended to blur together. The same held for Kentucky's 1950-51 team.

And our ranking of the teams that *did* make the list is just as open to question. Boston Celtics President Red Auerbach shook his head when told that the Lew Alcindor-led UCLA team was ranked above Bill Russell's San Francisco squad.

"I don't know," he said. "I like Kareem (Abdul-Jabbar, as Alcindor has long been known). He's a hell of a guy. I am a little prejudiced, a lot preju-

diced, to Russell. But Russell came out with the greatest statement of all. The media once asked him, 'Well, how do you think you'd do against Kareem?' Russell said, 'You've got the question wrong. The question is, how do you think Kareem would do against me?' And that was right. You never know. It's like who was the best fighter, Joe Louis or Muhammad Ali. There is no way of telling."

Told that we had received some assistance from a computer, Auerbach again shook his head. "Computers," he said, "can never creep into people's competitive attitudes. Not that Abdul-Jabbar wasn't a great competitor. But Russell continually rose to occasions. Abdul-Jabbar did, too. Abdul-Jabbar was a giant among men, he was so much bigger than everybody else. What would have happened if they were playing face-to-face? I don't know. Russell would have devised something to affect that sky hook. Look at how Russell adjusted against Wilt Chamberlain. To me, he outplayed Chamberlain nine out of 10 times."

Dick Harp, former Kansas coach, also questioned some of the findings. Informed that the Chamberlain-led Kansas team of 1956-57, a squad he had coached, made the list, Harp said those Jayhawks were no better than Phog Allen's 1951-52 Kansas team. The early-'50s Jayhawks, featuring Clyde Lovellette, won the NCAA championship.

Sagarin would be the first to admit that his computer was hardly infallible. But the technology allowed us to cross the decades for comparisons of legendary teams.

Until someone invents a time machine, our imaginations and the computers are the best we have. So, read on and dream. Dream of Russell vs. Kareem. Magic Johnson against Oscar Robertson. Chamberlain vs. Bob Kurland. Patrick Ewing against Jerry Lucas. Today vs. yesterday.

ONE

The Center Of Attention

UCLA

Kareem Abdul-Jabbar.

The name is charismatic, suggesting power and dominance. And for 20 professional seasons, 14 with the Los Angeles Lakers of the National Basketball Association, his play on the court supported that notion, perpetuating the almost-reverential predictions of stardom that can be traced back as far as Kareem's high school career at Power Memorial Academy in New York.

In those days, before his conversion to Islam, he was known by his given name—Lew Alcindor. Al-CIN-dor. That, too, conjured a vision of power, and the youngster provided plenty of that for three glorious seasons at UCLA in the late 1960s. The pairing of "Big Lew," as the writers dubbed the lanky 7-foot-1 center, with Coach John Wooden was like combining the Lakers with the Boston Celtics. The rest of the college basketball world simply did not have a chance. They formed the heart and soul of the greatest college team ever assembled.

To Wooden, Alcindor was just plain "Lewis." He went out of his way to treat the youngster as just another member of the team and only in retrospect would he accord Alcindor his due, calling him "the most valuable college player ever." Even then Wooden qualified his praise, emphasizing that "most valuable" didn't necessarily mean most talented or most outstanding. It simply meant that Alcindor was a gifted, versatile athlete who was able to take his team beyond the sum of its players.

Wooden's distinction, however, falls short. Without doubt, Alcindor was the best college-age center in history, the kind of player to whom all the adjectives apply. Complete. Well-schooled. Intelligent.

Dominating. He was the once-in-a-lifetime player around which a dynasty could be built.

There was, of course, another reason behind UCLA's dominance. The Bruins had the best coach.

Perhaps more than anyone, Wooden set the age of modern college basketball in motion. His UCLA teams popularized the sport and attracted national television. His zone press foreshadowed the age of high-tech defenses.

Wooden was an enigma, combining his liberal basketball ideas with an old-school personality. A deeply religious man (he was a deacon in his Santa Monica, Calif., church), Wooden's horn-rimmed glasses and slight stature (5-10) gave him the appearance of an English professor and, indeed, he liked to inspire his players with well-chosen verse. Writers, always looking for new adjectives, reached for idyllic images, turning to the Bible and Wooden's rural Indiana upbringing. He once was described as "the only basketball coach from the Old Testament."

This image cloaked the fact that Wooden was an intense competitor, one of the most intense in the history of the game. With his great eye for detail, he focused those competitive energies into a laserlike precision, which he used to cut the hearts out of opponents. In the dozen seasons between 1963-64 and 1974-75, his teams won 10 NCAA championships. This competitiveness as a coach was an extension of his intensity as a player. He had been an all-state high school performer in Indiana, and later a three-time All-America at Purdue under Coach Piggy Lambert.

His understanding of the game grew from the lessons Lambert had taught him about up-tempo bas-

The pairing of Coach John Wooden and big Lew Alcindor was fortuitous for UCLA, foreboding for the rest of college basketball.

ketball. After 11 years as a high school coach and a stint in the Navy during World War II, Wooden coached two years at Indiana State before accepting the UCLA job in 1948. It was an unheralded urban school at that time, with a losing basketball team and a small gym. But Wooden quickly turned that around. He did it with his knack for precision, which was especially evident in his carefully choreographed practices.

"I am not a strategic coach," he once said. "I am a practice coach." Each session was organized tightly to run his players through a barrage of drills, conditioning and scrimmaging. He always saved the scrimmaging for the end so that his players would learn to function when they were most tired.

Like a computer-aided design system, his mind seemed to view the game from every angle. Often he would watch his practices from the upper seats in a gymnasium to get a view of the entire floor. As Marv Harshman, the former Washington State coach once said, Wooden made adjustments during a game better than anyone. It was his complete view of the game that aided these adjustments.

But the hidden factor in Wooden's success was the soft-spoken coach's intense, almost consuming, desire to win an NCAA championship. He admitted later that he almost wanted it too badly. His early teams at UCLA were good (the Bruins never experienced a losing season under Wooden), but during his first 15 years, he failed to rise above the regional competition. Either he was falling short against Phil Woolpert's San Francisco powerhouses (featuring Bill Russell) or Pete Newell's University of California teams.

But he learned and grew as a coach during those years. Then in the early 1960s, Wooden hired one of his former players, Jerry Norman, as an assistant. Wooden had never enjoyed recruiting and Norman proved invaluable in that capacity. He could handle the face-to-face work, the selling of the program to recruits, which Wooden was reluctant to do. Norman also urged Wooden toward the zone press, which the UCLA coach had used in one form or another over the years. That combination led to UCLA's first national championship in 1964.

The timing could not have been better. Alcindor was a junior at Power Memorial and the most-coveted high school player since Wilt Chamberlain a decade earlier. An only child, Alcindor was quiet and bookwormish. His mother, Cora, was a singer and his father, Lew Sr., studied at the Julliard School of Music while working as a transit policeman.

As Power Memorial kept winning (the Manhattan-based Catholic high school won 71 straight games over one stretch), the pressure of Alcindor's college selection mounted. "I'll trade two first-round draft picks for him right now," quipped Coach Gene Shue of the NBA's Baltimore Bullets.

Alcindor's high school coach, Jack Donohue, had announced that his player's recruitment would be tightly controlled. College coaches weren't allowed to so much as speak to Alcindor, who presumably spent plenty of time perusing the hundreds of recruiting brochures and pamphlets sent by colleges.

Those circumstances aided Wooden and Norman. Based 3,000 miles away, they played by Donohue's rules and pursued the youngster in a low-key, unassuming manner. The fact that the reputations of both Wooden and the UCLA program were rapidly growing was simply a matter of good timing.

Donohue phoned Wooden early in the spring of 1964 and informed him that UCLA was one of the five schools Alcindor wanted to visit. Several weeks later, the two coaches met when Wooden flew east for a speaking engagement. "When I talked to Jab-

The 1966-67 Bruins combined the intimidating presence of Alcindor (left) in the middle with the lightning-quick moves of guard Lucius Allen (above).

UCLA's super sophomores of 1966-67: (left to right) Alcindor, Allen, Kenny Heitz and Lynn Shackelford.

bar's coach," Wooden said, "I asked him a favor: to let UCLA be the last of Jabbar's five visits, if possible. He said nobody else had asked for that, and he thought it would be all right."

That next year, Alcindor traveled to Los Angeles, where he was impressed by Wooden's unassuming manner, by the California culture and by UCLA's new arena under construction—Pauley Pavilion.

"At the conclusion of his 48-hour visit, he said, 'I'm coming to UCLA,'" Wooden recalled. "Then, to show you what kind of individual he is, sometime later he called me and asked me if I would come and visit his folks. He said his parents would

like to meet the coach for whom he was going to play.

"I talked to our athletic director and he said, 'They're Catholic, so why don't you take along Jerry Norman because he's Catholic and they might want to ask you some questions.' So Jerry and I took the trip, and we met Kareem's parents at 1 o'clock in the morning because his father was working the noon-to-midnight shift.

"I think what probably swayed Kareem more than anything was that we had just won our first national championship and had gone undefeated that year. The next year, his senior year, we won

The outmanned Dayton Flyers did everything they could to stop Alcindor in the 1967 NCAA Tournament championship game, but the Bruins coasted to their 30th straight victory.

It was celebration time for Mike Warren (left), the only junior starter in UCLA's sophomore-dominated lineup, and Alcindor after the Bruins' 1967 title-game victory over Dayton.

again. Now we really had his attention. Then, when he came out to UCLA, he saw that he would be playing in the new building, Pauley Pavilion. We would never have gotten him if we'd still been playing in that old gym with only two baskets, where I swept the floor every day before practice, and if we were still playing our home games at Santa Monica City College or Venice High School.

"So, as far as recruiting was concerned, I hardly recruited Kareem at all. He more or less just came to UCLA on his own."

On May 4, 1965, Alcindor announced his decision at a press conference in the Power Memorial gym. "This fall, I'll be attending UCLA in Los Angeles," he told a large assembly of reporters.

From the perspective of two decades, it is obvious that the young Alcindor made just the right decision—good for himself, good for Wooden, good for the game. Arguably, Alcindor could have gone to other schools and won three NCAA championships. But more than any other coach, Wooden was the best man to appreciate Alcindor's bountiful tal-

ent and to mold a system to help him reach his potential.

That doesn't mean Alcindor's transition from New York City to Los Angeles, from high school to college, was easy. He had been well protected from the outside world and immediately suffered a serious case of homesickness. He told reporters at one point that he wished UCLA could be transported to Times Square.

Fortunately for Wooden, the youngster weathered his personal storm and focused his attention on basketball. To develop his presence around the basket, Wooden had Alcindor spend much of his freshman year working with Jay Carty, a 6-8 graduate student who had played at Oregon State. Other members of an exceptional freshman team were Lucius Allen, a lightning-quick shooting guard, forward Lynn Shackelford, a deadly corner shooter, and Kenny Heitz, a 6-3 swingman who excelled on defense.

The college basketball world got its first foreboding glimpse of the future when this group met the

UCLA varsity in a 1965-66 preseason scrimmage and pounded out a 75-60 victory. The varsity, ranked No. 1 in most preseason polls that year after winning the national championship in 1964-65, couldn't handle Alcindor, who scored 31 points, grabbed 21 rebounds and blocked eight shots. It was no great surprise when the freshmen went on to enjoy a perfect season.

Wooden offered praise sparingly, but even he conceded early that Alcindor could be awesome. "At times, he even frightens me," the coach told reporters.

When they got their first exposure to prime-time basketball in 1966-67, the sophomores were everything they were cracked up to be—and more.

The four young Bruins combined with junior guard Mike Warren to create a starting unit that made a mockery of opponents. Alcindor ran through a variety of dunks and bank shots in his first varsity game against Southern Cal, setting a school record with 56 points in the Bruins' 105-90 victory. The Bruins' lethal zone press and up-tempo offense set the tone for what would become a three-year reign of terror.

Wooden set Alcindor in a low-post offense that season, maximizing the advantage of his skills and height. On defense, his rebounds and strong outlet passes keyed a quick break. When the zones became a little too tight around the big man, Allen and Shackelford loosened things with their perimeter shooting.

Allen was UCLA's Mr. Outside and a perfect complement to Alcindor. And like Big Lew, he was the target of a massive recruiting campaign in 1964 and '65 as his career at Wyondotte High School in Kansas City, Kan., wound to a close.

Playing as a 6-2 forward, Allen helped Wyondotte compile a 66-3 record in his three varsity seasons en route to two Kansas state championships. Like Alcindor, he was attracted by UCLA's recent success and the opportunity to play for a winner.

"The winning tradition," he told reporters when asked why he had chosen UCLA. "I like their style of play. It's a real team brand of ball."

Teaming in the Bruins backcourt with the equally quick Warren, who would go on to greater fame as police officer Bobby Hill in the hit television series "Hill Street Blues," Allen became a big part of that winning tradition, as did the 6-4 Shackelford, another highly recruited youngster who played his high school ball in beautiful downtown Burbank (Calif.), averaging 25 points his senior year.

The only obstacle in UCLA's path to a perfect 1966-67 regular season was the stall tactics adopted by some opponents. Southern Cal, victimized by the Bruins' relentless running attack in two prior games, slowed the ball down in a later meeting and almost pulled off a major upset. After leading, 17-14, at the half, the Trojans took the game to over-

After losing to Houston at the Astrodome in 1968, Alcindor (33) and the Bruins avenged the defeat with a victory over Elvin Hayes (44) and the Cougars in the NCAA Tournament semifinals.

time before falling, 40-35.

Beyond that game and another slowdown effort by Oregon, UCLA's progress was unimpeded. The Bruins entered the NCAA Tournament undefeated in 26 games and continued to roll, defeating Wyoming, 109-60, and Pacific, 80-64, to set up a meeting with Houston and junior consensus All-America Elvin Hayes, "the Big E," in the national semifinals at Louisville.

It would be the first of three highly publicized meetings between the two teams during the Alcindor era, meetings that would bring a new luster to the evolving image of college basketball. Hayes, an outspoken 6-8 forward, commented before the game that the UCLA center was overrated. But the rest of the basketball community was busy debating if there was any realistic way for anybody to stop him.

Bob Boyd, the coach at Southern Cal, maintained that the slowdown game was the only chance. Boston Celtics Coach Red Auerbach suggested that opponents might want to clog the middle—with the reservation that this method might result in excessive fouling. Double-teaming was another alternative, but Newell said that would be a waste of time because Alcindor would score any-

Alcindor's last hurrah in a UCLA uniform came in 1969 when he led the Bruins past Purdue in the NCAA championship game and then celebrated for the third straight year by cutting down the net.

way.

Houston Coach Guy Lewis decided his best strategy was to go directly at Alcindor with the idea of getting him in foul trouble. The Cougars boasted a burly front line of Hayes, 6-8 Don Kruse and 6-7 Melvin Bell with 6-5 guard Don Chaney running their offense. Houston literally lived and died with its inside game.

Lewis' strategy worried both Wooden and Norman, who spent the days before the game reminding Shackelford and Heitz that they would have to do their share of the muscle work. And, as expected, the Cougars came out strong, crashing the boards and forging a slight lead early in the game.

But Alcindor did not foul and observers sat on the edge of their seats waiting for the inevitable explosion. It happened at about the eight-minute mark when Shackelford hit on a long-range shot and the UCLA press forced a turnover. From there, the Bruins opened a lead and went on to win with ease, 73-58.

Hayes was less than gracious in defeat, claiming

that his teammates had choked and repeating his opinion that Alcindor was overrated. "He's not aggressive enough on the boards, particularly on offense," Hayes said. "Defensively, he just stands around. He's not all, you know, all they really put him up to be."

Alcindor did not comment as he and his teammates focused on the national championship game against Dayton, a Cinderella team with a 6-6 center (Dan Sadlier) and a high-scoring forward (Don May). As expected, the Flyers, who had stunned North Carolina in the semifinals, could not match up with Alcindor and fell behind early, 20-4. With the skinny, bespectacled Heitz doing a masterful defensive job against May, UCLA coasted to the national championship, 79-64. The victory allowed the Bruins to match the 30-0 record of Wooden's 1964 team and provided UCLA with its third national title in four years.

Alcindor was the obvious choice as the tournament's outstanding player. He completed his first season with a 29-point average, making 66.7 percent of his field-goal attempts, an NCAA record. Allen (15.5 points), Warren (12.7) and Shackelford (11.4) also averaged in double figures.

Even in victory, the Bruins got an unsettling taste of how life in the winner's circle would become. When May fell hard to the floor after colliding with Heitz early in the championship game, the crowd of 18,892 became vocal and derisive against UCLA. Suddenly they were being perceived as the bully Bruins—a perception that helped draw them closer together.

"We're not very popular, are we?" asked Heitz, an honors student. "You know, we're even starting to feel hurt. We're not a bully team at all. You practically have to smash Lew in the mouth before he gets tough."

The NCAA did exactly that before the 1967-68 season, outlawing the slam dunk in an apparent attempt to neutralize Alcindor. Ironically, the move actually worked in his favor because the slam was the only shot he found difficult to defend. With opponents forced to shoot from short range, Alcindor was able to swat more of their attempts to the hinterlands.

"Kareem was amazing," Wooden said. "As a freshman, he was largely instrumental in beating our varsity. I think he amazed a lot of people in his early career, and I think a lot of them got so interested in watching him that they forgot to play on occasion. But he was a very unselfish player, and he made every player on our team much better at each end of the court."

Wooden found himself with something of a traffic jam in 1967-68. Talented forwards Edgar Lacey and Mike Lynn, starters on the 1965-66 team, returned after missing a year because of injury (Lacey) and suspension (Lynn). So Wooden switched to a double-post offense, with Lynn and Lacey alternating at the high post.

In the season opener, Purdue and high-scoring Rick Mount pushed the Bruins to the limit before UCLA reserve Bill Sweek scored at the buzzer for a 73-71 victory that preserved the Bruins' win streak. It would continue through 47 games, until UCLA met Houston and Hayes in the Astrodome before 52,693 fans (an NCAA record) and a national television audience.

Houston was ranked second behind UCLA and had run up a 17-game streak of its own. The Cougars, last beaten in the 1967 NCAA Tournament semifinals by UCLA, had not lost at home in 48 games. It was one of the most ballyhooed basketball games ever, the big-talking Hayes finally getting his chance for revenge against UCLA's giant center.

Alcindor, unfortunately, was only operating at three-quarters speed. He had suffered a scratched eyeball the week before and had sat out two games. He elected to play against Houston, however, and quickly discovered that he was no match for the pumped-up Hayes on this day.

Alcindor, wearing an eyepatch, connected on only four of 18 field-goal attempts while Hayes scored 39 points, grabbed 15 rebounds and blocked eight shots in Houston's 71-69 victory. Hayes sealed the verdict when he sank two free throws with 28 seconds remaining. Houston, at least temporarily, was king of the basketball hill.

"I don't think it was a great basketball game," Wooden recalled, "but it was a great spectacle in which Elvin Hayes had one of the greatest individual performances I've ever seen. But, generally speaking, individual performances don't win basketball games. We felt that we were a better basketball team, and we sincerely hoped we would play them again. And when we did, we were ready."

Houston continued through the season undefeated, as did UCLA. But in the aftermath of the loss to Houston, Lacey had quit the team. The talented forward had been angered at his benching in the second half of that game. With Lacey gone, Wooden

Season Results
1966-67 (30-0)

105	Southern California	90	
88	Duke	54	
107	Duke	87	
84	Colorado State	74	
96	Notre Dame	67	
100	Wisconsin*	56	
91	Georgia Tech*	72	
107	Southern California*	83	
76	At Washington State	67	
83	At Washington	68	
96	California	78	
116	Stanford	78	
122	Portland	57	
119	UC Santa Barbara	75	
82	Loyola at Chicago	67	
120	Illinois at Chicago	82	
40	At Southern California (OT)	35	
76	Oregon State	44	
100	Oregon	66	
34	At Oregon	25	
72	At Oregon State	50	
71	Washington	43	
100	Washington State	78	
75	At Stanford	47	
103	At California	66	
83	Southern California	55	
109	Wyoming at Corvallis, Ore.†	60	
80	Pacific at Corvallis, Ore.†	64	
73	Houston at Louisville†	58	
79	Dayton at Louisville†	64	

*Los Angeles Classic
†NCAA Tournament

1967-68 (29-1)

73	At Purdue	71	
120	Wichita State	86	
121	Iowa State	80	
109	Bradley	73	
114	Notre Dame	63	
95	Minnesota*	55	
108	St. Louis*	67	
104	Wyoming*	71	
97	Washington State	69	
93	Washington	65	
94	At California	64	
75	At Stanford	63	
93	Portland	69	
69	At Houston	71	
90	Holy Cross at New York	67	
84	Boston College at N.Y.	77	
101	Southern California	67	
55	At Oregon State	52	
104	At Oregon	63	
119	Oregon	78	
88	Oregon State	71	
84	At Washington	64	
101	At Washington State	70	
100	Stanford	62	
115	California	71	
72	At Southern California	64	
58	N.M. State at Albuquerque†	49	
87	S. Clara at Albuquerque†	66	
101	Houston at Los Angeles†	69	
78	N. Carolina at Los Angeles†	55	

*Los Angeles Classic
†NCAA Tournament

1968-69 (29-1)

94	Purdue	82	
84	At Ohio State	73	
88	At Notre Dame	75	
90	Minnesota	51	
95	West Virginia	56	
98	Providence at New York*	81	
83	Princeton at New York*	67	
74	St. John's at New York*	56	
96	Tulane	64	
93	At Oregon	64	
83	At Oregon State	64	
100	Houston	64	
81	Northwestern at Chicago*	67	
84	Loyola at Chicago	65	
109	California	74	
98	Stanford	61	
62	Washington	51	
108	Washington State	80	
83	At Washington State	59	
53	At Washington	44	
91	Oregon State	66	
103	Oregon	69	
81	At Stanford	60	
84	At California	77	
61	At Southern California (OT)	55	
44	Southern California	46	
53	N.M. St. at Los Angeles†	38	
90	Santa Clara at Los Angeles†	52	
85	Drake at Louisville†	82	
92	Purdue at Louisville†	72	

*Holiday Festival
†NCAA Tournament

With the loss of Allen to academic problems, John Vallely took over as a starting guard in 1968-69 and averaged 11 points per game.

returned to the low-post offense with Alcindor as the single center.

The Bruins' defensive teeth were their 2-2-1 and 1-2-1-1 zone presses. Playing with renewed vigor, they literally hammered their competition en route to a rematch with Houston in the national semifinals at the Final Four in the Los Angeles Sports Arena.

Again it was No. 1 versus No. 2, but this time the payback was more than a bit unpleasant for the Cougars. Allen, Lynn and Alcindor shared scoring honors with 19 points apiece and Big Lew added 18 rebounds as UCLA humiliated Houston, 101-69, dispelling any doubts about its superiority. Hayes, who had averaged 41 points per game in the tournament, managed only 10, spending most of the night frustrated by the Bruins' diamond-and-one defense. Shackelford got the defensive assignment against college basketball's 1967-68 Player of the Year and did a splendid job of denying him the ball. The Cougars, also victimized by UCLA's intense full-court press, shot only 28.2 percent from the field.

"Houston was a great basketball team," Wooden recalled. "They had a lot of talent, and Hayes was a great individual player. Early in the second half, we led them by 44 points, and we could have won by a lot more than we did. Our starting five all scored something like 14 to 18 points.

"Our players still felt from the loss to them in the Astrodome earlier in the year. We felt we were a better basketball team, and from the time they beat us they were the No. 1-ranked team, as far as the polls were concerned. Polls are only man-made types of things and aren't all that meaningful, but, nevertheless, we knew about them.

"I felt my biggest problem would be to keep us from becoming too emotional, because the players really wanted that one. After that game, I thought we might have a tremendous letdown against North Carolina in the championship game. Fortunately, we didn't."

North Carolina, featuring Charlie Scott and Larry Miller, had ousted Ohio State in the other semifinal, but the Tar Heels didn't have the talent to stay with UCLA. Alcindor scored 34 points and grabbed 16 rebounds in the Bruins' 78-55 victory, sealing his second tournament MVP award and handing Wooden his fourth championship in five years.

The supporting cast changed considerably for Alcindor's third varsity season, but the final result didn't. Gone were Warren, Lynn and Allen, a victim of academics. Taking their place were a pair of talented sophomore forwards, Curtis Rowe and Sidney Wicks, and junior college transfer John Vallely, whom Wooden paired in the backcourt with Heitz.

This was not a particularly happy season for the introspective Alcindor, who generated a lot of criti-

1967 UCLA

Head Coach—John Wooden   Final Record—30-0

Player	Pos.	Hgt.	Wgt.	Cl.	G	FG	FGA	Pct.	FT.	FTA	Pct.	Reb.	Pts.	Avg.
Lew Alcindor	C	7-1	230	So.	30	346	519	.667	178	274	.650	466	870	29.0
Lucius Allen	G	6-2	180	So.	30	187	390	.479	92	129	.713	175	466	15.5
Mike Warren	G	5-10	160	Jr.	30	144	310	.465	94	124	.758	134	382	12.7
Lynn Shackelford	F	6-5	190	So.	30	143	298	.480	55	67	.821	177	341	11.4
Ken Heitz	F	6-3	180	So.	30	78	154	.506	27	45	.600	95	183	6.1
Bill Sweek	F-G	6-3	192	So.	30	58	121	.479	26	46	.565	85	142	4.7
Jim Nielsen	C-F	6-7	205	So.	27	54	104	.519	15	33	.455	91	123	4.6
Don Saffer	G	6-1	170	Jr.	27	32	71	.451	13	24	.542	22	77	2.9
Gene Sutherland	G	6-1	175	Jr.	20	15	33	.455	7	12	.583	15	37	1.9
Neville Saner	F-C	6-6	212	Jr.	24	12	39	.308	10	15	.667	46	34	1.4
Joe Chrisman	F	6-3	185	Jr.	19	8	25	.320	4	11	.364	28	20	1.1
Dick Lynn	F	6-2	177	So.	9	4	13	.308	2	21	.095	7	10	1.1
Kent Taylor	F	6-2	180	So.	4	1	5	.200	0	0	.000	1	2	0.5
Team												153		
UCLA					30	1082	2082	.520	523	801	.653	1495	2687	89.6
Opponents					30	779	1989	.392	352	570	.618	1196	1910	63.7

1968 UCLA

Head Coach—John Wooden   Final Record—29-1

Player	Pos.	Hgt.	Wgt.	Cl.	G	FG	FGA	Pct.	FT.	FTA	Pct.	Reb.	Pts.	Avg.
Lew Alcindor	C	7-2	230	Jr.	28	294	480	.613	146	237	.616	461	734	26.2
Lucius Allen	G	6-2	178	Jr.	30	186	403	.462	80	118	.678	181	452	15.1
Mike Warren	G	5-11	155	Sr.	30	152	353	.431	58	76	.763	111	362	12.1
Edgar Lacey	F	6-6	190	Sr.	14	72	125	.576	22	32	.688	110	166	11.9
Lynn Shackelford	F	6-5	192	Jr.	30	146	293	.498	28	33	.848	151	320	10.7
Mike Lynn	F	6-7	205	Sr.	30	128	280	.457	54	79	.684	156	310	10.3
Ken Heitz	G	6-3	181	Jr.	27	59	118	.500	26	35	.743	62	144	5.3
Jim Nielsen	F	6-7	205	Jr.	30	58	117	.496	23	35	.657	99	139	4.6
Bill Sweek	G	6-3	186	Jr.	27	40	85	.471	17	26	.654	32	97	3.6
Gene Sutherland	G	6-1	177	Sr.	27	10	24	.417	23	26	.885	15	43	1.6
Neville Saner	C	6-6	212	Sr.	24	16	43	.372	3	5	.600	38	35	1.5
Team												187		
UCLA					30	1161	2321	.500	480	702	.684	1603	2802	93.4
Opponents					30	781	2029	.385	453	688	.658	1238	2015	67.2

1969 UCLA

Head Coach—John Wooden   Final Record—29-1

Player	Pos.	Hgt.	Wgt.	Cl.	G	FG	FGA	Pct.	FT.	FTA	Pct.	Reb.	Pts.	Avg.
Lew Alcindor	C	7-1	235	Sr.	30	303	477	.635	115	188	.612	440	721	24.0
Curtis Rowe	F	6-6	216	So.	30	144	287	.502	99	146	.678	237	387	12.9
John Vallely	G	6-2	177	Jr.	28	116	234	.496	77	102	.755	91	309	11.0
Sidney Wicks	F	6-8	220	So.	30	84	193	.435	58	100	.580	153	226	7.5
Lynn Shackelford	F	6-5	190	Sr.	30	94	203	.463	22	44	.500	121	210	7.0
Ken Heitz	G	6-3	180	Sr.	30	84	180	.467	26	38	.684	69	194	6.5
Bill Sweek	G	6-3	188	Sr.	30	80	158	.506	30	48	.625	66	190	6.3
Steve Patterson	C	6-9	221	So.	29	58	110	.527	30	40	.750	112	146	5.0
Don Saffer	G	6-1	170	Sr.	8	13	25	.520	3	5	.600	4	29	3.6
Terry Schofield	G	6-3	186	So.	24	27	65	.415	11	18	.611	39	65	2.7
John Ecker	F	6-6	188	So.	20	12	24	.500	8	12	.667	24	32	1.6
Bill Seibert	F	6-6	175	So.	15	6	23	.261	5	7	.714	12	17	1.1
George Farmer	F	6-4	215	So.	6	2	3	.667	2	2	1.000	1	6	1.0
Lee Walczuk	G	6-0	175	So.	10	3	17	.176	0	0	.000	6	6	0.6
Jim Nielsen	F	6-7	204	Sr.	3	1	2	.500	0	0	.000	1	2	0.7
Team												137		
UCLA					30	1027	2001	.513	486	750	.648	1513	2540	84.7
Opponents					30	758	2026	.374	399	591	.675	1141	1915	63.8

Seniors Alcindor and Heitz flank the championship trophy as the triumphant Bruins hold up three fingers representing their three straight NCAA titles.

cism when he chose to join other prominent black athletes in their boycott of the 1968 Olympic Games and lashed out at critics who charged him with racism and even questioned his loyalty as an American. As he became more and more caught up in the general unrest that was sweeping the country and his religious leanings toward Islam, Alcindor's basketball concentration wavered.

Still, the Bruins coasted through their first 23 games before struggling in two overtime victories against California and Southern Cal. Then they were shocked by the deliberate Trojans in the regular-season finale, dropping a 46-44 decision that ended their winning streak at 44 games and marked the first time a UCLA team ever had lost at Pauley Pavilion.

They recaptured their momentum with big wins in the first two games of the NCAA Tournament, 53-38 over a stalling New Mexico State and 90-52 over Santa Clara. But they played poorly against Drake in the national semifinals in Louisville, barely escaping with an 85-82 victory. Vallely's 29 points helped offset Drake's strong man-to-man defense against Alcindor and put the Bruins in the national championship game against Rick Mount and Purdue.

Alcindor was never more dominating than his

final college game, scoring 37 points on 15 of 20 from the floor and pulling down 20 rebounds as UCLA won its fifth championship and third straight, 92-72. The UCLA big man was named the tournament's outstanding player for an unprecedented third time.

"Purdue had Rick Mount, a great player," Wooden recalled, "and I had Kenny Heitz, a 6-3 guard play him. Kenny did a tremendous job of controlling Mount until we had the game well in hand. All our team wanted to see Kareem finish his college career with an outstanding game, and he did in every aspect."

Alcindor's 37-point effort gave him 2,325 points and a 26.4-point average in his three-year college career. And nobody doubts that those totals could have been much higher. Shackelford, who played alongside the talented big man for those three glorious seasons, once was asked what the unselfish Alcindor could score if he really turned on the offensive gun for a full 40 minutes.

"Lew's never really used all his potential," he answered. "I heard Coach Wooden say once that Alcindor could average 50 points a game. And he could, easily—but I'd never get a shot."

And UCLA of the Alcindor era might never have qualified as the greatest *team* ever.

A Perfect Example

I N D I A N A

1975-76

It was one of those rare, rare occasions when everything fit perfectly.

The coach was perfect for the players, and the players dedicated to the coach. And on their way to a perfect 32-0 season, the 1975-76 Indiana Hoosiers set the standard for what team play was all about.

There is the vivid image of Coach Bob Knight, then just 35 years old but wise beyond his years. And driven—passionately. And there is the not-so-vivid image of the players, a collection of determined athletes with lots of substance and very little flash. The defense always seemed infallible, the offense structured and precise.

In college basketball history, there are celebrated instances of single, dominating players who lifted their teams to the pinnacle of greatness. But the 1975-76 Hoosiers found greatness as a group, as an aggregation of players whose blend of skills kept attention riveted on the team's whole and not its parts.

Scott May, the scoring forward, suited Knight's motion offense in every way. "He has to be the best all-around player I've ever been associated with and probably ever seen play the game," Knight said that season. "He handles the ball, screens, passes, sets up other guys as well as himself, can bring the ball down against the press, is an excellent free-throw shooter—what else can you say?"

May played an aggressive brand of defense, as well, which was the hallmark of a Knight-coached team. It was May's job, as an underclassman, to cover the opposition's top forward and hold him in check. With that emphasis on total performance, he was accorded consensus All-America recognition in

both his junior and senior seasons.

Playmaking point guard Quinn Buckner had played football two years at Indiana and looked like it. He was muscular, determined and experienced, too, having started as a freshman on the 1973 Indiana team that went to the Final Four. Buckner was the Hoosiers' vocal leader on the floor and perhaps the closest of any player to Knight. Athlete and coach understood and trusted each other completely.

Though a streaky shooter, Buckner established the Hoosier career record for assists and, with guard Bobby Wilkerson, put withering pressure on opposing backcourts. Wilkerson had the quickness to stifle other guards and the height (6-foot-7) to offset opposing forwards. A tremendous leaper, he jumped center, doubled at forward and excelled as a rebounding guard.

At the other forward position, Tom Abernethy had a knack for garbage buckets and offensive boards, and an unmistakable talent for blocking out opponents and defensive positioning. When May took on more offensive responsibility as a senior, it was Abernethy who was assigned to check the other team's top forward.

Center Kent Benson didn't meet with perpetual glory in the National Basketball Association, yet he was regarded as one of the top big men in the college game, a back-to-back All-America in 1976 and 1977. At 6-11, 245 pounds, he was a force to be reckoned with inside, certainly a bear of a rebounder (No. 2 behind Walt Bellamy on Indiana's career list) but also an accurate shooter with a first-rate hook shot. Best of all, he and May presented an inside-outside offensive challenge that demoralized

Bob Knight, the 35-year-old architect of Indiana's 1975-76 powerhouse, gives instructions to backup guard Jim Wisman.

defenses.

Had he not left the Indiana campus in the fall of 1974, uncomfortable with life at the big university, Larry Bird would have been a sophomore on this same Hoosier team—a team, incidentally, with four senior starters and one junior, Benson. Would he have even cracked the veteran lineup? Bird believes he would have contributed, and with the legend he built as a franchise player, few would dispute that. But how do you improve on perfect?

Dynasty, Hoosier fans say.

Regardless of what-might-have-been, Indiana came very close to winning the national championship in 1975, posting a 31-1 mark. To this day, Knight rates that team superior to his undefeated 1976 national champions. In addition to the '76 regulars, Knight had forward Steve Green, one of the best shooters in the nation, and supersub John Laskowski, a smooth offensive player whom Knight called "the most valuable unknown player I've ever seen."

The 1974-75 Hoosiers tore through the schedule like a runaway train, getting a surge of momentum with an early 98-74 rout of Kentucky that was notable for a confrontation between Knight and Wildcat Coach Joe B. Hall. Knight hit Hall on the back of the head and later laughed that it was a playful gesture. "If it was meant to be malicious," Knight told one reporter, "I would have blasted the (expletive) into the stands."

Hall, however, fumed about the incident and claimed he was humiliated. "All I want is another chance to play Knight," he said.

As fate would have it, Hall was granted that opportunity in the NCAA Tournament's regional championship. The Hoosiers were a perfect 31-0, though not quite the same team after May suffered a broken arm in game No. 26 against Purdue. May started against Kentucky but was ineffective, and Knight watched the season end with a 92-90 loss.

"That year," Knight recalled, "I think I made the biggest mistake I've ever made in coaching. When May broke his arm in the Purdue game, I had to decide whether to replace him with Tom Abernethy or John Laskowski. Abernethy was the normal replacement for May because he was a helluva defensive player and rebounder, but Laskowski was a great scorer. So I played Laskowski at the point against Illinois (the game after Purdue).

"At the workout, I told John to shoot the first three times he got the ball, and I told him that I would let him know if I wanted him to shoot any more. He scored 28 points against Illinois. We won, 112-89, and I remember thinking, '112 points is great, but we shouldn't be giving up 89 points.'

"We had two regular-season games left, and I'm struggling trying to decide whether to play Abernethy or Laskowski. If I play Laskowski, I've got to break up our guard combination of Wilkerson and

High-scoring forward Scott May was a two-time All-America who fit perfectly into Knight's motion offense.

Muscular guard Quinn Buckner, a former member of the Indiana football team, was the Hoosiers' playmaker and vocal leader on the floor.

Buckner because Wilkerson has to guard the opposition's high-scoring forward. With Abernethy I don't have that problem because he can guard whoever is at forward. Abernethy's our best defensive forward, even better than May."

Knight's agonizing over May's replacement carried right into the NCAA Tournament. "We're playing Texas-El Paso in our first-round game at 12:30," Knight said, "and I'm sitting there at quarter till 12 undecided about who is going to start. I think I should start Abernethy, but Laskowski is just too good a scorer. So we go with Laskowski, and that broke up our guard combination and really hurt us.

"When we played Kentucky, we started May, who was on the verge of being ready to play, but he

couldn't handle the ball or throw it at all with his left hand. So . . . we took him out (for Laskowski). We struggle, struggle, struggle, and they keep scoring against us and end up beating us, 92-90. Nobody should score 92 points against us, and I think if we had played Abernethy, he could have played Kevin Grevey. . . . Abernethy would have done a good job on Grevey (who scored 17 points). We might have held the score down in the 70s. I'm not positive we would have won, but we would have been a much better team.

"Not going back to the best defensive team we ever had was the biggest mistake I made in coaching. And that '75 team might have been good enough to have won it all."

Reserve center Mark Haymore remembered returning to the locker room to retrieve a gym bag after the loss. Inside, he discovered Knight crying in the bathroom.

"We should have won it," Knight said later of his reaction. "That team was a great one, one of the best I've been around, including the teams I was on and the teams I've seen play. There just hasn't been a better one. It was a tremendous disappointment not to win the title."

Knight had been intense before the loss, but it sparked his determination even more. Returning to Bloomington, he focused his energies on the next season, confident that anything a basketball team had to do, his would do. The final factor would be his unwavering will and, more important, preparation. ("The will to win is grossly overrated," Knight often said. "Everyone wants to win. The will to *prepare* to win is far more important.")

"Coach wasn't going to leave it up to us to be as great a team as we could be," Buckner said. "He was going to push, be it psychological, physical, whatever it took, to be the best team we could be."

Knight carried a reputation as a brilliant teacher and coaching martinet from his years at Army, where he coached the Cadets to a 102-50 record in six seasons, from 1965-66 through 1970-71. In this environment, he developed a keen appreciation of discipline and how it could be applied to basketball. If when Knight arrived at Indiana the boosters were apprehensive about his bringing defense, heaven forbid, to the land of run-and-shoot, they quickly understood that Knight's way would be Indiana's way. That was made abundantly clear when he discussed the matter of player-coach relations.

"Say that this is civilian discipline," he intoned, holding his hand chest high. "And this," he said, his hand at chin level, "is military discipline." Knight raised his hand above his head. "This is my discipline."

Knight was frequently depicted as a hot-tempered, belligerent coach prone to raging tirades, but for all his bullying and instruction, the morale of the team never suffered.

"We don't take it as a personal thing, that he is mad at us," Benson said. "The attitude of the team is that to awaken us deep down mentally, the coach has to do that. I think Coach Knight is the best coach who ever lived and he will go through a brick wall for his players."

"He gives so much of himself," said one former Hoosier, "that the least we can do is give our fullest effort."

If Knight's character was shaped while coaching at West Point, so was his devotion to a relentless man-to-man defense. Without a player taller than 6-6 due to academy height restrictions, Army led Division I schools in scoring defense three consecutive seasons and played in four National Invitation Tournaments.

There was nothing flashy about 6-11 All-America center Kent Benson, but he intimidated, scored, rebounded—and won.

The 1974-75 Hoosiers, with hot-shooting reserve John Laskowski filling in for the injured May, were undefeated until falling to Kentucky in an NCAA regional final.

And Knight, who had been a reserve on the John Havlicek-Jerry Lucas Ohio State squad that won the 1960 NCAA title and was runner-up in 1961 and 1962, was, according to Buckeye Coach Fred Taylor: "Frankly, never a strong defensive player. I suppose some kind of reverse psychology must have taken effect."

Knight had a reason as solid as the Hoosier defense itself. "Defense," he explained, "can be the most consistent and constant part of the game because you've got more control over it. You can't will the ball into the basket, so you work hardest on those things you have the most control over."

Driven by Knight's demanding expectations and unyielding preparation, the 1975-76 Hoosiers understood it would not be enough simply to play

against opponents. To realize their potential, they had to play against themselves. They were drilled to execute every play to perfection. Execution, Knight explained, would take care of the final score.

The rewards of such dedication would pay off in Indiana's first test of the new season, against the UCLA Bruins, the defending national champions, the holders of a title Knight believed should have been Indiana's. The Hoosiers would gain a measure of revenge—and then some.

With Gene Bartow making his debut as the successor to retired John Wooden, the Bruins were left for dead, 84-64, effectively paralyzed by the swarming Hoosier defense. Buckner and Wilkerson shut off the UCLA guards. The inside was dominated by Abernethy, May and Benson, who limited 7-foot-2

Bruin center Ralph Drollinger to two points and two rebounds. Indiana's tuned offense, meanwhile, passed and picked and set up May for 33 points. A total team effort, execution at its best.

Indiana would immediately face a series of stiff challenges but manage to respond in pressure situations. In their third game, the Hoosiers blew a 14-point lead against Notre Dame and Adrian Dantley before winning, 63-60. Days later, Benson hit a jump shot with nine seconds left to send a game against Kentucky into overtime. Indiana prevailed again, 77-68. Opening the Big Ten Conference schedule against Ohio State, the Hoosiers escaped with a two-point victory.

"We're just not going to blow anyone out," Knight said, "but people seem to be amazed when we play a close game."

The Hoosiers were winning with consistency but, quite often, not scoring with much. In an overtime victory over Michigan, they shot 37 percent for the game, with the five starters making only 22 of 69 field-goal attempts.

"Last year we beat people offensively, but this year we don't have shooters like Steve Green and John Laskowski," May said. "That's a lot of points we lost. This year, we have to pick up their points on steals, fast breaks and just playing good, basic defense. At times I think we have.

"When we're playing a game the way we can play it, I think we're better than last year. And yet there are times when we don't play as well. Yeah, we've been pretty good most of the time when we had to be, but the game is not played like that. You've got to concentrate each and every game, and that's not what we've been doing."

Once Knight gave his Hoosiers a late-season refresher course, they responded by breezing to their fourth straight Big Ten title. Indiana polished a fast break to overcome the zone opponents had used to bedevil its calculated offense. More shots found their mark, boosting the club's field-goal percentage to .517, sixth among Division I schools. Knight began using a bench that was once questionable but

Season Results
1975-76 (32-0)

84	UCLA at St. Louis	64	72	Michigan (OT)	67
83	Florida State at Indianapolis	59	85	Michigan State	70
63	Notre Dame	60	58	Illinois	48
77	Kentucky at Louisville (OT)	68	74	At Purdue	71
93	Georgia*	56	76	Minnesota	64
101	Virginia Tech*	74	101	Iowa	81
106	Columbia at New York†	63	96	At Wisconsin	67
97	Manhattan at New York†	61	76	At Northwestern	63
76	St. John's at New York†	69	96	Ohio State	67
66	At Ohio State	64	90	St. John's at S. Bend, Ind.‡	70
78	Northwestern	61	74	Alabama at Baton Rouge‡	69
80	At Michigan	74	65	Marquette at Baton Rouge‡	56
69	At Michigan State	57	65	UCLA at Philadelphia‡	51
83	At Illinois	55	86	Michigan at Philadelphia‡	68
71	Purdue	67			
85	At Minnesota	76	*Indiana Classic		
88	At Iowa	73	†Holiday Festival		
114	Wisconsin	61	‡NCAA Tournament		

Buckner's backcourt mate was Bobby Wilkerson, an outstanding leaper who excelled on defense while providing rebounding help.

The 1975-76 season culminated with two Big Ten coaching rivals, Knight and Michigan's Johnny Orr (left), doing battle in the NCAA championship game.

proved to be solid. In the overtime win over Michigan, reserve Wayne Radford made six of seven shots from the field on his way to 16 points and five rebounds. Against Minnesota, guard Jim Wisman had 12 points and seven assists.

"This team's neat because other teams can't concentrate on one individual star," Benson said. "They've got to respect all of us. As long as you play to your potential and everyone plays to his potential, there's no way they're going to stop the team by stopping one guy."

The Hoosiers unsettled their share of opponents with that kind of confidence. Much of it emanated

directly from Knight, who was usually blunt but not beyond subtlety. Network basketball analyst Billy Packer treasures one such instance when Michigan, dogging just behind Indiana in the conference standings, visited Bloomington. "Billy," Knight called from across the gym, "come here a minute. I want you to meet Johnny Orr, the coach of the second-best basketball team in America."

Indiana remained the team to beat heading into the NCAA Tournament. Dispatched to Baton Rouge, La., for the Mideast Regional, the Hoosiers encountered not Southern hospitality but Louisiana quicksand with a draw that pitted them against

St. John's (23-5), Alabama (23-4) and Marquette (27-1). Indiana overran all three opponents, however, and joined undefeated Rutgers, Michigan and UCLA in Philadelphia, site of the 1976 Final Four in recognition of the U.S. Bicentennial.

After the season-opening pasting by Indiana, UCLA had plenty to prove in a rematch in the semifinal round. But denied an inside game by the sagging Hoosier defense, the Bruins made only 34.4 percent of their shots and lost, 65-51, after having won 10 of the previous 12 NCAA titles. "They made us feel helpless," the Bruins' Marques Johnson said wearily.

Benson led four Hoosiers in double figures with 16 points, but the real hero, according to Knight, was Wilkerson. "Bobby got 19 rebounds," he remembered. "You think of our front line of Benson, Abernethy and May, all three NBA players for at least five years. And UCLA's front line was (All-America) Richard Washington, Marques Johnson and David Greenwood (the latter two 10-year pros). In that choice company, Bobby was the leading rebounder in the game by far."

Hopes for a title bout between undefeated teams were dashed when Michigan dismissed Rutgers, 86-70, in the other semifinal. The Spartans' victory did, however, set up another championship game first— a finale contested between two teams from the same conference.

Led by guard Rickey Green, the 25-6 Spartans had only narrowly been beaten by Indiana in two regular-season meetings, losing by six and five points. "A lot of people didn't believe me when I kept saying Michigan was probably the best team we've played all season," Knight said. "They're physical, fast and play offense and defense together."

The extent to which Knight had prepared and shaped this team for this one moment was made manifest in a scene only minutes before the game. "I'm walking down the ramp behind Benson, who is squeezing a rubber ball I'd given him as a freshman when I told him, 'Goddamn it, get some strong hands,'" Knight said. "And here we are two years later and he's still squeezing that rubber ball going into the championship game."

Less than three minutes into the game, Knight watched Wilkerson, the UCLA hero, get knocked cold in a collision. Searching for a replacement, he sent out Radford "because we expected a zone," then senior Jim Crews "for his experience" and finally, with seconds remaining in the half and Michigan leading, 35-29, Wisman "because he's got more quickness."

The difference in the second half? "Wisman," said Michigan guard Steve Grote. "Indiana wasn't hitting its first pass and was throwing it away. He came in and ran their game."

The Hoosiers answered with a burst of offensive power in the second half, pouring in 57 points to streak to win No. 32 and the national championship, 86-68. May, the team's leading scorer with a 23.5-point average on the season, erupted for 18 second-half points to finish with a game-high 26, and Benson, the team's No. 2 man all season, chipped in 15 for a game total of 25.

"This was a two-year quest," Knight said afterward. Yet his mission was far from complete. "I'll be on the train tomorrow morning—recruiting."

Looking, undoubtedly, for the same kind of players that had just given him his first national championship—players who would not beat themselves.

"The type of player we look for," Knight would say, "is first of all a good person with good character traits, because that's the kind of person who becomes an unselfish and team-oriented basketball player."

Knight, of course, went on to coach Indiana to

1976 INDIANA
Head Coach—Bob Knight   Final Record—32-0

Player	Pos.	Hgt.	Wgt.	Cl.	G	FG	FGA	Pct.	FT.	FTA	Pct.	Reb.	Pts.	Avg.
Scott May	F	6-7	218	Sr.	32	308	584	.527	136	174	.782	245	752	23.5
Kent Benson	C	6-11	245	Jr.	32	237	410	.578	80	117	.684	282	554	17.3
Tom Abernethy	F	6-7	220	Sr.	32	133	237	.561	55	74	.743	169	321	10.0
Quinn Buckner	G	6-3	203	Sr.	32	123	279	.441	40	82	.488	91	286	8.9
Bobby Wilkerson	G-F	6-7	200	Sr.	32	111	225	.493	29	46	.630	156	251	7.8
Wayne Radford	G-F	6-3	194	So.	30	49	87	.563	42	59	.712	64	140	4.7
Jim Crews	G	6-5	195	Sr.	31	36	77	.468	30	35	.857	23	102	3.3
Jim Wisman	G	6-2	175	So.	26	22	60	.367	21	29	.724	21	65	2.5
Rich Valavicius	F	6-5	215	Fr.	28	29	60	.483	10	16	.625	49	68	2.4
Bob Bender	G	6-3	178	Fr.	17	13	23	.565	9	12	.750	13	35	2.1
Mark Haymore	F-C	6-8	220	So.	13	11	27	.407	2	7	.286	28	24	1.8
Jim Roberson	F-C	6-9	185	Fr.	12	7	12	.583	5	6	.833	16	19	1.6
Scott Eells	F	6-9	185	Fr.	12	4	13	.308	3	4	.750	9	11	0.9
Team											1	158		
Indiana					32	1083	2094	.517	462	662	.698	1324	2628	82.1
Opponents					32	837	1921	.436	400	572	.699	1143	2074	64.8

Knight has reason to smile as May (center) and Buckner celebrate Indiana's 1976 NCAA title-game victory over Michigan.

two more NCAA titles, in 1981 and 1987. Like other great coaches such as John Wooden and Henry Iba, Knight was a consummate student of the game who developed into an exceptional teacher. Unlike the others, Knight had a private persona that created success and a public one that often took away from it.

Knight has come across as an egocentric genius who throws chairs and bullies the basketball world. But that image isn't wholly accurate.

Certainly he has a unique intensity. Knight is demanding—of himself, his players and the officials. As trite as it sounds, what Knight demands is not winning but the absolute best possible effort. When he gets that, he can be even peaceful after an Indiana loss. Conversely, there have been victories that left him disgusted.

After the 1976 championship, there was no need for re-evaluation. "One of the major emotional feelings in '76 was relief at winning the championship,"

Knight said. "I was just so pleased that the team won because it was one of the truly great college basketball teams.

"You know your team will always identify with that accomplishment. That stays with you, and you like to see kids have a part of it. I tell our players that someday they will be watching the tournament with their kids or grandchildren and they'll say, 'Hey, I played in that.' And it's a helluva lot better to say you won it.

"When we have a team with a chance to go to the finals, I put up a mathematical equation that shows a player's chances of winning the national title. The odds are a little over 4000-1. You take 280 or so teams and you're up to 4200 players in the division. Only 30 will play for the championship, and just 15 are going to win it. I've seen how winning the title has affected our kids. It gives them something."

In fact, it gives all of basketball something. Just a little better idea of the perfect team.

THREE

Walton Gang Rides High

UCLA

**1971-72
1972-73**

Five straight national championships and seven titles in eight years. A 221-15 record over that span with winning streaks of 47 and 41 games. A reputation as a relentless factory of basketball talent.

So read the legacy of UCLA basketball success when the Walton Gang came riding into Westwood. The gang's leader was a tall, skinny, gangly youth with floppy red hair and freckles. "An elongated Tom Sawyer," was how many writers described this unlikely savior. But beneath that boyish exterior lied an intense, almost ruthless, killer instinct that would result in 2½ more seasons of UCLA basketball domination and a controversial off-court image that would confound both his coach, John Wooden, and the conservative gurus of college basketball.

Walton arrived at UCLA without the immense fanfare that had accompanied Lew Alcindor six years earlier. But the 1971-72 season was barely underway when the talented sophomore began generating comparisons to his illustrious predecessor.

Alcindor, at 7-foot-1, could dominate a basketball game like nobody before him. Walton, at 6-11, was equally as intimidating. Alcindor could pass and shoot. So could Walton, maybe even better. Alcindor was an agile, quick, superior athlete with poise and confidence beyond his years. So, too, was Walton.

But that's where the comparisons end. Whereas Alcindor operated with an almost cold, calculated efficiency, Walton was an emotional buzzsaw, extolling his teammates to greater heights, shrieking at officials and angering opponents with his constant complaining. Off the court, Alcindor was shy,

withdrawn and private while Walton was a visible product of his radical era, whether protesting with political activists or championing the causes of various minorities.

Alcindor had arrived as part of a talented sophomore class that included Lucius Allen, Lynn Shackelford and Kenny Heitz. That was the heart of a team that went on to win three straight NCAA championships. Walton's arrival coincided with the departure of Sydney Wicks, Curtis Rowe and Steve Patterson, the heart of a team that followed the Alcindor era with two more NCAA titles. The Walton Gang had some tough acts to follow.

But the one thing that Wooden did not lack was talent. Positioning Walton in the middle, he opened the 1971-72 season by teaming his big man with fellow sophomores Keith Wilkes (forward) and Greg Lee (guard), senior Henry Bibby (guard) and junior Larry Farmer (forward). Through the next three seasons, Walton also would play with such impressive stars as Dave Meyers, Marques Johnson, Richard Washington, Swen Nater, Ralph Drollinger and Andre McCarter. The Bruins were so deep in talent that Nater, a backup center, became a first-round pick in the National Basketball Association draft despite the fact that he never started a college game.

That Walton chose to attend UCLA over a huge list of other colleges was largely a tribute to Bruin assistant Denny Crum, who would go on to greater fame as the coach at Louisville, and the school's growing basketball mystique. Walton was a sophomore playing for Helix High School in the San Diego area when he first came to Crum's attention.

"Coach Wooden didn't like to recruit, didn't like

Coach John Wooden and assistant Denny Crum (left), the man most responsible for UCLA's recruitment of dominating center Bill Walton.

to travel," Crum recalled. "He liked to be home with his wife. He enjoyed the coaching and teaching, but he didn't enjoy recruiting."

A UCLA alumnus in San Diego alerted Crum to the talented young center, and Crum discovered that Bill's older brother, Bruce, was attending UCLA on a football scholarship.

"I started corresponding with Bill," Crum said, "and I finally went down and watched him play. I came back and told Coach Wooden that this Walton kid was the best high school player I'd ever seen. I think he was a junior at the time.

"We were sitting in his office and Coach Wooden got up and closed his door and said, 'Denny, don't you ever make that stupid statement again. It makes you look like an idiot to say that some redheaded, freckle-faced kid from San Diego is the best high school player you've ever seen. First of all, there's never ever been, since I've been here, a major college prospect from San Diego, let alone the best player you've ever seen.'

"And I said, 'Coach, there's a lot of them I haven't seen play in high school, but he's still the best I've seen.'"

Crum said he almost had to trick Wooden into seeing Walton play.

"I asked him what he was doing on a certain night," Crum said. "He said nothing, so I told him to tell his wife that he wouldn't be home for dinner. I told him I needed him to go somewhere with me. He didn't know where we were going, and he didn't ask. We went to Bill's high school and Coach Wooden wanted to sit way up in the corner of the gym to be obscure. Of course, everybody recognized him anyway.

"When the game was over and we were in the car, I asked him, 'Well, what did you think about him?' He said, 'He is pretty good, isn't he?' And that was a real compliment because he didn't say real positive things about high school kids. He was usually real low key about that kind of thing."

What the UCLA coaches didn't know at the time

was that Walton, as a youngster, had attended one of Wooden's basketball camps.

"Without a doubt, UCLA was the only place to go," Walton said. "I wanted to go there even before they contacted me. I went to a John Wooden basketball camp for a day as a kid in San Diego. He and Bill Sharman came down to San Diego and gave a one-day clinic.

"I was young, 10 or 12. I came from a family that wasn't able to afford to send their kids to camp, and really there weren't that many camps when I was a kid. I wouldn't have been in a financial situation to go anyway. But I got to go to this one-day camp.

"I had watched UCLA in the early '60s when they were playing for the national championship with (Walt) Hazzard and (Gail) Goodrich. I loved the way they played. I loved the fast-break style and the pressure defense. UCLA was the first school to recruit me. I got my first letter from Denny Crum, the assistant coach, when I was a sophomore in high school."

Rather than frighten him away, the UCLA tradition and the idea of following in Alcindor's footsteps intrigued Walton.

"I wanted to go to UCLA," he said, "not only because of Coach Wooden, but because Pauley Pavilion was the nicest basketball building in the country. Equally important were the guys I would be playing with. I knew Greg Lee, and I knew he was a great player. I knew Keith Wilkes, and I knew he was a great player. I figured that to be most effective, I needed to play with that caliber of player.

"I also loved the enthusiasm and intensity of the fans."

It didn't take long for this group to let it be known that the 1971-72 season, and the two that would follow, would be anything but ordinary. Long-time broadcaster Curt Gowdy remembers his first meeting with the big redhead very well.

"I wrote a story for a magazine and it came out in 1971, predicting the All-America team," Gowdy said. "UCLA was playing its first game of the season that night, and I went out to watch them play. Some guy from the team comes to me and asks, 'You know Bill Walton?' I said, 'Yes, he's a new center.' The guy said, 'He wants to see you.'

"Well, I talked to Walton and he tore into me for not picking him for the All-America team. He was a sophomore and he was going to play his first varsity game that night. He pointed out that his freshman team had beaten the varsity by 20 points. I said, 'No, I didn't pick you. I didn't know much about you.' He said, 'Well, you should have done better research.'

"He really jumped all over me. I watched him play that night, and I could tell he was going to be great. He was a very emotional type. Every time he'd come down the court, he'd look over at Wood-

With the intimidating Walton flashing his considerable offensive skills, the 1971-72 Bruins obliterated opponents at a record pace.

en to see if he'd done all right, and Wooden would shake his head at him."

With Walton providing the physical power and Bibby, the only returning starter, keeping his young teammates on a steady course, the Walton Gang embarked on its record-breaking journey. This group set an NCAA record for obliterating opponents, running up an average victory margin of 30.3 points over 30 games. They scored more than 100 points in their first seven games, setting the tone for a season in which they would seldom be tested.

Walton drew most of the accolades, but Wooden pointed to Wilkes as a major factor in his team's success.

"He was a great player," the coach said, "so smooth and silky that he never got due credit, in my opinion. Players have a tendency to nickname teammates, and they gave Keith the name 'Silk.'"

With Walton in the low post, Wilkes was a perfect high-post scorer. In the Bruins' 1-3-1 offensive alignment, Farmer and Bibby worked at the wings while Lee ran the offense from the point. Lee, a master at throwing the lob pass to either Walton or Wilkes under (or over) the basket, was backed up by Tommy Curtis, Nater was the reserve center and Larry Hollyfield filled in at forward.

"We had very few set plays," Walton recalled. "Basically we had positions on the court. I played low post, Larry Farmer played the left box, Henry Bibby played the left wing. Basically, it was a 1-3-1 offense, with Bibby and Farmer as the wing players and Wilkes and myself at the double low post.

"Wilkes would break to the middle to make it a 1-3-1. Lee was right in the middle of the court, and he would set up the plays. Coach Wooden, Henry Bibby, Keith Wilkes and I always demanded that Lee bring the ball to our side, and Larry Farmer just got shafted in terms of the number of opportunities he had to score.

"So we ran our offense to the left side of the court. It wasn't complicated; just get the ball to people in good spots and let them do what was best with the ball. There wasn't a lot of screening, but there was a lot of cutting and passing; not many trick plays."

The Bruins didn't need tricks. In their ninth game of the season, Oregon State stayed close, 78-72, but from there the Bruins zoomed off again, leaving 17 more teams strewn in their wake. They entered the NCAA West Regional with a 26-0 mark. At Provo, Utah, they zapped Weber State and Long Beach State and headed back home for the Final Four at the Los Angeles Sports Arena.

The semifinal game would pit UCLA against Louisville—teacher, Wooden, against student, Crum, who already had left Westwood to try his hand at coaching. Louisville was no match for the Bruins and Walton, who almost singlehandedly dismantled the Cardinals with 33 points, 21 rebounds

Guard Henry Bibby, the only returning starter in 1971-72, provided the senior leadership UCLA needed in a 30-0 season.

and six blocked shots. Crum watched in awe as the players he had recruited for UCLA toyed with Louisville in a 96-77 victory, admitting later that his team never had a chance.

In the other semifinal, second-ranked North Carolina, featuring consensus All-America Bob McAdoo, was a big favorite against Hugh Durham's Cinderella Florida State team. The Seminoles had upset Kentucky in what would be the last game coached by Adolph Rupp.

Durham had a gifted scorer in Ron King, and he put him to work against the Tar Heels. Carolina shot poorly and struggled early. Down by 23 points, they rallied late before falling short, 79-75.

Nobody expected Florida State to provide UCLA with much of a challenge. But the upstart Seminoles had other ideas.

"We were behind at the beginning," Farmer recalled. "My junior year, our average winning margin was 30.3 points a game. Nobody had touched us. The Bruin Blitz, our press that generated momentum for us, betrayed us. They threw the ball upcourt, and we dared them to shoot out of the corner. They did and hit the shots.

"I don't remember what the final margin was, but it was one of the closest games we played."

With King lofting deadeye jumpers, Florida State opened a 21-14 lead, the first time all season the Bruins had trailed by seven points. But UCLA fought back to grab a 50-39 halftime margin. When Walton got into second-half foul trouble, however, the Seminoles cut the deficit and managed to stay within striking distance the rest of the way.

The Bruins' 81-76 victory was their closest call of the season. Wooden had produced his third 30-0 team and eighth NCAA champion (sixth straight) in nine seasons. The Bruins' winning streak now stood at 45 and the NCAA-record 60-game streak compiled by Bill Russell's San Francisco team in the mid-1950s was in sight.

Walton capped his first varsity campaign by scoring 24 points and grabbing 24 rebounds while being named the tournament's outstanding player. His final averages of 21.1 points and 15.5 rebounds were team-leading marks. Bibby (15.7), Wilkes (13.5) and Farmer (10.7) also averaged in double figures.

It was during the off-season that Walton stepped into the spotlight as a student radical. He grew his hair a little longer, tied it back with a headband and sported a scraggly beard. He made national headlines when he was arrested and fined $50 for his participation in an anti-war demonstration on the UCLA campus.

Crum recalled that even as a high school student, Walton had been different. Most recruits were eager to earn money through summer jobs, but Big Bill wanted to spend his summer reading and meditating at a beach house he had rented with his brother.

"That tipped me off that material things never meant anything to Bill Walton," Crum said. "He always ran around campus with cutoff Levis and T-shirts and thongs, or whatever you call them, on his feet. He rode a motor scooter and was a champion of all the minority classes on campus. He had a different philosophy and he and Coach Wooden clashed a number of times, not about basketball, but other things."

"Bill was a rebel," Wooden recalled with a smile. "Of course, during Bill's playing days, it was probably a little more rebellious time. He was fighting to end the Vietnam war and had various other causes. In between practices, I was always concerned about him."

Farmer, who would return later to coach UCLA for three seasons, said the players were always watching to see what their talented teammate would do next. And to see just how far Wooden would let him go.

"Wooden's concern was understandable, Farmer said. "Coach knew that Bill was a very impression-

'Silky smooth' was the description most often applied to classy forward Keith Wilkes.

Tommy Curtis (left) was a reliable backup guard who contributed eight points and six assists against Florida State in the 1972 NCAA Tournament championship game. Larry Hollyfield (right) replaced Bibby as a starting guard in 1972-73 and averaged 10.7 points per game.

able guy. If some guy talked to Bill one day and told him the sky was pink, Bill would believe that. And then if he talked to someone the next day who told him the sky was red, Bill would believe that, too.

"Coach wanted us to be individuals and experience college as students, not just as basketball players. In his system, he had rules off and on the court, but within that system he let us be ourselves. I don't think Coach minded Bill expressing his views on war at all. I think he was mad at Bill when Bill got arrested for voicing his views, and I'm sure he told Bill that.

"I know they had disagreements about length of hair from time to time. Bill thought that because it was fashionable to wear hair on his shoulders he should be able to do that during the season. I know Coach told him one day that if it was more important for him to wear his hair long, he should wear it long. He believed in a person being able to take a stand.

"But he told him if he was going to wear his hair long, not to come out for the team. Needless to say, Bill cut his hair. But he did give us freedom to be

our own person within his system."

That freedom carried over onto the court, where the free-wheeling Bruins marched relentlessly in 1972-73 toward their date with destiny. With Hollyfield replacing the graduated Bibby in the starting lineup, thirteen opponents were methodically dismantled before the Bruins embarked on a midwest road trip that would take them to Loyola of Chicago and Notre Dame in search of consecutive victories Nos. 60 and 61.

Loyola fell without a struggle, 87-73, allowing UCLA to tie San Francisco's record. The mark fell two days later when the Bruins routed Notre Dame, 82-63. Ironically, the Irish had been the last team to defeat a UCLA squad in the 1970-71 season.

With that little matter out of the way, the Bruins continued their drive toward another championship. They finished the regular season at 26-0 and then easily pushed their way into the Final Four with routs of Arizona State and San Francisco.

The string continued in St. Louis, where Bobby Knight's young Indiana team fell to the Bruins, 70-59. In the other semifinal, Gene Bartow's Memphis

State team featuring Larry Finch, Larry Kenon and Ronnie Robinson pulled off a 98-85 upset of a Providence team that included Ernie DiGregorio and Marvin Barnes.

Bartow's Tigers came out firing on all cylinders in the championship game, but Walton turned this contest into his personal showcase for the national television audience. Scoring off offensive rebounds, lobs from Lee and short turnaround jumpers, the UCLA big man connected on 21 of 22 field-goal attempts and a pair of free throws to score 44 points. His shooting performance was nothing short of awesome and he added insult to injury by grabbing a game-high 13 rebounds in the Bruins' 87-66 victory.

Memphis State, which had fought to a 39-39 half-time deadlock, was powerless to stop UCLA's seventh consecutive NCAA title victory and 75th straight win overall. And Walton, for the second straight year, was named the tournament's outstanding player.

His season totals were equally impressive. He shot 65 percent from the floor while averaging 20.4 points and 16.8 rebounds. Walton also led the team with 168 assists and his 506 rebounds broke the UCLA single-season record. Wilkes was the Bruins' second-leading scorer with a 14.8 average.

The temperamental Walton refused to talk to reporters after the Memphis State game, but later reflected on his most outstanding college performance.

"Memphis State had a powerful front line," he said, "but they were not particularly tall, so we

Walton at his dominating best, rejecting a shot against Florida State in the 1972 NCAA final.

Season Results
1971-72 (30-0)

105	The Citadel	49	81	Southern California	56
106	Iowa	72	89	Washington State	58
110	Iowa State	81	109	Washington	70
117	Texas A&M	53	100	At Washington	83
114	Notre Dame	56	85	At Washington	55
119	Texas Christian	81	92	Oregon	70
115	Texas*	65	91	Oregon State	72
79	Ohio State*	53	85	At California	71
78	At Oregon State	72	102	At Stanford	73
93	At Oregon	68	79	USC at Los Angeles	66
118	Stanford	79	90	Weber St. at Provo, Utah†	58
82	California	43	73	L. Beach St. at Provo, Ut.†	57
92	Santa Clara	57	96	Louisville at Los Angeles†	77
108	Denver	61	81	Florida State at L.A.†	76
92	Loyola of Chicago	64	*Bruin Classic	
57	At Notre Dame	32	†NCAA Tournament	

1972-73 (30-0)

94	Wisconsin	53	79	At Southern California	56
73	Bradley	38	88	At Washington State	50
81	Pacific	48	76	At Washington	67
98	Santa Barbara	67	93	Washington	62
89	Pittsburgh	73	96	Washington State	64
82	Notre Dame	56	72	At Oregon	61
85	Drake at New Orleans*	72	73	At Oregon State	67
71	Illinois at New Orleans*	64	90	California	65
64	Oregon	38	51	Stanford	45
87	Oregon State	61	76	Southern California	56
82	At Stanford	67	98	Arizona State at L.A.†	81
69	At California	50	54	San Francisco at L.A.†	39
92	San Francisco	64	70	Indiana at St. Louis†	59
101	Providence	77	87	Memphis St. at St. Louis†	66
87	Loyola of Chicago	73	*Sugar Bowl Tournament	
82	At Notre Dame	63	†NCAA Tournament	

Senior forward Larry Farmer, who later would become coach at his alma mater, performs cord-cutting duty after UCLA's 1973 NCAA Tournament victory over Memphis State.

tried to go to the hoop with the ball. I was feeling great and we were really moving the ball around. People talk a lot about my scoring, but it was really our team offense that had to click perfectly for me to get 21 baskets in that game.

"Our starting guards, Greg Lee and Larry Hollyfield, had 22 assists between them. Most of those were to me. We had the kind of offense that really thrived on passing the ball. Most of my shots were very short, so I had a very fortunate day.

"Normally, we had a fast-break team that relied on pressure defense to get our offense going. We would score bunches of points on the fast break after our defense forced turnovers. Then, after we scored, we would get into our press. This game was different. We weren't fast breaking that much because they were able to control the flow, and they weren't going to let our defense take them out of their game. So we had to rely on our set offense.

"Everybody was moving and passing at a faster pace than Memphis State, and once I got hot shooting, the guys found me for easy baskets underneath. Although I was hot, I missed three of five free

throws. I still get teased by all my teammates for going 21 of 22 from the floor and only two of five from the line."

One gnawing question remained after UCLA's title victory. Were the Bruins better than North Carolina State, another undefeated team (27-0) that had been denied entry into the NCAA Tournament because of recruiting violations? With David Thompson and 7-4 Tom Burleson leading the way, the Wolfpack would get its shot at tearing down the UCLA mystique in the 1973-74 campaign—a roller-coaster season that would punch a hole in UCLA's aura of invincibility.

With Meyers replacing Farmer and Curtis replacing Hollyfield in the Bruins' starting lineup, the Walton Gang opened strong with victories over Arkansas, Maryland and Southern Methodist, setting up an early-season dream meeting with N.C. State in St. Louis. UCLA, however, shocked a national television audience by soundly thrashing the Wolfpack, 84-66, as Wilkes performed a masterful defensive job on the high-scoring Thompson. Nine more lopsided victories lifted the Bruins' winning streak to 88 and basketball fans were ready to concede another national title when the express was suddenly derailed.

The shocker, ironically, occurred in South Bend, Ind., on January 19, 1974, when Notre Dame, UCLA's record-setting victim No. 61, took advantage of a late Bruin swoon to wipe out an 11-point deficit and record a 71-70 victory, bringing the streak to an unceremonious halt. That marked the first loss in Walton's varsity career, but it wouldn't be the last.

UCLA hit a snag four weeks later when it dropped consecutive Pacific-8 Conference games at Oregon State and Oregon before rebounding to win the league title and another invitation to the NCAA Tournament. The Bruins struggled to a three-overtime victory over Dayton and cruised past San Francisco to set up a Final Four showdown against North Carolina State in the Wolfpack's own back yard—Greensboro, N.C.

N.C. State, undefeated since its early-season loss to UCLA and ranked No. 1, was ready, willing and able. In a titanic struggle, the teams played to a 65-65 regulation deadlock and a 67-67 overtime tie before UCLA jumped out to a seven-point lead in the second overtime. But the Wolfpack fought back, taking advantage of Bruin mistakes, and eventually prevailed, 80-77. The Walton Gang had failed to match the three-championship success of Alcindor's Bruins.

"Those are the days you never forget," Walton said of his final college defeat. "You forget the great days like the Memphis State game and winning championships, but the ones you can never get out of your mind are the ones you lose when you should have won."

Still, there's no denying that the Walton and Alcindor eras formed the backbone of UCLA's dynastic run in the 1960s and '70s. And there's no denying that the common thread that connected the two eras was John Wooden.

"He (Wooden) was the perfect motivator for the kids," Farmer recalled. "Coach could figure out what it would take to get each kid on his team motivated to play and get the most out of him.

"I played with Dave Meyers (1972-73). He was a very sensitive kid and Coach got him to play hard by patting him on the back and giving him the attention he needed. By the same token, I was just the opposite. Had I been given a pat on the back I probably would have folded up shop, thinking I was God's gift to basketball. But Coach ignored me, and that kept me working hard.

"As I look back, I can see where he would do little things for everyone to maximize his ability. So, not only did he get great players, but he got the greatness out of them. He made us think as a team."

And he was able to make even his talented substitutes feel like they were part of the team.

"You look back," Farmer continued, "at some of the great players we had, players who could have averaged 30 points a game, who could have been great individual players. They were always part of a team. Coach Wooden taught us a system and made us play within that system.

"He treated us all the same when we were on the basketball court. He had us in great shape and we were fundamentally sound players. I guess the combination of all those things, and the fact that he was a great teacher, led to his incredible win streaks that I don't think will be matched in any sport.

"The guys who weren't playing obviously weren't

1972 UCLA

Head Coach—John Wooden   Final Record—30-0

Player	Pos.	Hgt.	Wgt.	Cl.	G	FG	FGA	Pct.	FT.	FTA	Pct.	Reb.	Pts.	Avg.
Bill Walton	C	6-11	210	So.	30	238	372	.640	157	223	.704	466	633	21.1
Henry Bibby	G	6-1	185	Sr.	30	183	407	.450	104	129	.806	106	470	15.7
Keith Wilkes	F	6-6	174	So.	30	171	322	.531	64	92	.696	245	406	13.5
Larry Farmer	F	6-5	195	Jr.	30	141	309	.456	39	71	.549	164	321	10.7
Greg Lee	G	6-4	195	So.	29	98	199	.492	56	68	.824	57	252	8.7
Larry Hollyfield	F	6-5	210	Jr.	30	95	185	.514	28	43	.651	98	218	7.3
Swen Nater	C	6-11	238	Jr.	29	83	155	.535	28	46	.609	139	194	6.7
Tommy Curtis	G	5-10	175	So.	30	55	126	.437	14	22	.636	63	124	4.1
Andy Hill	G	6-0	175	Sr.	26	16	45	.356	39	55	.709	20	71	2.7
Vince Carson	F	6-6	190	So.	28	26	65	.400	16	24	.667	72	68	2.4
Jon Chapman	F	6-6	210	Sr.	28	20	43	.465	6	12	.500	45	46	1.6
Gary Franklin	F	6-5	185	So.	26	14	34	.412	7	16	.438	26	35	1.3
Team												2	146	
UCLA					30	1140	2262	.504	558	803	.695	1647	2838	94.6
Opponents					30	766	2003	.382	396	578	.685	1140	1928	64.3

1973 UCLA

Head Coach—John Wooden   Final Record—30-0

Player	Pos.	Hgt.	Wgt.	Cl.	G	FG	FGA	Pct.	FT.	FTA	Pct.	Reb.	Pts.	Avg.
Bill Walton	C	6-11	220	Jr.	30	277	426	.650	58	102	.569	506	612	20.4
Keith Wilkes	F	6-6	180	Jr.	30	200	381	.525	43	66	.652	220	443	14.8
Larry Farmer	F	6-5	215	Sr.	30	160	313	.511	47	67	.701	150	367	12.2
Larry Hollyfield	G	6-4	215	Sr.	30	146	313	.466	29	59	.492	88	321	10.7
Tommy Curtis	G	5-11	170	Jr.	24	64	125	.512	26	39	.667	41	154	6.4
Dave Meyers	F	6-7	205	So.	28	52	109	.477	34	45	.756	82	138	4.9
Greg Lee	G	6-4	191	Jr.	30	44	93	.473	49	62	.790	38	137	4.6
Swen Nater	C	6-11	230	Sr.	29	39	85	.459	15	23	.652	95	93	3.2
Pete Trgovich	G-F	6-5	175	So.	25	34	89	.382	10	25	.400	43	78	3.1
Vince Carson	F	6-5	195	Jr.	26	18	35	.514	8	17	.471	58	44	1.7
Gary Franklin	F	6-4	187	Jr.	24	16	33	.485	6	12	.500	31	38	1.6
Casey Corliss	G	6-6	197	Fr.	2	0	0	.000	2	2	1.000	0	2	1.0
Bob Webb	G	6-2	160	Jr.	21	4	27	.148	5	6	.833	4	13	0.6
Ralph Drollinger	C	7-0	210	Fr.	2	0	1	.000	0	0	.000	1	0	0.0
Team												112		
UCLA					30	1054	2030	.519	332	525	.632	1469	2440	81.3
Opponents					30	794	2006	.396	214	315	.679	1014	1802	60.1

The Walton Gang poses with the 1973 championship trophy, its second and last, after dispatching Memphis State in the NCAA final.

real thrilled about it. Coach made no bones about telling us right at the beginning of the game that he would play the best eight players until the game was won or lost. It didn't take long to learn who those eight were.

"In a situation like UCLA, with the team winning every game, it's difficult to walk into a coach's office and say you think you ought to be playing more. Coach was very sensitive to the fact that there were guys who were not happy about their playing time, and he tried to make us aware that you had to pay your dues. When the opportunity came to play, he said we should have our heads screwed on right and not be disgruntled, and make the most of the opportunity.

"He was bluntly honest, and if you went to one of those meetings where you wanted to find out why or when or what, you might walk out of there with your tail between your legs wishing you hadn't gone in."

Wooden, asked to compare Alcindor (later known as Kareem Abdul-Jabbar) and Walton, began by describing Kareem as the most valuable ever to play the game.

"That doesn't necessarily mean the same thing as saying he is the best player," Wooden said. "But I believe Kareem caused opponents more problems at each end of the court than any other center I know of. Bill probably was a better basketball player than Kareem. He passed a little better, not that Kareem was a bad passer, and I would say that Bill could probably shoot a little better.

"But he still wasn't that tremendous threat in there. Bill could rebound and initiate the fast break with the outlet pass better than anybody I have ever coached. Overall, I would say our set offense might have been better with Walton because we had people to fill all the roles. But our overall game was probably a little bit stronger in the Jabbar era just because I think he was tremendously valuable."

FOUR

A Defensive Machine

SAN FRANCISCO

**1954-55
1955-56**

The world of sports never seems to lack for beauty contests. There are the All-America teams and the Most Valuable Player awards, and there are the statistical crowns and the sportsmanship honors.

Those things count, to be sure. However, they often amount to little more than salve for the losers. It is the winning of championships that really matters.

By the simple-but-bottom-line standard of titles produced (or at least contributed heavily to), Bill Russell stands as the most successful athlete in the history of basketball. He led the San Francisco Dons to NCAA championships in 1955 and 1956, then helped the United States to the gold medal in the '56 Olympic Games in Australia. From there, he put together an unparalleled professional career as the heart of a Boston Celtics team that won 11 National Basketball Association titles in 13 seasons. Not a bad run for a guy who struggled to get playing time on his high school team.

Even the greatest players are targeted for some criticism, though, and the one "charge" leveled against Russell was that he couldn't shoot. He scored adequately enough, but he came into prominence at a time—the mid-1950s—when the basketball ideal was a deadeye marksman. The jump shot was coming into vogue, and coaches everywhere seemed infatuated with acrobatic gunners.

Russell was the first of a new breed, the athletic big man. His shot-blocking skills were revolutionary, and his rebounding abilities controlled most games he played in. Far more important, he had a heart and a will dedicated solely to winning. As Bob Cousy, his Boston Celtics teammate, once said, "Bill Russell was the ultimate team player." By that, Cousy explained, Russell was willing to forgo the ego-inflating thrill of scoring to concentrate on the defense and rebounding that made his team successful. As it worked for the Celtics, that mindset earlier lifted San Francisco above the competition during Russell's collegiate days. From December 1954 through March 1956, Russell and the Dons set an NCAA record by winning 55 consecutive games.

Under Coach Phil Woolpert's guidance, center Russell and guard K.C. Jones were the key components of a defensive machine that ultimately changed the face of basketball. The happenstance manner in which this success occurred—in the days of hit-and-miss recruiting, Russell and Jones somehow found their way to USF—is startling.

Russell and Jones were fortunate because Woolpert was a coach with different ideas about the game, and most of them were defensive. "It just isn't good basketball," Woolpert once remarked of the up-tempo offense that was beginning to take hold in other programs. "I wouldn't know how to go about coaching it. You can't expect to execute scoring plays when you're running up and down the court like mad men."

Woolpert, a successful Bay-area high school coach, took over the top job at San Francisco in the fall of 1950 after the legendary and popular Pete Newell moved on to coach at California. Newell's shoes hadn't been easy ones to fill; he had coached the Dons to the National Invitation Tournament championship in 1949.

In Woolpert's first three seasons as the Dons'

coach, USF compiled 9-17, 11-13 and 10-11 records. Woolpert didn't make things any easier, in terms of attracting interest in his team, by emphasizing defense. His approach created more than a bit of grumbling among San Francisco fans. Still, Woolpert had the courage of his convictions. And circumstance brought him the unique players to execute what he believed in. The pairing of Jones, the backcourt sparkplug, and Russell, the dominant center, under Woolpert's tutelage brought together three people who believed in defense almost out of desperation.

Jones was the first major piece to the puzzle. In the San Francisco high school ranks, he set a Class AAA scoring record in his senior season, 1950-51. Despite that accomplishment, college scouts didn't appear interested in the Commerce High star until a newspaper reporter friendly to Jones wrote a story claiming that numerous colleges were recruiting him. Woolpert read the story, figured he better take a look at Jones and wound up offering a scholarship. A year after Jones' arrival on campus, Russell appeared on the scene.

Russell wasn't exactly a prize athlete at McClymonds High in east Oakland. In fact, he recalled in his autobiography, "Second Wind," that he was a troubled adolescent searching for a reason to be positive about himself. At McClymonds, he tried out for the football team but quit after one practice because he thought the coach was abusive. From there, he shifted his efforts to the cheerleading squad but failed to make the cut. His consolation, supposedly, would be junior-varsity basketball.

Season Results
1954-55 (28-1)

84	At Chico State	55	
54	At Loyola of Los Angeles	45	
40	At UCLA	47	
60	Oregon State	34	
56	UCLA	44	
94	Wichita at Oklahoma City*	75	
75	Oklahoma City at O.C.*	71	
73	George Washington at O.C.*	57	
70	San Diego State	56	
51	At St. Mary's	37	
56	San Jose State	30	
54	Santa Clara at Oakland	44	
62	Pacific	49	
76	Stanford	60	
84	California	62	
65	Loyola of Los Angeles	55	
69	St. Mary's	48	
72	At Pacific	52	
59	At San Jose State	49	
66	At Santa Clara	52	
65	St. Mary's	57	
64	At San Jose State	40	
67	Pacific	57	
73	Santa Clara	61	
89	West Texas State at S.F.†	66	
78	Utah at Corvallis, Ore.†	59	
57	Ore. St. at Corvallis, Ore.†	56	
62	Colorado at Kansas City†	50	
77	La Salle at Kansas City†	63	

*All-College Tournament
†NCAA Tournament

1955-56 (29-0)

70	Chico State	39	
58	Southern California	42	
72	San Francisco State	47	
65	Marquette at Chicago	58	
82	DePaul	59	
75	At Wichita	65	
61	At Loyola of New Orleans	43	
79	La Salle at New York*	62	
67	Holy Cross at New York*	51	
70	UCLA at New York*	53	
62	Pepperdine	51	
74	Santa Clara	56	
69	At Fresno State	50	
33	At California	24	
67	San Jose State	40	
68	Loyola of Los Angeles	40	
77	At Pacific	60	
79	Fresno State	46	
76	At San Jose State	52	
74	At St. Mary's	63	
80	At Santa Clara	44	
87	Pacific	49	
68	At Pepperdine	40	
65	At Loyola of Los Angeles	48	
82	St. Mary's	49	
72	UCLA at Corvallis, Ore.†	61	
92	Utah at Corvallis, Ore.†	77	
86	SMU at Evanston, Ill.†	68	
83	Iowa at Evanston, Ill.†	71	

*Holiday Festival
†NCAA Tournament

San Francisco's Bill Russell, an offensive player of limited skills, used his intimidating height and jumping ability to become a defensive giant.

More a ballhawk than a scorer, K.C. Jones was one of the driving forces behind San Francisco's record-setting 60-game winning streak.

Starting forward Stan Buchanan, not much of a scoring threat, mostly boxed out and played defense for the 1954-55 Dons.

The fact is, the gangly Russell didn't even possess the skills to make the JV squad. Enter George Powles, varsity basketball coach and noted American Legion baseball coach in Oakland.

Powles knew plenty about sports, but perhaps his greatest strength was in encouraging young people. For starters, he made Russell go out for the McClymonds varsity basketball team after he was pared from the junior varsity.

"What good will it do?" Russell wondered. "I can't even make the jayvees."

"I think you've got the makings of a good basketball player," said Powles, "and I want you to come out for the varsity."

"Those guys are better than I am," Russell shot back.

"Son, remember this," the coach said, "if you think the other guy is better than you, he will be."

Properly inspired, Russell found something toward which to direct his energies. Still, it wasn't an automatic thing. A bit awkward, he could run and jump quite well, but he froze with fear any time the ball came near him. When Russell made an infrequent appearance as a varsity substitute, students from his own school hooted. That, in turn, drove him to work harder.

By the latter part of his senior season, Russell had begun to make substantial progress, only by then it was too late for college scouts to take notice. However, he had caught the attention of Hal DeJulio, a former USF player, who asked Woolpert to give him a tryout. The coach agreed and, after taking a look at Russell, offered a scholarship. The coach wasn't completely sold on the big youngster, but Russell had height and a degree of agility. Plus, playground sessions with Powles had improved Russell's coordination and jumping and shooting skills.

There was little chemistry at the outset between Russell and Jones. Jones was quiet and painfully shy —not exactly traits that set off sparks in his relationship with Russell. But they roomed together, and Russell eventually drew Jones out from under his shell. Russell was a bookworm, but he was far from silent. He had an easy laugh that at times could rise to a screech. His thoughts on a wide variety of matters opened a world of fascination, Jones recalled.

The early-1950s time frame was not an easy period for blacks, and Russell and Jones were thrust into the middle of things. Both came from rural families that had migrated to California, Russell from Louisiana, Jones from Texas. Both were using basketball as a tool to escape poverty and the restrictions of race. Like Russell, Jones had found that basketball offered a solution to his identity problems.

"There's something that gives you confidence," Jones said. "That's what basketball did for me. In it,

I could escape into my own little world of being good at something."

The only problem was, Jones sprouted three inches over the summer after his senior year in high school, from 5-foot-10 to 6-1, and the spurt ruined the trajectory of his shot. He arrived at USF totally frustrated and confused by the loss of his offensive weapon. Perplexed by what had occurred, Jones, over the next two years, went from a scorer to a defensive hawk.

The Dons might have reached national-championship heights during the 1953-54 season had Jones not suffered an appendicitis attack that almost killed him just after the first game. With Jones out of action, the Dons played reasonably well but not at a level that some observers anticipated. Contributing to the less-than-expectations result was conflict on the team between the seniors and sophomore Russell. The veterans appeared to have an "elitist" attitude, Jones said. "We (the younger players) were just considered beneath them. It showed in our performance. As far as talent was concerned, our best team was 1954, but we wound up 14-7."

Still, the season brought a major chapter in the development of Russell, who was in the process of growing from 6-7 to 6-10. Russell's first varsity appearance was against Newell's California team, which featured center Bob McKeen. Early in the game, the Dons' center blocked a McKeen shot— and Newell was duly impressed. "Now where did he come from?" exclaimed the Cal coach. It was a question that would be posed time and again in the years ahead.

Jones returned to the lineup for the 1954-55 season, but the team's No. 2 and No. 4 scorers of the previous year—forward Frank Evangelho and guard Rich Mohr—had graduated. "...We came up with these no-shooters, no-talent guys like myself, (forward) Stan Buchanan and Russell," Jones said, "and then all of a sudden we came alive with this total team thing."

In December 1954, the unranked Dons faced a strong UCLA team on the Bruins' home court and Woolpert's charges were sizable underdogs. Russell played Bruins standout Willie Naulls tightly, though, and San Francisco turned in a highly creditable performance before falling, 47-40. The game changed the way the Dons looked at themselves. "That (the good showing) just flip-flopped our minds," Jones said. "Almost overnight, we became arrogantly confident, and we just rode that confidence."

After that game, Woolpert shuffled the starting lineup, inserting Hal Perry, a black, at guard in place of Bill Bush, a white, meaning that San Francisco would start more blacks than whites. To say the least, it was an unusual situation for the 1950s— anywhere.

"The beauty of it," Jones remembered, "was that

Sophomore Mike Farmer was a welcome addition to the Dons' frontcourt in 1955-56, when he averaged 8.4 points and 7.7 rebounds per game.

Bill Bush said, 'That's well and good.' There was no hassle about him being demoted. He said, 'This is best for the team, and I'll do it coming off the bench.' "

Along with his three juniors—Perry and Jones at guard and Russell at center—Woolpert started two seniors—forwards Buchanan and Jerry Mullen. Mullen was a good scorer—he would average 13.6 points per game for the season—but Buchanan possessed few offensive skills and therefore spent his time boxing out and playing defense.

"He just ran and hustled and did the best he could," Jones said of Buchanan. "That's what we all did. We were more into blue collar than talent. If we happened to score, fine. Our defense was so good, it took pressure off us offensively."

The Dons would not lose another game for two years. They rolled through their 1954-55 schedule with a defense that dismantled opponents. Woolpert explained his strategy to reporters: "If your opponents can't shoot, they can't score." In the backcourt, Jones and the cat-quick Perry were a high-pressure duo. "We just had this approach of getting up and getting all over people," Jones explained. Of course, having Russell at center allowed Jones and company to gamble defensively. If someone broke through the defense, Russell often blocked the shot or intimidated the shooter into missing.

"Heck," Russell told reporters, "I'd rather block a shot any day than score. It seems to do more for team morale."

Perry, reflecting many years later on his USF days, said "the country wasn't really ready for us...People who didn't know our team did not understand the tremendous human relationship we shared. Whenever we got into crisis situations, we'd call time out and Russell would say, 'All right, let's go do it!' So, we'd start shooting and he'd stuff our missed shots into the basket. He'd block shots and we'd run off eight points and the other team would say, 'My God! What happened?' "

Not a street-smart youngster like big-city products Jones and Russell, Perry, who was from the small Northern California town of Ukiah, had to prove he could play with the big guys—and he did just that.

"We'd go over to St. Ignatius High and play one-on-one, trying to learn from each other," said Perry, recalling his association with the biggest guy, Russell. "Russell wanted me to take him into the corners, then drive to the basket. This is how he practiced defense. He was always trying to get better. He knew his strengths and limitations. I remember him telling us, 'Look, guys, don't ever do what you can't do. Just do what you can do—and do it well.' "

Russell was fueled by a natural high-octane intensity that helped make him a quick leaper. And he

Forward Carl Boldt arrived at San Francisco in 1955 with the belief that he could be part of something special.

was ambidextrous. His left hand shut down many righthanded shooters. In fact, much of San Francisco's offense came from fast-break opportunities created by Russell's defense. "If Russell blocked the shot, we tried to determine which way it was gonna go," Jones said. "And then we were off to the races."

About the only relief opponents got was when Russell took a shot. He had very little range. However, there was no such thing as offensive goaltending at the time, so Russell often used his height and jumping ability to "guide" errant shots into the basket. He did that often enough to lead the team in scoring in the 1954-55 campaign, averaging 21.4 points per game.

Boasting a 23-1 regular-season record, USF entered the Western Regional of the NCAA Tournament and sliced up West Texas State, 89-66, and Utah, 78-59. Only in the regional title game were the Dons tested, when Oregon State and 7-3 center Swede Holbrook pushed them to the final buzzer before losing, 57-56. Oregon State adopted a strategy of double-teaming Russell while leaving Buchan-

The last big piece to the 1955-56 puzzle was sophomore Gene Brown, who saw plenty of playing time at a guard position.

an unguarded. Buchanan lacked confidence as a shooter and passed up several open shots until Woolpert ordered him to fire away. To his teammates' relief, Buchanan hit a couple of baseline jumpers, forcing Oregon State to shift strategy. That created just enough of an opening for the Dons to escape.

At the Final Four in Kansas City, Russell scored 24 points as San Francisco beat Colorado, 62-50, in a semifinal game and won a berth in the NCAA championship game against defending national kingpin La Salle. The Explorers, led by Tom Gola, had thrashed West Virginia, Princeton and Canisius in the East before edging Iowa in the other national semifinal. They clearly were the favorites of the Eastern basketball establishment.

"The West Coast was not a prominent factor in NCAA basketball," Gola said of the mid-'50s college game. "People aren't going to believe me, but Bill Russell was not a big name on the East Coast until they beat us in that tournament. Of course, the next year they went undefeated because Russell and K.C.

Jones went right through everybody. But the year that I went out there (Kansas City), Russell didn't know me and I didn't know him. In fact, I had never seen Bill Russell until we met in the lobby of the hotel. He was coming in and I was going out.

"I'll be honest with you. I've always said that Bill Russell is a great athlete. But in those days, I didn't think he could shoot, and I don't think he shot that well in the pros except for that little hook shot. But he had defensive ability that nobody could match. In those days. . .when somebody took a shot, he could jump up and guide it into the basket. He would get maybe 20 points a game just steering in all the shots."

The press predicted a giant showdown between Russell and the 6-6 Gola, but at the pregame meal, Woolpert informed the 6-1 Jones that he would be playing Gola. While Jones was shocked at the news, Woolpert knew Jones was a strong leaper and he figured that if Gola got by K.C., Russell would always be around. Primarily, Woolpert didn't want the task of guarding Gola to take Russell away from the basket.

After a few moments of apprehension, Jones calmed down. "I was out of my mind once the game started," he said. "I knew guarding him would be difficult, but I also knew that if he posted up or got by me, Russell would be there. And he did get by me a couple of times. But you're never going to stop a great player one-on-one. The important thing is, I was not intimidated."

The 1955 NCAA title game was tight in the early going as both teams performed in a near trance. In the second half, Woolpert's strategy paid off in a big way as the Dons steadily outdistanced La Salle for a 77-63 triumph. Jones finished with 24 points and Russell, recipient of the tournament's Outstanding Player Award, contributed 23 points and 25 rebounds. Gola wound up with 16 points, but he went without a field goal over one 21-minute stretch.

"The guy who hurt us that night was K.C. Jones," Gola said, "and K.C. was not known for his shooting ability. Russell guarded (backcourt standout) Alonzo Lewis and also sagged off back into the pivot on me. Alonzo just couldn't hit his shots (Lewis made only one field goal). If he had, it would have been nip-and-tuck all the way. But that was one of those things.

"There's always a guy on the team who sacrifices, who plays good defense, who moves the ball, and that was K.C. He was the catalyst for those San Francisco teams."

Playmaker Perry returned with Russell and Jones for the 1955-56 season. However, forwards Mullen (the team's No. 2 scorer the previous year) and Buchanan had used up their eligibility. No problem. Woolpert had able recruits on hand in touted sophomore Mike Farmer and Army veteran Carl Boldt, who also was a junior-college transfer. Another

Phil Woolpert, the coach and architect of San Francisco's two-year reign of terror, receives an award from professional great George Mikan after the Dons' 1955 national-championship season.

sophomore, guard Gene Brown, joined the Dons' rotation.

Farmer, a 6-7, 210-pounder from Richmond, Calif., was projected to fill the frontcourt power void created by the loss of Mullen, who in 1954-55 had averaged 7.1 rebounds per game in support of Russell's 20.5 mark. Boldt arrived on the Hilltop with the reputation as a strong offensive player—and with the belief that he was going to be part of something special.

"When I was recruited out of the Army, Ollie Matson (former Dons football star) told me to go to USF because of Russell," Boldt said. "Ollie said I'd be playing for the greatest winner of all time. We were a great team, but so much came down to Russell. . . ."

As San Francisco prepared for the new season, things looked bright for the foreseeable future, all right, but there was one disquieting note. While Jones had been granted an extra year of varsity competition because of the appendicitis attack that limited his 1953-54 season to one game, his eligibility extended only through the regular season. If the

Dons made a repeat appearance in the NCAA Tournament, they would do so without their main spark.

Also, over the off-season, the NCAA had adopted what became known as the "Russell rule," widening the free-throw lane from six feet to 12 in an effort to keep the USF star and other collegiate big men farther away from the basket. It had little effect.

"This is a hungry team," Woolpert said just before the season. "Their appetites are such that they can do a lot of eating before they're filled up." The Dons proceeded to gorge themselves.

San Francisco blitzed 25 opponents during the regular season and won plaudits from Joe Lapchick, the esteemed St. John's coach, in the process. "They're the best college team I've ever seen," said Lapchick, who in December 1955 had watched Woolpert and company make off with the Holiday Festival tournament championship at New York's Madison Square Garden, a tournament in which Lapchick's Redmen had competed.

San Francisco's greatness was mostly Russell's, said Iowa center Bill Logan. "You jump as high as you can and you're still only high enough to tap Russell on the shoulder," the 6-7 Logan cracked.

"Yes, it's Russell," Woolpert said, "but it's more than just him. Why, this is the finest college basketball team I've ever seen."

Any doubters remaining in the East ended their holdout early in the season. In winning the Holiday Festival, the Dons blew away some of the best teams in the country. La Salle fell the first night, 79-62, as Russell wiped 22 rebounds off the boards and scored 26 points. In its next outing, San Francisco thumped Holy Cross and Tom Heinsohn, Russell's future teammate on the Celtics, by a 67-51 score. Russell again grabbed 22 rebounds; this time, he

scored 24 points. In the Festival's championship game, the Dons' defense thoroughly frustrated one of John Wooden's fine UCLA teams and USF frolicked, 70-53. Russell turned in a 17-point, 18-rebound night.

A month later, San Francisco visited Pete Newell's California team, and the former Dons coach was ready with a slowdown. The Dons still won with comparative ease, 33-24, for their 40th straight victory. By tournament time, their winning streak had reached 51 games.

Jones, of course, would now have to watch from the bench. "No man will miss K.C. during the tournament as much as I will," Russell said. "You take a

1955 SAN FRANCISCO
Head Coach—Phil Woolpert   Final Record—28-1

Player	Pos.	Hgt.	Wgt.	Cl.	G	FG	FGA	Pct.	FT.	FTA	Pct.	Reb.	Pts.	Avg.
Bill Russell	C	6-10	205	Jr.	29	229	423	.541	164	278	.590	594	622	21.4
Jerry Mullen	F	6-5	195	Sr.	27	136	359	.379	94	129	.729	192	366	13.6
K.C. Jones	G	6-1	202	Jr.	29	105	293	.358	97	144	.674	148	307	10.6
Hal Perry	G	5-10	172	Jr.	29	73	196	.372	54	72	.750	55	200	6.9
Stan Buchanan	F	6-3	180	Sr.	29	48	159	.302	54	76	.711	93	150	5.2
Bob Wiebusch	F	6-3	180	Sr.	28	38	118	.322	25	35	.714	60	101	3.6
Rudy Zannini	G	5-7	152	Sr.	27	15	50	.300	21	29	.724	10	51	1.9
Dick Lawless	F	6-3	185	Sr.	26	17	63	.270	12	20	.600	29	46	1.8
Warren Baxter	G	5-8	165	Jr.	19	11	21	.524	12	17	.706	9	34	1.8
Bill Bush	G	6-0	165	Jr.	25	10	30	.333	20	36	.556	25	40	1.6
Steve Balchios	G	6-0	170	So.	8	2	3	.667	4	8	.500	5	8	1.0
Jack King	F	6-3	170	So.	16	4	12	.333	7	10	.700	7	15	0.9
Tom Nelson	F	6-4	195	So.	10	2	8	.250	1	2	.500	5	5	0.5
Gordon Kirby	C	6-4	205	Sr.	20	3	15	.200	1	5	.200	13	7	0.4
Team												81		
San Francisco					29	693	1750	.396	566	861	.657	1326	1952	67.3
Opponents					29	513	1611	.318	489	743	.658	977	1515	52.2

1956 SAN FRANCISCO
Head Coach—Phil Woolpert   Final Record—29-0

Player	Pos.	Hgt.	Wgt.	Cl.	G	FG	FGA	Pct.	FT.	FTA	Pct.	Reb.	Pts.	Avg.
Bill Russell	C	6-10	215	Sr.	29	246	480	.513	105	212	.495	609	597	20.6
K.C. Jones*	G	6-1	205	Sr.	25	76	208	.365	93	142	.655	130	245	9.8
Hal Perry	G	5-10	160	Sr.	29	107	293	.365	51	70	.729	57	265	9.1
Carl Boldt	F	6-4	190	Jr.	28	94	288	.326	54	69	.783	140	242	8.6
Mike Farmer	F	6-7	210	So.	28	101	272	.371	34	62	.548	218	236	8.4
Gene Brown	G	6-2	170	So.	29	78	207	.377	50	78	.641	127	206	7.1
Bill Mallen	F	6-3	230	So.	11	19	48	.396	8	15	.533	38	46	4.2
Mike Preaseau	F	6-5	191	So.	29	45	123	.366	28	46	.609	91	118	4.1
Warren Baxter	G	5-8	171	Sr.	26	22	73	.301	14	21	.667	18	58	2.2
Harold Payne	G	5-11	160	So.	15	6	17	.353	3	5	.600	2	15	1.0
John Koljian	F	6-3	190	So.	11	4	12	.333	3	7	.429	11	11	1.0
Bill Bush	G	6-0	170	Sr.	22	5	24	.208	10	16	.625	17	20	0.9
Jack King	F	6-3	170	Jr.	22	6	37	.162	6	13	.462	21	18	0.8
Tom Nelson	C	6-4	192	Jr.	19	3	15	.200	3	5	.600	13	9	0.5
Steve Balchios	G	6-0	162	Jr.	13	3	5	.600	0	0	.000	3	6	0.5
Vince Boyle	C	6-5	190	So.	10	0	0	.000	1	5	.200	4	1	0.1
Team												74		
San Francisco					29	815	2102	.388	463	766	.604	1573	2093	72.2
Opponents					29	509	1599	.318	496	742	.688	1069	1514	52.2

*Ineligible for NCAA Tournament as fifth-year player.

After leading San Francisco to consecutive national titles, Russell signed a contract (above) with the Boston Celtics and went on to help them win 11 NBA championships.

sling shot. I'm the forks and K.C. is the rubber band. He makes the operation go."

Fortunately for USF, though, Brown filled in admirably for Jones. San Francisco turned aside Wooden's UCLA team a second time, 72-61, as Brown tossed in 23 points. Utah was the Dons' next tournament victim, a 92-77 loser, with Russell and Brown combining for 45 points as Woolpert's crew earned a return to the Final Four.

In a national semifinal game at Evanston, Ill., four Dons scored in double figures—sophomore Farmer led the way with 26 points—and the West Coast crew exploded past Southern Methodist, 86-68. Now, USF was one victory from its second straight NCAA championship.

Standing in the Dons' path to another national crown was an Iowa team led by front-line stars Logan and Carl (Sugar) Cain. The Hawkeyes had left tourney victims Morehead State, Kentucky and Temple in their wake, but they were no match for Russell and friends. San Francisco prevailed, 83-71. Russell scored 26 points in the final, but didn't win the Outstanding Player Award. That honor went to Temple's Hal Lear, who had broken the tourna-

ment's single-game scoring record with a 48-point spree in the consolation game against SMU.

Only Russell, at 20.6, posted a double-figure season scoring average for San Francisco, which boasted a per-game victory margin of 20 points (compared with the 15.1 mark produced by the previous year's team). Jones finished his 25-game season with a 9.8-point scoring figure, while Perry wound up at 9.1. Boldt and Farmer combined for 17 points per outing, with Farmer contributing a 7.7 rebound average as well.

With Russell and Jones having graduated, Brown stepped to the fore as USF's main man and the Dons extended their winning streak to 60 games during the 1956-57 season before being bushwhacked at Illinois, 62-33. Russell and Jones, of course, went on to greatness with the Boston Celtics and Farmer enjoyed a six-year career in the pro ranks.

Asked recently how Bill Russell would fare in today's game, Gola was quick to answer. "Nobody," Gola said, "could touch Russell." And, for two years, no one could touch the San Francisco Dons.

FIVE

Perfect, But No Cigar

KENTUCKY

1953-54

"I hold no love for Kentucky," St. Louis Coach Ed Hickey said in December 1953 after watching Adolph Rupp's Wildcats beat his Billikens, 71-59. "But they're the sweetest-operating team to watch that I've ever seen. And that Frank Ramsey—I've said it before and I'll say it again—is the best college player in the country."

Hickey knew more than a little about college basketball and far more than most about how to compete against the nation's premier program. In an NCAA Division I coaching career that would end a decade later, he would win 435 games in 26 years. And, of the seven total losses that mighty Kentucky suffered in the 1948-49, 1950-51 and 1951-52 seasons, three of the defeats came at the hands of Hickey's St. Louisans. The first two of those Kentucky teams were NCAA champions; the third finished atop both final wire-service polls of the season.

The 1953-54 edition of the Kentucky Wildcats, though, might well rank as the best of Rupp's gifted teams in the noted coach's 41-season career at the Lexington-based university. Those Wildcats went undefeated in 25 games and outscored opponents by an average of 27.2 points per game.

The performance turned in by Rupp's athletes would have been remarkable under any conditions, but the circumstances under which Cliff Hagan, Frank Ramsey, Lou Tsioropoulos and company excelled stagger the imagination. Winners of 29 of 32 games in the 1951-1952 campaign and NCAA titlists in three of four seasons previous to that, the Wildcats were forced to sit out the 1952-53 season because of major rules infractions dating to 1948. First the Southeastern Conference and then the NCAA

came down hard on the Kentucky program, and the result was a season of nothing more than intra-squad games for Rupp's players. It wasn't exactly the time-tested way of keeping a team at peak efficiency.

While Rupp may have been effectively barred from competing, he wasn't about to stop building his team. "I will never be satisfied," Rupp reportedly said, "until the men who suspended us hand us the national championship trophy."

To that end, the Kentucky mentor conducted practice sessions three or four times per week during his team's suspended season. The point-shaving scandal of the late-1940s—made public in 1951—and other wrongdoing (including payments to Kentucky basketball players by various team backers) had taken their toll on the Wildcats' program, and Rupp wasn't about to let Wildcat basketball plummet even further.

At the end of the 1951-52 season, Kentucky had only nine varsity players on scholarship, an unusually low number because Rupp followed the practice of bringing in as many as two dozen freshmen each year and letting them battle for a spot on the varsity. Although the Wildcats were on probation, Rupp restocked the program with young talent.

"Coach Rupp brought in 12 to 15 freshmen," Ramsey recalled. "We had a tremendous group. We practiced three or four times a week. I thoroughly enjoyed the year as a student."

Academically, Ramsey, Hagan and defensive standout Tsioropoulos were all seniors. Thinking they would retain full athletic eligibility for the 1953-54 season, the players continued with sizable

Adolph Rupp, stung by a one-season suspension handed to his Kentucky program, was determined to guide his 1953-54 Wildcats to a national title.

course workloads. Tsioropoulos would earn his degree in the summer of 1953; Ramsey and Hagan were on target to receive their degrees early in 1954.

Four times during the 1952-53 season, beginning in December and ending in February, Rupp set up intrasquad games and invited Kentucky's basketball-crazy public to attend. The four events drew a little more than 36,000 people. One scrimmage was held the night of an ice storm, the worst weather of the winter, and still 6,000 fans showed up to cheer the Wildcats. The squads were named the Hagans and Ramseys after the two co-captains.

Already a master motivator and strategist, Rupp turned what appeared to be a minus into a plus. He used the adverse circumstances to build his team's mental toughness for the following season. "I think he felt the judge in New York had taken some very unwarranted potshots at him (in the wake of the point-shaving mess)," Ramsey said when asked about Rupp's desire for vindication.

Rupp's long-fixed image was that of an unsmiling dictator. But Rupp had a sense of humor, which he didn't lose even in the darkest hours, Ramsey said. As a spoof, the coach prepared a news release during the year of probation that focused on a play he supposedly had devised, a "front-back block." Then he sat back and hooted as news organizations inquired about his new secret weapon.

In reality, there were few gimmicks in the Baron's approach. He recruited the best athletes he could find and drilled them relentlessly in fundamentals.

"Mostly he took a bunch of raw country boys out of small towns," Ramsey said. "He would demand more than they thought they could do. He was a stern, demanding disciplinarian."

The soft side of the staff consisted of Harry Lancaster, longtime Rupp assistant, who would listen to the players' personal and academic problems.

Rupp also listened to his players, but mostly on basketball matters, Ramsey said. "You could tell him some things wouldn't work," the Madisonville, Ky., product said. "He would listen, but then he'd be able to convince you that they would (work)."

The Kentucky coach was a fiercely proud, unbending man, not the type to endear himself to opposing coaches (Hickey or anyone else). Many considered Rupp arrogant and aloof. His tremendous success after the war only increased these feelings.

By the time December 1953 rolled around, Kentucky's players, coaching staff and legion of fans were champing at the bit, to say the least.

With a year's practice, the '53-'54 Wildcats opened the season as if loosed from a cage. Along with Rupp's motivation, they had talent and experience. At 6-foot-4, Hagan played center and possessed a smooth hook shot and a solid rebounding game. The young man from Owensboro, Ky., had been a consensus All-America in 1951-52 when he

Quick and talented Frank Ramsey was a good outside shooter who was particularly adept at going to the basket.

averaged 21.6 points for Kentucky.

Ramsey, too, had gotten some All-America recognition that season—he was a first-team selection of two news outlets—while contributing stellar play from his guard spot. At 6-3, he was an unusually big backcourt player for that era. He had quickness to go with his size and scored frequently (15.9 average in Kentucky's last competitive season) in Rupp's fast-breaking offense. He was a fine outside shooter, but his quickness made him particularly effective going to the hoop. If he saw an opening, he usually was gone.

The 6-5 Tsioropoulos, amazingly the club's tallest starter, served as the frontcourt "stopper" on de-

Cliff Hagan, a smooth 6-4 center with a deadly hook shot, was Kentucky's leading scorer, averaging 24 points per game.

Season Results
1953-54 (25-0)

86	Temple	59	106	Georgia	55
81	At Xavier	66	100	Georgia at Owensboro, Ky.	68
101	Wake Forest	69	97	At Florida	55
71	At St. Louis	59	88	Mississippi	62
85	Duke✩	69	81	Mississippi State	49
73	La Salle✩	60	90	Tennessee	63
74	Minnesota	59	76	At DePaul	61
77	Xavier	71	100	Vanderbilt	64
105	Georgia Tech	53	109	Auburn at Montgomery, Ala.	79
81	DePaul	63	68	At Alabama	43
94	Tulane	43	63	LSU at Nashville†	56
97	At Tennessee	71			
85	At Vanderbilt	63	✩Kentucky Invitational		
99	Georgia Tech at Louisville	48	†SEC Playoff		

fense. He was the team's tough guy, emphasizing rebounding and defensive pressure from his forward position. Bill Evans and Phil Grawemeyer held down the other corner spot, with Evans playing considerably bigger than his 6-1 stature would suggest. Ramsey's companion at guard in this deep lineup was either Gayle Rose or Linville Puckett.

While Kentucky's "Big Three" standouts were seniors eligibility-wise, Evans and Rose were juniors and Grawemeyer and Puckett were sophomores. Six of the seven heavy-duty Wildcats were from the Bluegrass State, with Tsioropoulos the lone "import" (he was from Lynn, Mass.).

Each member of the starting five had played center in high school, Ramsey said, and thereby rebounded and moved the ball well. Rupp had recruited the players solely on athletic ability, and they could run and jump.

Kentucky's fast break was a thing of beauty, and when the Wildcats needed another weapon they could flash into a demoralizing full-court press. The only thing was, they seldom needed any extra dimensions to their game.

The Wildcats' return to the basketball wars was marked by an outburst of energy and confidence.

"We had sat out a year," Ramsey explained, "and we were coming back with that great Kentucky tradition, with Coach Adolph Rupp and our system. We were very confident in our system and our ability to execute it.

"When Hagan took a hook shot, I knew that thing was going in. When we had a tough opponent like Tom Gola (La Salle) or Bob Pettit (Louisiana State), I knew Lou Tsioropoulos would shut 'em down, or Billy Evans would shut 'em down."

This confidence permeated every arena the Wildcats entered, leaving opponents in awe. In no facility was the confidence level higher than Memorial Coliseum in Lexington, where Kentucky reopened play on December 5, 1953. The building was crammed with 12,000 fans, who grew only louder as the game progressed. Temple had the misfortune to be the first opponent in Rupp's path toward vindication. The Owls got steamrolled, 86-59, as Hagan set a school scoring record with 51 points.

After drubbing Xavier, Wake Forest and Hickey's St. Louis team, the Wildcats staged their first-ever UK Invitational on December 21-22. With the gambling scandal cutting into New York college basketball, particularly at Madison Square Garden, there was a movement across the country "to return the game to the college campuses." The holiday tournament in Lexington was part of that movement, and Rupp didn't cheat the fans with low-grade competition.

On the first night, Kentucky ran past a good Duke team, 85-69. Then, in the final, the Wildcats dispatched La Salle and All-America Gola, 73-60. The Wildcats were 6-0 and rolling.

In the next month, Rupp's talented and vengeful crew marched inexorably—or so it seemed—toward its objective: success in the NCAA Tournament. The Wildcats beat up on Minnesota, got by Xavier for the second time and then pounded Georgia Tech, DePaul, Tulane and Tennessee into submission (the four-game victory margin was 147 points). However, three days after the latter triumph—a 26-point SEC romp at Knoxville, Tenn.—the Kentucky program was sent reeling. Again.

In its January 26, 1954, edition, the Louisville Courier-Journal reported that in all likelihood Hagan, Ramsey and Tsioropoulos would be ineligible for the NCAA Tournament because of a little-known NCAA rule prohibiting graduate students from competing in the tourney.

Tsioropoulos, the story pointed out, had received his bachelor of arts degree the previous August, while Hagan and Ramsey would earn their degrees by the end of the current semester (and thus before the start of NCAA Tournament action). "Apparently there is only one way Ramsey and Hagan can remain eligible (for NCAA postseason play)," Courier-Journal sportswriter Larry Boeck reported. "That would be for them to flunk a subject they now expect to pass. This would deny them their bachelor degrees."

Rupp, at first, was disbelieving. "Why, I'm sure all three of these boys are eligible," he said with apparent certainty and undeniable hope.

The rule—long since changed—was indeed on the books at the time, and Kentucky subsequently got the grim news from the NCAA.

"The rest of these boys and I were in high school when those things happened," said Ramsey, referring to the point-shaving and payment scandals that had precipitated the 1952-53 suspension of Kentucky basketball and led to the eligibility problems. "Why'd they take it out on us?"

Ramsey, Hagan and Tsioropoulos all had worked diligently toward graduation, prompting a disappointed Hagan to point out that if the three had dogged it academically, they would have been eligible for the 1954 NCAA Tournament. NCAA rules requiring athletes to make "normal progress" toward degrees came under a barrage of criticism from Kentucky supporters, who charged that college athletics' governing body had made a farce of its own laudable dictum.

Shaken but still playing at full throttle, Kentucky proceeded to bash Vanderbilt by 22 points, Georgia Tech by 51, Georgia by another 51 and then by 32 and Florida by 42. A week and a half into February, the Wildcats boasted a 17-0 record but didn't quite know what the postseason gods had in store for them.

The picture became a little clearer on the night of February 11 when Kentucky Athletic Director Bernie Shively announced that his university would

Gayle Rose, a member of Kentucky's deep and talented supporting cast, spent most of his time in the backcourt alongside Ramsey.

not ask the SEC to waive its rule against league participation in the National Invitation Tournament. The NIT, badly in need of a box-office attraction, had hoped to land the No. 1-ranked Wildcats, whose NCAA Tournament quest appeared doomed because of the judgment against its graduate-student stars.

At the same time, the NCAA did give Kentucky officials one bit of good news. Should Kentucky and Louisiana State, both unbeaten in Southeastern Conference play to that point, continue undefeated in league competition and thereby be matched in a playoff game to determine the SEC's representative in the NCAA Tournament, Hagan, Ramsey and Tsioropoulos would be eligible for such a tie-breaker contest. The reasoning, an NCAA official said, was that conference playoffs were governed by conference rules despite the fact an NCAA berth would be at stake. And the SEC had no rule against the use of graduate students.

Ramsey puts the ball on the floor and heads to the basket in Kentucky's 1953-54 season opener against Temple.

Kentucky and Louisiana State, who wouldn't meet during the regular season because of a scheduling disagreement, were on track for just such a playoff. The Wildcats held up their end of the bargain by finishing 14-0 in league play and 24-0 overall as a result of a 68-43 laugher at Alabama on March 1. LSU, unbeaten SEC titlist the year before when Kentucky watched from the sidelines, was 13-0 in conference play at this juncture and needed to beat Tulane in its regular-season finale to force a showdown with Rupp's 'Cats.

Rupp, meanwhile, was lavish in his praise of the Kentucky squad, the first Wildcat team in more than 40 years to complete the regular season with a perfect record.

"There is no question this is the best team we've ever had at Kentucky and the finest team I have ever seen," said Rupp, who called the perfect season "what everybody in Kentucky wanted."

Folks in Louisiana wanted something, too: another NCAA Tournament berth. A Final Four participant in 1953 behind the scintillating play of Bob Pettit, LSU forced a playoff to decide the SEC's 1954

representative in the big show when it fended off Tulane.

The Kentucky-LSU battle for a spot in the NCAA tourney was contested at a neutral site, Nashville, Tenn. In a classic struggle played before a capacity crowd of 7,200, the Wildcats and Tigers fought to a 46-46 deadlock after three quarters of play (college basketball's time structure was changed to two 20-minute sessions the next season). The 'Cats, sparked by Ramsey's outside shooting and Hagan's consistent play inside, finally pulled away for a 63-56 triumph. Ramsey wound up with 13 field goals and 30 points, while Hagan scored 17 points. LSU's Pettit, who later would team with Hagan to form a potent 1-2 scoring punch with the National Basketball Association's St. Louis Hawks, matched Cliff's output.

Having won the right to represent the SEC in the NCAA Tournament but facing the prospect of playing in the meet without their "Big Three," Wildcat players were asked to vote on the NCAA bid. They voted overwhelmingly to accept.

"I had hoped you would vote not to go and not to put this record (25-0) in jeopardy," Rupp told his

Not everything went right for the Wildcats in 1953-54, as this reaction by Rupp (center) and the Kentucky bench will attest.

1954 KENTUCKY

Head Coach—Adolph Rupp   Final Record—25-0

Player	Pos.	Hgt.	Wgt.	Cl.	G	FG	FGA	Pct.	FT.	FTA	Pct.	Reb.	Pts.	Avg.
Cliff Hagan	C	6-4	200	Sr.	25	234	514	.455	132	191	.691	338	600	24.0
Frank Ramsey	G	6-3	185	Sr.	25	179	430	.416	132	181	.729	221	490	19.6
Lou Tsioropoulos	F	6-5	200	Sr.	25	137	390	.351	89	129	.690	240	363	14.5
Bill Evans	F-G	6-1	170	Jr.	25	86	231	.372	49	63	.778	180	221	8.8
Gayle Rose	G	6-0	155	Jr.	23	56	162	.346	42	65	.646	31	154	6.7
Phil Grawemeyer	F-C	6-7	180	So.	25	64	172	.372	19	35	.543	152	147	5.9
Linville Puckett	G	6-0	165	So.	24	44	149	.295	35	52	.673	53	123	5.1
Jerry Bird	F-C	6-6	200	So.	4	4	17	.235	6	8	.750	12	14	3.5
Bill Bibb	F	6-4	180	So.	16	10	32	.313	7	12	.583	25	27	1.7
Hugh Coy	F	6-1	185	So.	10	4	14	.286	6	10	.600	11	14	1.4
Willie Rouse	G	6-0	160	Jr.	5	2	9	.222	2	4	.500	1	6	1.2
Dan Chandler	G	5-11	160	So.	7	2	5	.400	3	3	1.000	0	7	1.0
Jess Curry	G	5-11	165	So.	9	2	17	.118	4	8	.500	4	8	0.9
Harold Hurst	C	6-7	190	So.	7	2	9	.222	2	12	.167	19	6	0.9
Clay Evans	G	5-9	165	So.	7	2	5	.400	0	4	.000	2	4	0.6
Pete Grigsby	G	5-10	165	So.	3	0	2	.000	1	2	.500	2	1	0.3
Others							1	4	.250	0	1	.000		2	
Others & Team													27		
Totals					25	829	2162	.383	529	780	.678	1318	2187	87.5
Opponents					25	481	1574	.306	546	872	.626	851	1508	60.3

The 1953-54 Kentucky Wildcats: Front row (left to right)—Rupp, Linville Puckett, Jess Curry, Rose, Clay Evans, Willie Rouse, Dan Chandler, Pete Grigsby, assistant coach Harry Lancaster. Second row—Manager Mike Dolan, Hugh Coy, Hagan, Lou Tsioropoulos, Jerry Bird, Phil Grawemeyer, Harold Hurst, Bill Bibb, Ramsey, Bill Evans.

team. "If we can't play with our full team. . .we're not going." Instead, LSU carried the SEC banner into the tournament.

So, Rupp and his players, ever-hopeful at midseason of rebounding for a national championship after an agonizing year-in-waiting, would watch once more from the sidelines. And what they saw proved particularly difficult to take. La Salle, a team Kentucky had handled by 13 points in December, rose up and emerged as the NCAA kingpin.

As good as Tom Gola and the Explorers were—and their 26-4 record was worthy of the utmost respect—the specter of the Kentucky Wildcats could not be ignored. The final United Press poll of the season, released nearly two weeks before the NCAA Tournament concluded, listed Indiana as No. 1 (the Hoosiers fell to Notre Dame in the tourney), Kentucky No. 2 and La Salle No. 11. The Associated Press' final rankings, voted upon after the NCAA title game, showed Kentucky in the top spot, La Salle as the runner-up and Indiana as No. 4.

Hagan, who in Rupp's view had "the greatest natural touch of any player I've seen," won consensus All-America honors in his second straight competitive season. Making extraordinary use of his hook shot, he scored 24 points per game and further aided the 'Cats' cause with a 13.5 rebound average. Ramsey, bound for sixth-man fame with the Boston Celtics, contributed 19.6 points and 8.8 rebounds

per outing, while Tsioropoulos pitched in with averages of 14.5 points (nearly double his output of 1951-52) and 9.6 rebounds. The "Big Three" had enjoyed a big season.

Backboard strength was a particular forte of these Wildcats, who despite a starting front line measuring only 6-4, 6-5 and 6-1 collected 52.7 rebounds per game compared with opponents' 34.0 mark.

The 6-1 Evans, a tenacious defender, picked off 7.2 rebounds per contest as he waged war under the basket with much taller opponents. Called "one of the most underrated players we ever had at Kentucky" by longtime assistant coach Lancaster, Evans also had his moments offensively. He averaged 8.8 points and was the team's top marksman from the foul line. Forward Grawemeyer and guards Rose and Puckett chipped in with a combined 17.7 points per game.

All the great numbers, of course, couldn't and didn't make up for the crushing blow of Hagan, Ramsey and Tsioropoulos being denied participation in the NCAA Tournament and Rupp's subsequent decision to keep his team out of the tourney. After all, the Wildcats had entered the season hellbent on revenge and wound up being foiled.

To their credit, though, the 1953-54 Kentucky Wildcats were never foiled on the court. They were, in fact, seldom even challenged.

SIX

Three Glorious Seasons

OHIO STATE

1959-60
1960-61
1961-62

When Fred Taylor became head basketball coach at Ohio State in 1958, he watched helplessly as opposing offenses ran roughshod over his first team. It didn't take long for the former Buckeye center to realize that he had a lot to learn.

So he went right to the top. He approached California Coach Pete Newell, the master defensive strategist of the era, at an off-season clinic in Moorhead, Minn. Newell, whose Bears had just won the 1959 NCAA championship, listened to Taylor's plea for help, thought about it for about 10 seconds and then began a succession of one-on-one coaching clinics that later would come back to haunt him. His student's final grade would not be handed out until the following March, when Newell's Bears and Taylor's Buckeyes would meet in San Francisco for the national title.

"Freddie had taken over the year before at Ohio State," Newell recalled, "and they (the Buckeyes) had the worst defensive record in Big Ten history. He comes to my clinic and says, 'Pete, I really want to talk to you. I'd like to pick your brain on defense. Will you help us?'

"I said fine. So I spend about three hours every afternoon going over just defense with Fred. In December the next year, I'm playing against Jerry West's team (West Virginia) in the L.A. Classic. And Fred's assistant comes to me. He's got a list of questions a foot long that he says Fred needs answers to. I answer all his questions and later in the season Fred meets me somewhere, and he's got a few more questions.

"What do you think happens? I end up playing Ohio State in the NCAA finals and he beats me with some of the defensive things we talked about."

"What Coach Taylor learned paid off," said Indiana Coach Bobby Knight, who was a sophomore substitute on Ohio State's 1959-60 team, "because as the '60 season wore on, we became a better and better defensive team."

Those defensive lessons certainly played a big part in Ohio State's rise to national prominence, but the real key to success was a crop of talented sophomores that would wreak havoc on opposing teams for three glorious seasons. When Jerry Lucas, John Havlicek and Mel Nowell were pronounced ready for varsity duty in 1959, they joined holdovers Larry Siegfried and Joe Roberts to comprise one of the greatest shooting teams in college basketball history.

The headliner of this group was Lucas, an enigmatic and reluctant star who moved his 6-foot-8 frame around the court with incredible fluidity, passed like a point guard, set the fast break in motion with his quick outlets and shot with amazing accuracy. And while basketball observers marveled at the youngster's vast array of talents, sportwriters were startled by his down-to-earth off-court demeanor. He was, literally, too good to be true.

"First come my studies," Lucas constantly told curious interviewers, "and then basketball."

That attitude was not the ploy of an image-conscious youngster. Image meant nothing to Jerry Lucas.

In a prep career that drew national attention, Lucas had led Middletown (Ohio) High School to a pair of state championships and 76 consecutive victories, tasting his only defeat in his last high school

Fred Taylor learned his lessons well and coached Ohio State to the 1960 national championship.

Season Results
1959-60 (25-3)

77	Wake Forest	69	
94	Memphis State	55	
94	Pittsburgh	49	
99	Butler	66	
81	At St. Louis	74	
96	At Butler	68	
92	At Utah	97	
91	At Brigham Young	79	
93	At Kentucky	96	
97	Illinois	73	
96	Indiana	95	
109	Delaware	38	
81	Northwestern	64	
85	At Purdue	71	
111	Michigan State	79	
99	Michigan	52	
77	At Northwestern	58	
106	At Wisconsin	69	
75	Iowa	47	
109	At Illinois	81	
84	At Michigan State	83	
93	Wisconsin	68	
83	At Indiana	99	
75	At Minnesota	66	
98	W. Kentucky at Louisville*	79	
86	Georgia Tech at Louisville*	69	
76	NYU at San Francisco*	54	
75	California at San Francisco*	55	

*NCAA Tournament

1960-61 (27-1)

85	At Ohio University	64	
81	St. Louis	66	
103	Army	54	
93	At Wichita	82	
90	At Loyola of Chicago	65	
84	Detroit	73	
97	Seton Hall at New York*	57	
70	St. John's at New York*	65	
84	St. Bonaventure at N. York*	82	
91	Illinois	65	
86	Evansville	59	
79	At Northwestern	45	
75	Minnesota	56	
92	Purdue	62	
100	At Wisconsin	68	
80	At Michigan	58	
100	Indiana	65	
83	At Michigan State	68	
89	Northwestern	65	
62	At Iowa	61	
73	At Indiana	69	
97	Wisconsin	74	
91	Michigan State	83	
95	At Illinois	66	
56	Louisville at Louisville†	55	
87	Kentucky at Louisville†	74	
95	St. Joseph's at K.C.†	69	
65	Cincinnati at K.C.† (OT)	70	

*Holiday Festival
†NCAA Tournament

1961-62 (26-2)

72	Florida State	57	
99	At Pittsburgh	79	
85	Wichita	62	
84	At Wake Forest	62	
92	Loyola of Chicago	72	
61	At St. Louis	48	
92	Penn State	49	
59	Washington at Los Angeles*	49	
105	UCLA at Los Angeles*	84	
76	USC at Los Angeles*	66	
85	At Northwestern	62	
89	Michigan	64	
90	At Minnesota	76	
91	Purdue	65	
94	At Purdue	73	
97	Northwestern	61	
89	Iowa	63	
91	Minnesota	66	
72	At Michigan	57	
80	At Michigan State	72	
102	Illinois	79	
72	At Iowa	62	
67	At Wisconsin	86	
90	Indiana	65	
93	W. Kentucky at Iowa City†	73	
74	Kentucky at Iowa City†	64	
84	Wake Forest at Louisville†	68	
59	Cincinnati at Louisville†	71	

*Los Angeles Classic
†NCAA Tournament

game in the state semifinals. In three varsity seasons, he scored 2,466 points and, understandably, became the target of one of the most frantic recruiting blitzes in college basketball history.

But Lucas was more than just a basketball phenom. He also was an honor student, the president of his senior class and a kid who was no more impressed with his basketball talents than he was with the reputations of some of his high-profile recruiters. A story that appeared in the 1960 Saturday Evening Post describes just how unimpressed he was.

Lucas, one day, was eating lunch in the high school cafeteria when the school's football coach approached and told him that Adolph Rupp, the Kentucky coach and presiding king of college basketball, was in town and would like to talk to him.

"I don't want to see him," Lucas replied.

"Well, give him a few minutes," the coach implored.

"All right, I've got a class down on the second floor," Lucas said. "Tell him I'll talk to him down there before class."

One of Lucas' high school teammates witnessed the scene.

"Rupp came down," he said, "and Jerry walked over and listened to him for 10 seconds, then went into class. Imagine! Adolph Rupp, the greatest coach in the world, and he gives him 10 seconds. If Rupp had wanted to talk to me, I'd have dropped dead."

When Lucas finally announced that Ohio State had won the recruiting war, he startled everybody by also announcing that he would be going to Columbus on an academic scholarship, with no extras thrown in for athletics. The reason he had chosen Ohio State? Because nobody else had stressed the importance of getting an education.

That sense of priority carried over to his college career. Maintaining an A average in his studies, Lucas played basketball with a totally selfless style. He shied away from publicity and seemed much more comfortable dishing off to open opponents than scoring himself. Using his quickness, deadly one-hand jumper and hook shot to score almost at will, Lucas averaged 26.3 points and led the nation with his 63.7 percent field-goal accuracy in 1959-60. But teammates and coach were quick to point out that he could have scored a lot more.

"Just because I've scored a lot of points on a basketball court doesn't make me something special," Lucas told one writer. "It doesn't prove a darn thing. I just want to be Jerry Lucas, average guy, just one of the kids. That's all."

The word "average" never would apply to Lucas. Neither would it apply to Havlicek, another high school phenom who, ironically, was better known for another sport.

"Woody Hayes (Ohio State's legendary football

The real force behind Ohio State's leap into national prominence in the early 1960s was Jerry Lucas (11), who could score almost at will with his large repertoire of slick moves.

coach) had talked at our high school sports banquet and tried to talk me into playing football," recalled the former prep quarterback and baseball star who also had averaged 31.2 points for Bridgeport High in Lansing, O. "However, my mother wasn't very happy about me playing football, and I decided I liked basketball better.

"When Woody realized I wasn't going to play football, he told me he still wanted me to come to Ohio State. Fred Taylor had been involved in the recruiting process also, because he was about ready to take over the basketball job from Floyd Stahl, who was retiring. He had recruited a great class, including Jerry Lucas, Mel Nowell and Gary Gearhart, players I had played against in high school

all-star games. And I had a great feeling for State, being an Ohio person.

"Of course, the other prominent fellow on our team was Bobby Knight. I met him in 1958 at a barn used for recruiting parties and that sort of thing. He had that line-drive jump shot that he took from about 35 feet, and I thought this guy can really shoot. He wasn't the quickest man on foot, but defensively he played hard. When you got fouled by Bobby, you knew you had been fouled."

Young, eager and talented, this sophomore cast joined forces with veterans Siegfried, a junior, and Roberts, a senior. With Siegfried and Nowell at the guard positions, Havlicek and Roberts at forward and Lucas manning the middle, Taylor's Buckeyes

Forward John Havlicek, who would go on to professional fame with the Boston Celtics, was a hustling, do-everything performer in his three Ohio State seasons.

embarked on a long journey that would take them to championship heights.

"Larry had been the leading scorer for Ohio State the year before (1958-59) with a 19.6-point average," Havlicek said of Siegfried, "and Joe Roberts was a seasoned veteran. He was a great rebounder. Siegfried had great confidence and, of course, Jerry never played like a sophomore. He always played beyond his years."

Gaining more confidence as their defense improved, the Buckeyes charged to the Big Ten championship with only three regular-season losses.

"When we played Indiana tough on their home floor (a 99-83 loss), we knew we could play with just about anyone in the country," Havlicek said. "We also lost out in Utah (97-92) and to Kentucky (96-93). All those teams were highly ranked and we played them pretty competitively. As sophomores, we really didn't fear anything. We just went out and played as hard as we could."

From the momentum of their conference title, the third-ranked Buckeyes sliced apart their competition in the NCAA Tournament's Mideast Regional—Western Kentucky, 98-79, and Georgia Tech, 86-69. The Final Four would be a showcase of college talent featuring the top three teams in the national polls.

Joining the Buckeyes in the Final Four were Newell's California team, Cincinnati and New York University. California was ranked No. 1 by United Press International and No. 2 by the Associated Press. Cincinnati, rated No. 1 by AP and No. 2 by UPI, featured Oscar Robertson, whose talent encompassed all of the game, from playground razzle-dazzle to team strategy. He seemed to see everything on the court and understand it. After falling short of a national championship in his sophomore and junior seasons, the "Big O" and his Cincinnati teammates were hungry.

Both the Bearcats and Golden Bears were 27-1 when they met in a semifinal game, which many thought would determine the national champion. Defense proved to be the key. Newell's deliberate game plan held Robertson in check (he scored 18 points) and resulted in a 77-69 Cal victory.

Ohio State, which had shot 49.7 percent from the floor while compiling a 23-3 record, was matched against NYU in the other semifinal. The Violets' best player was Tom (Satch) Sanders, who later would become Havlicek's teammate and roommate with the Boston Celtics.

"Tom Sanders was on that team," Havlicek said, "and two fellows named Ray Paprocky and Al Filardi. Filardi was known as a garbage man, a guy who gets a lot of cheap baskets inside. My assignment was to keep Filardi away from the boards so he couldn't come up with all the loose balls. We played a similar style, so I ended up doing a decent job on him.

"Tom Sanders was a person who looked like he came from outer space because he wore wire-rim glasses with a big rubber piece between them and an eyeglass band that wrapped around his head. He also had those huge, long knee guards that were quite unusual at that time. And Satch just had such a distinctive style and flavor all his own.

"He had a fairly decent game against us. He was 6-6 and had to play Jerry Lucas. There was no way he could defend against Jerry's hook shot. Siegfried and Mel Nowell played very well that particular game."

The Buckeyes humbled NYU, 76-54, setting up the meeting of student and master. Defense may have been the lesson, but the Buckeyes, who averaged 90.4 points per game, killed the Bears with blistering shooting. They hit 16 of their 19 first-half shots en route to a 37-19 halftime lead. Just as impressively, Ohio State held California to a shooting mark under 30 percent. In the locker room, a stunned Newell mentioned to his players that they needed to get more defensive rebounds. Star center Darrall Imhoff reportedly answered, "Coach, there have only been three, and I got all of 'em."

"The final ball game was really over at halftime," Havlicek said. "That first half may have been the most awesome half a team ever had in a championship game. It was really over very quickly, and it was very surprising to us to find that we were that far ahead of them. As sophomores, you always feel like someone is going to come back on you.

"Fred Taylor had been a student of Pete Newell's, and I think the tables were sort of reversed that night because Fred utilized a lot of things he had learned from Pete. The great thing about Pete is that he really loves for people to learn more about the game, and he was one of the masters. He wasn't afraid to give pointers to other people, and I think we benefited from it greatly."

Havlicek said he was about the only damper on the Buckeyes' first-half offense.

"I cut two fingers on my shooting hand two days before we went to California," he explained. "The cuts required 10 stitches. But in the championship game, we shot a phenomenal percentage the first half. I missed two of the four shots I took, and I felt I was a real burden to the team."

Although California cut into the lead early in the second half, Ohio State surged again and won, 75-55. Nearly 30 years later, Newell said he still doesn't regret helping Taylor.

"Believe it or not, we had a defensive plan," Newell said. "But they beat us with their quickness, especially Mel Nowell (who scored 15 points on 6-of-7 shooting from the field). That was the only time I felt our defense was a step slow."

Lucas led five Buckeyes in double figures with 16 points and 10 rebounds, enough to sew up the tournament's outstanding-player citation. His postsea-

Havlicek flashes his dexterity with a reverse lefthanded layup in 1961-62 action.

Sophomore guard Mel Nowell (3) maneuvers for a shot (left) against California in the 1960 NCAA Tournament title game. At right, Larry Siegfried scores an easy basket as teammate Joe Roberts (right) watches in the Buckeyes' victory over the Golden Bears.

son honors included the first of three consensus All-America selections and he earned a gold medal by playing for the United States in the 1960 Summer Olympic Games.

"Joe Roberts (10 points on 5-of-6 shooting from the field) had a great game, too," Havlicek said of the title contest. "I remember a long hook shot he hit from the top of the key."

Siegfried (13.3), Nowell (13.1), Havlicek (12.2) and Roberts (11) all joined Lucas as double-digit scorers for the season.

With four starters returning (Roberts was replaced at forward by Richie Hoyt), Ohio State's 1960-61 opponents prepared for the worst. And

they weren't disappointed. The Buckeyes ran through their schedule like a well-oiled machine, averaging 85.1 points while shooting at a .498 clip. Lucas continued to dominate opposing centers, Havlicek, now known affectionately as "Hondo," continued his excellent all-around play and Nowell and Siegfried continued to form one of the best backcourts in the nation.

As Ohio State steamrolled opponent after opponent, Nowell described the feeling that comes with being part of something special.

"I don't think a basketball player could ever ask for more," he said. "It's really overwhelming to be a part of something so fabulous. Here I was, as a

It was celebration time for the Buckeyes and their coach after their convincing title victory in 1960. Squatting (front right) is future coaching great Bob Knight.

sophomore, on a Big Ten and national championship team. Here we are, this year, doing things no other teams have ever done—or not many of them, anyway.

"But the best thing about it is the high quality of the guys on the team. The pride they have is wonderful. Each guy knows the other guy has terrific pride within himself and you know they're all going to be doing their part out there."

By the end of the regular season, Ohio State was

24-0 and ranked No. 1 in both polls. The Buckeyes' closest call was a one-point victory at Iowa. Only two other teams—St. Bonaventure and Indiana— had managed to stay within four points. The nation's No. 2 team was surprising Cincinnati, a 23-3 squad now playing without Robertson. Nobody doubted that the Buckeyes were the best team in the nation. The real question was whether they were the best of all time.

Fate would have something to say about that.

And so would state-rival Cincinnati, a starless, almost nondescript team that knew how to win.

With the graduation of Robertson, Bearcat Coach George Smith had moved up to the athletic director's post, handing the coaching reins to assistant Ed Jucker. Not much had been expected from a team that started two seniors (Bob Wiesenhahn and Carl Bouldin), two juniors (Paul Hogue and Sandy Pomerantz) and a talented sophomore (Tom Thacker). But the Bearcats had something to prove. Ohio State, they claimed, was not even the best team in Ohio, much less the nation.

In its wisdom, the 1961 NCAA Tournament selection committee sent Ohio State to the Mideast Regional and Cincinnati to the Midwest. The Buckeyes struggled to a 56-55 victory over Louisville in the second round, advancing only after Havlicek hit a jumper with six seconds left and Louisville missed a crucial free throw. But the Buckeyes rebounded to rout Kentucky, 87-74, in the regional final.

The Bearcats had an easy second-round game, defeating Texas Tech, 78-55. But the regional final against Kansas State was another matter. With 10 minutes remaining, Cincinnati trailed by seven. But the Bearcats' deliberate offense somehow generated a flurry of baskets and Cincinnati outdistanced the Wildcats down the stretch, 69-64, for its 20th consecutive victory.

The tournament semifinals in Kansas City proved nothing more than a warmup for an Ohio State-Cincinnati showdown. The Buckeyes pounded St. Joseph's, 95-69, and the Bearcats blitzed Utah, 82-67. Most observers were ready to concede a second straight national crown to Ohio State.

But not Cincinnati. The Bearcats scrapped, pounded the boards and literally dictated the title game's tempo. As the crowd watched in disbelief, Cincinnati kept pace with the powerful Buckeyes, finally grabbing a 61-59 lead with less than two minutes to play. But Ohio State gained a temporary reprieve when Knight drove for a layup, his only two points, to tie the game with 1:41 remaining. That's the way it stayed through regulation.

As the overtime unfolded, Cincinnati slowly took control. As Ohio State rooters watched in stunned silence, the Bearcats built a lead and forced the Buckeyes to foul. When all was said and done, Cincinnati had a 70-65 victory and its first-ever national championship. Lucas, who had scored 27 points and grabbed 12 rebounds after scoring at a 24.9 clip during the season, earned his second straight Outstanding Player Award. But that was small consolation to a team that had just watched its hopes for a perfect season wash away.

Strangely, circumstances would repeat themselves in 1961-62, with a few minor changes in script.

Ohio State, with Richard Reasbeck (guard) and Douglas McDonald (forward) replacing Siegfried and Hoyt, again rampaged through its regular-season schedule, compiling a 23-1 record while earning the No. 1 nod in both polls. The Buckeyes dominated their competition, no team coming closer than eight points before a late-season trip to Wisconsin resulted in an 86-67 defeat.

Cincinnati suffered two early-season conference losses and struggled to earn its berth in the NCAA Tournament. The Bearcats, with newcomers George Wilson and Ron Bonham replacing Wiesenhahn and Bouldin, finished the regular season at 24-2 and then met Bradley in a one-game playoff to break a tie for the Missouri Valley Conference champion-

1960 OHIO STATE
Head Coach—Fred Taylor   Final Record—25-3

Player	Pos.	Hgt.	Wgt.	Cl.	G	FG	FGA	Pct.	FT.	FTA	Pct.	Reb.	Pts.	Avg.
Jerry Lucas	C	6-8	220	So.	27	283	444	.637	144	187	.770	442	710	26.3
Larry Siegfried	G	6-4	195	Jr.	28	145	311	.466	81	108	.750	107	371	13.3
Mel Nowell	G	6-2	174	So.	28	156	330	.473	56	73	.767	72	368	13.1
John Havlicek	F	6-5	196	So.	28	144	312	.462	53	74	.716	205	341	12.2
Joe Roberts	F	6-6	214	Sr.	28	135	281	.480	38	56	.679	194	308	11.0
Richard Furry	F	6-7	208	Sr.	28	61	134	.455	20	33	.606	92	142	5.1
Robert Knight	F	6-4	186	So.	21	30	74	.405	17	27	.630	42	77	3.7
Howard Nourse	C	6-7	183	Sr.	17	24	47	.511	5	5	1.000	46	53	3.1
Gary Gearhart	G	6-2	167	So.	19	21	52	.404	7	16	.438	22	49	2.6
Richie Hoyt	G	6-4	194	Jr.	23	22	52	.423	14	18	.778	19	58	2.5
David Barker	G	6-2	174	Sr.	16	11	27	.407	1	6	.167	13	23	1.4
John Cedargren	F	6-5	183	Sr.	13	7	12	.583	2	5	.400	14	16	1.2
James Allen	G	5-9	164	Jr.	7	1	9	.111	5	6	.833	2	7	1.0
Nelson Miller	F	6-3	187	So.	6	2	5	.400	1	3	.333	4	5	0.8
J. T. Landes	G	5-11	165	So.	6	2	8	.250	0	2	.000	1	4	0.7
Gary Milliken	G	5-11	171	Jr.	2	0	3	.000	0	0	.000	1	0	0.0
Team												139		
Ohio State					28	1044	2101	.497	444	619	.717	1415	2532	90.4
Opponents					28	753	1941	.388	447	645	.693	1032	1953	69.8

ship. Cincinnati, its defense now working in full gear, prevailed, 61-46.

Everything was in line for a championship-game rematch as Ohio State sailed through its preliminary-round games and then pounded Wake Forest, 84-68, in the national semifinals at Louisville. Cincinnati received a scare from UCLA in the semifinal, finally scratching out a 72-70 victory and setting up its second straight title meeting with the Buckeyes.

There was, however, a subplot to the unfolding drama—a twist of fate that would doom Ohio State to another second-place finish. In the semifinal game against Wake Forest, Lucas wrenched his left knee while pursuing a rebound and had to be helped off the court. When Cincinnati and Ohio State tipped off the following night, Lucas was there in spirit, but he was unable to perform up to his usual standards. The Bearcats won again, 71-59.

"I was rooming with Jerry at that time," Havlicek recalled, "and I really didn't know how effective he was going to be. It was one of those things where you couldn't tell what was going to happen until he got on the floor. In those days, you played back-to-back games in the tournament, Friday and Saturday.

1961 OHIO STATE
Head Coach—Fred Taylor　　　　Final Record—27-1

Player	Pos.	Hgt.	Wgt.	Cl.	G	FG	FGA	Pct.	FT.	FTA	Pct.	Reb.	Pts.	Avg.
Jerry Lucas	C	6-8	224	Jr.	27	256	411	.623	159	208	.764	470	671	24.9
Larry Siegfried	G	6-4	192	Sr.	28	151	314	.481	123	143	.860	141	425	15.2
John Havlicek	F	6-5	192	Jr.	28	173	321	.539	61	87	.701	244	407	14.5
Mel Nowell	G	6-2	166	Jr.	28	155	317	.489	70	90	.778	80	380	13.6
Richie Hoyt	F	6-4	191	Sr.	28	60	140	.429	33	43	.767	80	153	5.5
Robert Knight	F	6-4	180	Jr.	28	54	136	.397	15	26	.577	77	123	4.4
Gary Gearhart	G	6-2	170	Jr.	24	25	66	.379	17	26	.654	24	67	2.8
Richard Reasbeck	G	6-0	171	So.	20	22	45	.489	6	11	.545	24	50	2.5
Douglas McDonald	F	6-5	191	So.	22	18	43	.419	4	12	.333	48	40	1.8
Kenneth Lee	C	6-5	174	So.	20	9	38	.237	9	10	.900	45	27	1.4
J. T. Landes	G	5-11	168	Jr.	13	6	17	.353	3	5	.600	8	15	1.2
Donald Furry	C	6-2	185	Jr.	3	1	2	.333	1	2	.500	2	3	1.0
Nelson Miller	F	6-3	187	Jr.	16	6	20	.300	1	2	.500	14	13	0.8
James Allen	G	5-9	170	Sr.	7	1	5	.200	2	4	.500	1	4	0.6
Raymond Apple	F	6-3	184	Sr.	8	1	6	.167	1	2	.500	4	3	0.4
John Noble	F	6-4	176	So.	6	1	3	.333	0	0	.000	3	2	0.3
Gary Milliken	G	5-11	168	Sr.	4	0	2	.000	0	0	.000	1	0	0.0
Team												152		
Ohio State					28	939	1886	.498	505	671	.753	1418	2383	85.1
Opponents					28	690	1895	.364	460	691	.666	1053	1840	65.7

1962 OHIO STATE
Head Coach—Fred Taylor　　　　Final Record—26-2

Player	Pos.	Hgt.	Wgt.	Cl.	G	FG	FGA	Pct.	FT.	FTA	Pct.	Reb.	Pts.	Avg.
Jerry Lucas	C	6-8	223	Sr.	28	237	388	.611	135	169	.799	499	609	21.8
John Havlicek	F	6-5	205	Sr.	28	196	377	.520	83	109	.761	271	475	17.0
Mel Nowell	G	6-2	174	Sr.	28	140	358	.391	72	92	.783	80	352	12.6
Richard Reasbeck	G	6-0	178	Jr.	27	97	218	.445	19	29	.655	63	213	7.9
Douglas McDonald	F	6-5	203	Jr.	28	92	180	.511	34	53	.642	99	218	7.8
Gary Bradds	C	6-8	207	So.	27	50	72	.694	23	40	.575	72	123	4.6
Gary Gearhart	G	6-2	172	Sr.	19	32	86	.372	21	36	.583	40	85	4.5
James Doughty	F	6-4	211	Jr.	26	39	92	.424	23	31	.742	61	101	3.9
Robert Knight	F	6-4	191	Sr.	25	35	89	.393	9	11	.818	38	79	3.2
Richard Taylor	G	6-4	193	So.	23	9	24	.375	10	15	.667	12	28	1.2
Donald Flatt	G	6-4	205	So.	24	9	28	.321	8	16	.500	18	26	1.1
Gene Lane	F	6-8	209	So.	18	8	23	.348	2	4	.500	16	18	1.0
Donald Furry	F	6-3	198	Sr.	2	1	1	1.000	0	1	.000	0	2	1.0
LeRoy Frazier	G	6-5	167	So.	21	7	24	.292	1	5	.200	11	15	0.7
John Noble	C	6-4	190	Jr.	5	0	0	.000	0	0	.000	2	0	0.0
Donald DeVoe	F	6-5	183	So.	5	0	1	.000	0	0	.000	1	0	0.0
Team												108		
Ohio State					28	952	1961	.485	440	611	.720	1391	2344	83.7
Opponents					28	706	1848	.382	443	622	.712	971	1855	66.3

Mel Nowell (right) comforts a disconsolate Siegfried after Ohio State was forced to settle for a second-place trophy in 1961.

"When we went out on the floor, I knew right away he wasn't going to be as effective as usual. I know that I could have taken over more offensively, and it kind of bugs me that I didn't. The night before, in the game against Wake Forest when Jerry got hurt, I played well and got 20 points or so (25).

"If I had shot 20 times against Cincinnati, maybe it would have been a different ball game. But I played my role. I remember that the Cincinnati coach did not want me involved defensively while they were running their patterns. So my assignment, Ron Bonham, and I more or less held hands at half court while the other guys played four on four."

Taylor later acknowledged that even with Lucas at full strength, the outcome might have been the same because Cincinnati had developed into a superior team.

Lucas, who led the Buckeyes in scoring average, rebounding and field-goal percentage in all three of his varsity seasons, went on to a distinguished 11-year career with several National Basketball Association teams. Havlicek and Siegfried both went on to become key figures in the Boston Celtics' NBA domination during the 1960s. Nothing, however, could ease the memory of those two championship-game losses to Cincinnati.

"It was very disappointing to lose the last two years after we had won the first," Havlicek said.

And still unbelievable to many who thought that the Lucas-Havlicek Ohio State teams of the early 1960s were the best ever.

In 1962, an appreciative Ohio State crowd gave Lucas a well-deserved standing ovation as he took a seat during his final home game in a Buckeye uniform.

The Fabulous Wildcats

K E N T U C K Y

**1947-48
1948-49**

The Kentucky basketball teams of 1947-48 and 1948-49 rolled to 68 victories and suffered only five defeats, a record that qualifies as pretty heady stuff.

Just how good were Coach Adolph Rupp's Wildcats? Probably even better than their gaudy won-lost mark would indicate.

The fact is, even while key players were shaving points in the second of those seasons, Rupp's team was on the way to its second consecutive NCAA championship.

It was a strange era in college basketball, one that left hundreds of unanswered questions, not the least of which was: How good would this Kentucky team have been had it played straight up?

Known as the "Fabulous Five," the 1947-48 Wildcats posted a 36-3 record, finished second in the Olympic Trials and placed five players on the '48 U.S. Olympic team. The Kentucky team of the following season could well have been the first in history to win both the NCAA Tournament and National Invitation Tournament in the same year, but Kentucky lost in the NIT as prominent members of the squad acquiesced to gamblers.

The tragedy surrounding the gambling scandal hit hardest not on the team's standing, but on the individuals involved—including Rupp himself. At the 1952 court proceedings involving three Kentucky players, a New York judge lambasted Rupp's personal relationship with a bookmaker and accused the Kentucky program of a "ruthless exploitation of athletes." The university later conducted an internal investigation that cleared the coach, but his reputation remained somewhat besmirched despite a dazzling coaching career (he finished with an NCAA-record 875 victories in 41 seasons).

Still, it was the athletes who shaved the points and paid the ultimate price. Paying most dearly as a result of the transgressions were center Alex Groza and guard Ralph Beard, All-America players whose pro careers were terminated in October 1951 once word of their point-fixing roles was made public.

In the players' defense, the United States was in the throes of dealing with the complex aftermath of World War II. The country wasn't exactly standing firm at its moral center, the war having shaken up millions of lives, including those of the Kentucky players, many of whom were service veterans.

Rupp, meanwhile, had used the wartime circumstances to help make Kentucky basketball one of the nation's most dynamic sports operations. Before the 1945-46 season, the U.S. Army had invited Rupp to develop a recreation program for American forces in Europe. While overseas, the Baron of the Bluegrass took full advantage of the opportunity to recruit the best basketball players among the servicemen soon to return from the war. Among his finds were Dale Barnstable and Jim Line, both of whom starred in service leagues and later would provide tremendous boosts to the Kentucky program.

Joe B. Hall was one of the enrollees at the Lexington campus in the postwar period.

"It was a time when veterans were flooding the colleges," said Hall, who went on to succeed Rupp as Kentucky coach more than a quarter of a century later, "so you had a backlog of about four years of athletes who had been in the service. So

Adolph Rupp, the legendary guru of Kentucky basketball, with Alex Groza, the center who led his 1947-48 and 1948-49 Wildcats to NCAA championships.

those were great years, not only in Kentucky, but at a lot of schools. Sports in general took a big step forward with . . . all those veterans."

The influx of service returnees added to the already large number of high school seniors seeking college scholarships to play basketball. The Depression had abated for most regions of the country prior to the war, but poverty remained pervasive in the hills of Kentucky. Young players were desperate for a way out. Most colleges offered tryouts, which were legal under existing NCAA rules, and Kentucky's sessions probably were the most extensive and competitive in the country.

"It was dog-eat-dog," Hall recalled. "The players came in by bus, by train, or their families drove

down. I can remember some great players who came in and tried out and didn't make it, guys like Frank Selvy, who went on to Furman and became a top scorer."

Hall himself was a participant.

"About all that I had ever known growing up was Kentucky basketball and Coach Adolph Rupp," said Hall, who was from Cynthiana, Ky. "And I guess that as a high school player, to have Coach Rupp in the stands was about as big a thrill as you could have. Every kid who loved basketball in the state of Kentucky followed the University of Kentucky. I was no different. I was a fan long before I was a player at Kentucky. I kept my scrapbook on Kentucky basketball from the time I could remember anything about the game. And I'm sure that many other aspiring players did, also.

"Coach Rupp had been at the University of Kentucky since 1930-31, so when I arrived on the scene, he'd been there 17 years. When I was a high school player, he attended one of my games. I didn't find that out until the game was over, but that was a great thrill to me as a young man."

For the most part, assistant coach Harry Lancaster and the team manager conducted the tryouts.

"Coach Rupp sat up high in the stands," Hall recalled. "I just remember that I was on the campus one weekend with high school all-staters from all over the nation, and we were on the floor when Coach Rupp and Coach Lancaster were coming out of their office. Coach says, 'Harry, let's go upstairs since you can see so much damn better.' And I guess that was the first thing I ever heard him (Rupp) say. After about 70 of us scrimmaged the whole Saturday morning, the manager came down and called my name and asked me to come back the next weekend. I came back, and there was a new group of players and we went at it again. That's the way recruiting was done back then."

This traffic jam of talent produced predictable results—namely, overwhelming success on the court and more than a bit of frustration for the players who lost out. No fewer than three first-rate players found it impossible to crack an ever-improving Kentucky lineup.

As a Kentucky freshman, Bob Brannum had earned All-America distinction in 1943-44, but after returning from the service, he sat on the bench until deciding to transfer to Michigan State. Guard Jack Parkinson played three years at Kentucky, went into the service and then was relegated to limited duty upon his return. Jim Jordan, a West Virginian, was a service-ball standout who saw sparse playing time at Kentucky after entering the university with four years of collegiate eligibility remaining.

Like Brannum, numerous other players left Lexington. But the effect was almost nil. Rupp had selected a core of skilled athletes unmatched by other schools. As a judge of talent, he had few peers.

"Nobody would give me credit for this, but the first thing I look at is that academic record," Rupp once said, reflecting on his recruiting technique. "If you're taking a poor student, you're wasting your time. Next you would like to have size, then you would like to have speed. The desire to compete, you can't measure that. They can look nice on parade, but you can't measure desire except under fire."

Asked about his principles of coaching, Rupp had a ready reply. "It's getting five men and teaching them how to play together," he said, "and giving them a pattern to play by and practicing that pattern over and over until they know how to meet any situation, with a good coach sitting on the bench to remind them now and then."

Rupp, a native Kansan who played basketball for the Kansas Jayhawks under the legendary Phog Allen, was a stern taskmaster who wasn't kidding about the "over-and-over" routine. Once, when a young Kentucky player messed up three consecutive possessions during a workout, Rupp commented, "That's all right. You can't make every play perfect. If you did, you'd score a basket every time. But let's work at it a few thousand times."

Rupp's Wildcats emerged as the superior team in postwar America, running off a blur of victories and championships that mesmerized their fans in the Bluegrass. Rupp, the man in the brown suit (supposedly his lucky attire on game days), became a folk hero across the down-on-its-luck state.

Basketball had become "a kind of a salvation for Kentucky," Hall explained. "The small rural communities on the high school level did not play football in the state of Kentucky. Many of the schools were so inaccessible back in the hollows that they just couldn't get that many kids together to have a football team. Basketball became a way of life in the Kentucky mountains and in eastern Kentucky."

A man of immense pride, Rupp had begun coaching basketball at the school in the fall of 1930

Season Results

1947-48 (36-3)

80	Indiana Central	41	82	At Vanderbilt	51
80	Ft. Knox	41	69	Tennessee	42
72	Tulsa	18	63	Alabama	33
71	Tulsa	22	79	Vanderbilt	43
74	DePaul at Louisville	50	78	Georgia Tech	54
67	At Cincinnati	31	58	Temple at Louisville	38
79	Xavier	37	59	At Xavier (O.)	37
59	At Temple	60	87	Florida at Louisville*	31
52	At St. John's	40	63	LSU at Louisville*	47
65	At Creighton	23	70	Tennessee at Louisville*	47
98	Western Ontario	41	54	Georgia Tech at Louisville*	43
67	At Miami of Ohio	53	76	Columbia at New York†	53
47	At Michigan State	45	60	Holy Cross at New York†	52
79	At Ohio	57	58	Baylor at New York†	42
65	At Tennessee	54	91	Louisville at New York‡	57
71	At Georgia Tech	56	77	Baylor at New York‡	59
88	At Georgia	51	49	Phillips Oilers at New York‡	53
70	Cincinnati	43			
68	At DePaul	51	*SEC Conference Tournament		
55	At Notre Dame	64	†NCAA Tournament		
41	At Alabama	31	‡Olympic Trials		
69	Washington (Mo.) at Mem.	39			

1948-49 (32-2)

74	Indiana Central	38	96	Xavier (O.)	50
67	DePaul at Louisville	36	74	Alabama	32
81	Tulsa	27	85	Mississippi	31
76	Arkansas	39	78	Georgia Tech	32
51	At Holy Cross	48	95	Georgia	40
57	At St. John's	30	51	At Xavier (O.)	40
51	Tulane at Louisville	47	70	Vanderbilt	37
78	Tulane at New Orleans*	47	73	Florida at Louisville†	36
40	St. Louis at New Orleans*	42	70	Auburn at Louisville†	39
63	Bowling Green at Cleveland	61	83	Tennessee at Louisville†	44
66	At Tennessee	51	68	Tulane at Louisville†	52
56	At Georgia Tech	45	56	Loyola of Chicago at N.Y.‡	67
56	At DePaul	45	85	Villanova at New York§	72
62	Notre Dame at Louisville	38	76	Illinois at New York§	47
72	At Vanderbilt	50	46	Oklahoma A&M at Seattle§	36
56	At Alabama	40			
75	Mississippi at Memphis	45	*Sugar Bowl Classic		
62	Bradley at Owensboro, Ky.	52	†SEC Conference Tournament		
71	Tennessee	56	‡NIT		
			§NCAA Tournament		

Groza could handle the basketball, but his biggest attribute was an ability to put points on the board.

and by the opening of the 1947-48 season, his awards case lacked only an NCAA-championship trophy. In the previous five years, Kentucky had compiled records of 17-6, 19-2, 22-4, 28-2 and 34-3 and included an NIT title (1946) in its nonstop success. The Wildcats were coming off a season in which they had gone unbeaten in the Southeastern Conference and finished second in the NIT to Arnie Ferrin and Utah.

For the 1947-48 season, Rupp had three particularly gifted players in 6-foot-7 pivotman Groza, greyhound backcourt operative Beard and forward Wallace (Wah Wah) Jones. Beyond that junior trio, Kentucky boasted such talented players as guard Ken Rollins and forwards Cliff Barker, Barnstable and Line. Rollins was a senior, Barker a junior and Barnstable and Line sophomores.

Rupp had attracted Groza, a skinny high school senior, from Martins Ferry, O., in 1944. The younger brother of pro football player Lou Groza, Alex arrived in Lexington with no pretenses of greatness.

Groza, before leaving Martins Ferry, had asked a hometown journalist for a photograph of a player about half Groza's size stealing a rebound from the collegian-to-be. "I want to tack it on my wall at UK," Groza explained, "so I'll always have something to put me in my place in case I'm ever tempted to get big-headed."

Alex appeared in 10 games for the Wildcats during his freshman season, 1944-45, before entering the service. Two years later, he returned to the Wildcats as a mature physical specimen well on his way to becoming an imposing inside player.

"Groza was the big man," Hall recalled, "and certainly one of the finest in the country. He was only 6-7, but he was a scoring machine. He understood the game, and he wasn't intimidated. Yet he wasn't interested in roughing up his opponent; he was interested in winning and contributing to the team's success. He got along well with the players and was very likable.

"That team had tremendous maturity, because they had a lot of Army veterans, including Groza. Cliff Barker was 27 years old and had been in a German prisoner-of-war camp for 16 months, and if that doesn't lend maturity to a ball club, then I don't know what would."

Barker's court presence was something to behold.

Dale Barnstable (left) and Jim Line were service veterans who made major contributions in Kentucky's run to consecutive national titles.

Guard Ralph Beard (left) was a strong, quick perimeter player who averaged in double figures in both championship seasons. Ken Rollins (right), a senior on the 1947-48 team, was a smooth-passing playmaker.

A story in Sportfolio magazine described Barker as a "real ballhawk . . . apparently gifted with a sixth sense. The man with the hands of a magician comes up with many loose balls, intercepted passes and clean steals and then demoralizes defenses by charging toward the basket and feeding mates with sharp passes over his shoulder, behind his back and between his legs . . . Extremely agile and smooth, Barker is a tough man in the front line of defense."

The forte of the late-1940s Kentucky teams, though, was offense. They regularly ran up about 70 points in an era when most games were settled with scores in the 50s. Kentucky was, assistant Lancaster once said, "a beautiful team. They had the finest fast break I have ever seen, before or since. It

was just magnificent the way Groza got the ball off the board."

Groza usually hit Jones or Rollins with the outlet pass, and one or the other would find Beard streaking to the basket.

"I've often said that Ralph Beard could step on the floor today and be an outstanding basketball player without changing skills at all," Hall said. "He was such a competitor, a defensive ballhawk and outstanding scorer, just a tremendous athlete. He had the greatest quickness of anyone I've ever seen on the basketball floor. Beard had ups and downs because he had games that the opposition really concentrated on stopping him. Many teams felt that if they could stop Ralph Beard, they could stop

Wallace (Wah Wah) Jones averaged better than nine points in both seasons, many coming on his specialty—the offensive rebound.

Kentucky."

The 5-10 Beard, whose scoring average in a four-season career at Kentucky was 10.9, showed a strong perimeter game as well that featured a deep set shot, a two-handed shot from over his head and a one-handed jumper.

Beard, who attended high school in Hardinsburg, Ky., before enrolling at Louisville's Male High when he moved to the state's major city preceding the start of his junior year, first developed his shooting skills in a rather strange locale—*inside* the family home.

"His first basket was his nursery chair," his mother said. "He was 3 then. We had bought him a round rubber ball, and his father taught him to

Forward/guard Cliff Barker (above) was a gifted defensive player, passer and rebounder who would amaze opponents with his agility and quickness.

pitch it at the nursery chair. Later, we got him a basketball goal and put it on his high chair. Next, when he got a little older, we put the basket above the kitchen door. You could hear the sound of breaking dishes in our house every day.

"When he was about 6, we made a regular court in a vacant room we had upstairs. Older boys would come in and play with him. Falling plaster was a daily occurrence. Next, we moved the basket outdoors on the garage. The dishes and plaster were safe then."

No opponents were safe, however, against the mighty Wildcats of the late '40s. When Kentucky went to a half-court offense, Groza was a terror in the post. He averaged 14.5 points per outing in his three-plus years in Lexington, going to the basket with a collection of pump fakes and power moves. And if he missed, the 6-4 Jones made a specialty of offensive rebounding.

Jones had come to Kentucky to play for Coach Bear Bryant's football team, but he became invaluable to Rupp's program.

By NCAA Tournament time, the 1947-48 Wildcats had won 31 of 33 games, the losses coming at the hands of Temple (one point) and Notre Dame (nine points). Most sportswriters figured that of the eight teams in the NCAA field, the only club capable of beating Kentucky was defending national champion Holy Cross.

Kentucky eased past Columbia, 76-53, in the first round of the Eastern playoffs. Then, in the Eastern title game, Rollins shut down Holy Cross standout Bob Cousy—the flashy guard was held to five points—and the Wildcats advanced with a 60-52 triumph as Groza, Beard and Jones combined for 48 of the Kentuckians' points. In the West, Baylor had beaten Washington and Kansas State.

In the East-vs.-West battle for the national crown (the Final Four format of representatives from four playoff sites gathering at one site was still four years away), Kentucky bolted to an early 17-point lead and cruised by Baylor, 58-42, at New York's Madison Square Garden. Groza, who scored 14 points, was named the tournament's Most Outstanding Player.

From there, the dream-like season continued. An eight-team field was chosen for the 1948 U.S. Olympic Trials, with both Amateur Athletic Union and collegiate entries competing, and the AAU champion Phillips Oilers and Rupp's Wildcats headed the cast. Kentucky and Baylor clashed once more, in the semifinals, and the Wildcats prevailed by 18 points this time around. The 'Cats fell to the Bob Kurland-led Oilers in the title game, but Kentucky's five starters made the U.S. Olympic team roster and helped the Americans breeze to the gold medal in London.

Having put together a phenomenal season, the Kentucky Wildcats seemed positioned to make an-

other run at national honors the following year. Among the departing seniors, only Rollins was a major loss. An 11.7 scorer for Kentucky in 1942-43 before entering the Navy, he was a steadying influence in the Wildcats' backcourt upon his return and contributed 8.4 and 6.6 scoring averages in his final two varsity seasons.

Rollins was replaced as a starter by the 6-3 Barnstable. However, Barnstable wasn't the passer that Rollins had been, so Rupp switched him to forward and moved Barker out to guard.

Hall recalled that during his freshman year, 1947-48, "Kentucky had the 'Fabulous Five.' Four of them returned my sophomore year, and we called our 12-man squad the 'Fabulous Five and the Sorry Seven.' I was so far down at the end of the bench that I didn't get into the games very often." (Twice to be exact, in 34 games.)

Even the "Sorry Seven" didn't hurt Kentucky's chances in 1948-49. For the first time ever, the Associated Press conducted a nationwide college-basketball poll that season, and the first team to sit atop the weekly rankings—the initial balloting was done in January—was St. Louis. A December loss to those Billikens in the Sugar Bowl Tournament convinced the Baron that his team needed to concentrate on getting the ball to Groza.

Once that adjustment was made, Kentucky's inside game became dominant until, that is, the team entered the NIT, where it was upset by Loyola of Chicago in the quarterfinals, 67-56. (More than two years later, it would be revealed that the Wildcats lost the game while some of their own were trying to shave points. But those developments were known only to the players and a small circle of gamblers in 1949.)

After its NIT misadventure, Kentucky then entered the NCAA Tournament and made quick work of the opposition. Villanova fell first, 85-72, in the Eastern playoffs. Rupp and company followed up by humiliating a strong Illinois club, 76-47, in the Eastern final. In the West, Henry Iba's Oklahoma A&M team moved through his brand of controlled paces. The Aggies nipped Wyoming, 40-39, then powered past Oregon State, 55-30.

The 1949 NCAA championship game was scheduled for Seattle, meaning the Kentucky squad faced the discomfort of a 3,000-mile train ride from the Eastern competition at Madison Square Garden. The Western survivor, meanwhile, had to make a considerably shorter haul—from Kansas City. The travel inequity didn't seem to bother the Wildcats, who rode Groza's 25-point performance to their second consecutive NCAA crown, achieved with a 46-36 triumph over Oklahoma A&M.

"It was a tough game all the way," Rupp told reporters afterward. "We had to play this one the hard way, almost to the finish."

Groza again was named the tournament's leading

player. He and Beard were consensus All-America selections, and Jones earned a spot on United Press' first team.

In addition to its NCAA title, Kentucky had been designated No. 1 in AP's final poll of the season. That voting had taken place almost three weeks before the championship game.

Groza had made tremendous strides in his final collegiate season. After averaging 11.6 points over 76 games in his sophomore and junior years, he scored at a 20.5 clip as a senior. Plus, he made 42.3 percent of his field-goal attempts and 72.6 percent of his free-throw tries in 1948-49, major improvements over the marks of his previous season (37.7 from the floor, 62.9 from the line).

"He just takes over under all circumstances," Rupp said of Groza late in the year. "He's a natural leader. He's extremely well-poised. Never ruffles much . . . It seems like he's always in front, leading the way for the other players, whether on the basketball floor, sightseeing or meeting people."

After their last season at Lexington, Groza, Beard, Jones and Barker would form the nucleus of a new pro team, the Indianapolis Olympians. With stock ownership in the National Basketball Association club, the former Wildcats saw their wealth

1948 KENTUCKY

Head Coach—Adolph Rupp   Final Record—36-3

(Statistics and record include three games in Olympic Trials [2-1 record] after NCAA Tournament.)

Player	Pos.	Hgt.	Wgt.	Cl.	G	FG	FGA	Pct.	FT	FTA	Pct.	Reb.	Pts.	Avg.
Alex Groza	C	6-7	220	Jr.	39	200	530	.377	88	140	.629	...	488	12.5
Ralph Beard	G	5-10	175	Jr.	38	194	536	.362	88	149	.591	...	476	12.5
Wallace Jones	F	6-4	225	Jr.	36	133	427	.311	69	103	.670	...	335	9.3
James Line	F	6-2	185	So.	38	107	296	.361	51	62	.823	...	265	7.0
Ken Rollins	G	6-0	175	Sr.	39	95	341	.279	67	92	.728	...	257	6.6
Cliff Barker	F	6-1	185	Jr.	38	98	317	.309	52	93	.559	...	248	6.5
Dale Barnstable	F	6-2	175	So.	38	76	280	.271	24	42	.571	...	176	4.6
Joe Holland	F	6-4	190	Jr.	38	58	207	.280	24	47	.511	...	140	3.7
Jack Parkinson	G	6-0	175	Sr.	29	43	214	.201	10	22	.455	...	96	3.3
Walt Hirsch	F	6-3	180	Fr.	13	16	55	.291	5	9	.556	...	37	2.8
Albert Cummins	G	5-10	160	So.	17	13	37	.351	6	9	.667	...	32	1.9
Jim Jordan	F	6-3	185	So.	30	13	88	.148	18	25	.720	...	44	1.5
Garland Townes	G	6-0	170	Fr.	13	7	22	.318	5	11	.455	...	19	1.5
Roger Day	F	6-3	185	Fr.	11	5	18	.278	7	9	.778	...	17	1.5
Wil Smether	G	6-2	180	Fr.	7	5	10	.500	0	3	.000	...	10	1.4
Robert Henne	G	6-1	165	Fr.	11	5	22	.227	3	7	.429	...	13	1.2
Albert Campbell	C	6-4	200	Sr.	15	6	27	.222	4	7	.571	...	16	1.1
Johnny Stough	G	6-0	170	So.	23	8	38	.211	5	10	.500	...	21	0.9
Kentucky					39	1082	3465	.312	526	840	.626	...	2690	70.0
Opponents					39	....		.232	...	...	....	...	1730	44.4

1949 KENTUCKY

Head Coach—Adolph Rupp   Final Record—32-2

Player	Pos.	Hgt.	Wgt.	Cl.	G	FG	FGA	Pct.	FT	FTA	Pct.	Reb.	Pts.	Avg.
Alex Groza	C	6-7	220	Sr.	34	259	612	.423	180	248	.726	...	698	20.5
Ralph Beard	G	5-10	176	Sr.	34	144	481	.299	82	115	.713	...	370	10.9
Wallace Jones	F-C	6-4	225	Sr.	32	130	440	.295	49	75	.653	...	309	9.7
Cliff Barker	G-F	6-2	185	Sr.	34	94	315	.298	60	88	.682	...	248	7.3
Dale Barnstable	F-G	6-3	180	Jr.	34	84	309	.272	41	57	.719	...	209	6.1
Jim Line	F	6-2	190	Jr.	32	70	195	.359	43	51	.843	...	183	5.7
Walter Hirsch	F-G	6-4	185	So.	34	67	209	.321	22	32	.688	...	156	4.6
Roger Day	F	6-3	185	So.	19	21	39	.538	9	17	.529	...	51	2.7
Al Bruno	F	6-3	185	So.	9	9	30	.300	2	3	.667	...	20	2.2
Garland Townes	G	6-0	180	So.	16	10	48	.208	11	20	.550	...	31	1.9
Johnny Stough	G	6-0	170	Jr.	25	13	56	.232	12	14	.857	...	38	1.5
Bob Henne	G	6-1	170	So.	9	2	19	.105	3	7	.429	...	7	0.8
Joe B. Hall	G	6-0	165	So.	2	0	3	.000	0	1	.000	...	0	0.0
Kentucky					34	903	2756	.328	514	728	.706	...	2320	68.2
Opponents					34	538	2216	.243	454	756	.601	...	1530	45.0

The 1948-49 Kentucky Wildcats: Front row (left to right)—Rupp, Line, Barker, Johnny Stough, Beard, Joe B. Hall, Garland Townes, assistant coach Harry Lancaster. Second row—Barnstable, Walter Hirsch, Jones, Groza, Bob Henne, Roger Day, manager Humzey Yessin.

and fame grow until the fall of 1951 when it was disclosed that Groza and Beard had accepted bribes to shave points while playing for Kentucky. Groza and Beard were denied further participation in the NBA and forced to sell their stock, and the Olympians folded after the 1952-53 season.

The two players—along with Barnstable, a high school coach in Kentucky when the news broke—confessed they had accepted money to trim points in the 1949 NIT game against Loyola. They later implicated several of their Kentucky teammates in the scandal. And the New York judge who imposed suspended sentences on Groza, Beard and Barnstable decried the fact that Rupp had allowed a Lexington bookmaker to travel with the team and fraternize with the players at a New York nightclub.

Rupp was stunned by the point-trimming disclosures. "They can't touch my boys with a 10-foot pole," he had said earlier of rumors that gamblers had gotten to some of his players.

The fact that Wah-Wah Jones knew nothing of his colleagues' misdeeds—"I guess it makes me look pretty stupid, but I didn't have any idea at all that

anything was going on"—left Rupp further nonplussed.

"If the boys who were playing on the same court with them didn't know it, how was I to know it?" Rupp wondered.

As the impact of the scandal reverberated—in the 1947-1950 time frame, the gambling mess had involved 32 players on seven teams nationwide—University of Kentucky President Herman L. Donovan ordered an internal investigation of his school's program. "From all we could learn," Donovan said after reviewing the results, "Coach Rupp is an honorable man who did not knowingly violate the athletic rules." The same couldn't be said for Rupp's players.

Rather than knowing how good they really were in view of their consecutive NCAA titles, some of the Kentucky coach's standouts were left only with their memories—many of which had been tarnished. Still, some of the luster went unmarred. After all, when it came to on-court skills, Wildcat opponents really couldn't touch Rupp's athletes—not even with a 10-foot pole.

EIGHT

The Bearcats 'Survive'

C I N C I N N A T I

**1960-61
1961-62**

Ed Jucker remembers feeling queasy in the spring of 1960 when he contemplated the passing of three-time All-America Oscar Robertson and two teammates from the Cincinnati basketball program.

Jucker, then a 41-year-old Cincinnati assistant, was just about to take over as the Bearcats' head coach, replacing George Smith. Smith was moving up to the athletic director's job.

"I was sick," Jucker recalled. "Our tickets were all sold out for 1961. Our opponents were thirsting for revenge. And I sat there and thought, 'There go 55 of our 87 points a game.' I asked myself where I was going to make up all those points."

More than half of those Cincinnati points—33.7, to be exact—in the recently completed season came from Robertson, who with considerable help from skilled guard Ralph Davis and a nice contribution from forward Larry Willey had led the Bearcats into the Final Four in 1959 and again in 1960.

Now, however, the fabulous Big O was graduating to the professional ranks. Things, apparently, would never quite be the same at Cincinnati.

Jucker's prescription for making up the points—or at least tempering the impact of the loss of Robertson and friends—was to make changes. Drastic changes.

With a run-and-gun offense, Cincinnati and Robertson had posted a 79-9 record in the previous three seasons and had finished atop the Associated Press' final poll of the 1959-60 campaign. The excitement provided by the Robertson teams had drawn throngs of supporters to Bearcat games.

"The fans had loved watching Robertson and his teams run up and down the floor," Jucker said.

However, in Final Four competition in both 1959 and 1960, Cincinnati had lost to Pete Newell's California Golden Bears. Those Cal teams featured uncompromising defense and controlled offense. Watching from the bench as Smith's aide, Jucker had come to admire Newell's style.

So, upon becoming head coach, Jucker decided that he would downshift Cincinnati's attack into a low-gear, patient offense, while emphasizing defense. At the time, he wasn't even thinking about trying to approximate the won-lost success of the Robertson years, Jucker said in an interview nearly three decades later. "The control game was really to survive, for myself, the players and the program," Jucker said.

At best, the coach figured his 1960-61 Cincinnati team might win 15 games. Never in his wildest imagination did Jucker dream of what would unfold in his first three seasons as the Bearcats' mentor.

"I was interested in being competitive," Jucker said. "I figured if we could hang in there and keep the games close, we would create enough excitement to keep most of our fans. I decided that maybe if we gave up only 40 points a game, we wouldn't need to score much. I figured if we were close at the half, we had a chance to win. I wanted to keep the program respectable. I also didn't want to have to put my house up for sale."

Calling the movers didn't seem like such a bad idea in the first few weeks of the 1960-61 season. His new approach brought arched eyebrows from nearly everyone, Jucker acknowledged.

"The fans didn't like it, and the players weren't

When Oscar Robertson took his amazing talents to the NBA after the 1959-60 season, Ed Jucker (above) took over as Cincinnati coach and guided the Bearcats to two straight national titles.

convinced either," the coach recalled. "We lost two conference games and three of the first eight we played. Those first eight ball games were almost unbearable because the kids were looking at me tongue-in-cheek. The fans were booing. It wasn't easy."

Compounding the Bearcats' problem was the box-office competition that the university faced from the city's professional basketball team. While Oscar Robertson was no longer a Bearcat, the lithe superstar was still in town plying his trade with the Cincinnati Royals of the National Basketball Association. To keep Bearcat fans from defecting in droves to the pro game, Jucker's athletes had to produce—and in a hurry.

Jucker nonetheless was determined to sell the players on what he called the "science of percentage basketball" or, in simpler terms, working for good shots. "The closer you are to the basket, the easier it is to score," was the point he drummed into his players. He wanted his teams to control the ball and wait for the other team to make a mistake.

"On defense, we try to pressure opponents into a pattern they are not used to playing," Jucker explained to reporters at the time. "We want them to play another game—a game they don't know."

Jucker wasn't fooling himself over the risks involved in his coaching philosophy.

"I knew I was asking for trouble," the coach conceded. "If it didn't work, I was dead."

Considering the pressures of modern college basketball, some coaches today might be reluctant to show such boldness. But Jucker was the old-school type. In addition to his duties on the basketball coaching staff, he was a professor in the school's physical-education department and had served as coach of Cincinnati's highly successful baseball team (for whom he had coached a hard-throwing lefthander named Sandy Koufax).

Jucker himself had played basketball and baseball at Cincinnati in the late 1930s, then served in the Navy during World War II, where he played more basketball. After the war, he coached basketball at the Merchant Marine Academy and at Rensselaer Poly, both in New York state, before moving to Cincinnati as an assistant.

By the time Jucker took over the Cincinnati program, he wasn't afraid to do things his way. And Smith, despite having been head coach, wasn't a meddlesome athletic director.

There were two primary obstacles to Jucker's success. First, Robertson's continued presence in the city was a reminder of the old, exciting style of play. And while Oscar remained very supportive of his old university, he couldn't help but attract a sizable segment of Bearcat fans to Royals games.

The second major problem, Jucker said, was his players' collective attitude. "They all wanted to be Oscar Robertson," he remembered. "But I finally convinced them that if we all played as one, they could add up to an Oscar Robertson. Some would shoot, some would dribble, all would play defense. In the end, we didn't have an All-America. But we had an All-America team."

As might be expected, the toughest players to convince were those who had played with Robertson under the old system, specifically senior co-captains Bob Wiesenhahn and Carl Bouldin. Wiesenhahn, a rugged 6-foot-4, 215-pound forward, shared playing time with Willey as a junior, but came on as a starter and emerged as Cincinnati's top scoring threat in 1960-61.

Wiesenhahn, from the Cincinnati area, had exceptional strength and was a fine high school football player, Jucker recalled.

"Nobody but Cincinnati had wanted him as a basketball player," Jucker said. "But he was a very determined defender and a good rebounder."

In an informal way, Wiesenhahn was responsible for keeping the '60-'61 team loose when it struggled in the early going. "Before each game, he would be over in the corner doing 50 to 100 pushups and situps," the coach explained. "This relaxed us, because the players would get around him and count and say, 'Come on, Bob.' That helped with the tension."

Bouldin was the team's best outside shooter. The only problem was, Jucker didn't go much for outside shooting. "It took them a while to adjust," Jucker said, "but they did." It helped that Bouldin, a guard, was an all-around athlete who had starred for Jucker's baseball team and would go on to pitch in the majors. Superb athletes, it seems, can adapt to any system.

Bespectacled and easygoing, 6-9 Paul Hogue was a key operative for these Cincinnati Bearcats. "Everything is jelly"—as in fine and sweet—was Hogue's trademark saying, and with the junior center proving a force up front, the saying wasn't an idle boast.

A power rebounder and excellent defensive player, Hogue also possessed good offensive skills, including a short jump shot and a "half hook."

Beyond that, he possessed good power moves in the post. And with Jucker's penchant for getting the ball inside, Hogue evolved into a good scorer. The new offense would mean nearly 400 field-goal attempts for Hogue in '60-'61, up from the 264 total he had as a sophomore in Cincinnati's high-speed offense.

Among the veteran players, the only casualty to the new style of Cincy basketball was junior forward Sandy Pomerantz, who would quit early in the season because of a lack of playing time.

While holdovers Wiesenhahn, Bouldin and Hogue were crucial to the team's success, newcomers also played pivotal roles. At 6-2, sophomore forward Tom Thacker was the one Cincinnati athlete who could play above the rim. Thacker,

Tom Thacker, a sophomore in the 1960-61 campaign, was the one Bearcat with the ability to play above the rim.

Burly Bearcat center Paul Hogue has position on Ohio State's Jerry Lucas as he reaches for a rebound during the 1961 NCAA Tournament championship game.

though, could do much more than jump. He was a tenacious defender and the kind of player who wanted the ball when the game was on the line.

The other newcomer, playmaker Tony Yates, was not a typical sophomore. A service veteran, Yates was 23 years old. "He was a leader and a great defensive player," Jucker said. "Being older, he had the experience. He was good with the other players. When they made mistakes, he gave 'em a pat on the back. He was the coach on the floor."

Paired with Bouldin in the backcourt, Yates would get few scoring opportunities. "I seldom allowed them to shoot," Jucker said of his guards. "They didn't like it. But at the end of the season, they did pretty well."

If the guards wanted to score, their opportunities would have to come from the Bearcats' trapping press. But there would be no reaching for the ball. Jucker didn't want the fouls. The press was there to force mistakes, particularly bad passes.

And if scoring wouldn't be a job for the guards, ballhandling rated as a high priority. Jucker despised turnovers. "The pride we had in ballhandling, that was a way of life," the coach said. "If somebody turned over the ball, it was almost a timeout. We wanted to find out what's going on here."

Jucker's precise offense required stellar passing and few mental errors. The coach always wanted to set up backdoor plays and inside shots, and the Bearcats would swing the ball around the defense looking for that special opening.

Cincinnati's problems in the first month of the 1960-61 season—the squad's three losses came in a five-game stretch—were most evident in a 17-point setback at St. Louis and a 19-point defeat at Bradley. The players obviously were slow in adjusting to Jucker's ways. However, in the ninth game of the season, the Bearcats seemed to come together in a 10-point triumph over a Dayton team bound for a 20-victory season.

From there, Cincinnati played like a team possessed. By mid-January, Jucker's Bearcats had stretched their winning streak to six games and boasted an 11-3 record. Interest was picking up, to say the least, as the city began to rivet its attention on a winner. Robertson was doing his thing across town, all right, scoring about 30 points per game for the Royals. However, the Royals were headed for a last-place finish in their division.

Winning, Jucker-style, didn't stop. After Wiesenhahn fueled a 17-point pasting of a rugged Iowa team in early February by going on a 26-point tear, Cincinnati had won 16 of 19 games. A month later, the Bearcats wound up the regular season with a 69-57 victory over Marshall, a decision that ran Cincy's winning string to 18 games and its record to 23-3. In Missouri Valley Conference play, Cincinnati, which had started out 0-2, wound up at 10-2.

George Wilson earned a starting forward job in 1961-62, but not until he understood Jucker's 'team' philosophy.

Tony Yates (left), a 23-year-old former serviceman, became the Bearcats' playmaker and floor general in 1960-61. Ron Bonham arrived a year later and averaged 14.3 points.

And, incredibly, after a what-do-we-do-now reaction to Robertson's departure, Bearcat fans could bask in the glow of their team's No. 2 national ranking in both final wire-service polls. Still, Cincinnati was overshadowed in its own backyard. No. 2 in the nation, the Bearcats also were No. 2 in Ohio. The top-ranked team in the country entering the NCAA Tournament was unbeaten Ohio State, the defending national champion.

Led by the junior triumvirate of Jerry Lucas, John Havlicek and Mel Nowell and senior standout Larry Siegfried, Ohio State had roared to a 24-0 regular-season record and, over two seasons, boasted a 29-game winning skein. In the NCAA regionals, the Buckeyes would be competing in the Mideast and the Bearcats would be doing battle in the Midwest.

Ohio State survived a big scare in its first 1961 NCAA Tournament test, subduing Louisville by one point in a Mideast semifinal after trailing the Cardinals by five with the game clock under the three-minute mark. Cincinnati, meanwhile, bashed Texas Tech, 78-55, in a Midwest semifinal. In regional championship games, the tables were turned.

The Buckeyes breezed, beating Kentucky by 13 points, but the Bearcats had to scramble to knock off Kansas State, 69-64. Whatever the method, it was off to Kansas City and the Final Four for Ohio State and Cincinnati (plus Utah and St. Joseph's, winners of the West and East competition).

The national semifinals of 1961 bordered on boring as Ohio State dismantled St. Joseph's, 95-69, and Cincinnati stymied Utah, 82-67. However, the final offered a dream-time matchup: No. 1 vs. No. 2. That the teams were from the same state only added to the drama.

Jucker, as usual, wanted his Bearcats to stay close throughout and then win it at the end. Ohio State Coach Fred Taylor figured that forcing Hogue into foul trouble was the way to go. As it turned out, both coaches got their way. Ohio State led, 39-38, at the half, and Hogue had three fouls.

Cincinnati's strong man wasn't whistled for another foul, though, and, all the while, he made Lucas work for his shots. Hogue was on the way to a nine-point, seven-rebound performance; Lucas was en route to 27 points and 12 rebounds. While Lucas managed a significant statistical edge in his head-to-head duel with Hogue, the Bearcats crashed the backboards and halted the Buckeyes' fast break. It was enough, as Jucker had hoped, to put Cincinnati in position to win.

With two minutes left in regulation play, the Bearcats guarded a two-point lead. Ohio State tied the score at 61-61 with 1:41 remaining as junior reserve Bob Knight (future Indiana coaching great) made a driving layup. And that's where the score stood when time expired.

Thirty seconds into the extra period, Hogue broke the deadlock by sinking two free throws. Then, after a Wiesenhahn field goal gave Cincinnati a 65-62 edge, Yates tossed in three foul shots in the final 1:06 and Thacker scored on an outside jump shot. Cincinnati won going away, 70-65.

"We did nothing special," Jucker said of his Bearcats, who finished with a 36-32 rebound edge. "All we did was a job. Each person did a job. No All-Americas. Just a bunch of great defenders, shooters and hustlers."

Rather than gloat over the school's first national title, Jucker acknowledged his low expectations for the 1960-61 season. "I would have settled for 15 victories, really, I would have," he told the media. "I kept saying to myself, 'Well, we'll lose the next one.' We'd win and I'd think, 'Well, the next time.' We just kept winning, and pretty soon I was convinced myself."

Back home, the fans no longer were yearning for the run-and-gun days. A Cincinnati city councilman, caught up in the frenzy of the moment, called the Bearcats' triumph "the greatest event that has ever happened in the city of Cincinnati. This is the greatest team in the world."

Athletic Director Smith said, "The championship was way beyond my expectations. Seven years ago, Jucker and I started planning. We had hoped, but we didn't know it would come to this so quickly."

Little did they know that the show had just begun.

With Wiesenhahn (a 17.1 scorer for the 1961 national champions) and Bouldin having completed their eligibility, Jucker needed two fresh faces in the Bearcats' starting unit for 1961-62. He found them in sophomores Ron Bonham and George Wilson, standouts who two years earlier had been named the No. 1 high school players in Indiana and Illinois, respectively. But Jucker didn't just give jobs to Bonham and Wilson. He had to straighten out their thinking first.

A 6-5, 200-pound forward, Bonham had a smooth offensive game. "One of the greatest pure shooters I've ever seen," Jucker said.

Bonham wasn't fast, but he had a quick first step. He was best at shooting off the screen. But as a typical young player, he liked to let fly with long-range shots. Jucker, of course, demanded an inside focus.

Thacker goes high to drop in a basket in the first of Cincinnati's consecutive championship-game victories over Ohio State.

Hogue (left) and Thacker battle Buckeyes Jim Doughty and John Havlicek (right) during the 1962 NCAA title game.

Season Results

1960-61 (27-3)

90	Indiana State 51	80	Drake 70
85	Western Michigan................. 54	73	Bradley 72
70	Miami of Ohio........................ 62	77	At Iowa 60
76	At Seton Hall 84	61	St. Louis................................. 52
74	Loyola of Los Angeles 53	67	Wichita State 64
40	At St. Louis 57	81	Tulsa 52
75	Nebraska 60	85	At Houston............................. 80
53	At Bradley 72	73	At North Texas State........... 43
71	Dayton 61	89	Xavier (O.) 53
84	George Washington 61	69	At Marshall 57
74	Houston (OT)......................... 71	78	Tex. Tech at Lawr., Kan.*.... 55
83	North Texas State................. 34	69	Kansas St. at Lawr., Kan.* ..64
80	At Wichita State.................... 57	82	Utah at K.C.*......................... 67
92	At Tulsa 75	70	Ohio State at K.C.* (OT)......65
64	Duquesne............................... 53		*NCAA Tournament
86	At Drake................................. 64		

1961-62 (29-2)

86	Indiana State 63	60	At Houston............................. 52
63	Miami of Ohio........................ 30	77	At North Texas State........... 50
86	At Wisconsin.......................... 67	54	At St. Louis 48
60	At Drake 59	70	At Tulsa 52
77	Marshall................................. 49	83	George Washington 43
51	At Wichita State.................... 52	59	Houston.................................. 47
84	Colorado 67	72	Bradley 57
97	St. John's at New York*........ 68	84	Wichita State 63
64	La Salle at New York*........... 56	61	Xavier (O.).............................. 58
101	Wisconsin at New York*....... 71	61	Bradley 46
62	St. Louis................................. 47	66	Creighton at Manhat. Kan.†.46
72	Tulsa 43	73	Colorado at Manhat., Kan.† .46
68	At Bradley (OT) 70	72	UCLA at Louisville†.............. 70
80	Dayton 61	71	Ohio State at Louisville†....... 59
62	At Duquesne 54		*Holiday Festival
89	North Texas State 61		†NCAA Tournament
73	Drake 52		

Wilson, on the other hand, was a 6-8 forward/center. He had good jumping ability and his own style on offense.

With Bonham and Wilson ticketed for duty in the frontcourt, Thacker was moved from forward to guard to supplant Bouldin. Despite the infusion of new firepower, the team was built around Hogue's power game, and both Bonham and Wilson found that hard to accept in the early going. Soon, they got the message.

In Cincinnati's Holiday Festival opener at Madison Square Garden in late December, Jucker kept Bonham and Wilson on the sideline and told the two players that when they were ready to play his way, "just whisper to me." As Jucker recalled, "It wasn't long before they whispered."

Bonham bounded off the bench and pitched in 27 points in 22 minutes, firing the Bearcats to an easy victory over St. John's. He was a starter thereafter. Wilson who contributed seven points in relief against the Redmen, eased into starting duty four weeks later.

After the Festival, which Cincinnati wrapped up in rousing fashion with a 30-point triumph over Wisconsin, the Bearcats were 9-1 and rolling. Subsequent Missouri Valley victories over St. Louis and Tulsa preceded an overtime loss to league rival Bradley, a defeat that loomed large at the time. Sure enough, at the end of the regular season, Cincinnati and Bradley were tied for first place in the league standings, necessitating a playoff to determine the conference's NCAA Tournament representative.

In a game contested at a neutral site, Evansville, Ind., the Bearcats put a 61-46 bear hug on a Bradley team that featured two-time All-America Chet Walker. The victory shot Cincinnati into Midwest Regional competition, where opponents proved no competition at all. Creighton fell, 66-46, as Hogue dominated play with 24 points and 19 rebounds, and Colorado went down to a 73-46 defeat as Cincy's front line of Hogue, Wilson and Bonham pounded the Buffaloes for 58 points. The Bearcats, ranked No. 2 in the country (as they had been the year before), were Final Four-bound once more. Joining them in Louisville would be Wake Forest, UCLA and top-rated (again) Ohio State.

UCLA Coach John Wooden's first Final Four team, featuring Walt Hazzard, John Green and Gary Cunningham, pushed the Bearcats to the brink of elimination in one national semifinal. Cincinnati prevailed, however, when Thacker drilled a 20-foot jump shot after UCLA lost the ball on an offensive foul whistled against Hazzard. Cincinnati 72, UCLA 70. The winning field goal accounted for Thacker's only points of the night, an evening that clearly belonged to veteran center Hogue. Playing the finest game of his career at an opportune time, Hogue netted 36 points and snatched 19 rebounds.

In the other bracket, Ohio State, about to close

out its Lucas-Havlicek-Nowell era, bested Wake Forest, 84-68, but the Buckeyes' title hopes suffered a jolt when Lucas took a nasty spill against the Demon Deacons and injured his left knee.

With Lucas hobbled, Cincinnati seemed primed to claim a second straight championship. And the Bearcats did just that, sweeping to a 71-59 triumph over the Buckeyes in a game in which Cincy mounted leads of up to 18 points. Most observers, including Ohio State Coach Taylor, thought that even a healthy Lucas probably wouldn't have changed the outcome. Cincinnati had become the best team in college basketball.

"The key again was our ability to get the ball in to Hogue," Jucker said, "and our control of the boards. I also thought our defense was terrific. This was a real satisfying victory. We have a dedicated team, and we proved to the world it is the greatest."

Lucas, while not at his best physically, nonetheless played the entire game. "My knee didn't hurt," a candid Lucas said, "but Hogue bothered me."

Hogue, who finished with 22 points and 19 rebounds in the final compared with Lucas' marks of 11 and 16, was named the top player of the 1962 Final Four.

Cincinnati, once and for all, had shaken free from Ohio State's giant shadow. Back-to-back national championships had been accomplished only three times previously, and now the Bearcats had earned their place among college basketball's storied teams. Adding to the euphoria surrounding the Cincinnati program was the fact that four starters

1961 CINCINNATI

Head Coach—Ed Jucker

Final Record—27-3

Player	Pos.	Hgt.	Wgt.	Cl.	G	FG	FGA	Pct.	FT	FTA	Pct.	Reb.	Pts.	Avg.
Bob Wiesenhahn	F	6-4	215	Sr.	30	206	428	.481	101	149	.678	299	513	17.1
Paul Hogue	C	6-9	235	Jr.	30	208	391	.532	87	168	.518	374	503	16.8
Tom Thacker	F	6-2	170	So.	30	139	351	.396	91	133	.684	284	369	12.3
Carl Bouldin	G	6-1	174	Sr.	30	140	327	.428	72	90	.800	85	352	11.7
Sandy Pomerantz	F	6-6	205	Jr.	2	6	10	.600	3	4	.750	7	15	7.5
Tony Yates	G	6-0	175	So.	30	84	173	.486	53	88	.602	106	221	7.4
Dale Heidotting	F-C	6-8	190	So.	26	39	91	.429	15	23	.652	96	93	3.6
Fred Dierking	F-C	6-6	210	Jr.	25	29	60	.483	7	15	.467	55	65	2.6
Jim Calhoun	G	6-0	175	Jr.	17	14	37	.378	7	13	.538	9	35	2.1
Tom Sizer	G	6-2	180	Jr.	24	18	48	.375	12	16	.750	23	48	2.0
Larry Shingleton	G	5-10	158	So.	20	7	24	.292	4	10	.400	11	18	0.9
Mark Altenau	F	6-3	195	So.	18	6	14	.429	4	9	.444	11	16	0.9
Ron Reis	C	6-10	240	Jr.	11	1	7	.143	1	4	.250	6	3	0.3
Frank Turner	F	6-7	191	So.	3	0	1	.000	0	0	.000	0	0	0.0
Team												187		
Cincinnati					30	897	1962	.457	457	722	.633	1553	2251	75.0
Opponents					30	693	1844	.376	437	662	.660	1153	1823	60.8

1962 CINCINNATI

Head Coach—Ed Jucker

Final Record—29-2

Player	Pos.	Hgt.	Wgt.	Cl.	G	FG	FGA	Pct.	FT	FTA	Pct.	Reb.	Pts.	Avg.
Paul Hogue	C	6-9	235	Sr.	31	211	424	.498	99	175	.566	383	521	16.8
Ron Bonham	F	6-5	200	So.	31	174	382	.455	95	125	.760	156	443	14.3
Tom Thacker	G-F	6-2	170	Jr.	31	134	331	.405	74	121	.612	266	342	11.0
George Wilson	F-C	6-8	210	So.	31	109	216	.505	67	101	.663	248	285	9.2
Tony Yates	G	6-1	175	Jr.	31	97	253	.383	61	91	.670	94	255	8.2
Fred Dierking	F	6-6	210	Sr.	28	42	97	.433	30	51	.588	81	114	4.1
Larry Shingleton	G	5-10	158	Jr.	25	42	101	.416	14	25	.560	34	98	3.9
Dale Heidotting	F	6-8	195	Jr.	22	24	47	.511	20	35	.571	50	68	3.1
Tom Sizer	G	6-2	180	Sr.	25	26	57	.456	15	24	.625	33	67	2.7
Jim Calhoun	G	6-0	175	Sr.	18	14	38	.368	2	3	.667	7	30	1.7
Bill Abernethy	F	6-5	200	So.	3	1	4	.250	0	0	.000	2	2	0.7
Ron Reis	C	6-10	235	Sr.	15	3	10	.300	2	4	.500	2	8	0.5
Larry Elasser	G	6-2	185	So.	10	2	7	.286	1	4	.250	5	5	0.5
Team												175		
Cincinnati					31	879	1967	.447	480	759	.632	1536	2238	72.2
Opponents					31	663	1799	.369	381	556	.685	1142	1707	55.1

The triumphant Cincinnati Bearcats celebrate their second straight championship in 1962.

would be returning for the 1962-63 season.

Gone, of course, was Hogue, who had averaged 16.8 points in both his junior and senior seasons and was a behemoth on the boards. Wilson shifted to center and senior Larry Shingleton moved in at guard, and the Bearcats missed nary a beat. They won their first 19 games of the '62-'63 season, stretching their two-season winning streak to 37 games, and advanced to the Final Four with a 25-1 record.

Ranked No. 1 in both wire-service polls this time, Cincinnati inspired awe.

"I saw Cincinnati beat Kansas (early in the season)," Tulsa Coach Joe Swank said, "and they just looked invincible. I couldn't sleep after I watched them play." Swank's Golden Hurricane was a conference rival of the Cincinnati club.

Ultimately, the 1963 NCAA championship would come down to a confrontation between the nation's highest-scoring team, Loyola of Chicago, averaging 91.8 points per game, and the country's stingiest team, Cincinnati, yielding 52.9 points per game.

Led by Bonham, an All-America selection (as was Thacker), the Bearcats bolted to an eight-point half-time lead in the national title game and held a 15-point edge—at 45-30—with 12 minutes remaining. Cincinnati appeared a shoo-in for an unprecedented third consecutive national crown.

However, the usually calm-and-collected Bearcats began to unravel. The Loyola press took its toll, forcing numerous Cincinnati turnovers, and Jucker's crew found itself in foul trouble. Loyola went on a 24-9 blitz, a run capped by Jerry Harkness' game-tying jump shot that sent the game into overtime at 54-54. In the extra session, Vic Rouse's last-second tip-in gave the Ramblers a stunning 60-58 victory.

"Our game plan worked for us 99 out of 100 times," Yates said afterward. "On this night, it didn't."

The Cincinnati-Loyola battle was the last game in Bearcat uniforms for Yates and Thacker, players whose court savvy would be sorely missed (Cincinnati's record fell to 17-9 the next year).

Sitting in his South Carolina retirement home years later, Jucker reflected on the 1963 NCAA championship game. "We got into foul trouble and missed our free throws," he said. "It was as simple as that. I guess that's what makes the sport so great."

The matter-of-fact appraisal was typical of a man who wasn't afraid to make decisions and live with the results. And living with two NCAA title banners—the result of Ed Jucker's decision to implement a down-tempo brand of basketball at Cincinnati—proved a mighty comfortable existence.

The Wolfpack Gets Revenge

NORTH CAROLINA STATE

1973-74

The old saying that it's better to be lucky than good is often used to describe the North Carolina State basketball team of 1973-74.

There seems to be little doubt that the Wolfpack was the recipient of more than its share of luck that season, particularly in terms of scheduling, en route to ending UCLA's run of consecutive NCAA championships at seven. But often forgotten—or at least overlooked—is the fact that Coach Norm Sloan's squad was indeed good. In fact, it was very, very good. Excellent, even.

Sloan would be the first to acknowledge that his Wolfpack got some breaks along the way. Never having to leave the state of North Carolina during postseason play surely ranked high among them.

But all the peripheral stuff aside, the 1973-1974 North Carolina State Wolfpack put one talent-laden club on the floor. It had a jumping-jack superstar in 6-foot-4 forward David Thompson, the kind of guy who could let fly with a silky jump shot or power his way to the basket, depending on what defenses gave him. It boasted a quality big man in 7-4 Tom Burleson, a fine passing center who also was an effective scorer and rebounder. And it possessed a skilled playmaker in 5-7 Monte Towe, a guard who could hit the outside shot and break full-court presses.

Plus, the Wolfpack featured a superb defensive guard in Moe Rivers, who could turn up the pressure and get a steal or stick in a medium-range jumper, and a muscleman in Tim Stoddard, who offset meager statistical contributions by being a force up front and supplying all the tough defense you'd ever want. Stoddard had other athletic skills,

too: Within a year and half after the '73-'74 season, he would make his debut as a major league pitcher.

Off the bench, North Carolina State had a pair of 6-8 players. Sophomore forward Phil Spence could rebound and score, while senior Steve Nuce could play forward and center. Perhaps the best thing about the reserve corps was that it was dissension-free. Since it was obvious who deserved to start, the reserves filled their roles happily. "And it's unique to have something like that," Sloan said.

Beyond all the individual talent, North Carolina State—in Sloan's view—had a collective golden attitude.

"They were up for every game," Sloan said of his players. "I had no difficulty with that team. That's the most fun I've ever had coaching."

The catalyst for this attitude, the coach said, was Thompson. "What a tremendous individual David Thompson was," Sloan gushed. "He got so much publicity, but he was so humble and shared it with everybody."

The son of a custodian, Thompson grew up near Shelby, N.C., in conditions that bordered on poverty. He was the 11th of 11 children. But he possessed athletic talent, and his 42-inch vertical leap made him an instant star at Crest High School in Shelby.

Sloan remembered that he first heard about Thompson during David's sophomore year at Crest. The NCAA had no restrictions on recruiting visits, telephone calls and other contacts with recruits in those days.

"We worked awfully hard on David," Sloan said. "We spent a lot of time up there." So did other

Norm Sloan directed his powerful North Carolina State team to an undefeated season in 1972-73 and a national championship the next year.

schools, particularly North Carolina. Thompson's decision came down to N.C. State and Carolina, and finally he chose Sloan's program.

Despite having spent considerable time watching Thompson, N.C. State's coach was in for a major surprise. Sloan knew Thompson had a work ethic that would at least rival his talent, but he just didn't realize the extent of that ethic. "The thing that made David so great," Sloan explained, "is that he was very gifted, yet he never really knew in his own mind how good he really was."

Sloan said many of the athletes he had come in contact with over the years thought they were better than they really were. In turn, they had a tendency not to work as hard as necessary.

"David," Sloan said, "always had something to

work on because he thought he should. Plus, he loved to play the game. Our team would finish practice, and he would go out and get a manager or somebody and play another 45 minutes."

Thompson had a knee operation after his sophomore season of 1972-73, but was ready to compete with the U.S. team in August 1973 at the World University Games in Moscow. The Americans, for whom Sloan served as an assistant coach, won the University Games title by defeating a Soviet Union squad that featured six members of the Russian team that had won the Olympic gold medal a year earlier.

The Americans left immediately after the championship game, Sloan recalled, and arrived home umpteen hours later with little sleep. Sloan stopped

The most lethal weapon in Sloan's offensive arsenal was jumping-jack David Thompson, a multi-talented athlete who could destroy defenses in many ways.

by his office, and an associate came in and asked how Thompson's knee had held up. "I told him the knee must have been fine," Sloan said, "because David was over in the gym shooting baskets. After one month of solid competition (including a pre-University Games tour), he flies home, gets no sleep and goes immediately to the gym to shoot. David truly loved the game."

Thompson was coming off a stunning sophomore season at North Carolina State. Averaging an Atlantic Coast Conference-leading 24.7 points, the sensational leaper made the consensus All-America team and was a landslide winner in balloting for ACC Player of the Year (he polled 116 votes, compared with four for runner-up George Karl of North Carolina). More important, the N.C. State

team soared as high as he did. The 1972-73 Wolfpack won all 27 of its games.

Perfect season or not, the Wolfpack did little celebrating. Because of an NCAA penalty for recruiting infractions, N.C. State was not a member of the 25-team field for the NCAA Tournament. The facts of the probation still irritate Sloan a decade and a half later.

"They (NCAA officials) put Duke on probation because an alumnus of theirs gave a player a sport-coat to graduate in," Sloan said. "We got probation for violating four administrative rules. Today, at worst, what we did would bring a private repri-mand from the NCAA.

"At the time, I told an NCAA official, 'This is the most unfair thing that has ever happened to me,

Tom Burleson used his 7-foot-4 frame to average 18.1 points in 1973-74 while also proving to be an effective passer and rebounder.

something I'll be answering to as long as I am in the business.'"

Most accounts of the probation state that N.C. State received the penalty for violations concerning Thompson, a claim that might be technically correct but still disturbs the coach. After an intense recruiting battle between North Carolina State and North Carolina, Thompson signed with the Wolfpack in May 1971. That August, the player visited friends at N.C. State's basketball camp and stayed in their room overnight. "We knew he was there," Sloan said of an action that the NCAA deemed illegal.

While at the camp, Thompson also participated in a pickup game that included one of N.C. State's assistant coaches. "The NCAA decided that game amounted to an illegal tryout," Sloan said. "We had signed him three months earlier."

All eyes were riveted on Thompson when he arrived on the Raleigh campus in the fall on 1971. However, freshmen nationwide weren't eligible for varsity competition for another year, meaning that the Wolfpack had to make do (translation: a 16-10 record) while waiting for David to join the big team.

Second-year man Thompson was indeed a superstar on that unbeaten 1972-73 club, but he received plenty of help from junior Burleson and fellow sophomores Towe and Stoddard. Burleson, from Newland, N.C., was fourth in ACC scoring with a 17.9 average and tops in the league in rebounding with a 12.0 mark. Towe and Stoddard, both from Indiana, chipped in with 10 and 7.9 points per game, respectively.

An Indiana native who had played for N.C. State in the late 1940s under the legendary Everett Case, Sloan used his home-state connections to recruit Towe and Stoddard. At first, Sloan had scoffed when someone suggested that he go after the diminutive Towe, who had lettered in football, basketball, baseball and golf in high school. But the guard quickly made Sloan—and the rest of the country—a believer.

"It's something inside," Sloan would say when asked how Towe managed to compete in a big man's game. With the ball, the little guy would challenge taller players; on defense, he would draw the offensive foul, which meant that he sometimes had to play hurt. That didn't bother Towe, either.

With leadership from Thompson and Towe, N.C. State had charged through its 1972-73 schedule. But the Wolfpack's season ended with a victory in the ACC Tournament championship game. "It wasn't until the end of their sophomore year that I realized what a tremendous group they were," Sloan said of the Thompson-Towe-Stoddard class. "Greatness is a difficult thing to predict. So much goes into it in terms of leadership."

For the next season, the coaching staff filled a

void in the backcourt by landing Rivers out of Gulf Coast Junior College in Florida. In another key personnel matter, Spence moved into heavy duty as a sophomore. Beginning with Sloan, the entire N.C. State program felt it had something to prove to college basketball.

The 1973-74 schedule offered North Carolina State a put-up-or-shut-up opportunity. In the third game of the season, the Wolfpack was matched against Bill Walton-led UCLA. The Bruins had been non-stop NCAA champions beginning with the 1967 tournament, but many thought a tourney-eligible N.C. State team might well have upended John Wooden's athletes in 1973.

While fans would never know what might have happened had UCLA and North Carolina State clashed in March 1973, they would get the second-best thing: A December 1973 matchup between the two powerhouses.

North Carolina State was eager to shake loose the shackles of NCAA restriction and mount its bid for the national championship. The Walton Gang, featuring the red-haired giant for whom it was named and standout forward Keith Wilkes, was out to match the incredible feat of the Lew Alcindor-paced UCLA teams of the late-1960s by winning a third straight NCAA crown. Of course, such an accomplishment would push the Bruins' overall NCAA-title string to eight.

N.C. State met Wooden's Bruins in St. Louis. It was a classic matchup, UCLA entering the contest with a record 78-game winning streak and the Wolfpack boasting a 29-game victory run. The Wolfpack, benefiting from the fact Walton got into early foul trouble, managed a 33-32 halftime lead but found itself in a 54-54 tie when Walton returned from a 21-minute respite. Upon the 6-11 center's return to action, the Bruins went on a 19-2 rampage and breezed to an 84-66 triumph before a throng of 18,461 fans.

Wilkes' play proved crucial in the clash of the titans. Not only did he break loose for 27 points, he also harassed Thompson into one of his poorest shooting performances as a collegian. In the face of Wilkes' defensive pressure, Thompson made only seven of 20 field-goal attempts and wound up with 17 points.

Needless to say, the Wolfpack players were crushed over their big-game failure.

"Coming back after the loss, the players wouldn't talk to anybody," Sloan recalled. "I remember Towe lay down and put his face in the crack of the seat."

Back in Raleigh, Towe paid Sloan a visit and asked that the team tighten its training rules and impose a curfew. The coach was opposed. He liked to begin each season without rules, as if he expected his players to act maturely. "Why start off treating players immaturely?" he asked.

Burleson's opposite was 5-7 guard Monte Towe, a skilled playmaker and a good outside offensive threat.

Season Results
1973-74 (30-1)

79	East Carolina	47	111	Furman at Charlotte	91
97	Vermont	42	105	Davidson	78
66	UCLA at St. Louis	84	111	Wake Forest	96
94	Georgia	60	113	Duke	87
97	Villanova at New Orleans*	82	80	At Clemson	75
98	Memphis St. at N. Orleans*	83	83	North Carolina	72
78	N. Carol. at G'boro, N.C.†	77	72	Wake Forest	63
91	W. Forest at G'boro, N.C.†	73	87	Virginia at G'boro, N.C.‡	66
96	Clemson	68	103	M'yland at Gr., N.C.‡ (OT)	100
80	Maryland	74	92	Providence at Raleigh, N.C.§	78
90	At Virginia	70	100	Pittsburgh at Raleigh, N.C.§	72
104	UNC Charlotte	72	80	UCLA at Gr., N.C.§ (2 OT)	77
83	At North Carolina	80	76	Marquette at G'boro, N.C.§	64
86	At Purdue	81		*Sugar Bowl Classic	
86	At Maryland	80		†Big Four Tournament	
105	Virginia	93		‡ACC Tournament	
92	At Duke	78		§NCAA Tournament	
98	Georgia Tech at Charlotte	54			

Burleson uses his gigantic arm span to control a rebound during a 1974 game as teammate Tim Stoddard watches the action.

But Towe and the players insisted. Sloan warned that such rules could cause problems and that players might eventually regret the guidelines.

Sure enough, Sloan said, it wasn't long before Rivers had car trouble that caused him to miss a basketball-related deadline. As a result, the transfer guard was forced to sit out a game at Virginia. Rather than hear Sloan say, "I told you so," the players hustled their way to a 20-point victory over the Cavaliers. That triumph came on the heels of a six-point triumph over Maryland in a Super Bowl Sunday game in which Thompson went on a 41-point scoring spree.

With their record at 10-1 after the rout of Virginia, North Carolina State seemed to be playing with great skill and confidence. The Wolfpack's approach was simple. On offense, Thompson would head down low to the left, then cut to the basket. From there, he slashed to the high post. If the defenses overplayed him, he would cut to the basket, where Towe would find him with the team's trademark Alley-Oop pass.

If the defenses didn't overplay Thompson, they were in trouble, Sloan said. "Once he got it at the top of the key, he would either shoot his jumper or go right by them."

Zone defenses weren't much of a problem, either. When the opposition collapsed on Thompson, he easily hit an open teammate, Rivers or Towe on the wings, or Stoddard on the baseline.

Bobby Jones, North Carolina's All-ACC forward and a defensive wizard, perhaps summed up Thompson's skills best.

"David is so much better than everyone else he must get bored," Jones said. "Yet he never plays bored. He does just enough to get the job done at his own pace. You can't stop him; he can only stop himself.

"Sometimes I think he's teasing us, playing down or something. The first time I played against him he made a beautiful shot and I said, 'Nice shot.' He turned, smiled and said, 'Thank you.' I think he might have winked."

Burleson was a force on the boards and, as the season progressed, his offense improved as he gained confidence.

Five days after Notre Dame supplanted UCLA at the top of the rankings following the Fighting Irish's termination of the No. 1-rated Bruins' 88-game winning streak, No. 3 North Carolina State showed its own mettle by rallying from a 15-point deficit and winning by five points at Purdue. On the same day that the Wolfpack staged its comeback against the Boilermakers, UCLA avenged its loss to Notre Dame by hammering the Irish by 19 points. In the next balloting, the Bruins were back atop the polls and North Carolina State was second.

Sloan's Wolfpack ascended to the No. 1 position three weeks later after UCLA lost two games in the

Northwest. And N.C. State retained that head-of-the-pack ranking heading into the Atlantic Coast Conference Tournament, the league's qualifying competition for the NCAA Tournament. In those days, a loss in the postseason tourney meant the end of any NCAA Tournament hopes (it wasn't until 1975 that the NCAA field was expanded to include more than one team from a conference).

North Carolina State drew a bye in the first round of the ACC meet, held in Greensboro, N.C., then clipped Virginia in the semifinals. In the tourney final, the Wolfpack would be matched against a Maryland juggernaut that featured Tom McMillen, Len Elmore and John Lucas. Lefty Driesell's Terrapins had compiled a 23-4 record to that point, with two of their losses being inflicted by David Thompson and company and the other defeats coming against mighty UCLA and North Carolina. The N.C. State-Maryland pairing had the potential for greatness—and the game didn't disappoint.

After 20 minutes of action, the Terrapins guarded a 55-50 lead. With seconds left in regulation play, the score was tied, 97-97, and Maryland owned the ball. However, a Terps shot missed the mark as time ran out and North Carolina State prevailed in overtime, 103-100. Burleson, voted the ACC Tournament's Most Valuable Player for the second straight year, put on an amazing show. The towering pivotman tossed in 38 points and picked off 13 rebounds. Thompson, who had scored 37 points in the semifinals, added 29 against Maryland.

Both teams shot well and committed few turnovers in a game many observers call the finest in ACC history, but only one club could go on. North

Thompson and Steve Nuce team up against Virginia's Wally Walker in ACC play.

1974 NORTH CAROLINA STATE

Head Coach—Norm Sloan   Final Record—30-1

Player	Pos.	Hgt.	Wgt.	Cl.	G	FG	FGA	Pct.	FT	FTA	Pct.	Reb.	Pts.	Avg.
David Thompson	F	6-4	195	Jr.	31	325	594	.547	155	208	.745	245	805	26.0
Tom Burleson	C	7-4	235	Sr.	31	228	442	.516	106	162	.654	377	562	18.1
Monte Towe	G	5-7	145	Jr.	31	168	325	.517	60	74	.811	67	396	12.8
Moe Rivers	G	6-1	165	Jr.	30	155	320	.484	53	81	.654	86	363	12.1
Phil Spence	F	6-8	215	So.	30	74	149	.497	32	52	.615	188	180	6.0
Tim Stoddard	F	6-7	225	Jr.	31	74	178	.416	23	33	.697	141	171	5.5
Steve Nuce	F	6-8	210	Sr.	28	51	110	.464	22	28	.786	89	124	4.4
Mark Moeller	G	6-3	175	Jr.	30	30	69	.435	21	23	.913	36	81	2.7
Greg Hawkins	F	6-5	185	Sr.	25	23	49	.469	25	34	.735	36	71	2.8
Dwight Johnson	G	6-0	160	So.	19	9	18	.500	11	18	.611	14	29	1.5
Bill Lake	C	6-11	190	Fr.	14	6	16	.375	3	5	.600	11	15	1.1
Steve Smith	F	6-10	210	So.	8	3	4	.750	1	2	.500	5	7	0.9
Ken Gehring	F	6-9	203	Fr.	8	2	6	.333	1	2	.500	4	5	0.6
Mike Buurma	C	6-10	220	Fr.	13	3	14	.214	1	2	.500	7	7	0.5
Craig Kuszmaul	G	6-5	181	Jr.	18	3	8	.375	2	5	.400	6	8	0.4
Bruce Dayhuff	G	6-2	175	Fr.	16	2	14	.143	3	4	.750	6	7	0.4
Jerry Hunt	F	6-5	200	So.	5	1	3	.333	0	0	.000	1	2	0.4
Team												134		
North Carolina State					31	1157	2319	.499	519	733	.708	1452	2833	91.4
Opponents					31	957	2198	.435	403	608	.663	1249	2317	74.7

The signs tell the story as Wolfpack fans in Greensboro, N.C., await the start of the UCLA-N.C. State matchup in the NCAA Tournament semifinals.

Carolina State, frustrated by NCAA sanctions a year earlier and coming dangerously close to missing out on an NCAA Tournament bid in the stemwinder against Maryland, was that team.

"Our emotions were at their peak after the Maryland game," Sloan said. "I've never had an emotional experience like that. I remember being down on the floor with my wife and Monte (Towe, who sank two key free throws at the end of the overtime). We were all hugging. Monte said, 'To heck with it. I feel like crying. I'm gonna cry.' We and Maryland had played each other so many times. The few weaknesses that each team had we knew about them."

It wasn't that a national championship would be anticlimactic. But the team's emotions had no higher level, Sloan emphasized.

In the East Regional on N.C. State's home floor, Reynolds Coliseum, the Wolfpack turned away Providence and Pittsburgh—but not before enduring a harrowing experience against the latter opponent.

Midway through the first half of the regional final, Thompson fell to the floor after a leaping attempt to block a Pitt shot. He landed on the back of his head and did not move for four minutes. The N.C. State star regained consciousness, was taken to

a hospital and, after needing 15 stitches to close a head wound, was pronounced all right. In fact, he returned to Reynolds Coliseum with about seven minutes left in the game, by which time the Wolfpack had built a 20-point lead en route to wrapping up a berth in the Final Four. Heavily bandaged, Thompson weakly acknowledged the cheers of the Raleigh crowd.

The Final Four was held just down the road in Greensboro. College basketball's premier event would feature North Carolina State, UCLA, Kansas and Marquette. In most people's minds, the semifinal matchup of N.C. State vs. UCLA qualified as the battle for the national championship.

UCLA had lost its aura of invincibility after going unbeaten in the 1971-72 and 1972-73 seasons. Not only had the Bruins lost in South Bend, Ind., and suffered subsequent defeats at Oregon State and Oregon, they also had been extended to three overtimes in a 111-100 triumph over Dayton in the West Regional. Still, beating UCLA was perceived as a task of immense proportions.

The North Carolina State-UCLA clash was nothing less than spectacular. Wilkes encountered foul trouble early. Walton was grand with 29 points and 18 rebounds. So was Thompson, with 28 and 10. Both coaches played conservatively, using only

Two high-flying forwards, N.C. State's Thompson and UCLA's Keith Wilkes, battle during action in the Wolfpack's double-overtime victory over the Bruins.

seven men. At halftime, the score was 35-35. At the end of regulation, it was 65-65. The first overtime ended in a 67-67 knot. UCLA then shoved off with a seven-point lead in the second overtime, and it seemed settled. Somehow, the Wolfpack found the fuel for one final, miraculous acceleration and blew past the Bruins at the wire, 80-77.

Sloan was surprised over his team's response to the monumental victory.

"The dressing room was kind of down, from what I thought it would be," he said. "They were excited, but not as much as I thought they'd be. I

thought back at the hotel maybe they'd celebrate a little more. But it never really did reach the emotional pitch I thought it would."

The Bruins, meanwhile, had every reason to be down. Their dynasty had ended. "Those are the days you can never forget," said Walton, alluding to UCLA's 74-67 lead in the second overtime. "The ones you can never get out of your mind are the ones you lose when you should have won. You can't take anything away from N.C. State . . . but I do feel we beat ourselves in that game."

Wooden was gracious in defeat and said the

NCAA championship game, pitting the Wolfpack against Marquette (a 64-51 winner over Kansas), would be well worth watching. It was, at least for N.C. State fans. Two technical fouls against Marquette Coach Al McGuire late in the first half helped ignite the Wolfpack, which built a nine-point halftime bulge and wound up winning, 76-64.

The title triumph was North Carolina State's 30th victory of the year against one loss, that early-season setback at UCLA's hands.

"We won the wrong one," Wooden said of the two UCLA-North Carolina State games of the 1973-74 season. "But they were a fine basketball team."

For Sloan and his players, the emotions didn't hit the high side again until they returned to Raleigh and found 10,000 fans waiting to greet them. N.C. State's supporters certainly appreciated what the team had accomplished. Not only had the Wolfpack won it all, but it had done so impressively. In the final wire-service rankings, UCLA had been rated No. 2 in both polls, Marquette was No. 3 in one and No. 5 in the other, Maryland was No. 4 and North Carolina boasted a No. 8 spot in one survey. Top-ranked N.C. State had beaten UCLA in the stirring NCAA Tournament semifinal, downed Marquette in the national final and beaten Maryland and North Carolina three times each.

Thompson, voted the NCAA Tournament's best player and also selected as the Associated Press' national Player of the Year, wound up with a 26-point scoring average for the season. Burleson scored at an 18.1 clip and collected 12.2 rebounds per game. Towe and Rivers also were double-figure scorers for the Wolfpack.

Of the top six point producers on the national-championship squad, only Burleson was a senior. The Wolfpack, with its host of returnees, nonetheless struggled a bit in 1974-75—if a 22-6 record could be called struggling. Thompson went on a 29.9 season scoring binge and was a consensus pick as national Player of the Year, but N.C. State failed to qualify for the 1975 NCAA Tournament.

Still, the disappointment of 1975 couldn't dim the luster of 1974.

One summer, Sloan and Wooden happened to meet as they took early-morning walks during a West Coast coaching clinic. They shared a stroll and their memories of that great game in Greensboro. For Sloan, who in 1980 left North Carolina State to take over the coaching duties at Florida, the memories remain vivid.

What makes the 1974 NCAA championship so special, Sloan says today, "are the teams that we beat. I defy anybody to beat more Top 10 teams on the road to the championship and knock off a team the caliber of UCLA.

"I don't remember a down cycle with my guys. We were just good all the way."

Lucky, too. But most of all, *good*.

Thompson, the spoils of victory hanging around his neck, signals his feelings after N.C. State's title-game victory over Marquette.

One Magic Season

M I C H I G A N
S T A T E

1978-79

A college basketball team's success is transitory, but the impact of its star players endures. That impact can be measured by the emotions they stir and the memories they leave behind in short careers. Earvin Johnson's college career was shorter than most, but his impact on the game and its fans will last forever.

He was, simply, pure Magic.

That nickname was no accident. Every ounce of his 6-foot-8 frame oozed magic as he moved around the collegiate basketball courts like a young gazelle. There was magic in his uncanny passing ability and his unorthodox push shot. There was magic in his knack for playing any position on the court and his penchant for always being in the right place at the right time. There also was magic in his infectious emotion and personality as well as his dancing eyes and broad, beaming smile. But most of all, Earvin Johnson was Magic because of his ability to somehow transform good teams into great ones.

That was the case when he led Lansing's Everett High School to a Michigan state championship in his senior season. That was the case when he led the Michigan State Spartans to the NCAA title in 1978-79. And that certainly was the case when, after declaring hardship and turning professional following his sophomore season, he led the National Basketball Association's Los Angeles Lakers to five championships in the 1980s.

"I'm asked a lot what was the greatest thing Earvin did," said Jud Heathcote, Johnson's coach at Michigan State. "Many say passing the ball, his great court sense, the fact that he could rebound. I say the greatest things Earvin did were intangible.

"He always made the guys he played with better. In summer pick-up games, Earvin would take three or four non-players and he'd make those guys look so much better and they would win, not because he was making the baskets all by himself, but because he just made other players play better."

Magic's reputation as a high school phenom was well established when he arrived at East Lansing in the fall of 1977 as part of a recruiting class that included 6-8 center Jay Vincent and 6-4 forward Mike Brkovich. Heathcote, who had just finished his first campaign at Michigan State after five seasons as head coach at Montana, combined that threesome with senior guard Bob Chapman, junior forward Greg Kelser, sophomore forward Ron Charles and sophomore guard Terry Donnelly.

"I'd heard about him (Johnson) at Everett High School," Donnelly recalled, "and I'd even seen him play. But it didn't really hit me until I got in the backcourt with him, on the first day of practice. You're running down the floor and you're open and most people can't get the ball to you through two or three people, but all of a sudden the ball's in your hands and you've got a layup."

The lessons his teammates learned quickly by playing with Johnson took longer to sink in with opposing coaches and players. The amazing thing about the youngster was that the whole of his game was much greater than the sum of its parts. Magic was not particularly quick and his jumping ability was only average. He was never known during his college career as an outside marksman and his defensive ability was questionable.

But, oh, could this kid pass, and his ballhandling

Although just a freshman in 1977-78, Earvin Johnson already possessed the poise and offensive skills that would lead Michigan State to a national championship a year later.

abilities were nothing short of amazing for some- one his size. But his biggest asset was his on-court presence, his ability to control the flow of a game. As one writer noted after watching Michigan State's Magic act, "He doesn't play basketball as much as he orchestrates it."

Such intangibles were not lost on Heathcote who, despite his need for big bodies under the basket, didn't hesitate to run Johnson at the point.

"I still remember the first game that Earvin played," Heathcote said. "We were playing Central Michigan. I think he had seven points and about eight turnovers, and everyone said, 'Heathcote's crazy. He's got Earvin handling the ball on the break, he's got him playing guard out there on of- fense, he's got him running the break, he's got him doing so many different things. Nobody can do all those things.'

"It's just that Earvin was nervous playing that first game and he didn't play like he played in prac- tice. Actually, he was very comfortable in all those areas. When he went to the pros and right away they had him playing forward, I said sooner or later they'll realize that Earvin can play anywhere on defense and he has to have the ball on offense."

That's because Johnson had always had *the ball.* As a youngster, he would rise early and head for the local playground where he would spend the better part of the day doing his Dave Bing and Oscar Rob- ertson impressions. Basketball was his life, along with sharing household chores with his three older brothers and six sisters, all of whom played basket- ball.

"I dribbled the ball everywhere from third grade on," Magic once said. "If I went to the store, went to the movies. I just had it in the streets and all over the place. I think by handling it on those cracks and those rocks and everything else, it just made me a better ballhandler."

His passing skills surfaced naturally, but not without a light tug from his high school coach.

"In the first three games of his senior year, he averaged 45 points a game and got 54 in one of them," Heathcote said. "His coach, George Fox,

With Johnson providing his special brand of magic, forward Greg Kelser (above) and the Spartans soared to great heights in 1978-79.

Season Results
1978-79 (26-6)

71	Central Michigan	54	61	Northwestern	50
92	Cal State Fullerton	89	85	Kansas	61
109	At Western Michigan	69	60	At Iowa	57
69	At North Carolina	70	73	At Ohio State	57
63	Cincinnati at Pontiac, Mich.	52	59	At Indiana	47
98	Washington St. at Portland*	52	80	Michigan	57
65	Oregon State at Portland*	57	73	Purdue	67
74	Indiana at Portland*	57	76	Illinois	62
84	Wisconsin	55	76	At Minnesota	63
69	Minnesota	62	81	At Wisconsin	83
55	At Illinois	57	95	Lamar at M'fr'boro, Tenn.†	.64
50	At Purdue	52	87	LSU at Indianapolis†	71
82	Indiana	58	80	Notre Dame at Indianapolis†	68
83	Iowa (OT)	72	101	Pennsylvania at S.L. City†	67
48	At Michigan	49	75	Indiana St. at S. Lake City†	.64
65	At Northwestern	83		*Far West Classic	
84	Ohio State (OT)	79		†NCAA Tournament	

called him in and said, 'If we're going to win the state, you can't continue to play the way you're playing. You've got the entire crowd watching you, and the opponents all watching you, and that's fine. But you've also got your four teammates watching you.'

"Earvin said, 'I got you, coach.' The next game he scored 12 points and had 18 assists."

And from there, it was off to the races, for both Everett High and Johnson. The youngster handled the inevitable recruiting mayhem with his typical poise and charm and eventually narrowed his choices to Michigan and Michigan State.

When Johnson joined Vincent, another local high school star, in committing to Michigan State, the reaction around Lansing was predictable. The day after Johnson's announcement, Spartan fans purchased 100 season tickets before noon and sell-outs at Jenison Field House became fashionable, everybody wanting to get a look at Heathcote's new magic show.

The arrival of this dynamic duo was welcome news for the upperclassmen who had just struggled through a 10-17 campaign. (The record later was changed to 12-15 because of two forfeits.) The man who would benefit most was Kelser, a tall, wiry leaper out of Detroit who had averaged 21.7 points in his sophomore season.

"Everything really came together when we got Johnson and Vincent," Kelser said. "When I first got here (1975-76), we were a young club and picked to finish ninth or 10th (in the Big Ten). But we finished fourth behind Purdue.

"The next year was Jud's first year and we were rebuilding. We ended up 10-17, but easily could have been 17-10 because we lost so many close games. Then Jay and Earvin came.

"When we got Earvin and Jay, we knew that we were ready to go places."

Nobody expected the Spartans to go anywhere in 1977-78, but Heathcote's young charges had other ideas. With Kelser (who later would be dubbed "Special K") providing the inside firepower and Johnson providing the magic, Michigan State captured its first Big Ten championship since 1966-67 and advanced all the way to the regional finals of the NCAA Tournament before losing a close game to eventual national champion Kentucky. To say that the young, inexperienced Spartans, who did not have a player taller than 6-8, raised a few eyebrows is a massive understatement.

"We won the Big Ten title very easily, winning our first seven games by kind of sneaking up on everybody," Heathcote said. "No one gave us any credit. We were picked to be about fifth in the league. We played Providence, Dave Gavitt's club, first in the NCAA Tournament and just ran them right off the floor. And he said, 'Watch out for Michigan State, they may go all the way.'

Jay Vincent, a 6-8 center, was another talented sophomore and double-figure scorer on Michigan State's 1979 championship team.

"We did not play particularly well against Western Kentucky (a second-round tournament game), but managed to get 90 points. We were looking past them to the Kentucky game. Kentucky had been rated No. 1 all year and it was the big game for us."

The regret in Heathcote's voice is evident when he recalls the regional final.

"We had a lead (27-22) at halftime," he said. "We came in and said, 'Let's gamble on the tipoff play.' We scored on the tip-off in the second half. I think we're up by seven or nine points, then our 'Magic Man' picked up his fourth foul with 10 minutes to go. We knew we couldn't win the game with him sitting on the bench, so he kept playing and played very conservatively, very cautiously.

"They put a 1-3-1 zone trap on us. Everyone says we lost that game defensively because Kentucky's Rick Robey would come up and set the screens for Kyle Macy against Terry Donnelly. They would call the fouls on us and Macy would go to the foul line and he just killed us. But we lost the game, in our minds, on the offensive end. We did not generate

Terry Donnelly (left) provided consistency, depth and good outside shooting for Michigan State's backcourt, which thrived on the slick passing and other all-around skills of the talented Magic Man (right).

the offense against that 1-3-1 zone.

"My assistant and I have talked about that game and thought that maybe if we'd done a little better coaching job, we would have won a national championship that year. We were in the final eight, and when I looked at Arkansas and Notre Dame in the Final Four, neither of those clubs was as good as we were. Not only that, the fact that Kentucky waltzed to the championship maybe indicated that we had played the championship in the final of the regionals."

That 52-49 loss, however, set the stage for 1978-79. Now everybody knew about the electrifying slam dunks of Kelser and the crowd-pleasing showmanship of Johnson. Kelser had averaged 17.7 points per game while Johnson had checked in with averages of 17 points and 7.9 assists in his freshman campaign. Vincent (11.3 points), Charles, Donnelly and Brkovich also were returning to a 25-5 team that figured to challenge for a national championship.

But the Spartans pulled another surprise, stum-

bling through the early part of their schedule like a worn-down thoroughbred that has seen better days. Heathcote recalls that the biggest problem was that his team had practiced through September for a basketball trip to Brazil and, by the time the regular season began, his players were getting burned out.

"Earvin did not want to go (to Brazil)," Heathcote said. "He had been playing all summer, and he had just got back from Russia. He had played on some junior national team, and yet he knew he had to go if the team was going. We went down and played eight games. We won seven, and we won the Governor's Cup in Sao Paulo after we lost to the Brazilian national team in Rio de Janeiro.

"So it was a great trip for us, and an emotional trip. But in all honesty, our kids came back tired of basketball."

The Spartans did not look tired when they dismantled a strong Soviet team, 76-60, in a November exhibition game, but they looked lethargic as they opened their schedule with three victories before

Michigan State Coach Jud Heathcote gives courtside instruction to Mike Brkovich, another of his talented 1978-79 crop of sophomores.

losing to North Carolina.

"Suddenly, I thought we came to life in the Far West Classic, and we just demolished a pretty good Washington State team," Heathcote said. "I think it was 98-52, and the kids said, 'Hey coach, that one was for you.'"

State went on to beat Oregon State and Indiana to win the tournament and was rewarded with a No. 1 ranking in the national polls. But. . . .

"We kept that rating for a week," Heathcote said. "Then we played Illinois on the road when they were rated No. 3 in the country. They beat us with a last-second shot. We went to Purdue and they beat us with a last-second shot. And it looked like we were snake-bit or unlucky.

"But then if you look at the stats, we were out-rebounded 2-1 in both places. We were just not playing well. We weren't playing good defense. Then

(after two conference wins at home) we went down and lost to Michigan on a foul shot after time had run out. From there, we went to Northwestern and lost by 18. By that time we're 4-4 (in the Big Ten).

"So we started talking that, 'Maybe it's our team, maybe we're not going anyplace, maybe this is the year that nothing goes.'"

The 83-65 loss to Northwestern was the low point of the season. Fans were grumbling, coaches were scratching their heads and players were doing some serious soul-searching. There were rumors of dissension among the players, primarily because Magic was getting all the headlines while his teammates were being shoved into the background.

"That has had its effect," Heathcote admitted at the time. "They like to play with Earvin, but they'd also like more publicity than they get.

"At first, we thought Earvin got all the press because of his newness, but it has continued with our success. We talk about it, and they understand it. They don't begrudge Earvin his publicity, they'd just like more for themselves.

"They feel—and I feel—they have earned it."

Kelser, however, claimed that there was no animosity among the players toward Johnson.

"Earvin is a super ballplayer and has his local following because he played high school ball in Lansing," he told one writer. "I'm one of his biggest fans.

"If we're winning, everyone gets publicity. That's the general attitude on our team. There's no jealousy. When one person gets publicity, we take it as a team thing whether or not the person's name is mentioned."

With Northwestern still fresh on everybody's mind, the Spartans called a team meeting to clear the air.

"We went in and said, 'Let's talk about what the season has been. Let's talk about where we are going,'" Heathcote said. "And we sat down and one of my all-time favorite players, Mike Longaker, a sub who ended up No. 1 in his class at Harvard Medical School, had a lot to say. He was the only guy that Earvin would listen to.

"The consensus was, 'Hey, we haven't worked hard enough; we haven't played hard enough; we're a lot better than we're playing and the season isn't over.'"

With that meeting of the minds, the remainder of the season unfolded like a well-organized script. The Spartans won 10 of their last 11 regular-season games and captured a share of the Big Ten title (with Iowa and Purdue). They had pulled together as a team, but much of the leadership and sacrifice had come from Magic.

"He injured his ankle against Ohio State," Heathcote recalled, "then we had to play Northwestern and Kansas. He was averaging 17 or 18 points a game. With about 2½ minutes left in the Northwest-

Johnson had good cause to dance after the Spartans' 80-68 victory over Notre Dame in the Mideast Regional final had earned them a spot in the 1979 Final Four.

ern game, they cut our lead to about six. So, I told Earvin it was time to go in, and he says, 'Yeah Coach, time to get in there.'

"He went in and controlled the ball for the last 2½ minutes and scored two points. He couldn't have cared less that going into the game was going to lower his scoring average. He cared next to nothing about scoring."

That attitude showed itself consistently, from the daily practice routine to game situations.

"Earvin was a unique player in that he would practice hard," Heathcote said. "He and Gregory Kelser were our hardest working players in practice. Jay Vincent and Ron Charles were, I don't want to say lackadaisical, but there were times when they just didn't want to practice. I finally got

Kelser dribbles around Indiana State phenom Larry Bird (left) in the 1979 NCAA Tournament championship game, and then celebrates Michigan State's 75-64 victory (right) by cutting down the net.

to the point where, instead of the assistant coaches or myself, I'd say, 'Earvin, get Jay and Bobo to practice harder today.'

"He was the coach out there on the floor."

The Spartans' stretch run allowed them to slip into the NCAA Tournament field with a 21-6 record. It didn't hurt that the NCAA field had been expanded that season to accommodate the burgeoning number of competitive college programs. Critics claimed the new format would be awkward. But history and further expansion have proved otherwise.

Playing with renewed vigor in their "second season," the Spartans began steamrolling their way toward a championship. Kelser poured in 31 points and grabbed 14 rebounds in a 95-64 thrashing of Lamar. Magic scored 24 points and dished out 12 assists in an 87-71 victory over Louisiana State. Kelser scored 34 points and grabbed 13 rebounds and Johnson added 19 points and 13 assists in an 80-68 win over a Notre Dame team that featured Kelly Tripucka, Orlando Woolridge and Bill Laimbeer.

The biggest Spartan rampage was witnessed by a stunned Pennsylvania team in the national semifinals at Salt Lake City. The Cinderella Quakers, who

had upset North Carolina, Syracuse and St. John's en route to the Final Four, were no match for Michigan State. The Spartans rolled up a 50-17 halftime advantage and cruised past Penn, 101-67, as Kelser scored 28 points and Magic posted a triple-double—29 points, 10 rebounds and 10 assists.

"It's amazing," Heathcote said, "because we played the five games in the NCAA playoffs just like we were starting over. Our guys said, 'We're where we should have been, so let's take advantage of it.'

"The Notre Dame game—the regional final—was the key game. Notre Dame had had a lot of publicity, and our guys kind of resented that because they felt the Irish got more publicity than they deserved."

The victory over Penn resulted in Michigan State's first-ever berth in the national championship game. The Spartans' opponent would be Indiana State, another first-timer that had ridden the enormous talents of Larry Bird to a 33-0 record and the nation's No. 1 ranking. The subplot for this unfolding drama was perfect: Magic versus the Birdman.

Bird had arisen as college basketball's debatable phenomenon. Like Johnson, Bird was an excellent passer whose physical skills did not seem to add up to his superstar billing. The jury was out. Some thought the 6-9 forward, who averaged 28.6 points and 15.8 rebounds in his senior season, was a great, great player headed for a Hall-of-Fame professional career. Others thought he was a product of the Sycamore's second-rate schedule.

Indiana State answered some of its critics by disposing of Virginia Tech, Oklahoma and Arkansas in regional play, and then slipped past a tough DePaul team in the national semifinals, 76-74, as Bird connected on 16 of 19 field-goal attempts while scoring 35 points and grabbing 16 rebounds.

Even those who questioned Bird's abilities had to agree that there was something special about the coming matchup. The flamboyant Magic would be orchestrating Michigan State's rampaging offense while the quiet, shy, sensitive kid from French Lick, Ind., would be trying to drive the small and unheralded Sycamores to an unlikely national championship. What nobody realized at the time was that this would be the first of many key matchups between the two players who would go on to dominate professional basketball during the 1980s.

Unused to the publicity (and criticism), Bird was sheltered from the media by Coach Bill Hodges and the Indiana State staff. With his shyness, he projected to the college basketball audience a silent and sullen image, which contrasted greatly the free-wheeling and talkative Magic. Bird loosened up a bit when he reached Salt Lake City.

"To me, it's a serious game," he said when asked by reporters about the difference between himself and Magic. "Now you wouldn't expect me to be havin' all kinds of fun when the score's tied, two seconds are left on the clock and the other guys have the ball. It's nice that Magic laughs a lot. I just hope he won't be laughing in my face after he makes a big play."

This championship contest earned the highest television rating of any college basketball game ever as a massive audience tuned in and showed its sixth sense for history. Heathcote solved the Bird riddle with a matchup zone. The Indiana State star was snared every way he turned. Hassled into missing 14 of 21 shots, he scored only 19 points. And while Michigan State got into early foul trouble, the Sycamores made only 10 of 22 free throws.

The Spartans led by nine points at halftime and, when Indiana State threatened in the second half, Donnelly doused 'em with five long-range jump shots. He would finish with 15 points on five-for-five shooting from the floor and the Spartans closed out their dominating tournament performance with a 75-64 victory.

Johnson finished with 24 points and seven rebounds to capture the tournament's Most Outstanding Player Award. As much as his offense, Magic had been a key to the Michigan State defense—a 1-3-1 matchup zone—because of his wing span, his anticipation and his ability to rebound and take the ball up the court himself.

"Our feeling after winning the national championship was not extreme elation like you would think, but relief," Heathcote said. "It was like the Kentucky team the year before. They were just expected to do so. I figured our guys would go out and celebrate, but you know what our guys did? They all went home and went to bed. They said, 'Coach, we're worn out. We'll celebrate when we get back home.'"

Rather than resolving the Bird versus Magic debate, the game only served to fan the flames.

"Bird had put on a tremendous performance in the semifinals against DePaul," Heathcote said,

1979 MICHIGAN STATE
Head Coach—Jud Heathcote   Final Record—26-6

Player	Pos.	Hgt.	Wgt.	Cl.	G	FG	FGA	Pct.	FT.	FTA	Pct.	Reb.	Pts.	Avg.
Greg Kelser	F	6-7	190	Sr.	32	246	451	.545	110	164	.671	278	602	18.8
Earvin (Magic) Johnson	G	6-8	207	So.	32	173	370	.468	202	240	.842	234	548	17.1
Jay Vincent	C	6-8	228	So.	31	170	343	.496	54	93	.581	161	394	12.7
Ron Charles	F	6-7	190	Jr.	32	115	173	.665	51	82	.622	162	281	8.8
Mike Brkovich	F	6-4	183	So.	32	85	167	.509	53	66	.803	56	223	7.0
Terry Donnelly	G	6-2	159	Jr.	32	83	155	.535	46	61	.754	50	212	6.6
Gerald Busby	F	6-4	168	Fr.	13	12	26	.462	6	8	.750	12	30	2.3
Rob Gonzalez	F	6-7	218	Fr.	28	18	31	.581	12	15	.800	27	48	1.7
Greg Lloyd	G	6-1	166	Jr.	19	8	16	.500	11	16	.688	10	27	1.4
Mike Longaker	G	6-1	182	Jr.	19	9	14	.643	8	12	.667	6	26	1.4
Rick Kaye	F	6-7	201	So.	16	8	11	.727	4	9	.444	10	20	1.3
Don Brkovich	F	6-6	183	Fr.	11	3	5	.600	1	4	.250	6	7	0.6
Gerald Gilkie	F	6-5	182	So.	5	1	4	.250	1	3	.333	4	3	0.6
Jaimie Huffman	G	6-3	173	So.	7	1	3	.333	0	2	.000	5	2	0.3
Team												93		
Michigan State					32	932	1769	.527	559	775	.721	1186	2423	75.7
Opponents					32	830	1912	.434	343	510	.673	1116	2003	62.6

(Team totals include dead-ball rebounds.)

Heathcote is mobbed by Michigan State well-wishers after his team's triumphant return to the Spartans' East Lansing campus.

"and that was the first I'd seen him in person. We'd seen him in film clips and on TV once. You know, it's amazing when you get into the Final Four. There are lots of freelance writers looking for any angle, anything that's bizarre, different or controversial.

"The way the format was set up, you had to pick two players to interview and then you'd have individual interviews. So, I took Gregory Kelser and Earvin to the interview room, and I told them, 'Hey, when we go in, someone will try to get you to say something negative about Larry Bird so they can make an issue about it. Say what a great player he is and this and that.'

"When they came back they said, 'Coach, you can't imagine the questions they asked us to try to trap us; how Larry Bird is overrated and things like that.' The guys handled it beautifully, but the writers were trying to trap them, which I resent."

After the season, Johnson, who had set a Michigan State one-season record with 269 assists, claimed hardship status and gave up his final two years of college eligibility to enter the NBA draft. He was selected by the Los Angeles Lakers while Bird took his talents to the Lakers' biggest rival, the Boston Celtics. The destinies of the two players had

become inextricably linked.

Each year Johnson comes home from the NBA wars and makes his way to the Michigan State gym where he can usually find Heathcote. Asked how Magic had changed over the years, the Michigan State coach said, "The pro game has turned it into a kind of a business rather than fun. The first three or four years Earvin was in the NBA, it was just like it was at Michigan State, like it was in high school—fun.

"The day he'd get home, he'd be in our gym. Now, a hundred games or whatever it is, takes its toll. Now he's just frazzled when the season's over. But he still comes and plays in the summer. He still probably prepares harder and better for the pro camp than the rookies do.

"Earvin is a dedicated player. I kid him every summer. I say, 'Earvin, maybe this is the summer you should learn to shoot a jump shot.' He says, 'Maybe I should, but I don't quite need it yet.' We kind of laugh about it as he zeros in with that long, one-handed shot.

"But when I say Earvin has changed, I mean he's matured. Basketball is still fun, he still plays it with flair and enthusiasm. He hates to lose."

And he doesn't very often.

Cougars Rise Fast, Fall Hard

H O U S T O N

1967-68

The fidgety coach was known for wearing incandescent sport coats, chewing on red and white polka-dot towels and gulping down 20 cups of water on a good night. The team wasn't regarded as the greatest in college basketball history—yet it was the first of only two teams to defeat the one that was.

The year was 1968. The coach, Guy Lewis. His team, the Houston Cougars, led by Elvin Hayes and Don Chaney. The greatest team in the history of college basketball? Well, if you don't recall the UCLA Bruins of Lew Alcindor, perhaps you're in the wrong book, or at least on the wrong page.

The meeting was billed as the "Game of the Century," a title that perhaps only barely did the event justice. Not just the game itself, which saw Houston snap UCLA's 47-game winning streak, but its role in the growth of college basketball as a ubiquitous television event of the 1980s. Staged in the sold-out Houston Astrodome, the game was played before college basketball's largest audience ever—in person (52,693) and on television (150 stations in 49 states).

But enough of the big picture for the moment. The story here is Guy V. Lewis and his 1967-68 Cougars, a team whose greatness can be attributed, by and large, to the integration of the Houston basketball program. Hayes and Chaney, both the product of segregated black high schools in Louisiana, broke the basketball color line at Houston, thereby ensuring the school's transition from basketball respectability to prosperity as an NCAA independent.

Chaney, a 6-foot-5 guard, was the better known of the two recruits, having received acclaim as a high school All-America at McKinley High in Baton Rouge. "Chaney was a super leader—a quiet leader, but a super one all the same," Lewis said. "He knew the game of basketball in and out."

Chaney, of course, went on to become a defensive star for the Boston Celtics and coach the Los Angeles Clippers and Houston Rockets. But coming out of high school, he was an offensive wheel who would average 21.6 points per game on Houston's 1964-65 freshman team.

"My responsibilities were changed at the varsity level," he explained. "I became more of a specialist. My job was to get the ball inside to Hayes as much as possible. Actually, it made a lot of sense, because not many teams could stop Elvin inside.

"I might have resented my role a little if we hadn't been winning," he recalled. "Nobody wants to be a caddie all his life. But when you win, it makes everything seem all right. Besides, I acquired a reputation as the team's best defensive player and I liked that."

Hayes' basketball career began in the cotton country of northeastern Louisiana, where poverty was a way of life in his hometown of Rayville. The feats of segregated black schools were rarely noted in newspapers of the day, but reports of Hayes' ability were heard through the coaches' grapevine as he led Eula Britton High to a state championship during his senior season.

"I was shooting every shot imaginable," Hayes said of those days, "and from every spot on the floor. I was shooting from the corners, the top of the key, all over, with jumpers and hooks and layups."

Guy Lewis, his trademark towel in hand, watches the 1967-68 Cougars, his best team in a long tenure as Houston coach.

Houston assistant Harvey Pate's first look confirmed Hayes could do as much. The one thing the big center needed, Pate said, was to learn inside power moves in the post. He got those lessons when he enrolled at Houston.

"I liked the idea of going to Houston . . . of helping desegregate athletics here," he told a Cougar beat reporter. "I knew Coach Lewis wanted to do just that, so I went."

Lewis was one of the few college coaches who fully understood the post game, having been a forward for Houston's very first varsity team in 1946. He led the team in scoring that season and the next, crediting much of his success to the post moves and footwork he learned from former Auburn forward Frank Williams while they served together in World War II.

"What I learned made me a different player," Lewis said. And quite a coach, too, one who would coach the Cougars for 30 full seasons beginning with the 1956-57 campaign and win 592 games. Much of that success was derived from Lewis' ability to develop frontcourt players.

"Few people can play the center spot; I know I can teach a guy to do it," he said. "Learning the post game made guys who couldn't play basketball really outstanding players."

In Hayes' case, he was already a one-of-a-kind force. But the post lessons he learned as a freshman only made him better. "The big thing was to get him inside and teach him the power moves," Lewis recalled. "As a freshman, he loved to shoot that ball from the deep corner."

Lewis' instruction paid quick dividends. After shattering scores of freshman-team records (first-year players were then ineligible for the varsity), Hayes helped lead the 1965-66 Cougars to a 23-6 record as a sophomore, averaging 16.9 rebounds and a school-record 27.2 points per game.

Opponents' attempts to defense Hayes were exercises in frustration. At 6-9, 240 pounds, he had grown to be a bear of a young man, although he preferred the press guides list him at 6-8. ("A guy reads you're that tall and you outjump what he expects a 6-8 to do, he respects you. You have an edge on him," he explained.) Under the backboard, he was playing a devastating game. And having lost none of the polish from his trademark turnaround jump shot, he could hit from all around the key.

"I sure didn't think I'd be doing this well," Hayes marveled. "I knew this was the first time I'd be playing against guys my size and I just didn't know what to expect.

"My biggest adjustment? I'd have to say it's learning how to play with two and three men defensing me, learning how to move and when to shoot and when to pass the ball. When they sink on me like that, it's got to leave somebody open for a good shot."

Indeed, the 1965-66 Cougars still rank as one of the highest-scoring teams in NCAA history with an average of 98.1 points per game. Yet it was the big center, Hayes, who commanded the attention, on the hardwood and in the headlines. And what were they saying?

Gary Turner, Texas Christian forward: "He's only a sophomore! It makes me glad I'm a senior."

Johnny Swaim, TCU assistant coach: "A man sitting next to me at the Houston-LSU game wondered why LSU didn't drive more to the bucket when a man got open. I told him if a boy did drive, he was liable to get a 'Spalding' imprint across the forehead when Hayes batted the ball down."

By their junior years, Hayes and Chaney were the core of a Final Four team. Playing the low post underneath the basket, Hayes was listed as a forward in what essentially was a double-post offense, with Lewis rotating Leary Lentz, Don Kruse and Ken Spain at center. By this time, the Cougar starting lineup also featured another black, junior Melvin Bell at forward, and black reserves in Theodis Lee and Andrew Benson.

The integration of the Cougar team, Lewis recalled, had required some adjusting. "It was the smoothest transition for me," he said. "For the players, I can't say that, because they took some abuse on the road. But here in Houston and on our campus, the people loved them. And one of the things that impressed and amazed me about Elvin, any abuse he took on the road, it only made him play that much harder."

Hayes eclipsed his scoring record by averaging 28.4 points, and Houston wound up 27-4 after riding into the 1974 Final Four with a 10-game winning streak. Once there, the Cougars encountered unbeaten UCLA and a 7-foot-1 sophomore named Alcindor, who, Hayes said before their first-ever confrontation in the semifinals, was "just another guy"—and overrated at that.

In the game, Hayes outscored Alcindor, 25-19, and outrebounded him, 24-20. The Bruins, howev-

Season Results
1967-68 (31-2)

110	Sacramento State	79	108	Fairfield	76
90	Abilene Christian	75	102	Marshall at New York	93
121	North Dakota State	88	107	At Centenary	56
54	At Illinois	46	106	Miami (Fla.)	64
86	G. Washington at Houston*| 61	106	Air Force	82
113	Montana State at Houston*	67	130	Texas-Arlington	75
102	Brigham Young	69	158	Valparaiso	81
103	Minnesota	65	105	At Hardin-Simmons	82
81	At Arizona	76	120	Virginia Tech	79
94	At Nevada-Las Vegas	85	107	At West Texas State	76
69	Bradley at Honolulu†	52	94	Loyola of Chi. at S.L. City‡	76
77	Marquette at Honolulu†	65	91	Louisville at Wichita‡	75
45	N. Texas St. at Honolulu†	43	103	Texas Christian at Wichita‡	68
91	Michigan	65	69	UCLA at Los Angeles‡	101
118	Centenary	81	85	Ohio State at Los Angeles‡	89
98	West Texas State	53			
71	UCLA	69	*Bluebonnet Classic		
112	Lamar	79	†Rainbow Classic		
			‡NCAA Tournament		

Under the tutelage of Lewis, Elvin Hayes developed his inside game and became one of the greatest players in college basketball history.

er, smothered the Cougars, 73-58, a loss that stung the Houston star. In the locker room afterward, Hayes suggested his teammates had "choked up" and stuck by his comments about Alcindor. "I can't really say Alcindor should be the Number 1 basketball player in the country," he said. The Bruins' big center, on the other hand, was gracious in victory, saluting Hayes as "the best I've faced this year."

The Big E said he wanted another shot at Big Lew. The schedule-makers would give it to him the following January, but this battle would be waged with a revamped Houston lineup. Lentz and Kruse, the two primary centers on the 1967 team, and

starting guard Gary Grider all had completed their eligibility. Bell would sit out most of the 1967-68 season after undergoing knee surgery. As a result, the Cougars' depth had disappeared.

"We had more bench strength in '67," Lewis explained. "The '68 team was just a starting five—but that starting five was really, really something."

Theodis Lee, another Louisiana product, moved in at forward to replace Bell. Lee had been used only sparingly as a sophomore the season before but had flashed his talents on the freshman team, averaging 18.5 points and 10.8 rebounds per game. At 6-7, 210 pounds, he had the physical stature to play forward but the agility to make like a guard.

Spain, part of the revolving centers trio, had played at Houston's Austin High with Lewis' son, Vern, and spent a few afternoons on their backyard court, learning post moves from the past master. "He was strong as a bull," Lewis said. Not to mention an all-state football standout.

Spain served notice of his potential in the 1967 Final Four consolation game against North Carolina, scoring 24 points with 14 rebounds in an 84-62 rout of the Tar Heels. It was just the the performance he needed to boost his confidence coming into his junior season.

The open guard spot was filled by slick-passing junior George Reynolds, a transfer from Imperial Valley Junior College in California. "George was the greatest point guard I ever played with," Hayes would say years later. "He knew exactly what each player could do, where his best shots were.... If you were open at 10 feet but he knew you were better at five feet, he'd get the ball to you at five. That's how good he was."

Vern Lewis played the point whenever Houston employed a half-court offense—which wasn't very often. The Cougars relied on a wide-open floor game that churned out points and left opponents unstrung. If that wasn't enough, they made the full-court press an important part of the defense, forcing turnovers and general pandemonium.

"We had about nine different presses," Lewis said. "We charged up and down the floor so much.

"They say to have a good pressing team, you've got to have a good man on the ball and a good man guarding the basket. We had both with Hayes on the basket and Chaney on the ball. Chaney had long arms and great anticipation for a pass. We didn't keep steals in those days, and there's no telling how many he had, but it would have been some kind of record.

"We also didn't keep blocked shots," he noted, "and when (Akeem) Olajuwon came here in the 1980s, he set all the school records. But Hayes would have had three times as many as Olajuwon if we had kept statistics then. He was a natural shot-blocker. And he was a scorer. In his career here, Elvin scored over 30 points 52 times. By comparison, Olajuwon in three years with me scored over 30 twice."

Every shooter, big man or small, chose his shot carefully with Hayes swooping through the air, trying to pin their offerings against the backboard. Consequently, he was notorious for goaltending violations, an annoyance Lewis had more or less expected when he instructed his big man to swipe at *everything.*

"Referees know you can trap a shot on the way up," Lewis explained, "but they still, often, call goaltending on the same play. If they called them the way they should, we'd get more breaks. We still get our percentages anyway, because if E is batting away everything that goes up there, the shooters are going to think twice the next time."

Hayes did have to adjust to another rule that many believed was an attempt to neutralize players such as himself and Alcindor. Prior to the 1967-68 season, the NCAA outlawed dunking, a decision that Lewis mourned. Hayes' shuddering jams had been Houston's biggest psychological weapon. In fact, all of the Cougars had been encouraged to stuff at every opportunity.

Yet it proved to be an ill-considered rule, one that had little effect on Hayes' offense. Relying on his beautiful turnaround jumper, he would average 36.8 points per game over the season, receive consensus All-America honors for the second straight year and be voted the NCAA's Player of the Year. His season total of 1,214 points (still No. 2 in the Division I record books through 1989) boosted his three-year career total to 2,884 points, second only to Oscar Robertson at the time.

Altogether, the Cougars ran up buckets of points with their pressing defense generating easy offense. They scored more than 100 points in 18 games, peaking with a 158-81 flogging of Valparaiso, then coached by John Wooden's successor at UCLA, Gene Bartow. "He didn't know what to say afterward," Lewis recalled. "Elvin scored 62 in that game."

Houston was a physical team, too, given the fact that Reynolds was the smallest member of the starting five at 6-4, 205 pounds. With that kind of bulk, the Cougars averaged 62.8 rebounds per game to lead all Division I schools. More than 20 years later, their 2,074 total rebounds were still an NCAA record.

Houston opened the season with 16 straight victories and climbed to No. 2 in the wire-service polls behind UCLA. Beyond the artistry of Hayes, Lewis contended that much of the team's success was due to the improvement of Spain and Lee, and the presence of Reynolds, who added a strong passing dimension to the offense. Clearly, Chaney was now the Cougars' defensive star, but he hadn't gone into hibernation on offense. He would average 13 points per game over the schedule, fourth on the team be-

Houston's quiet leader was guard Don Chaney, who sacrificed his offensive talents for the good of the team.

hind Hayes and the two rising juniors, Spain (14.4) and Lee (13.9).

Confined to one simple line on the Houston schedule, Game No. 17 stood out in resplendent glory, as much then as it does now:

Jan. 20. . . .UCLA. . . .at Houston Astrodome.

The anticipation had been building since the rematch was announced the previous summer. By the time classes started at Houston for the fall semester, 30,000 tickets had been sold. Requests continued to pour in from all over the country. "If we hadn't run out, we would have sold 75,000 tickets," the Astrodome's ticket manager would speculate. "No

Junior center Ken Spain, a local prep recruit, battles Ohio State players for a rebound as forward Theodis Lee (40) looks on during the 1968 NCAA Tournament consolation game.

doubt about it."

It was only a 1968 version of sports hype, a practice that would grow to immense proportions over the ensuing decade, but much of the country was buzzing over the showdown. For two weeks before the game, Lewis' phone never quit ringing. Things got so bad that the Houston coach refused to allow his players to mention UCLA by name.

"We've been ripe for an upset because we can't get our minds off UCLA," Lewis, breaking his own rule, explained to a reporter.

The Astrodome was a giant facility meant for baseball and football. To convert to basketball, $10,000 was spent to truck in the court panels from the Los Angeles Sports Arena—coincidentally, the same floor on which the Final Four would be played. It was all a strange sight in the vast expanse of the dome, with center court located where second base normally would have been and the nearest seat 100 feet away. But television zeroed in and so did the 52,693 fans in attendance, an NCAA record for a regular-season game more than 20 years later.

The Bruins came to town riding a 47-game winning streak—and with legitimate excuses should the string be snapped. Guard Mike Warren was recovering from the flu. Alcindor had suffered a scratched eyeball in a game against California and hadn't played in the Bruins' last two victories. Both played against Houston.

"I had sent a scout out to take a look at UCLA on the West Coast before our meeting in January," Lewis recalled. "He came back and told me, 'No college team can beat this team.' I told my players that and they just laughed and told me, 'We'll beat them coach.'"

Hayes opened the scoring with a turnaround jumper, setting the stage for a first-half performance Lewis called "the greatest I've ever seen in college basketball." The Big E poured in 29 of his game-high 39 points, forcing UCLA to play catch-up virtually all night. Alcindor was scarcely a factor in the game, making only four of 18 shots from the field as Hayes, and at times Spain, kept him frustrated underneath in Lewis' 1-3-1 zone defense.

The Bruins did make a game of it in the second half. Trailing 46-43 at halftime, they stepped up an ornery full-court press and tied the score on three different occasions, the last time with 44 seconds to play. But with 28 seconds left, they put Hayes on the free-throw line, and he calmly sank his 38th and 39th points for a 71-69 Houston lead. When UCLA flubbed its inbounds play, the Cougars took over possession and ran out the clock.

Alcindor finished the game with 15 points and 12 rebounds to Hayes' 39 points and 15 rebounds. "I didn't feel as good physically as I should have," the Bruins' big man told reporters afterward.

"Maybe Lew had an off night," said Hayes, who

played the final 12 minutes with four fouls. "I was blocking some of his shots and I might have bothered him a little.

"I thought Lew couldn't be faked, but this time I faked him out twice. He's a good player, but it doesn't make any difference to me how tall he is. You can't say enough about what a great job Kenny Spain did on him. He played so well (11 rebounds) that we controlled the rebounding. That made the difference in the game."

The loss burned deeply for UCLA. "I hope they come back to L.A. undefeated," Bruin guard Lucius Allen said. "That would be very nice."

The Cougars did, indeed, arrive at the Final Four with a 31-0 record and the No. 1 ranking in the polls. But now they were missing their best passer, Reynolds, who was ineligible for the NCAA Tournament because of a shortage of credit hours lost in his transfer to Houston. In spite of that, the Cougars were upbeat.

"We've improved I don't know how much since the UCLA game," Hayes said. "They couldn't play us as close now as they did then. If we played 'em again, we'd beat 'em worse, and it couldn't matter if it was on their own floor."

Hayes would get the chance to prove his point. The Bruins, bracketed for a rematch in the semifinal game, were unbeaten since the battle royal in the Astrodome and playing in the friendly surroundings of the Los Angeles Sports Arena, their former home court. And they were ready for Hayes with a "diamond-and-one" defense.

The "one," in this game, was Bruin forward Lynn Shackelford, who draped himself all over Hayes all night. Hayes was held to 10 points and five rebounds, and Houston—the Division I leader in offense with 97.8 points per game—was drubbed, 101-69, as UCLA advanced to its fourth NCAA championship in five years.

"It was devastating, there's no question about that," Lewis remembers.

Lee typified Houston's shooting woes, making only two of 15 attempts from the field. The Cougars shot only 28.2 percent from the floor and appeared sluggish from the opening tipoff. "We just weren't up for it," Lee said afterward. "I figured before the game that the best we could shoot would be 35 percent. Our mental attitude wasn't right."

Lewis would coach the Cougars through the 1985-86 season and make three more trips to the Final Four. Yet he has no trouble identifying the biggest event of them all. "The UCLA game in the dome not only helped us at Houston," Lewis said, "it helped basketball. It proved basketball was a national product. That was the greatest game I was ever in, ever coached in."

Nothing was more representative of the burgeoning growth of college basketball than the Houston program itself. The Cougars had been playing their

Forward Melvin Bell, a key member of the Cougars' 1967 Final Four team, missed the 1967-68 season after undergoing knee surgery.

Though Chaney (left) would average 13 points per game, his primary responsibility was getting the ball to Hayes, who took apart Lew Alcindor and UCLA in a classic midseason showdown at the Astrodome (right).

home games at Delmar Field House, a high school facility located 10 miles off campus. To practice, they had to compete for gym time at four other sites around town. That was set to change, however, as the university looked ahead to the completion of Hofheinz Pavilion, a new 10,000-seat arena that would host its first Cougar cage event on December 1, 1969.

But the one game that stands above all others, not only in the Houston annals but perhaps in all of

college basketball, is the one staged on that January night in 1968. And if UCLA proved a point by ousting Lewis' Cougars in the Final Four in both 1967 and 1968, so be it. "We were the second-best team in the United States," Lewis remembers fondly. "There's no doubt in my mind."

And being second-best to the Alcindor-era Bruins, a team that would lose its only other game to Southern Cal the next season, wasn't all bad. No doubt about it.

When Hayes and Alcindor met again in the NCAA Tournament semifinal, the tables were turned, with the powerful Bruins recording a 101-69 victory.

1968 HOUSTON

Head Coach—Guy Lewis   Final Record—31-2

Player	Pos.	Hgt.	Wgt.	Cl.	G	FG	FGA	Pct.	FT.	FTA	Pct.	Reb.	Pts.	Avg.
Elvin Hayes	F	6-9	235	Sr.	33	519	945	.549	176	285	.618	624	1214	36.8
Ken Spain	C	6-9	230	Jr.	33	191	406	.470	92	157	.586	422	474	14.4
Theodis Lee	F	6-7	210	Jr.	33	203	466	.436	54	99	.545	260	460	13.9
Don Chaney	G	6-5	210	Sr.	33	189	431	.439	50	84	.595	191	428	13.0
George Reynolds	G	6-4	205	Jr.	28	106	197	.538	68	93	.731	136	280	10.0
Tom Gribben	F-G	6-2	180	So.	30	38	116	.328	22	33	.667	70	98	3.3
Niemer Hamood	G	6-0	170	Jr.	25	31	65	.477	17	22	.773	17	79	3.2
Carlos Bell	C-F	6-5	220	So.	23	27	53	.509	17	24	.708	50	71	3.1
Vern Lewis	G	5-11	170	Sr.	33	35	91	.385	23	38	.605	34	93	2.8
Larry Cooper	F	6-6	210	So.	18	11	22	.500	3	10	.300	20	25	1.4
Kent Taylor	G	6-2	180	So.	8	1	8	.125	0	2	.000	6	2	0.3
Billy Bane	G	6-2	188	Jr.	11	1	9	.111	0	3	.000	9	2	0.2
Team												215		
Houston					33	1352	2809	.481	522	850	.614	2074	3226	97.8
Opponents					33	943	2449	.385	497	699	.711	1418	2383	72.2

Spain (left) scores two points against UCLA. Hayes (right) fights for a rebound against Ohio State.

The Makings Of a Dynasty

U C L A

1963-64

The "genius" of former UCLA Coach John Wooden can best be illustrated by the types of teams he directed to NCAA championships. He won with tall ones, middle-size ones, fast ones and even short ones. Of his 10 championship teams, none cemented his reputation as a winner more than the 1963-64 Bruins. The short ones.

Louisville Coach Denny Crum, asked to list the all-time best teams in college basketball history, was quick to include Wooden's first title team. Crum, who played for UCLA in the late 1950s and later served as Wooden's assistant, was lavish in his praise of a Bruin backcourt that featured Walt Hazzard and Gail Goodrich and the team's all-out, take-no-prisoners style of play.

"Talk about two great guards," Crum said. "That team didn't have the size, but they were relentless with the zone press, which was relatively new to college teams. As the game wore on, they started anticipating passes and moves. They might be down 15 points and, all of a sudden, boom, they'd be right back in the game and just beat you with their quickness."

Hazzard, the swift playmaker who later coached at UCLA, said the team drew its strength from a special chemistry. "We went 30-0," he said, "and we had no starter larger than 6-foot-5."

"Chemistry" is the operative word in describing what made the 1963-64 Bruin team tick. Wooden, the man who made it all work, recruited a competitive group of players who liked his style, wanted to win and were willing to accept their roles with pride. Hazzard, a senior, was the team's acknowledged floor general.

"My role was the leader, the spirit of the team," Hazzard said. "I had come from a great basketball tradition in high school in Philadelphia, where I had been a scorer. At UCLA, I became the playmaker and offensive quarterback. I accepted that role.

"I knew I could have been the leading scorer, but Gail Goodrich was a great scorer. If he missed five in a row, that was no big deal to him. He would just hit the next five. He was a hungry guy who liked to score points. The other players on the team realized that in the fast-break situations, if he was the guy in the middle, he was gonna take the shot."

Most of the offense came from UCLA's superlative backcourt, but much of the Bruin success was generated by the inside grinders and bench players who played to their strengths and sacrificed publicity for victories.

"Jack Hirsch, a 6-3 forward, was our top defender, always assigned to the other team's top scorer," Hazzard said. "He had the instincts, the tenacity. He knew how to shut a guy down. In junior college he had averaged 38 points a game, but at UCLA he was the defender.

"Fred Slaughter, our 6-5 center, weighed about 230 pounds. He was ideal for the high-post offense John Wooden ran. Even with that size, he was the high school 200-meter champion in Kansas. He played up front on our press, but when the ball crossed half court, he'd still beat everybody back.

"In retrospect, it was the team that epitomized Wooden's brilliance. He took the strengths of his individual players and adjusted his system to maximize those abilities. Keith Erickson, at 6-5, was our

UCLA Coach John Wooden was a master at adjusting his system to the strengths of his individual players.

fifth man on the 2-2-1 press. He was a great player and an athlete with great reactions, a great rebounder with excellent timing. Above all, he was a fierce competitor.

"To that, Wooden added his two players off the bench, Kenny Washington and Doug McIntosh. Coach Wooden just fit all these pieces together to make a great team."

Hindsight provides a clear picture of Wooden's coaching "brilliance," but, by the early 1960s, there was nothing to suggest that he would ever be known as anything more than a "good" coach. Although UCLA had recorded a winning record every season since Wooden's arrival in 1948, many fans were becoming frustrated by the program's lack of national success. Nobody was more frustrated than Wooden himself.

"I wanted to win a national championship very much," Wooden recalled, "and I think it's quite possible that, prior to winning one in 1964, I might have wanted it so much I hurt my players in one or two instances. I may have overworked them thinking that I had to really work hard, and that may have caused us not to play as well as we could.

"I never wanted to win one as badly as I wanted to win that first one. I never thought of winning it in terms of being accepted as a coach. But maybe I felt that without realizing it."

After a hitch in the Navy during World War II and two years at Indiana State, Wooden came to UCLA and immediately turned around a losing program.

But his instant success eventually became his worst enemy as he struggled for more than a dozen years to lift his teams above the regional competition. UCLA remained a low-profile program and its teams played and practiced in a tiny gym with inferior facilities. Although he won, Wooden's progressive coaching style remained suspect on the West Coast, where Phil Woolpert at San Francisco and Pete Newell at California were winning with disciplined, patient offenses.

Beyond that, Wooden's pious, philosophical personality did not endear him to his fellow coaches. That's not to say that he didn't have his admirers, one of which went on to sports broadcasting fame after a basketball career at Wyoming.

"The Wooden teams were all different but all alike in the regimen," said Curt Gowdy. "They ran those high-post offenses. I noticed little things about them, how they'd hold their arms up in the free throw lane ready for the rebound, how they always banked their side shots.

"When they practiced, they had a drill where they'd come down, bounce to the baseline and shoot a little bank shot outside the baseline. I asked Wooden about that. He just thought it was an easier way to shoot than aiming straight for the hoop. His teams had beautiful skills fundamentally.

"Wooden was a deceiving man in that he mildly rolled up his program during the games. In practice, he was tough. When he was a player (at Purdue) he was tough. He would drive and crash into the bleachers on layups and played the game hard. His teams played that way."

That toughness translated into a winning formula as Wooden patiently worked the pieces into place. Heading into the 1960s, he increased his player rotation to a working unit of seven or eight men. And he studied various forms of the full-court press, which he had used off and on during his early years at UCLA.

The big breakthrough came with the commitment of Hazzard.

The son of a Philadelphia minister, Hazzard caught the eyes of college recruiters with his play at Overbrook High School, the same prep factory that had produced Wilt Chamberlain and Wayne Hightower. Already a dominant scorer, Hazzard was quickly developing a reputation as an outstanding passer and superb ballhandler.

Those skills were the direct result of the youngster's fascination with the Harlem Globetrotters and his off-season playground scrimmages against such present and future National Basketball Association stars as Chamberlain, Willie Naulls, Wally Jones and Guy Rodgers.

Guard Walt Hazzard (42), UCLA's floor general, and Fred Slaughter (35), a 6-foot-5 center, during action in a 1962 NCAA Tournament semifinal loss to Cincinnati.

As a youngster, Hazzard watched the Globetrotters and immediately set out to emulate Marques Haynes, the team's dribbling wizard. He put in hours of practice and eventually took his skills to the high school courts and the Philadelphia playgrounds.

It was Naulls who first alerted Wooden to the budding star and actively pursued the youngster's talents for his alma mater. The combination of Naulls, Jackie Robinson and the enticing California sunshine won out over the aggressive pleas of hungry Eastern recruiters. Robinson, Hazzard's childhood baseball hero, had attended UCLA.

After one year of junior college, Hazzard and fellow sophomore Slaughter joined three seniors— forwards Gary Cunningham and Pete Blackman

and guard John Green—on UCLA's 1961-62 team. With the senior leadership, Hazzard's adjustment to the college ranks was made easier and the Bruins compiled an 18-9 record en route to a berth in the Final Four, where they extended eventual national champion Cincinnati in the semifinals before losing, 72-70.

Hazzard's junior year required more of an adjustment. With the three seniors gone, Hazzard had to assume more leadership responsibility and he spent much of the early 1962-63 season trying to determine his role. Scorer or playmaker?

"I called him into my office one day and asked him to pattern himself after (former college and NBA great) Oscar Robertson, who looks for the pass first and the shot second," said Wooden after

Gail Goodrich, UCLA's top scorer with a 21.5-point average, reaches for a loose ball during a 1964 game against Kansas State.

Season Results
1963-64 (30-0)

113	Brigham Young	71	
80	Butler	65	
78	Kansas State at Manhattan	75	
74	Kansas at Lawrence	54	
112	Baylor at Long Beach	61	
95	Creighton at Long Beach	79	
95	Yale*	65	
98	Michigan*	80	
83	Illinois*	79	
88	At Washington State	83	
121	At Washington State	77	
79	Southern California	59	
78	Southern California	71	
84	Stanford	71	
80	Stanford at Santa Monica	61	
107	At UC Santa Barbara	76	
87	Santa Barbara at S. Monica	59	
87	At California	67	
58	At California	56	
73	Washington	58	
88	Washington	66	
100	At Stanford	88	
78	At Washington	64	
93	Washington State	56	
87	California	57	
91	Southern California	81	
95	Seattle at Corvallis, Ore.†	90	
76	USF at Corvallis, Ore.†	72	
90	Kansas St. at Kansas City†	84	
98	Duke at Kansas City†	83	

*Los Angeles Classic
†NCAA Tournament

seeing his young star's dilemma. "I told him 100 players in the nation would outscore him and they wouldn't make All-America. But his passing could make him an All-America."

Hazzard took his coach's advice and started delivering the goods—sharp, deceptive, crisp passes to Slaughter and newcomers Goodrich, Hirsch and Erickson, a volleyball player of considerable renown. Everything suddenly began to fall into place.

"A lot of people don't realize that that team (the 1963-64 squad) was very good the year before," Wooden said. "I had instituted the 2-2-1 zone press, and we won the conference championship. We were knocked off in the regionals by Arizona State. They (the Wildcats) had a tremendously hot-shooting team. They just hit everything they shot, and we got behind early and couldn't catch up."

The Bruins finished the 1962-63 season with a 20-9 record, Hazzard indeed earned All-America honors and everything was in place for UCLA's run to its first-ever national championship. The starting lineup returned intact, a year older and wiser, and bench help was now available in the form of Washington and McIntosh, a pair of talented sophomores. But the biggest piece to the puzzle was provided by Goodrich, a junior who was ready to blossom into a major offensive threat.

The 1962-63 season had been a learning experience for the lefthanded sharpshooter, who had entered UCLA in 1961 without much fanfare after an outstanding prep career at Polytechnic High in Los Angeles. Ability was never a question. Size was.

He stood 5-7 as a high school junior and 5-11 a year later. His slender build did not endear him to college recruiters. But Wooden saw something special in the youngster and literally snatched him away from rival Southern Cal, where Goodrich's father had starred in the late 1930s.

However, his transition to the college ranks was anything but smooth.

"From freshman to varsity ball is a big jump, but Gail expected it would be easy," Wooden said. "He expected to do too well and, when he didn't, he put too much pressure on himself. For the first half of the season (1962-63), he didn't do as well as he should have.

"When he realized what the problem was, Gail quickly solved it."

Never lacking in confidence, Goodrich, now standing 6-1, came on strong in the second half and took a lot of pressure off Hazzard. Working together in the backcourt, this duo would carry UCLA to new heights.

The national publications all liked UCLA in their 1963 preseason predictions, but most agreed that the Bruins did not have enough height to accomplish Wooden's long-desired goal.

It quickly became apparent, however, that height was no obstacle for this group. Working their press

The quickness and athletic ability of Keith Erickson was the key to UCLA's devastating zone press.

with precision, the Bruins stripped and dismantled taller, slower opponents like a band of thieves working over a parked car. They struck like lightning.

Slaughter and Goodrich worked the front line, pressuring the inbounds pass. Hirsch and Hazzard were the second line—Hazzard in position to convert a steal into automatic offense. The safety valve was Erickson.

"Our five starters on that team had different personalities," Wooden said. "Keith Erickson was a great athlete. I've coached better basketball players, but never a better athlete. And to play that No. 5 position in the press, he was just tremendous. I've never seen anyone come close to being his equal.

"And other players filled their roles in the zone press. In the 1 and 4 positions in the press, I prefer lefthanders. And just by chance, I had lefthanders in Gail Goodrich and Jack Hirsch. In the 3 position, I like a ball-handler, and I put Hazzard there. In

the No. 2 position, I had Fred Slaughter, not tall, but big and quick of foot. I had two quality substitutes, Kenny Washington and Doug McIntosh.

"I didn't think they (Washington and McIntosh) were that good at the beginning of the year, but they came along very well and enabled us to have the type of rotation we needed. The players complemented each other extremely well, and they got to the point where being behind didn't mean anything to them. They knew they were going to get one of those spurts through our press, and they expected it. They expected a spurt in each half, and for the most part we got them."

Wooden's press was designed to force anxious opponents into ballhandling mistakes. "If you go for steals, you'll foul," he constantly reminded the Bruins. Quickness, agility and endurance were the elements that devastated UCLA's opponents while draining their confidence and creating numerous scoring opportunities.

Backup center Doug McIntosh was an excellent rebounder and one of Wooden's top players off the bench.

Goodrich was at his offensive best in the 1964 NCAA title game, when he scored 27 points in a 98-83 victory over Duke.

Wooden recruited the first two qualities, but he built stamina in his regimented, hard-driving practices. He said many times that he was, above all else, a practice coach, and it was during those daily sessions that he brought all of those elements together. He drilled his players until every game movement became a natural reaction.

The 1963-64 Bruins opened impressively with a 113-71 win over Brigham Young. But it wasn't until six victories later, in mid-December, that they really caught the national eye.

Playing in the second round of the Los Angeles Classic, the Bruins took apart second-ranked Michigan, a team that featured Cazzie Russell, 98-80. "The

greatest game I've ever seen my team play," Wooden told reporters afterward. The next night of the holiday tournament, UCLA whipped a solid Illinois team, 83-79, and vaulted to the No. 2 spot in the national polls behind Kentucky. It was the kind of recognition Wooden had sought.

The Wildcats stumbled in early January, but the Bruins continued to roll, attaining the top spot in the polls for the first time in UCLA basketball history. There was only one close call the rest of the way (a 58-56 win at California) as the Bruins remained undefeated through their 26-game regular-season schedule and prepared to put their top ranking on the line in the NCAA Tournament's West

Hazzard battles high-scoring Duke star Jeff Mullins for a loose ball during the game that would lift UCLA to its first-ever national championship.

Regional in Corvallis, Ore. They were understandably brimming with confidence, although observers around the country still were not convinced.

Duke, many said, was the favorite. UCLA was too small.

The Bruins did little to change that thinking as they struggled past Seattle, 95-90, and San Francisco, 76-72, surviving by virtue of their superior conditioning and their opportunistic press. But UCLA had reached the Final Four for the second time in three seasons and, sensing success, Wooden tightened his intensity and cracked the whip, driving Hazzard particularly hard in practice.

"I don't believe in artificial motivational things; maybe with some individual now and then," he explained. "For example, I might try to get Hazzard mad at me because, when he'd get mad at me, he'd show me. But if I tried to get Gail Goodrich mad at

me, he'd go into a shell. You have to learn the personalities of the players. But generally speaking, I don't agree with the emotional approach.

"I think for every peak, there is a valley. If you were standing in the hallway of our dressing room when we came out for warmups, you never had to worry about being run over. I wanted our team to walk out slowly and warm up and not expend a lot of energy. I wanted to save that energy for the game. I didn't want a lot of cheering and yelling in the dressing room. I wanted peace and quiet so we could consider things and analyze things.

"I think there's the tendency by many coaches to get players overly motivated. Once in a while it works, but I think for every time it works, there may be a couple of times it affected them adversely."

The grand event was to be staged at Municipal

Auditorium in Kansas City, where UCLA would be joined by Kansas State, Michigan—and Duke. Little did anyone realize that they would be witnessing the birth of a dynasty that would steamroll its way over the next dozen years to the top of the college basketball world.

In UCLA's semifinal game, Kansas State, which had lost by three points to the Bruins in the regular season, set up its zone defense and relied on 29 points from star Willie Murrell to take a 75-70 lead with 7:28 remaining. But as they had done so frequently during the season, the Bruins came from behind, putting together an 11-point spurt to carve out a 90-84 victory. Erickson led the UCLA charge with a 28-point effort.

Duke advanced from the other bracket, disposing of Michigan, 91-80. The Blue Devils were big and talented, Jeff Mullins providing the scoring punch and a pair of 6-10 monsters, Jay Buckley and Hack Tison, handling inside duties. The only real question was how Coach Vic Bubas' team would handle UCLA's press.

The Blue Devils did it well in the early going of the title game, using their height to pass downcourt and create mismatches. As a result, Duke enjoyed a 30-27 lead with 7:14 remaining in the first half. But then it happened. The pressing Bruins struck hard and fast, scoring 16 unanswered points for a 43-30 lead. They drained Duke's confidence and never looked back.

"I think that happened in the championship game against Duke," Wooden recalled. "They led us early, but it only took us two or three minutes to catch up, and we had a 12-point lead at the half (50-38). But the lead wasn't the thing; it was the look they had on their faces. They looked whipped."

With Goodrich scoring 27 points and Washington adding 26 points and a team-high 12 rebounds off the bench, UCLA coasted to a 98-83 victory. All of those observers who had predicted a Duke victory now were convinced.

"Most everyone felt Duke would win the game," Wooden said. "In the hotel Saturday afternoon before the game that night, a group of coaches were talking and some of them said, 'Johnny, Duke's a remarkable team. Remarkable and big. You've got a nice team, but it's amazing you've won 29.'

"There was a Czech coach there who had spent some time during the year at different schools around the country, and somebody asked him, 'What do you think about the game?' In cryptic English, he said, 'UCLA win.' And they asked him, 'How can you say that, Duke's a big team?' He said, 'Yeah, UCLA is team,' and he held up his hand to represent our team.

"That's about as nice a compliment as a coach can get. And that year, we really played as a team."

Hazzard, who scored only 11 points and fouled out in his final college game, was nevertheless honored after the season as a consensus All-America, College Player of the Year and the NCAA Tournament's outstanding player. He averaged 18.6 points and was one of four Bruins to reach double figures. Goodrich (21.5), Hirsch (14) and Erickson (10.7) were the others.

With the departure of Hazzard, Slaughter and Hirsch, many believed that UCLA would fold its tent in 1964-65 and live off the memories of their season in the sun. And, indeed, the Bruins stumbled out of the blocks, dropping a 110-83 decision to Illinois in their season opener.

But, with Goodrich silencing critics who claimed that his success was a product of Hazzard's playmaking and passing skills, it quickly became ap-

1964 UCLA
Head Coach—John Wooden   Final Record—30-0

Player	Pos.	Hgt.	Wgt.	Cl.	G	FG	FGA	Pct.	FT	FTA	Pct.	Reb.	Pts.	Avg.
Gail Goodrich	G	6-1	160	Jr.	30	243	530	.458	160	225	.711	156	646	21.5
Walt Hazzard	G	6-2	188	Sr.	30	204	458	.445	150	209	.718	142	558	18.6
Jack Hirsch	F	6-3	190	Sr.	30	160	303	.528	101	152	.664	227	421	14.0
Keith Erickson	F	6-5	181	Jr.	30	127	315	.403	66	106	.623	272	320	10.7
Fred Slaughter	C	6-5	230	Sr.	30	103	221	.466	30	62	.484	242	236	7.9
Kenny Washington	F-G	6-3	177	So.	30	71	155	.458	42	67	.627	126	184	6.1
Steve Brucker	F	6-4	201	So.	1	2	4	.500	0	1	.000	2	4	4.0
Doug McIntosh	C	6-6	196	So.	30	40	77	.519	28	56	.500	131	108	3.6
Kim Stewart	F	6-5	220	Sr.	23	22	56	.393	7	15	.467	45	51	2.2
Rich Levin	F	6-4	190	Jr.	19	16	43	.372	6	12	.500	12	38	2.0
Kent Graham	F	6-3	174	Jr.	1	1	2	.500	0	0	.000	1	2	2.0
Mike Huggins	G	5-11	165	Sr.	23	13	34	.382	11	23	.478	22	37	1.6
Chuck Darrow	G	5-11	183	So.	23	11	29	.379	14	24	.583	27	36	1.6
Vaughn Hoffman	C	6-7	223	So.	21	10	21	.476	5	10	.500	27	25	1.2
Team												238		
UCLA					30	1023	2248	.455	620	962	.644	1670	2666	88.9
Opponents					30	798	2080	.384	506	783	.646	1428	2102	70.1

parent that success had not spoiled UCLA. With guard Fred Goss, forward Edgar Lacey and center McIntosh joining Goodrich and Erickson in the starting lineup and Washington and sophomore Mike Lynn playing reserve roles, the Bruins ripped through the rest of their regular-season schedule, losing only to Iowa, 87-82.

In the NCAA's West Regional, UCLA numbed Brigham Young, 100-76, and then outlasted San Francisco, 101-93, earning its third trip in four seasons to the Final Four.

This time the event was in Portland, where the Bruins matched up against Wichita State in the semifinals. With Goodrich scoring 28 points and Lacey adding 24, they breezed, 108-89.

Cazzie Russell and Michigan had eliminated Bill Bradley and Princeton in the other semifinal, 93-76, despite Bradley's 29 points. The media expected a real showdown in the final, especially since Erickson would miss the game with a pulled groin muscle. But there was something about a national championship game that inspired Washington. He scored 17 points, Goodrich exploded for 42 and UCLA overpowered the Wolverines, 91-80. Goodrich ended his senior campaign with a 24.8 average while becoming the top career scorer in UCLA history.

"We were too quick for Michigan, even with Erickson hurt with a pulled groin muscle," Wooden said. "Kenny Washington came in, and, for the second national championship in a row, just played a beautiful game. And Goodrich had taken over as the leader, the way Hazzard had done the year before."

Ironically, Bradley was named the tournament's outstanding player in the wake of his 58-point performance in the consolation game against Wichita State. Wooden considered that an injustice.

"Bradley got his 50-some points in the consolation game against Wichita State," he said. "If you check the records, I think you will find that Goodrich got 42 in that championship final and played only half the game. I'm not saying that Goodrich is a better basketball player than Bill Bradley. I have nothing but great respect for Bill Bradley because I thought he was one of the all-time greats. But I did feel that, in that particular tournament, Goodrich was the most valuable player."

The prize for Goodrich, however, was the championship, and that was sweet enough. For Wooden, it was only the second of what would become many layers of icing on the cake.

"After the first win, I never wanted one as badly," he said of the national championships. "And, you know, they seemed to flow. Someone asked me, 'How come it took you 15 years to win your first one at UCLA?' I said, 'I'm a slow learner, but when I learn something, I get it down pretty good.'"

UCLA's key reserve was Kenny Washington (23), who always seemed to rise to the occasion during big games.

Wooden and his victorious Bruins—the first of many championship UCLA teams.

THIRTEEN

Sooners Take No Prisoners

O K L A H O M A

1987-88

They were big, bad and brutally efficient. They lit up scoreboards, humbled opponents and gloated. The 1987-88 Oklahoma Sooners were a lean, mean scoring machine, created in the brash image of Billy Tubbs and well-schooled in the art of inflicting victory. When they won, which they usually did, they made it hurt.

Offensively, these Sooners played without conscience, throwing down three-pointers and slam dunks with equal delight. Defensively, they pressed and undressed opponents like no team had ever done before. And they went about their task with a brashness seldom seen in amateur athletics, never showing mercy and always ramming home their unmistakable feeling of superiority.

They were, simply, an extension of their coach.

Early in the season, the Sooners ran over an out-manned Georgia State team, 124-81. Late in the game, State Coach Bob Reinhart sent a player to the Sooner bench to ask Tubbs to ease up. The Oklahoma coach responded by sending his team back into the full-court press.

"Damn guy wanted mercy," Tubbs said later, "wanted me to back off. That's against the law. They call it point shaving. I'm not going to jail. Damn."

That attitude was not exactly new to Big Eight coaches and fans, who had been witnessing Tubbs' take-no-prisoners antics since 1980, when he took over an Oklahoma program that had been mired in basketball mediocrity. He quickly turned things around and, in the process, turned on a fountain of resentment that would pour over the Sooners for the remainder of the decade.

Tubbs was accused of making obscene gestures at opposing crowds, he constantly baited officials, he argued with rival coaches and he allowed his players to taunt opposing players and crowds after victory had been assured. In 1984, after the Sooners had put the finishing touches on a victory at Kansas, the players celebrated by joining arms in chorus-line fashion at the free throw line. His fiery exchanges with Missouri Coach Norm Stewart became Big Eight legend. He was unbearable in victory, petulant in defeat.

But he also was charming. Bearing a strong resemblance to actor Jack Nicholson, right down to his smirking, side-winding smile, Tubbs disarmed interviewers with his down-home philosophies and Oklahoma drawl (he was raised in Tulsa). Once he stepped onto the court, however, he transformed into a pugnacious street fighter who would go to any length to win. And he usually did.

After a 9-18 first campaign, Tubbs set the stage for his 1987-88 team by guiding the Sooners to six straight 20-plus-win seasons, six straight postseason appearances and a pair of conference championships. His 1984-85 team, featuring high-scoring Wayman Tisdale, finished 31-6 and advanced to the Midwest Regional final of the NCAA Tournament before losing to Memphis State.

As the decade wore on, the Sooners, attracting such stars as Tisdale, Tim McCalister and Darryl Kennedy, became more and more lethal, crushing opponents and enjoying every tantalizing moment of their success. Their specialty became the 100-point game, which the 1987-88 Sooners turned into an artform.

There was nothing tactful or diplomatic about Oklahoma Coach Billy Tubbs, who set his 1987-88 Sooners on a course of destruction.

Lefthanded-shooting Stacey King came out of nowhere to lead the Sooners in scoring while becoming Tubbs' center of attention.

In their first 14 games, all victories, they averaged a whopping 115.5 points. Most of the scores read like Australian-rules football.

Texas A&M fell, 104-80. Loyola-Chicago, 123-73. Sam Houston State, 111-69. Centenary, 152-84. Georgia State, 124-81. Virginia, 109-61. Dayton, 151-99. Oral Roberts, 144-93. Illinois State, 107-56. Austin Peay, 109-69. Oklahoma State, 108-80.

By now, everybody knew about the run-and-gun Sooners, but this early-season rampage piqued curiosity and national publications began sending writers to Norman to find out what was going on.

Tubbs was only too happy to explain. The secret to his team's success, he lectured, was not offense. It was a pressing defense that generated points in a hurry. But underneath that technicality lied the story the writers really wanted to hear—Tubbs' concentrated effort to redefine sportsmanship. He was only too happy to explain that, too.

"One coach whined a little but I don't concern myself with it," Tubbs replied when asked about running up the scores. "My philosophy is that we're going to play hard every minute of the game, and there's no compromise on that. I don't know how to coach any other way.

"You work so hard at practice to get guys to play to their maximum capability. What should you do, call a timeout and say, 'Hey, let's slack off guys.' Every player wants to impress you and the crowd. What should I say, 'Go in and screw up the game.'"

And his players were only too happy to second that notion.

"I might feel sorry for these teams getting blown out by 40 or 50," guard Ricky Grace told reporters, "but I've been around Coach too long. He says, 'Remember where nice guys finish.'"

The goal was simple. Tubbs and his Sooners were not happy with just winning. They wanted to crush people. The means to that end seemed obvious.

"Think of the real crushers here in football at Oklahoma," Tubbs said. "They run back interceptions, block kicks, run back punts. They force fumbles and get it at the (opponent's) 20. It's a rare case where you crush anybody by taking it on your 20 and grinding it out. When I was in college, I remember hearing the statement that the only way you really crush people is to do it with your defense, to force things to happen.

"I didn't shape my philosophy to fit Oklahoma. But my philosophy fits well at Oklahoma. You can't play boring basketball here. The people are too used to exciting football."

His Richter scale for excitement was measured in points and records. He had to have 100 points a game, he told his players. And he wanted them to set records, lots of 'em. The 1987-88 Sooners went above and beyond the call of duty.

With center Stacey King averaging 22.3 points, forward Harvey Grant 20.9, guard Mookie Blaylock

Oklahoma guards Mookie Blaylock (left) and Ricky Grace unnerved opponents as part of the Sooner press and undid them with outside shooting.

16.4, Grace 14.7 and forward Dave Sieger 10.9, Oklahoma shattered the NCAA record for most points in a season—4,012 in 39 games, or 102.9 per outing. They also set NCAA records for most three-point field goal attempts (791) and steals (33 against Centenary) and tied the NCAA mark for most points against a Division I team (152 versus Centenary). They shattered five NCAA marks and 41 Big Eight Conference records ranging from scoring to blocked shots.

"I love records," said Tubbs, who had employed the same brand of racehorse basketball at Lamar before taking the Oklahoma job. "I'm intrigued by them. One game this year (a 134-84 victory over Colorado) we had 71 points in the first half and that tied a Big Eight record. But of course all the records we break are our own records. . . . My (1979-80) team at Lamar shared the NCAA record for points in a half with Artis Gilmore and that bunch from Jacksonville (1970-71) at 86. That's why I want 90 in a half now. I want that record."

There was just something about uncharted territory that lured Tubbs.

"I love to do things no one else has ever done," Tubbs explained. "If I was alive in the 1300s, I would have been on a ship trying to find the edge of the earth."

A product of the 20th Century, Tubbs' explorations were limited to a search for basketball talent. With the graduation of Kennedy, McCalister and burly David Johnson from a 24-10 team, prospects for a banner 1987-88 campaign did not appear bright.

But Tubbs already had dipped into the junior college ranks to get Grant and Grace in 1986 and he traveled that route again in '87 to get Blaylock. When he combined those talents with the fast-improving King and the versatile Sieger, the Sooners were ready to roll.

Grace and Blaylock were no strangers. They originally had been paired in the same backcourt at Midland (Tex.) Junior College. Grace moved on to Oklahoma in 1986, while Blaylock stayed for one more season at Midland, where he earned All-America honors. The Oklahoma coaches had looked at Blaylock, but they weren't as impressed as Grace. When Grace learned that his former teammate was considering Kansas and Florida, he took action.

"I said, 'uh oh. I don't want to play against him,' " Grace told reporters. He helped Blaylock arrange a visit to Norman and he made sure that he had a good time when he was there. Blaylock chose Oklahoma.

Paired together once again, the two guards executed just as they had at Midland. Although only 6-foot tall, Blaylock preferred to play shooting guard on offense while letting the 6-1 Grace handle the ball. Blaylock's real forte was defense, where he

High-scoring forward Harvey Grant was a natural for the Sooners' run-and-gun offense.

Season Results
1987-88 (35-4)

104	Texas A&M	80	92	At Nebraska	77
93	At Penn State	59	112	Kansas State	95
123	Loyola of Chicago	73	79	At Oklahoma State	75
111	Sam Houston State	69	120	New Mexico	100
89	At Florida State	87	95	Kansas	87
152	Centenary	84	134	Colorado	84
124	Georgia State	81	90	At Missouri	93
109	Virginia at Honolulu*	61	113	Nebraska	93
151	Dayton at Honolulu*	99	99	Colorado at Kansas City‡	66
93	Georgia at Honolulu*	90	102	Missouri at Kansas City‡	99
144	Oral Roberts at Okla. City†	93	88	Kansas St. at Kansas City‡	83
107	Illinois St. at Okla. City†	56	94	UT-Chat. at Atlanta§	66
109	Austin Peay State	69	107	Auburn at Atlanta§	87
108	Oklahoma State	80	108	Louisville at Birmingham§	98
77	Louisiana State	84	78	Villanova at Birmingham§	59
62	At Kansas State	69	86	Arizona at Kansas City§	78
96	At Colorado	76	79	Kansas at Kansas City§	83
86	Pittsburgh	83			
109	Iowa State	86	*Chaminade Christmas Classic		
96	At Iowa State	91	†All-College Tournament		
73	At Kansas	65	‡Big Eight Conference Tournament		
120	Missouri	101			

Forward Dave Sieger was a deadly three-point marksman who was versatile enough to fill any role that was necessary.

used his lightning-quick reflexes and the Sooners' aggressive style to wreak havoc on opposing guards. He stole and stole again, reducing opponents to nervous wrecks. He set an NCAA record in the Centenary game by making 13 steals and set another NCAA mark with 150 for the season.

"I think by him guarding me in practice, it made me a better player," Grace said.

"Mookie's speed and quickness may compensate for some of the things he can't do," added Tubbs.

In retrospect, this guard tandem complemented each other perfectly. Grace had set an assist record in his second season at Midland and had scored at an 11.2-point clip in his first season at Oklahoma (1986-87).

Grant also had considered attending Kansas after playing at Independence (Kan.) Community College, where he, too, earned All-America honors. The 6-8 Grant actually had started his career at Clemson with twin brother Horace, but transferred when Horace got most of the playing time. Horace went on to Atlantic Coast Conference stardom and was picked by the Chicago Bulls on the first round of the 1987 NBA college draft. Harvey, looking to find his niche with a big-time program, decided that Oklahoma had the atmosphere in which he could thrive.

"I thought, 'That's my team.' They'd run up and down the floor like they never got tired," he said of the Sooners. "I thought about going to Kansas because that's all you hear around Independence. But if I'd gone there, it would have been a slower pace, and everything would have been Danny Manning, Danny Manning.

"I knew Oklahoma and Coach Tubbs were for me. . . . They want to run, shoot the ball and get the fans excited. And once you get the fans excited, everybody on the team gets excited. And that's when basketball is really fun."

After averaging 16.9 points in his first season, Grant moved nicely into a leadership role while providing plenty of offense. He exploded for 40 points in an early-season game against Oral Roberts and hit the 30-plus-point plateau five more times over the course of the campaign. He also was the team's leading rebounder and top percentage shooter (.547). He was equally adept at shooting 17-footers and making inside moves against slower big men.

"We couldn't stop Grant," was the lament of Pittsburgh Coach Paul Evans after watching the forward score 28 points in Oklahoma's 86-83 victory over his sixth-ranked Panthers. "We tried three different people on him. We tried to front him and tried to play behind him. But they got the ball to him."

Grant's performance was enhanced greatly by the amazing improvement of King, a 6-10 center who would go on to consensus All-America honors in

Tubbs, charming off the court, transformed into a pugnacious street fighter once the game began.

1988-89 and become a first-round NBA draft pick. Nobody would have predicted such honors three years earlier.

A native of Lawton, Okla., King had fallen into academic trouble as a freshman and missed the second half of the 1985-86 campaign. He returned to earn a starting job at the beginning of his sophomore year, only to lose it because of miserable shooting.

"That was a learning experience," King said. "I grew up a lot and I did it quick. I became a lot more mature person. When I became ineligible, I let the team down, I let myself down and I let my family down. I felt like the lowest thing on earth. It really hit me. I knew I had to rededicate myself."

In the classroom, he raised his grade-point average from a 1.4 in his first semester to a 3.2 in his second, good enough to make the Dean's Honor Role. As an athlete, he focused on weightlifting, bulking up from 195 to 230.

"Stacey has come farther since high school than any player I've ever had," Tubbs told reporters.

At the end of his sophomore season, he scored 19 points and grabbed eight rebounds off the bench against Pitt in the NCAA Tournament.

"That gave me a taste of it," King said. "They were giving Harvey Grant a lot of attention, double-teaming him, so that left me open. They probably figured I couldn't score."

They were wrong.

He entered his junior season with a new confidence and started lighting up the scoreboard. King exploded for 40 points in one game against Missouri and struck for 37 against Auburn, 36 against Iowa State, 35 in another game against Missouri and 34 against Kansas State. Shooting at a 54.3 percent clip, the lefthander, using a deadly turnaround bank shot and a variety of short hooks, reached the 30-plus-point plateau eight times.

"If you don't push him out, he's automatic," Auburn Coach Sonny Smith said of King.

By March his brash confidence was zooming.

"I add a new dimension to this team with my quickness and running ability," he said. "Last year, we didn't have a center who could run up and down the court. This year we're beating people a lot more on fast breaks. . . I'm going down the floor and getting dunks.

"I'm like a juggernaut. I just keep getting better and better."

King's explosiveness was not limited to offense. Opposing players quickly got that message when he began swatting away their shots at a record pace. By season's end, he had become the first Big Eight player ever to block more than 100 shots (he finished with 103) in a season.

The other frontcourt starter, fifth-year senior Dave Sieger, filled a swing role. He had a solid outside shot that allowed him to score eight three-pointers in a game against Oklahoma State. But he also was a fine passer and a solid rebounder who played good defense. Whichever of those skills the Sooners needed at the time, the 6-5 Sieger provided. The only white player among the starting five, his teammates called him "Soul Man." Others called him the team's glue.

"I kind of watch what's going on in the early stages," Sieger said, "then provide what's needed. If some of our guys aren't shooting well, and I'm off to a good start, then I fill the scoring role. If defense is something we need to go on, then I'm more of a defensive player."

Sieger was blessed with a natural endurance that fit nicely into the Sooners' run-run-run scheme. He once ran a 4:40 mile without training. Track coaches had asked him to become a distance man, but Sieger said he wasn't interested. Too boring. Basketball, on the other hand, had plenty of action.

Particularly Sooner Ball, or Billy Ball, as the writers had taken to calling it. Despite their antics, the unrelenting Sooners were earning begrudging respect around the college circuit.

"This Oklahoma team has the best full-court pressure I've ever seen," Oklahoma State Coach Leonard Hamilton said after watching his team fall by 28 points. "They have great quickness. They have five great athletes who will pressure the ball. Even some of the great presses ever, like at UCLA, didn't have five people coming out and pressuring the ball. Even Stacey King comes out and challenges the ball."

Despite Oklahoma's fast-paced attack, Tubbs relied heavily on his starting five. Such talents as Tyrone Jones, Andre Wiley, Terrence Mullins and Anthony Martin saw only limited duty, usually at the end of a lopsided game or when one of the starters got into foul trouble. Their turn would come a year later and they appeared content with that prospect.

Riding their 14-0 record to the No. 3 ranking in both the Associated Press and United Press International polls, the Sooners hit a mid-January snag that brought them back to earth. Taking their prime-time act to New Orleans, the Sooners fell to Louisiana State, 84-77. Then the cold-shooting Sooners, forced into a slower pace by a solid Kansas State team, fell in Manhattan, 69-62.

As Tubbs had pointed out many times, the Sooners became vulnerable anytime the opposition held them under 100 points.

But they seldom looked vulnerable the rest of the way as they got back on track and reeled off 12 straight victories before falling in overtime at Missouri, 93-90. They rebounded in their regular-season finale, however, ripping Nebraska, 113-93, and

entered the Big Eight postseason tournament as the conference champion with a 27-3 record.

They humbled Colorado in the opener, defeated Missouri by three points in a semifinal matchup and then edged Kansas State, 88-83, for the tournament championship. After the title game, King mugged for the cameras and planted a kiss on the conference trophy.

Everybody in the talent-rich Big Eight was convinced. Oklahoma had the makings of a national champion. Observers outside the conference also took note, although nobody seemed to like the possibility. "Oklahoma's lust to run up the score is hard to watch," an Atlanta newspaper said on the eve of the NCAA Tournament.

Thriving on their high profile and laughing at their critics, Tubbs and his Sooners took a 30-3 record into the tournament. In order, they ripped Tennessee-Chattanooga (94-66), Auburn (107-87), Louisville (108-98) and Villanova (78-59) to earn a spot in the Final Four at Kansas City.

There, they were matched against second-ranked Arizona, a consistent, mistake-free team that featured forward Sean Elliot and hot-shooting guard Steve Kerr. The Wildcats were not mistake-free against the pressing Sooners, however, turning the ball over 15 times. Oklahoma ran to a 12-point halftime lead and held off two second-half charges, beating Arizona, 86-78.

In the other bracket, Kansas, with star forward Danny Manning, was the surprise survivor. The Cinderella Jayhawks, one of three Big Eight teams to make the final eight (Kansas State was the other), matched up in its semifinal against Duke at Kemper Arena—30 miles from their home base.

Kansas continued to mystify prognosticators, racing to a 14-0 lead against the Blue Devils and

1988 OKLAHOMA
Head Coach—Billy Tubbs   Final Record—35-4

Player	Pos.	Hgt.	Wgt.	Cl.	G	FG	FGA	Pct.	FT	FTA	Pct.	Reb.	Pts.	Avg.
Stacey King	C	6-10	230	Jr.	39	337	621	.543	195	289	.675	332	869	22.3
Harvey Grant	F	6-8	205	Sr.	39	350	640	.547	113	155	.729	365	816	20.9
Mookie Blaylock	G	6-0	175	Jr.	39	241	524	.460	78	114	.684	162	638	16.4
Ricky Grace	G	6-1	175	Sr.	38	199	442	.450	72	103	.699	137	559	14.7
Dave Sieger	F	6-5	210	Sr.	39	148	326	.454	43	64	.672	192	426	10.9
Tyrone Jones	F	6-5	215	Jr.	24	53	119	.445	27	35	.771	43	151	6.3
Andre Wiley	F	6-5	195	Jr.	30	66	124	.532	48	66	.727	103	180	6.0
Terrence Mullins	G	6-2	200	Fr.	37	48	112	.429	21	32	.656	53	136	3.7
Anthony Martin	F	6-7	230	So.	36	51	111	.459	30	37	.811	97	132	3.7
Art Pollard	G	6-2	185	Jr.	18	18	41	.439	5	10	.500	13	46	2.6
Mike Bell	F	6-5	205	Jr.	24	19	29	.655	11	19	.579	27	49	2.0
Jason Skurcenski	G	6-2	170	So.	14	3	10	.300	3	4	.750	5	9	0.6
Team												130		
Totals					39	1533	3099	.495	646	928	.696	1659	4012	102.9
Opponents					39	1208	2635	.458	606	865	.701	1686	3159	81.0

Three-Point Field Goals: King 0-1, Grant 3-14, Blaylock 78-201, Grace 89-248, Sieger 87-219, Jones 18-50, Wiley 0-1, Mullins 19-43, Martin 0-2, Pollard 5-18, Skurcenski 0-2; Opponents 137-410.

King was a master at the art of celebration. He mugs for the camera (right) after the Sooners' victory over Kansas State in the finals of the Big Eight Tournament and (left) after their victory over Villanova in the final of the Southeast Regional.

stretching its margin to 24-6 midway through the first half. With Manning scoring 25 points and Milt Newton adding 20, the Jayhawks held off a late Duke rally and defeated the Blue Devils, 66-59.

Kansas, now sporting a 26-11 record, had lost to Oklahoma twice during the regular season. And just about everybody figured the third meeting would produce the same result. But on its 50th anniversary, the NCAA Tournament provided an all-Big Eight championship game that would stir America's underdog soul.

The first half was full of surprises as the emotional Kansas players showed that they would not go down without a struggle. The Jayhawks came out running and successfully challenged the Sooners at their own furious pace. Shooting at a blistering 71 percent clip from the floor, Kansas withstood the intense Oklahoma pressure and a tight first half ended in a 50-50 deadlock.

With Manning, who would earn consensus All-America and Player of the Year honors, providing the offensive core and Coach Larry Brown making a series of deft substitutions, the Jayhawks' confidence mounted. The smell of upset was in the air.

The second half belonged to the Jayhawks. Brown wisely chose to slow the pace and Oklahoma made a series of strategic blunders that shifted the momentum in Kansas' favor.

First, Oklahoma's Grant dropped off his coverage of Kansas' Chris Piper to help King cover Manning. When that happened, Piper became the open outlet for the Jayhawks' passing attack and Kansas cracked the Sooner defense. Instead of pressuring five points, the Sooners pressured four.

The second biggest factor was Oklahoma's poor shot selection. Grace had a particularly poor game, taking one bad shot after another. He continued to loft from outside instead of going inside to Grant

Kansas star Danny Manning, the chief culprit in the Jayhawks' upset victory over the Sooners in the NCAA Tournament final, drives against Grant.

and King. When Oklahoma didn't score, it couldn't apply its pressure defense.

A third factor was Oklahoma's reluctance to push the ball inside after Manning had picked up his third foul early in the second half. The Sooners missed an opportunity to force him to the bench.

And with the pace slowed down, the Jayhawks' stamina was no longer a factor.

The Jayhawks faltered slightly midway in the second half when substitute Scooter Barry missed an inside shot and moments later had the ball stolen in open court. But even that trauma was resolved in the closing minutes when Barry hit a key free throw to preserve the win.

Manning and the University of Kansas upset Oklahoma, 83-79. Manning finished with 31 points, 18 rebounds and five steals and was named the tournament's outstanding player.

Did Oklahoma's problems stem from overconfidence? That's a hard one to answer. Tubbs said the fact that the teams were meeting for a third time was not a factor. Yet from the very outset, Kansas appeared to be one step ahead of the Sooners.

In the postgame press conference, Tubbs was uncharacteristically subdued. Yes, he admitted, he was bitter. "When you lose," he said, "it's easy to look back and say what we could have done differently."

Still, the Sooners finished the season as one of the most prolific offensive teams in the history of the game. Their 102.9 points per game was the fifth best mark in NCAA history and they outscored opponents by an average of 21.9. They averaged 7.7 three-point field goals and still shot a respectable 49.5 percent from the field.

It didn't take long for Tubbs and the Sooners to get over their bitterness. With only King and Blaylock returning to the starting lineup, the 1988-89 Sooners picked up where they had left off in 1987-88 and pounded their way to a 30-6 record.

En route, they captured another Big Eight championship and another Big Eight postseason tournament title before falling to Virginia in the semifinals of the NCAA Tournament's Southeast Regional.

And they continued to wreak havoc on opposing psyches. With King scoring 26 points per game, the Sooners again averaged better than 100 points (102.2). And they were as brash and unyielding as ever.

It merely served as a message to the college basketball world that Sooner Ball was here to stay. And that the newest wave of high-powered offenses would become a viable part of the game's history—and future.

FOURTEEN

The Start of Something Big

NORTH CAROLINA

1956-57

Serious students of Southern basketball have noted in jest that Everett Case is the father of basketball at the University of North Carolina. Case, of course, coached at North Carolina State.

In the late 1940s and into the 1950s, Case's Wolfpack teams ran roughshod over the rival Tar Heels, winning 15 consecutive meetings through six seasons. In retrospect, Carolina couldn't have been blessed with better luck. To compete with Case, university officials hired Frank McGuire away from St. John's before the 1952-53 season.

At North Carolina, McGuire proved to be much more than a remedy for the Wolfpack ailment. Within five seasons he coached the Tar Heels to a 32-0 record, the best in collegiate history, and the 1957 national championship.

The key to McGuire's success would be his ability to lure players from the New York playgrounds to the little academic community in Chapel Hill. McGuire was born-and-raised New York, a former player for St. John's and coach there for five seasons. In 1952, he took the Redmen all the way to the NCAA championship game against Kansas. Those memories would be his forever—along with the network of little-known talent scouts that would become part of his "underground railroad."

"All the people in New York are my friends," he explained. "No one gets paid for helping, but everybody looks out for me. The whole police department looks for players for me. So do the high school coaches, so do the brothers at the Catholic schools. Even the waterfront looks out for me."

The first of McGuire's recruiting successes would be his most significant, that being Lennie Rosenbluth, a willowy 6-foot-5 Jewish kid with a clear shooting conscience. Ironically, Rosenbluth had been recruited by Case but rejected after a tryout.

Being one of the first Northern players at the decidedly Southern school wasn't easy for Rosenbluth. North Carolina was Bible Belt, dominated by an intense Baptist culture. But the timing did afford him one of the more interesting perspectives of Carolina basketball history.

"I remember my first freshman game," Rosenbluth said. "We couldn't get into the gym. It was locked, and we had to get the custodians to open the doors so we could go out and play. The stands were completely empty. Maybe 100 people showed up. However, by our senior year the gym wasn't big enough to hold everybody.

"When I first went to Carolina, basketball was the furthest thing from people's minds. Frank McGuire's basketball office was behind an old ticket window, and you had to walk sideways to get in. It's changed, and I guess I was lucky enough to be there right from the beginning, as Frank McGuire was building the program that has become one of the greatest in the United States."

After his second season in Chapel Hill, McGuire imported another transfusion of talent from the New York area in Joe Quigg, Bob Cunningham, Pete Brennan and Tommy Kearns. Along with Rosenbluth, the four New Yorkers would fill out the starting lineup for McGuire's 1957 NCAA titlists. Moreover, five of the eight reserves on that team also would be brought down from the big city.

"When Frank went to Carolina, he just kept that

New York connection," Kearns explained. "It didn't matter if Frank were in Omaha or Tulsa or Chapel Hill, he was going to recruit New York kids."

McGuire made it clear he was doing only what was necessary to improve the Carolina program. "My job is to win and I get the boys who can do the job," he said. "If the scholarships go to the boys from New York, that's where I find the best basketball talent available."

Yet the native New York Irishman wasn't far wrong when he joked, "Down here boys are told, 'Don't play for McGuire—you won't understand a word he says.' "

McGuire's second recruiting class was strictly Catholic, which created a few difficulties at both ends of the recruiting process. "We had problems with the high school Catholic principals sending our grades down to a Southern Baptist-type school," Kearns recalled. "The lines were more clearly drawn back then than they are now. It was fairly difficult to make a commitment to a non-Catholic Southern school. It was a major concern for our parents.

"I remember very clearly when Coach McGuire came to my house to recruit me. He came with one of his good friends who lived fairly close to our family. Coach McGuire had a theme. We were going to go down South as missionaries. So now we were athletes and missionaries, and Catholicism was going to march through North and South Carolina. Frank was just a very charismatic guy."

Life on campus initially puzzled the transplanted denizens of the New York boroughs. "Everybody says hello to you," Brennan noted. "Imagine walking down Times Square and saying hello to people. They'd lock you up."

For Rosenbluth, life in New York had prepared him for the cultural clash—and some ethnic taunting—he found down South. "In some places, some of the players might say something to me," he said. "But I ignored it because in New York I had played in the church leagues and I played at the YMCA, the only white kid in an all-black YMCA. So that didn't bother me. I think it bothered the other players, but I just felt like putting points on the board and winning. Like Frank McGuire said, 'All you have to do is stay ahead of the teams and that hushes the crowd and hushes the players.' Basically, that's what I tried to do."

McGuire dressed his New Yorkers in blazers, schooled them in his basketball and turned them loose on the Atlantic Coast Conference. They didn't overwhelm Case's N.C. State teams, but they did find a footing, finishing the 1955-56 season with an 18-5 record. McGuire was bitterly disappointed by a 21-point loss to hated Wake Forest in the ACC Tournament, but that frustration would become one of the motivating factors the following season.

Frank McGuire, a former player and coach at St. John's, built his 1956-57 Tar Heel team around kids from the New York playgrounds.

Carolina would beat Wake four times, the last by two points in the all-important ACC tourney, where the conference's solitary NCAA bid was decided.

Early in the season, the 1956-57 Tar Heels showed signs of falling victim to dissension. The four junior starters—Quigg, Brennan, Cunningham and Kearns—had found a social life of their own in the university's fraternity system. There were suggestions that they were only reluctantly working the ball to Rosenbluth, the senior and captain.

McGuire ordered a team meeting to head off any tension. More than any other coaching move, that was perhaps his greatest achievement that season—to convince his talented juniors, all potential stars in their own right, to work with Rosenbluth as the designated scorer.

"We got so close on the court that we got to know exactly what everybody else was doing," Rosenbluth said years later. "For example, I knew that if Pete put the ball on the floor, it was going up."

A basic back-to-the-basket forward, Rosenbluth had a full complement of shots and a quick release. He was particularly effective flashing into the lane, taking the pass, then maneuvering for a quick, good shot. He never seemed bothered by misses. Over his three-year varsity career, Rosenbluth averaged 26.9 points per game (a standing school record through 1989) by shooting 46 percent from the floor, re-

McGuire (right) with three stars from his 1955-56 North Carolina team: (left to right) Lennie Rosenbluth, Joe Quigg and Jerry Vayda.

markably accurate for the era.

Rosenbluth's versatility as a shooter, McGuire said, made him the greatest player he ever coached. "He has an excellent jump shot, a good hook and he can drive," the coach said. "He can hit from the outside or the inside, and he can rebound. What more could you want from one of your players?"

While still in high school, Rosenbluth had been good enough to be invited to a Boston Celtics rookie camp by Red Auerbach. He had competed at the YMCA with the likes of Sihugo Green, later a two-time All-America at Duquesne, and played summer league ball in the Catskills, where pro, college and top prep players honed their skills. But Rosenbluth learned most of his basketball on the streets and playgrounds of the Bronx, where defense was played with elbows and knees and the king of the hill was the man with the most points—and bruises.

"It was murder for anyone to drive in those park games," he said. "Lots of times we had to quit because somebody slammed into the pipes under the backboard and got knocked cold."

Without the benefit of a referee, much less a coach, that background explained some of his defensive shortcomings and the blunt observation of one ACC coach: "We pass the ball to whoever Rosey is guarding—he sets our offense for us." Far more important, however, was the way he developed as a playground shooter.

"You changed positions according to who was playing," Rosenbluth said. "One day, I'd be the biggest kid, so I'd play the pivot. Next day there would be someone bigger than me, so I'd have to play outside."

McGuire went so far as to call him a "freak," strictly in a flattering sense. "I guess you'd have to call him a freak because he can do anything on a court you want him to do," McGuire said. "He can kill you from the corner, or from the middle of the court or from around the foul lane."

Rosenbluth wasn't selfish by nature, but when he received the ball, he had a mind to shoot it. "You learned he wasn't going to kick it back to you," one

Talented Tar Heel guard Tommy Kearns.

teammate said. All of them, however, grew to respect his ability to score in the clutch.

The four juniors settled into their roles as contributors, although Kearns, a flashy guard, was probably the most difficult convert. The players remember McGuire picking up two balls before one practice and throwing both on the court. "One's for Tommy," he said, "and one's for the rest of the team. Tommy, if you want to hog the ball, take one for yourself."

Kearns did adjust, but was still capable of taking over the scoring role, along with Brennan, when Rosenbluth was too closely guarded. Almost every opponent on the Tar Heels' schedule rigged its defense to stop Rosenbluth, often leaving his set-up men wide open. Some teams conceded he'd score regardless (he was Carolina's leading scorer in all but five games) and played their usual defense.

"We always go into a game figuring he's going to get a bundle," one coach said. "There's just no way to stop him. If you collapse around him in the pivot, he goes outside and kills you. He can jump shoot from beyond the range of the zone."

Cunningham, at 6-4, was one of the tallest guards in the country and, consequently, a key rebounder. He had been a prolific scorer early in his prep career but was never the same shooter after severely cutting his shooting hand in an accident during his senior year. At Carolina, he made his mark as a hustling defensive hawk, a physical player who took advantage of his size in the backcourt.

With the 6-9 Quigg at center and the forward spots manned by 6-6 Brennan and 6-5 Rosenbluth, the Heels put one of the nation's tallest front lines on the court. Each would average better than eight

Season Results
1956-57 (32-0)

94	Furman	66	
94	Clemson at Charlotte, N.C.	75	
82	G. Wash'ton at Norfolk, Va.	55	
90	At South Carolina	86	
70	Maryland	61	
64	At New York University	59	
89	Dartmouth at Boston	61	
83	Holy Cross at Boston	70	
97	Utah at Raleigh, N.C.*	76	
87	Duke at Raleigh, N.C.*	71	
63	W. Forest at Raleigh, N.C.*	55	
71	At William & Mary	61	
86	Clemson	54	
102	Virginia	90	
83	At North Carolina State	57	
77	At Western Carolina	59	
65	At Maryland	61	
75	Duke	73	
68	At Virginia	59	
72	Wake Forest	69	
86	North Carolina State	57	
75	South Carolina	62	
69	At Wake Forest	64	
86	At Duke	72	
81	Clemson at Raleigh, N.C.†	61	
61	W. Forest at Raleigh, N.C.†	59	
95	S. Carolina at Raleigh, N.C.†	75	
90	Yale at New York‡	74	
87	Canisius at Philadelphia‡	75	
67	Syracuse at Philadelphia‡	58	
74	Michigan State at K. C.‡	70	
54	Kansas at Kansas City‡	53	

*Dixie Classic
†ACC Conference Tournament
‡NCAA Tournament

rebounds per game, led by Brennan's 10.4 average. Firing his deadly jump shot, the big forward also would finish as the team's No. 2 scorer, averaging 14.7 points per game.

As the Tar Heels snaked their way through the schedule, McGuire contended they'd get even better—once they were beaten. "Everybody's trying to get up for us," he said. "They jump higher, shoot better and run faster."

Being undefeated, North Carolina brought out the best in opponents and survived its share of anxious moments. With a 16-0 record, the Heels traveled to Maryland and found themselves trailing by four points in the game's waning moments. McGuire called the team to the bench and prepared it for what seemed inevitable. "You've been gracious winners," he said, "now be gracious losers." Back on the floor, Carolina rallied to tie the score before winning in double-overtime, 65-61.

"The boys told me after that game that they did not intend to be beaten," McGuire said. "That victory gave them a tremendous lift."

Carolina didn't overpower its opponents but had a knack for pulling games out of the fire. In their next test after Maryland, the Heels squandered an eight-point lead over Duke before Kearns hit two free throws in the final seconds of a 75-73 victory. Two games later, they escaped with a three-point win over Wake Forest, which would provide the biggest test in the ACC Tournament. In the semifinal game, with under a minute remaining and the Deacons leading by a point, Rosenbluth completed a three-point play with a hook from the circle and a free throw to seal a 61-59 victory.

Arguably, that three-point play was the first great moment for ACC basketball, allowing the Tar Heels to advance into the NCAA Tournament and annex the four-year-old conference's first-ever national title.

North Carolina arrived at the Final Four with a 30-0 record and the top ranking in the wire-service polls. Newspapers already were playing up what appeared to be an impending collision with second-ranked Kansas, led by 7-foot sophomore center Wilt Chamberlain. The Jayhawks had lost only twice, on the road to Iowa State and Oklahoma State, but now had the homecourt advantage in Kansas City's Municipal Auditorium, just a short drive from the Lawrence campus.

For that championship game story line to develop, the Tar Heels had to get past Michigan State in a three-overtime thriller in the semifinal round. "We won several games we should have lost that season," McGuire said years later. "I thought sure we would lose at least four games we won."

This, indeed, was one of those games. Quigg attempted only one field goal before he fouled out. Overall, the Heels shot a dismal 31 percent from the floor.

Rosenbluth, a scoring threat from anywhere on the court, averaged 28 points in North Carolina's championship season.

Kearns drives toward the basket against rival Wake Forest, a team the Tar Heels defeated four times in the 1956-57 season.

From a 29-29 tie at halftime, the game moved to a 58-58 deadlock at the end of regulation. With 11 seconds left in the first overtime, Brennan rebounded a missed Michigan State free throw, drove the length of the floor and scored on a jumper with three seconds remaining to keep the Heels alive. The teams entered the third overtime tied at 66. Finally, Rosenbluth converted two steals into field goals and

Carolina outlasted the Spartans, 74-70.

In less than 24 hours, the Tar Heels would play for the title against Kansas, which walloped San Francisco, 80-56, in the other semifinal bracket.

"In the 1950s," Kearns said, "we played the tournament games on consecutive nights, Fridays and Saturdays, instead of on Saturday and Monday like it is today. In the semifinals we played Michigan

1957 NORTH CAROLINA

Head Coach—Frank McGuire   Final Record—32-0

Player	Pos.	Hgt.	Wgt.	Cl.	G	FG	FGA	Pct.	FT	FTA	Pct.	Reb.	Pts.	Avg.
Lennie Rosenbluth	F	6-5	195	Sr.	32	305	631	.483	285	376	.758	280	895	28.0
Pete Brennan	F	6-6	190	Jr.	32	143	363	.394	185	262	.706	332	471	14.7
Tommy Kearns	G	5-11	188	Jr.	32	138	318	.434	135	190	.711	100	411	12.8
Joe Quigg	C	6-9	205	Jr.	31	111	256	.434	97	135	.719	268	319	10.3
Bob Cunningham	G	6-4	190	Jr.	32	88	224	.393	55	92	.598	214	231	7.2
Tony Radovich	G	6-2	192	Sr.	16	21	40	.525	20	26	.769	29	62	3.9
Bill Hathaway	C	6-11	240	So.	15	16	48	.333	10	24	.417	75	42	2.8
Stan Groll	G	6-0	182	So.	12	10	27	.370	5	9	.556	18	25	2.1
Bob Young	C	6-6	200	Sr.	15	11	43	.256	7	13	.538	32	29	1.9
Ken Rosemond	G	5-9	150	Jr.	15	6	15	.400	5	9	.556	9	17	1.1
Danny Lotz	F	6-7	198	So.	24	7	20	.350	9	23	.391	39	23	1.0
Gehrmann Holland	F	6-3	200	So.	12	4	8	.500	0	1	.000	6	8	0.7
Roy Searcy	F	6-4	185	Jr.	11	0	3	.000	4	5	.800	11	4	0.4
Team												82		
North Carolina					32	860	1996	.431	817	1165	.701	1495	2537	79.3
Opponents					32	720	2043	.352	658	956	.688	1151	2098	65.6

State three overtimes, and then we played Kansas in the finals—for three overtimes.

"We played six overtimes in two days. That was like playing three and a half games in two days . . . and we all played virtually the whole game every game (that season)."

The analysts thought the Carolina players would be intimidated by Chamberlain, just like the other Kansas opponents before them. Kearns destroyed that myth as he strutted around the team hotel. "We're a chilly club," he said. "I mean, we just keep cool. Chamberlain won't give us the jitters like he did to all those other clubs."

Rosenbluth confirmed as much. "Most of us were playing in the Catskill Mountains during the summer," he recalled, "and we played against Chamberlain when he was in high school. So we were not awed by his back dunks or by how big he was.

"As we got ready for the game, we tried to remember that no matter if he dunked the ball over his head or whatever, it was still just two points. It counts the same as hitting a little jump shot from 10 feet out, so we tried not to be awed. We put a man in front of him, behind him and on either side of him and said, 'Hey, go ahead and do.' "

To be safe, McGuire had a plan to deflate the tension from the start. He sent the 5-11 Kearns out to jump center against the Jayhawk giant.

"McGuire's assistant coach had seen the play at the YMCA in the early '30s," Kearns remembered. "I really didn't know anything about the plan for me to jump center against Wilt until Coach McGuire said something to me five minutes before the game. I just passed it off, however. After the player introductions, we sat on the bench and he said, 'Tommy, you're going out to jump against Wilt.' I was just as surprised as anybody.

"I think Wilt was taken aback, as I think the whole team was. It set a tone for the game, and we jumped off to a very big lead as a result. I think it was a daring move by Coach McGuire, and it had an awful lot to do with us winning the game."

After disconcerting the Kansas center with comedy, the Heels surrounded him with a stifling zone. Chamberlain didn't score for nearly five minutes. Carolina, meanwhile, worked the ball for high-percentage shots and took a 19-7 lead.

"I said I didn't care if we didn't take a single shot in the first half if the shot opportunity wasn't a good one," McGuire said. The Heels executed superbly, shooting 65 percent from the field for the half, while Kansas shot terribly, making only 27 percent of its attempts. The half ended with Carolina in front, 29-22.

In the second half, Chamberlain shook loose from the zone, and the Jayhawks moved into position to claim the title. Carolina was tired, and its frontcourt was in foul trouble. But with 10 minutes left and the Tar Heels trailing by three, Kansas

Rosenbluth launches a jump shot as a pair of Clemson Tigers watch in vain.

The 1956-57 North Carolina Tar Heels: Front row (left to right)—Roy Searcy, Gehrmann Holland, Danny Lotz, Ken Rosemond, Bob Cunningham, Kearns. Second row—McGuire, manager Joel Fleishman, Bob Young, Rosenbluth, Quigg, Pete Brennan, assistant coach Buck Freeman, trainer John Lacey.

elected to stall. The crowd loved it, since North Carolina had played ball control all night. McGuire loved it even more than the fans.

"We stood at our end of the court and let Kansas play catch," he said. "At five minutes, I waved my hand and the boys went after them. They'd given us time to get our second wind and provided us a safety margin in the foul column."

With 1:45 remaining, however, Rosenbluth fouled out of his last college game with 20 points. Given Rosey's 28-point scoring average (a single-season school record through 1989), the Tar Heels— still down by three points—would have looked to their All-America for a few more buckets. But now he was gone, the man McGuire called his greatest ever, and his mates would have to carry on.

They did just that, getting a field goal from Quigg and a free throw from Kearns to tie the game at 46 at the end of regulation. After trading baskets in the first extra period, the teams played a scoreless second overtime. The third period started briskly, as Kearns hit a bucket and a pair of free throws for a 52-48 Carolina lead. The Jayhawks scratched back, however, and took a 53-52 advantage when Gene Elstun made a free throw with 25 seconds remain-

ing. More important, Elstun missed one, too.

Now Carolina would drive one last time—and directly at the big man himself. With less than 10 seconds left, Quigg hurtled down the lane as Chamberlain moved forward to meet him. As Quigg prepared to let fly, Kansas' Maurice King intruded, quite physically in the eyes of the officials. Quigg was awarded two foul shots with six seconds left.

"I just had a great feeling I would make the shots," Quigg said years later. "I told coach I would make them and he said, always confident, 'After Joe makes the shots, we'll go to a zone.' "

Quigg buried both attempts, then sealed the championship by slapping away a Kansas pass as time expired. Carolina had prevailed, 54-53, and completed the perfect season with 32 victories. Among the unbeaten clubs in NCAA history, only the 1976 Indiana Hoosiers have won as many.

McGuire and Rosenbluth flew off for an appearance on the Ed Sullivan Show. The rest of the Heels returned to Raleigh-Durham Airport and found a crowd of 10,000 waiting to celebrate. McGuire and his New York boys had started something big in Chapel Hill. Even today, folks remember they have Everett Case to thank for it.

FIFTEEN

Cinderella's Double Date

CITY COLLEGE OF NEW YORK

1949-50

College basketball has had its share of "Cinderellas," but none fit the glass slipper better than the 1949-50 team from City College of New York. For one glorious season, the Beavers captured the hearts and imaginations of New York's basketball fans while completing an unprecedented championship double.

Unfortunately, the Beavers were all too true to their media motif. Midnight struck in the February following their storybook season when key members of their starting five were arrested in a point-shaving scandal (involving games in the 1950-51 season), and a subsequent investigation revealed that grades had been changed to allow the admission of players to the academically prestigious school.

Perhaps the saddest part of the postseason development was that this team and its coach were the darlings of a city that badly needed an image of freshness and innocence to believe in. The 1949 Beavers, young, talented, exciting and New York born and bred, fit that description. And believe in them it did.

As CCNY marched improbably through first the National Invitation Tournament and then the NCAA Tournament fields, its student-body cheer echoed loudly through the canyons of Manhattan. "Allagaroo-garoo-gara; Allagaroo-garoo-gara; Ee-yah, Ee-yah; Sis, Boom, Bah, Team! Team! Team!" And when that double journey was completed, no one could deny New York City its long-awaited moment in the college basketball spotlight.

The Beavers were the epitome of the city-slick, racehorse brand of basketball that had taken root in the West before filtering into New York in the mid-1940s. They played a fast-break, up-tempo game that even included the new-wave one-handed style of shooting that their coach privately abhorred.

"If I see one of my kids doing that, I'll break his other arm," Nat Holman snapped when he first saw a ball lofted toward the basket with one hand. But by the end of the decade, even Holman, a basketball traditionalist in the truest sense, had come to grips with the necessity to keep pace with the game's evolution.

It was a difficult compromise. Holman, known reverently as Mr. Basketball around college circles, had long nurtured his strict principles of fundamental basketball. Control the ball. Set up offensive formations. Pass with painstaking care. Shoot only when there's a genuine opening. Never, ever get reckless.

Holman's principles were chiseled out of what he had done himself on the basketball court and what he *knew* to be effective. And there was no arguing that he had done plenty.

The native New Yorker was a star with the Original Celtics, the first great professional barnstorming team. The Celtics would play more than 100 games in a season, and they rarely lost. Every game was a basketball clinic. Holman was an expert marksman with his set shot, he was one of the best ballhandlers of his era and he was an outstanding student of what was then an evolving, uncomplicated game.

He became CCNY coach in 1920 at the tender age of 23 and kept an unrelenting schedule for 14 years in which he would coach basketball during the day, barnstorm on the professional circuit at night. And

City College of New York Coach Nat Holman, alias Mr. Basketball, with 1949-50 stars Ed Roman (left) and Ed Warner.

Warner had that special talent that allowed him to twist and turn through traffic while driving to the basket.

though his school never attracted top athletes, Holman attracted national attention with his ability to win—359 times going into the 1949-50 campaign.

Given that background, it's not difficult to understand how Holman became the guru of Eastern basketball. As a professional player with the Celtics, he was admired in New York and points north, south, east and west. A snappy dresser, he lectured and wrote extensively on the game, which naturally evolved in his image. He remained true to his philosophies, even when such Western rebels as the 1941-42 Stanford Cardinals introduced their revolutionary run-and-gun style. But by the late 1940s, other Eastern teams had seen the light and Holman, begrudgingly, decided to take the plunge.

He couldn't have picked a better time.

Blessed with a better group of athletes than he had ever coached before, Holman began blending in elements of the fast-break style with his still-fervent belief in precision passing and defense. His 1946-47 team reached the semifinals of the NCAA

Tournament before losing to Holy Cross, his 1947-48 team finished 18-3 without getting a postseason bid and his 1948-49 team played in the NIT. It was in 1948 that a special class of freshmen arrived to set the stage for what would become Holman's "season in the sun."

Irwin Dambrot, a freshman on the 1946-47 team and the only senior starter on the 1949-50 double-championship team, recalls his coach with a sense of reverence.

"Nat Holman was a very strong disciplinarian," Dambrot said. "When he talked, he wanted silence. When he showed somebody on the team a movement, he wanted no one to move. Everybody would just have to freeze and pay very, very close attention.

"Directly and indirectly, he demanded a lot of respect."

During the games he wanted movement, always movement. The key to Holman's new system was motion, always precise and deceptive; give the ball

Floyd Layne (3) was a defensive specialist who did most of his scoring from right under the basket.

to the pivotman and go to the basket. He particularly liked an offense that featured all five players rotating in and out of the pivot. That suited the 1949-50 starting five because all of them had played center in high school. The pivotman had to be versatile and a solid passer, able to hit his teammates as they cut off of him toward the basket. It was literally a game of hot potato.

"The ball would move, everybody would move," Dambrot said. "So if a defensive man turned his head, you were gone. We went in for back-door layups all the time."

Holman also appreciated the full-court running game, but he continued to drill his players on defense and fundamentals, never allowing himself to stray too far from his roots. His players, already well-schooled in the free-wheeling brand of ball played on the New York playgrounds, expanded their skills in Holman's unrelenting practices.

"If you didn't box out, he'd pull you right out of the game," Dambrot said. "Nat Holman taught you defense."

And unlike many coaches of his era, Holman was a fervent proponent of scouting reports that would help him dissect an opponent and prepare his players for each game.

Dambrot, as a senior, was the elder statesman and leader of a team that started four sophomores. It was a talented cast that featured 6-foot-6 Ed Roman at center, 6-4 Ed Warner and Dambrot at the forwards and a pair of 6-3 guards, Floyd Layne and Al (Fats) Roth. Centers Leroy Watkins and Joe Galiber, forward Norm Mager and guard Mike Wittlin gave Holman four solid seniors off the bench.

Warner, who would become a paraplegic as a result of an auto accident later in life, was the team's most natural talent. "When he got there, we just got better and better and better," Dambrot said.

"Warner's arms were three to four inches longer than most people's," Dambrot recalled, and, as a result, "he played as if he were 6-8." In addition to being a fine leaper, he was lightning quick, he could handle the ball and he was particularly efficient at

Season Results
1949-50 (24-5)

91	Queens	45	61	Niagara	68
76	Lafayette	44	75	At St. Joseph's	59
67	Southern Methodist	53	66	At Fordham	62
82	Kings Point	28	74	Syracuse	83
71	Brooklyn	44	57	Manhattan	55
63	Oklahoma	67	64	New York University	61
76	California	46	65	San Francisco at New York*	46
53	UCLA	60	89	Kentucky at New York*	50
54	St. John's	52	62	Duquesne at New York*	52
61	Loyola of Chicago	46	69	Bradley at New York*	61
80	West Virginia	55	56	Ohio State at New York†	55
95	At Muhlenberg	76	78	N.C. State at New York†	73
64	At Boston	56	71	Bradley at New York†	68
56	At Princeton	46			
68	At St. Francis	46	*NIT		
49	At Canisius	53	†NCAA Tournament		

Guard Al (Fats) Roth was a solid playmaker who also was known for his ability to rebound and push through opposing teams' picks.

driving to the basket, often twisting his body between two or three defenders. He also was an excellent student of Holman's philosophies, developing into one of the best defensive players in the country.

One coach called Warner, who averaged 14.8 points in the 1949-50 season, the best sophomore he had ever seen. St. John's Coach Frank McGuire said he had "hands like an octopus—fine, educated hands." Holman himself called Warner "the toughest bucket man (scorer) in college."

Roman, not as natural and fluid as Warner, was the team's true pivotman. He checked in at a beefy 220 pounds and was not adverse to throwing his weight around under the boards. He was a versatile shooter who could hook with either hand or turn quickly for a jump shot. When Warner moved inside, Roman would move out for his deadly one-hand set shot. The big man led the Beavers with a 16.4 average his sophomore season while shooting at a 41.6 percent clip—a high figure in those days.

Dambrot was the other scorer, averaging 10.2 points after a 1948-49 season in which he had set a CCNY season scoring record with 276 points. The

6-4 forward, one of the city's early jump shooters, was a leaper who possessed a nice lefthanded shot.

Layne was the defensive specialist who usually was assigned to the opposing team's big scorer. One of the most popular players on the team, the tall, lanky Layne averaged 6.9 points, most of them coming on moves to the basket. Layne would survive the scandals at CCNY and later become head coach at the college.

Roth was a 200-pounder who earned his nickname (Fats) with his ability to rebound and push through opposing picks. His primary job was to handle the ball and play defense, and when he shot, he did so from the set position. He connected on only 28.8 percent of those shots while averaging 6.4 points.

This was the cast that would wave its magic wand and transform New York into a one-season basketball mecca. Fans of CCNY, a public education system that offered free tuition to motivated students, knew that Holman had the makings of a good team, and preseason newspaper reports were generous in their praise. But nobody suspected that it could challenge for national honors. Nobody, that is, except Holman himself and one New York newspaper that commented early in the 1949-50 season that CCNY might well become the greatest team that New York City had ever produced.

The Beavers' home base was Madison Square Garden, where many of the city's colleges played their games. But it didn't take long for CCNY to become the crowd favorite in the 1949-50 campaign.

"New York basketball in those days was unreal," Dambrot said. "There would be 18,000 fans in Madison Square Garden, packed to the rafters."

Holman had expressed concern that his team would be affected by its early-season press clippings, but that didn't seem to be the case as the Beavers won 13 of their first 15 games, losing only to Oklahoma (67-63) and UCLA (60-53). One of their victims was city-rival St. John's (54-52), a team expected to contend for a national title.

But, suddenly, Holman's Beavers hit a late-season snag. They dropped consecutive games to Canisius and Niagara before falling to Syracuse three games later. That slump almost cost the Beavers a postseason bid. Two more victories brought their final regular-season ledger to 17-5 and they were awarded one of the final spots in the NIT field only because of their sweep in the so-called "subway series" among metropolitan New York schools.

The prospects for success in the tournament did not appear good. Most observers were inclined to dismiss CCNY as a young group of overachievers that was still a year away. But Holman had other ideas. He pulled his kids together, calming his sophomores and needling his seniors. He reestablished the winning attitude that had carried them through the early part of their schedule while preparing

Warner (8) goes for the opening tip as Irwin Dambrot (right) holds his ground during a game against Loyola of Chicago.

them for the job that lay ahead.

And just as quickly as the Beavers had fallen off course, they righted themselves and served notice that they were not a team to be taken lightly. The first opponent to learn that lesson was defending NIT champion San Francisco, which succumbed meekly to the Beavers, 65-46, in the opening round. Warner, who had scored 26 points in CCNY's regular-season finale against New York University, matched that total against the Dons. The result raised a few eyebrows, but nothing compared to the one that would follow.

CCNY's second-round opponent would be third-ranked Kentucky, the team that had captured the last two NCAA championships. "Just play your game," Holman told his players, and they did, shocking the basketball community by racing past the Wildcats, 89-50. It was the most lopsided defeat ever experienced by an Adolph Rupp-coached team and the kind of confidence booster that can lift a team to great heights. After the massacre, Rupp predicted the Beavers would take the title.

The victory was predicated by a slick coaching maneuver by Holman. After Bill Spivey, Kentucky's 7-foot center, had opened the game by

blocking several of Roman's shots, Holman shifted Warner into the post, and the quicker little man literally ran circles around Spivey. Warner hit the 26-point mark for the third straight game and his slick inside maneuvers opened up the court and allowed the Beavers to work their fast break against the slower Wildcats.

"We just ran them off the court and made every shot," Dambrot recalled. "They just couldn't handle our fast break."

The state of Kentucky was so devastated by the shocking result that its legislature considered a resolution that the capitol's flag be lowered to half staff. According to Dambrot, an unspoken incentive in the minds of the CCNY players was the fact that Kentucky, an all-white Southern team, avoided, whenever possible, playing against teams with black players. Warner, Layne, Galiber and Watkins all were black.

CCNY's outburst was enough to get the attention of the press, and the interest increased when the Beavers outlasted Duquesne, 62-52, in the tournament's third round. That victory not only lifted the Beavers into the NIT championship game, but it also earned them a spot in the upcoming NCAA

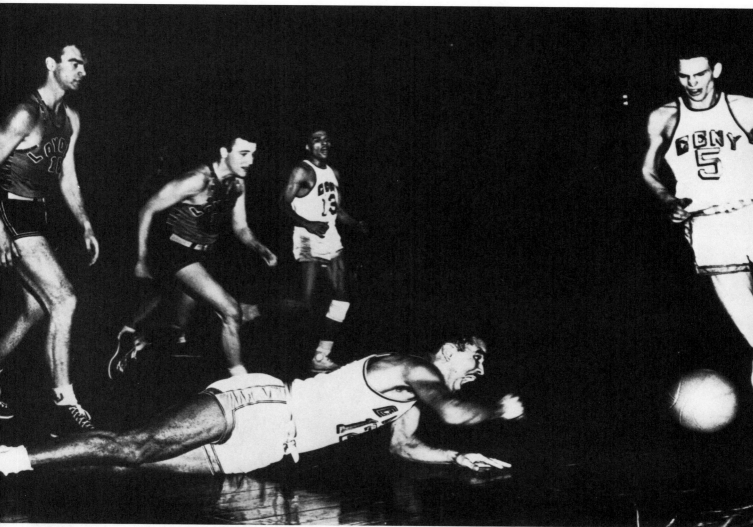

Loyola players watch helplessly as backup center Joe Galiber falls to the floor and
Dambrot chases down the loose ball.

1950 CCNY

Head Coach—Nat Holman   Final Record—24-5

Player	Pos.	Hgt.	Wgt.	Cl.	G	FG	FGA	Pct.	FT.	FTA	Pct.	Reb.	Pts.	Avg.
Ed Roman	C	6-6	220	So.	29	207	497	.416	61	95	.642	....	475	16.4
Ed Warner	F	6-4	205	So.	29	157	365	.430	115	203	.567	....	429	14.8
Irwin Dambrot	F	6-4	185	Sr.	29	124	334	.371	47	81	.580	....	295	10.2
Floyd Layne	G	6-3	175	So.	29	68	243	.280	63	104	.606	....	199	6.9
Al Roth	G	6-3	200	So.	29	68	236	.288	50	97	.515	....	186	6.4
Herb Cohen	G	6-1	170	So.	24	50	122	.410	30	57	.526	....	130	5.4
Norm Mager	F	6-5	185	Sr.	29	41	116	.353	22	35	.629	....	104	3.6
Ronald Nadell	G	5-11	170	Jr.	19	17	44	.386	13	20	.650	....	47	2.5
Seymour Levy	G	6-1	170	Sr.	6	4	19	.210	4	7	.571	....	12	2.0
Mike Wittlin	G	5-10	165	Sr.	22	16	51	.314	6	10	.600	....	38	1.7
Leroy Watkins	C	6-7	185	Sr.	11	9	18	.500	1	4	.250	....	19	1.7
Joe Galiber	C	6-4	205	Sr.	24	11	46	.239	12	23	.522	....	34	1.4
Arnie Smith	G	6-1	170	Jr.	14	4	22	.182	7	8	.875	....	15	1.1
Larry Meyer	G	5-8	170	So.	8	3	23	.130	2	7	.286	....	8	1.0
Arthur Glass	G	6-1	185	Jr.	9	1	14	.071	0	0	.000	....	2	0.2
CCNY					29	780	2150	.363	433	751	.577	....	1993	68.7
Opponents					29	...	.....	.....	...	.....	.....	....	1610	55.5

North Carolina State's Sam Ranzino follows the flight of his shot as CCNY's Layne and Norm Mager look for a rebound in an NCAA Tournament semifinal game.

Tournament. The NCAA selection committee, unable to choose from among CCNY, St. John's and Duquesne, had decided to take the team that advanced furthest in the NIT. That berth went to the Beavers when St. John's fell to Bradley in the other NIT semifinal.

Most predictions were that CCNY, like St. John's, would fall to the top-ranked Braves in the NIT final. The clock was about to strike midnight for the Cinderella Beavers. Holman's pregame speech was short and sweet. "You've grown up," he told his youngsters. "You can do it. I know you can do it."

The task at hand indeed appeared formidable. The Braves featured All-America forward Paul Unruh and a pair of little big men in 5-8 Gene Melchiorre and 6-1 Bill Mann. Bradley boasted a 29-3 record and appeared ready to cap its banner season with a national championship.

And that script seemed to be accurate as the Braves controlled their upstart opponents in the early going.

"Against Bradley, they were destroying us the first half," Dambrot said. "It was like a snake pit they were so good. At one point we were down 10 to 12 (11) points, but we closed to three by the half (30-27) and won it from there."

Once CCNY got its fast break into full gear, Bradley was in trouble. The Beavers methodically built their lead and coasted home with a 69-61 victory and their first-ever national title. Dambrot led the way with 23 points and Warner was named the tournament's Most Valuable Player.

Holman had been battling a high fever during the final, but the outcome provided a nice cure. "The team just seemed to arrive in the Kentucky game," he told reporters. "I don't think they have been lucky and I don't think they've just been hot. They simply found themselves. And if they stay hale and hearty, I think we can beat anybody, and that includes Bradley again."

As fate would have it, the Beavers would get their chance to find out. Ironically, many New Yorkers were critical of Holman for accepting the NCAA bid. "Not a smart move," they said, "because lightning doesn't strike twice in the same place." They expressed serious doubts that the coach could get his team to play at the same fever pitch that it had in pulling off the NIT upset.

They underestimated both Holman and his now-determined players.

First up for CCNY would be Ohio State, the nation's second-ranked team. The Buckeyes were ready for the Beavers and almost ended their dream of a double championship. Using a tight zone defense and scoring from inside, the Buckeyes extended CCNY, and only some good outside shooting enabled the Beavers to escape with a 56-55 victory.

The Beavers returned to Madison Square Garden

Roth (25) battles North Carolina State players for a rebound as Layne stands ready to help.

for their semifinal matchup against North Carolina State and rewarded their "Allagaroo" chanting fans with a 78-73 victory. Roman led the way with 21 points and Warner added 17 as CCNY advanced to the final and its date with destiny. Only three teams had won one of the major championships and competed in the other in the same season, and no team had ever won both.

Their opponent? Bradley, of course, which had advanced to the final with victories over UCLA and Baylor.

The Braves were better prepared for the Beavers, but at this point nothing could stop the express. CCNY built an 11-point lead midway through the second half and only a desperation surge by Brad-

Warner lays the ball into the basket, despite the effort of Bradley's Charley Grover in the 1950 NCAA championship game.

ley put the final result in doubt. Two Melchiorre steals and layups brought the score to 69-68 and, after another turnover, Melchiorre again drove for what could have been the go-ahead basket. But Dambrot blocked the shot and the Beavers scored an easy layup to seal their 71-68 victory.

Dambrot, named the tournament's outstanding player, led the way with 15 points, but the real hero of the title game was Mager, who came off the bench to score 14. In the locker room after the game, Holman pronounced the Beavers "the greatest team I ever have coached at CCNY."

Students and city residents mobbed the New York streets the next day, chanting "Allagaroo." The college shut down classes for the day and the

players were introduced at a celebration. College President Harry N. Wright told the ecstatic crowd, "This is one of the proudest days of my life. This team came here to study, not to play basketball. I am proud of the team and what it has done for the college. I want to point out that they are given no scholarships to play ball, and they have not been imported to play ball. I am particularly proud of their high scholastic rating."

The jubilation carried right through to the next February, when, abruptly, a number of CCNY and other New York-based players were arrested and charged with point shaving. They became part of the nationwide investigation into gambling in college athletics that revealed numerous "fixes" in 23 different cities in the late 1940s and early '50s. The CCNY players admitted point-shaving activity in three games, all in the season that followed their double-championship campaign.

The 1951 gambling scandal brought an end to regular-season NCAA games at Madison Square Garden. It was widely believed that the atmosphere there played a big part in fomenting corruption.

As for CCNY, the investigation revealed that grade records had been falsified to allow several of its talented basketball recruits admission to the university, enough of an embarrassment to silence the "Allagaroo" cheers.

"That's sort of tough to talk about," Dambrot said when asked the effect on the team. Several players had made youthful mistakes and paid a stiff price. Warner might have felt the sting more than anybody because he had the talent to play in the NBA—a dream that died as a result of the scandal.

The other unfortunate victim of this story was Holman himself. For years, he had represented what was right in college athletics, and the scandal blindsided him as much as anyone. He was suspended from the coaching ranks for two years before he was finally cleared of any wrongdoing, but the damage clearly had been done.

In 1989, he was 92 years old and living an active life in an adult home in New York, where he painted portraits for relaxation. But, as Dambrot explained, the former coach screened his interviews, adamantly refusing to discuss the scandal.

Sadly, just as the fast-break style of play evolved as an art form, the gambling investigations virtually wiped out the city's thriving basketball culture. The major programs at Long Island University, CCNY, Manhattan and NYU never recovered.

Perhaps that was for the best. The memories of the 1949-50 CCNY Beavers concern only what they did on the court.

"We were a team that moved very well," said Dambrot, who went on to become a New York dentist. "We used all the best of modern basketball.

"I think our team would do pretty good today. We were the best of our era."

SIXTEEN

Oscar-Winning Performance

1959-60

Over the years, the language of basketball has settled on the term "complete," as in "the *complete* player," to describe the ultimate, the best. It means the guy who can do everything. Shoot. Dribble. Pass. Rebound. Play defense. Win.

In other words, Oscar Robertson.

At least that's what UCLA's renowned coach, John Wooden, has said of Robertson many times. Innumerable players and coaches alike have agreed.

"In his time, he was the greatest," said Ed Jucker, an assistant at Cincinnati when Robertson played his collegiate basketball for the Bearcats. "No one was the equal to him. I always called him a complete ball player, and there are not many truly complete players. But he could play any position."

For being a so-called complete player, Robertson was almost nonchalant about the scope of his skills, former Kansas Coach Dick Harp said. "He had unbelievable control of a basketball game, and many times he looked like he was taking a walk in the country when he did it," Harp said. "He was so much in control of things. He had the size, the quickness, everything. He had all those great blessings, but among them he had great judgment about what to do with the ball."

Robertson led the nation in scoring three straight years as a collegian, starting off with a gaudy 35.1 average in his sophomore season of 1957-58. On top of that, he averaged 15.2 rebounds in 88 games in a Cincinnati uniform, a figure that still stands as a Bearcat career record. And, as a senior he averaged 7.3 assists per game, a single-season Cincy record that remains intact.

The scoring was nice, the 6-foot-5 Robertson said

nearly 30 years after playing his last collegiate game, but it was the rebounding in which he took the most pride "because I know how hard it was. It was tough going in there against guys 6-10 or bigger. To rebound against them, you had to outquick them, out-think them."

Some observers have attempted to compare Robertson to modern players of extraordinary talent, such as Magic Johnson or Michael Jordan. But Pete Newell, who coached California to an NCAA championship, says Robertson actually has more in common with Larry Bird.

Most people think of Robertson as a guard, Newell said, because he played in the backcourt as a professional with the Cincinnati Royals and Milwaukee Bucks. But as a collegian, Robertson was a forward.

"Oscar played forward more like Larry Bird plays forward," Newell said. "He was such a great passer. He brought the ball up even though he was playing forward. He was so tough when he got the ball. Oscar would go down and get it. Then they'd clear for him, and he'd just take it on his own. There was no way you could stop Oscar one-on-one from penetrating and getting his shot."

Ultimately, however, the bottom line for players like Jordan, Bird and Robertson is not how complete they make themselves, but how complete they make their teams.

Robertson's impact cannot be denied.

In a three-year varsity career, he propelled Cincinnati to a No. 2 final ranking in both major wire-service polls in 1958 and led the Bearcats to a No. 1 rating in the Associated Press' final balloting of

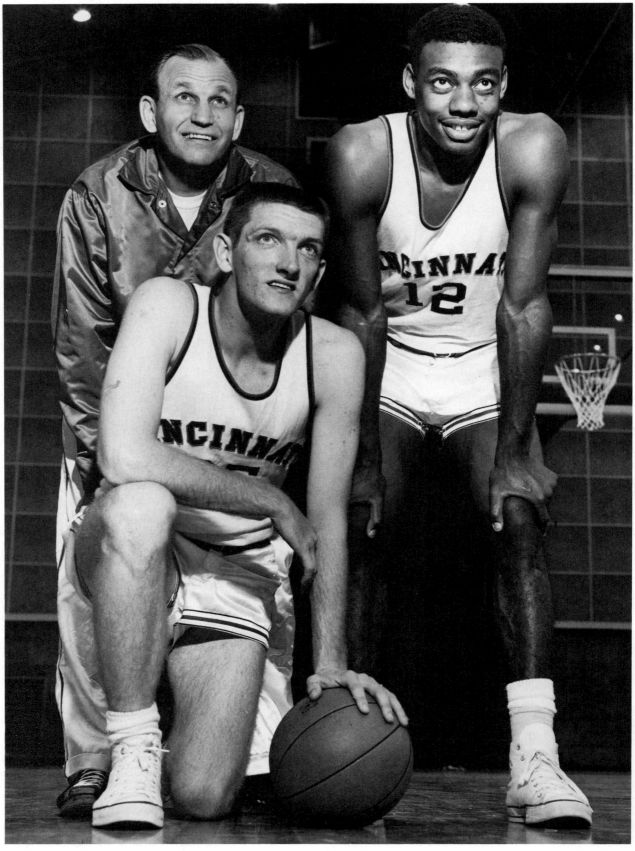

Cincinnati Coach George Smith and his top two scorers—forward Oscar Robertson (12) and guard Ralph Davis.

1960. In 1959, Cincinnati wound up No. 4 in one survey. Twice he took the Bearcats to the Final Four.

"We didn't have much size," Robertson said. "Our strength was our quickness up and down the court. But we didn't dodge anybody, I'll tell you that. We played the best teams of the era—St. Louis, Bradley, St. Bonaventure, Louisville, North Carolina, North Carolina State. We were like Louisville is today. We took on everybody."

There remains the impression that Robertson was a one-man team at Cincinnati. If so, the Bearcats' one-man team was far better than the vast majority of the nation's five-man teams.

"He didn't want to be a one-man team," Jucker said. "But he dominated play, and the other players did give him the ball. His teams were running teams. Oscar filled the middle. He was a great passer and had beautiful moves. Quite often he would get the rebound and take it the length of the court to score."

Addressing the one-man-team issue, Robertson said simply, "I passed the ball and I hustled. When I shot it, I went to get the rebound. I took what the defenses gave me. That allowed me to create for other people."

As a prep junior, Robertson had carried Crispus Attucks High School in Indianapolis to the state championship in 1955, the first time an all-black team had ever won an Indiana state crown, and the school repeated in 1956. Crispus Attucks' success featured a 45-game winning streak.

Robertson's success went beyond the game of basketball. A fine student, he was a member of the National Honor Society. Considering his athletic prowess and academic capability, Oscar was eye-balled by virtually every college that had integrated its athletic programs or was willing to integrate them.

He chose Cincinnati for several reasons. It was close to home and had a solid academic reputation. Plus, the school's rigorous basketball schedule offered him the opportunity to play against the best competition in the country. The only negative about the school came with the complexity of the times.

Robertson was the first black to ever play basketball for the Bearcats, and the pressure of integration would weigh heavily at times. Although located in Ohio, Cincinnati is, in some ways, a Southern town. The city sits on the Kentucky border, and many of its residents have ties—emotional and otherwise—to the South. Furthermore, the school scheduled numerous games with Southern schools in the late 1950s and early 1960s.

"A lot of people thought that I should open doors," Robertson once said of integration. "But I didn't feel it was up to me to do it. It's for everybody to do." (His message was clear: People of all

Robertson, the epitome of the complete player, was impossible to stop once he got his hands on the ball.

'The Big O' poses with the Cincinnati Bearcat (left) and with teammates Bob Wiesenhahn (21) and Davis (right).

races shared responsibility.)

Oscar shook off any distractions, however, and made an enormous impact on the game. Cincinnati Coach George Smith went to the team's strength and ran a high-speed attack that churned out points. Across the country, Oscar Robertson quickly became known as "The Big O."

Before the beginning of the 1957-58 season, Smith called a special team meeting. All the Bearcat players were invited—except Robertson.

"I want you fellows to understand something, and I don't want Oscar to hear what I have to say," Smith said. "You were a good team before, but with Robertson you're going to be a better one, maybe a

great one. He'll get all the headlines and all the publicity—you might as well make up your minds to that. But if you'll play with him, he'll take you farther than you've ever gone before."

Sophomore Robertson teamed with fellow frontline players Connie Dierking and Wayne Stevens, both seniors, to boost the '57-'58 Bearcats to a 7-0 start. Cincinnati then suffered losses in two of the next three games, preceding what would be a landmark game for its gifted newcomer from Indianapolis.

Game No. 11 of the season afforded Cincinnati the opportunity to showcase Robertson in the nation's major media center. It matched the Bearcats against Seton Hall on January 9, 1958—at the fabled basketball palace, New York's Madison Square Garden. While the turnout was disappointing—4,615 fans were on hand—the press was out in force. And it got an eyeful.

Hitting on 22 of 32 field-goal attempts and all 12 of his free-throw tries, Oscar established a Garden scoring record with 56 points in a 118-54 annihilation of the Pirates. Additionally, he garnered 15 rebounds. It was a performance that left the college basketball world raving.

"There's never been one like him," gushed St. John's Coach Joe Lapchick. "Fabulous! Until this kid came along, I thought Tom Gola was the best soph I'd ever seen. . .He does everything. How can you stop a guy like that?"

Season Results
1959-60 (28-2)

107	Indiana State	62	67	Houston	55
102	Marshall	61	123	North Texas State	74
89	Miami of Ohio	58	60	At St. Louis	57
123	St. Joseph's (Pa.)	79	57	At Houston	47
97	At Louisville	74	85	At North Texas State	54
86	Bradley	71	97	Wichita State	76
96	St. Bonaventure at N.Y.*	56	110	Tulsa	64
86	St. Joseph's (Pa.) at N.Y.*	77	71	At Drake	56
96	Iowa at New York*	83	86	Xavier (O.)	68
70	Dayton	63	99	DePaul at Manhattan, Kan.†	59
76	At Wichita State	69	82	Kansas at Manhattan, Kan.†	71
83	At Tulsa	50	69	California at San Francisco†	77
79	St. Louis	57	95	NYU at San Francisco†	71
90	At Bradley	91	*Holiday Festival		
61	At Duquesne	58	†NCAA Tournament		
64	The Citadel	43			
96	Drake	61			

Robertson during game action against North Carolina State in December 1958: N.C. State's John Richter grabs the rebound (left) and Lou Pucillo shoots over Robertson (right) as Carl Bouldin (34) watches.

Added Lapchick: "He's oil-slick. The pros here tonight have got to be gasping."

The New York press, never particularly quick to sing the praises of an outsider, could hardly contain itself.

New York Post sportswriter Gene Roswell, having caught Oscar's Garden party, wrote:

"Looking for the perfect basketball player? Oscar Robertson is your man, the 19-year-old Cincinnati soph who took the Garden apart and threw the pieces away last night.

"Greater than Tom Gola...than Guy Rodgers...than Wilt Chamberlain. These were the names that toppled after one glimpse of the kid who has been the rage of the Midwest since his high school days in Indianapolis.

"One glimpse is enough for anyone who ever has seen a basketball bounce...."

Columnist Jimmy Cannon, commenting on New York fans' introduction to the greatness of the Big O, remarked: "They knew right away, soon as the kid handled the ball. It was the way he dribbled, crouching, shielding the ball with his body. There was the quickness of his hands, the agility of his body...They knew, and most of them will never forget it because this was a big night...Not many were there either, but as Oscar Robertson's legend increases, the liars will put themselves in the Garden on the big night of Thursday, January 9."

Robertson had three other scoring binges in the 50s during his sophomore season, a year in which Cincinnati won 25 of 28 games. Any NCAA-title hopes the Bearcats may have had, though, died in a Midwest Regional semifinal game in Lawrence, Kan., when Cincinnati fell to Kansas State, 83-80, in overtime. Robertson, Dierking and Stevens, who scored 61 of the Bearcats' points, all fouled out against the Wildcats.

When the Bearcats arrived in San Francisco for the 1960 Final Four, Davis (holding white coat), Robertson and Smith (right) led them off the plane.

The NCAA Tournament appearance in 1958 was the first ever for Cincinnati, a three-time National Invitation Tournament participant in the 1950s. Clearly, Oscar Robertson was taking the Bearcats places.

Robertson didn't just do as he pleased, however —although it probably seemed that way to most observers. He conceded the defenses grew tougher with each season he was in college, as coaches devised more ways to contain him.

"They did everything," Oscar said. "Double-teams, triple-teams, diamonds, boxes, all kinds of zones. But that's what made basketball what it is, those coaches coming up with new defenses."

And if the defenses weren't enough, it seemed to Robertson that referees had become overly intrigued by his moves. He recalled officials watching him intently as he warmed up. They would go to his coach and remark that some of Robertson's moves seemed to constitute traveling.

Another major minus in Cincinnati's scheme of things was the loss of guard Spud Hornsby from the team. Hornsby, a sparkplug-type who had averaged 5.1 points as a sophomore in 1957-58, got married, a violation of team rules that forced him to leave the squad. To Robertson, the loss of Hornsby was a key element that hurt Cincinnati's championship aspirations the next two seasons.

None of this, however, stopped Robertson from

sparking Cincinnati to the Final Four in 1959, the school's greatest level of basketball achievement to that point. While the Bearcats had lost frontcourt firepower with the departure of the 6-10 Dierking and Stevens (who combined for 26.5 points per game in 1957-58), guards Ralph Davis and Mike Mendenhall stepped to the fore offensively in 1958-59. Davis notched 15.5 points per game that season and Mendenhall scored at a 13.5 clip, giving sizable support to Robertson, who notched 32.6 points per outing.

Despite the absence of a big man, the Bearcats lost only three regular-season games (two of them in the racially hostile environment of the Dixie Classic in Raleigh, N.C.), won a heated battle with Bradley for the Missouri Valley Conference championship and rolled into the NCAA Tournament.

Then, just as the Bearcats prepared to enter post-season play in March 1959, Mendenhall was declared academically ineligible. Accordingly, Robertson found himself faced with even more of the team burden, but his inspired play lifted the Bearcats past Texas Christian and Kansas State in the Midwest Regional. Robertson had totals of 58 points and 27 rebounds against the Horned Frogs and Wildcats.

At the Final Four, Cincinnati encountered the great defensive master, Pete Newell, and his California team led by 6-10 Darrall Imhoff. "We didn't have any size," Robertson said. "We played well and did the best we could. All of us were about 6-5. We didn't do a bad job."

Cincinnati managed a 33-29 halftime lead against the Golden Bears, but Cal stormed back for a 64-58 victory (and went on to win the national championship against West Virginia). Like everyone else, California focused on Robertson.

"I thought we played excellent defense," Newell said. "We made Oscar work like the dickens for the ball. We made him bring the ball up, and we did really a good job of defensive rotation. We tried to deny Oscar the ball. If we're going to get beat, we wanted those other guys to beat us."

Robertson wound up making only five of 16 field-goal attempts against the Bears' harassing defense. While "held" to 19 points, he did his usual yeoman's service on the boards by collecting 19 rebounds.

"Everywhere Oscar went, we would throw a second guy at him," Newell said. "They were worried about our press, but we really just faked the press because we wanted Oscar to bring the ball up the court. There was no way we could steal the ball from Oscar, but we pecked at him in what I call our 'coward press.' We looked like we were pressing, but mostly we were making them worry.

"When Oscar got to midcourt, he'd give up the ball to the guard and move to the forward's spot. Then we denied him the return pass. We beat them because we just happened to have the style to handle their club."

Newell said he waited for the last minute before the game to make his defensive assignments. "I had a player named Rob Dalton," the coach said. "He was about 6-3, and he looked like the results of an X-ray. On a clear day, you could see right through him, but he was really a competitive kid. Really an excellent athlete, but he didn't have a very imposing physique. We always played man-to-man defense and, before a game, I might ask one of my guards how he would play the center or ask a center how he would play the small forward. They might get switched to another player on defense, and I wanted them to be aware of that.

"Anyway, just before the game I went over the assignments and the last player was Oscar. Well, Oscar was *the* player in college basketball. He was in every magazine that had anything to do with sports, and he had set all kinds of records and was truly one of the all-time great players. I called Rob 'Thunderbird,' because he was the only kid I knew rich enough to own a Thunderbird. So I said, 'Thunderbird, I'm going to give you Oscar.' And I can see him tense up; this is what he wanted. So we get out before the game, and you know how players shake hands and introduce themselves, my name is Smith and the other kid says he's Jones or whatever. Well, Bobby walked up to Oscar before the game and put his hand out and said, 'My name is Dalton, what's yours?' "

While Newell and the pesky Dalton had been effective in slowing Robertson, most opposing coaches and players weren't. As pro guard Dick Barnett once explained, "If you give Oscar a 12-foot shot, he'll work on you until he's got a 10-foot shot. Give him 10 and he wants eight. Give him eight, and he wants six. Give him six, he wants four. Give him

four, he wants two. Give him two, you know what he wants? That's right, baby, he wants a layup."

New York University Coach Lou Rossini once summed up the situation this way: "Put your four best men on Oscar. Then tell your fifth man to cover his teammates. That might stop him."

The next season, 1959-60, featured the best of Robertson's three teams at Cincinnati.

Davis gave the Bearcats an offensive threat on the wing. A good passer and a man capable of running the fast break with confidence, Davis, a senior, was paired at guard with junior Carl Bouldin.

"Carl was a very smart basketball player," Robertson said, "but I think he could have been more aggressive. He had a good shot and could handle the ball."

Robertson would have preferred to play in the backcourt himself.

"I could have done better as a guard," Oscar said. But Robertson admired and respected Smith, the kind of coach who listened to his players. Robertson played forward without complaining and saved his backcourt duties for the pros.

Robertson also would have preferred more playing time for senior forward Larry Willey, who teamed with junior forward Bob Wiesenhahn to give the Bearcats some inside strength. Willey wasn't a natural athlete, but he could have been better with more playing time, Robertson maintained.

The real difference for 1959-60 was that the Bearcats once again had a big man, although an inexperienced one. Paul Hogue, a 6-9 bull of a sophomore from Knoxville, Tenn., had moved up to the varsity. While he would become an integral part of back-to-back NCAA championship teams in the post-Robertson era, Hogue found himself undergoing a learning experience in '59-'60. Nevertheless,

1960 CINCINNATI
Head Coach—George Smith   Final Record—28-2

Player	Pos.	Hgt.	Wgt.	Cl.	G	FG	FGA	Pct.	FT.	FTA	Pct.	Reb.	Pts.	Avg.
Oscar Robertson	F	6-5	198	Sr.	30	369	701	.526	273	361	.756	424	1011	33.7
Ralph Davis	G	6-4	180	Sr.	30	182	364	.500	46	70	.657	60	410	13.7
Paul Hogue	C	6-9	240	So.	30	152	264	.576	63	130	.485	331	367	12.2
Larry Willey	F	6-6	210	Sr.	30	98	157	.624	46	71	.648	145	242	8.1
Bob Wiesenhahn	F	6-4	215	Jr.	23	70	157	.446	32	50	.640	156	172	7.5
Carl Bouldin	G	6-1	166	Jr.	30	72	160	.450	31	48	.646	54	175	5.8
Sandy Pomerantz	F	6-6	195	So.	26	37	74	.500	20	34	.588	48	94	3.6
Tom Sizer	G	6-2	180	So.	27	22	57	.386	9	17	.529	24	53	2.0
Mel Landfried	C	6-8	215	Jr.	12	8	21	.381	5	10	.500	30	21	1.8
Jim Calhoun	G	6-0	175	So.	19	15	35	.429	3	9	.333	16	33	1.7
John Bryant	G	6-3	170	Jr.	22	6	18	.333	3	5	.600	16	15	0.7
Ron Reis	C	6-10	230	So.	10	2	9	.222	1	6	.167	7	5	0.5
Fred Dierking	F	6-6	210	So.	14	2	8	.250	0	5	.000	26	4	0.3
Team												185		
Cincinnati					30	1035	2025	.511	532	816	.652	1522	2602	86.7
Opponents					30	738	1924	.384	466	693	.672	1165	1942	64.7

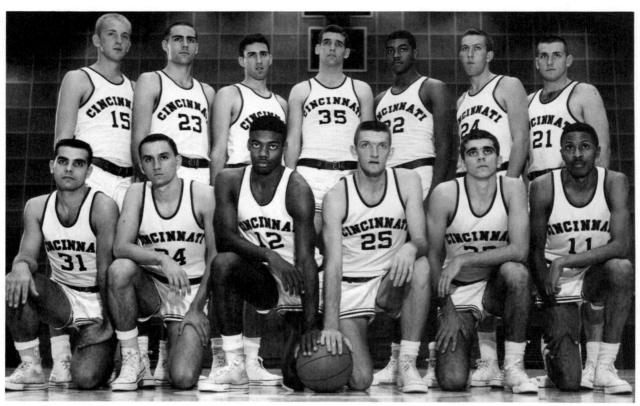

The 1959-60 Cincinnati Bearcats: Front row (left to right)—Jim Calhoun, Bouldin, Robertson, Davis, Tom Sizer, John Bryant. Second row—Fred Dierking, Larry Willey, Sandy Pomerantz, Ron Reis, Paul Hogue, Mel Landfried, Wiesenhahn.

the 240-pounder was a force.

"He probably wouldn't agree," Robertson said, "but his sophomore year at Cincinnati was probably Hogue's best. I think he learned the game of basketball. He learned the position, the fundamentals of playing inside. He was a big guy. They couldn't push him out of the post."

With this group, the Bearcats suffered only one regular-season defeat, a single-point loss to a Bradley team that finished fourth in both wire-service polls. At 25-1, Cincinnati embarked on the 1960 NCAA Tournament trail and promptly dispatched DePaul and Kansas in the Midwest Regional. Coach Ray Meyer's Blue Demons fell by 40 points; Harp's Jayhawks succumbed by 11.

Again, as in 1959, the Cincinnati Bearcats were two victories from a national championship. Again, as in '59, California and its crafty defense stood as a semifinal obstacle in the Final Four.

Pressured by the Golden Bears' tenacious defense, Robertson had another long night. This time, he sank only four of 16 floor shots—his teammates were a combined 22 for 42—and Cal carved out a workmanlike 77-69 triumph.

"You have to be able to put the ball in the basket, and we didn't do it," Robertson said. "We missed a lot of easy shots—five-foot shots around the basket."

The Bearcats went on to beat New York Universi-

ty for third place in the NCAA Tournament, the second straight such finish for Robertson and company. Overall, this 1959-60 unit won 28 of 30 games, outscored its opponents by an average of 22 points per game and had a season field-goal percentage of .511 compared with the opposition's mark of .384.

In averaging 86.7 points per game, Cincinnati got 33.7 points an outing from Robertson, 13.7 from Davis and 12.2 from newcomer Hogue. Two Bearcats were double-figure rebounders, with Robertson boasting a 14.1 average and Hogue pulling down 11 rebounds per game.

Bearcats aide Jucker, named Cincinnati head coach after the season, remembers Robertson in the locker room after the 1960 NCAA Tournament semifinals.

"He was very discouraged," Jucker said. "Anybody would feel the same way if you played 30 to 40 minutes of basketball with three or four guys in your face all the time."

Robertson, however, says he was far from devastated.

"I wasn't that upset about the loss," said Oscar, who went on to a sensational pro career. "We did the best we could. At least we got there (the Final Four). A lot of teams didn't."

A lot of teams didn't have the likes of Oscar Robertson, either, a complete player if there ever was one.

SEVENTEEN

From Agony To Ecstasy

GEORGETOWN

**1983-84
1984-85**

Like many of college basketball's finest teams, the 1983-84 Georgetown Hoyas had a greatness born of disappointment.

Coach John Thompson's team had suffered a painful loss to North Carolina in the 1982 NCAA championship game, a contest in which Patrick Ewing, completing an impressive freshman season, stood out for the Hoyas. Georgetown then struggled through a rebuilding season during Ewing's sophomore year, all the while carrying the sting of that defeat to North Carolina.

"Winning is a big satisfaction, and losing is a big disappointment," Thompson said when reflecting on the '82 setback, a 63-62 defeat in which an errant pass in the final seconds killed the Hoyas' chances. "The higher you climb, the more you feel the disappointment when you don't get it. But you know you've accomplished an awful lot to be one of the last two teams. The guy who loses on that last night feels just as bad as the guy who loses the first night.

"And he might even feel worse because he was so close. I can never forget the expression on Ewing's face after the North Carolina game. It's a deep pain, but everybody who tries to accomplish something big takes the chance of a big disappointment."

Thompson used the agony of March 1982 as the motivation to drive his team to NCAA glory in April 1984. For Thompson, the power of disappointment was a lesson he had learned years before while growing up in Washington, D.C., in a family struggling to keep above the poverty line. His father, John Thompson Sr., worked long hours for low pay at a tile company. His mother did domestic work—washing, ironing and cleaning—in other people's households.

Young John had a difficult time in the parochial school he attended. He failed "intelligence" tests and was labeled a slow learner. One teacher even suggested that he was retarded.

As Thompson's frustration deepened, his marginally acceptable behavior slid to the point that the parochial school finally dismissed him.

From there, he was sent to the then-segregated District of Columbia public schools and was placed in the sixth-grade room of a veteran educator, Sametta Jackson. She took an interest in John and was surprised to learn that he was a sharp thinker. He just couldn't read. And he couldn't see very well.

Once he was fitted with glasses, Thompson responded quickly to Mrs. Jackson's efforts. Still, by the end of the school year, she knew he wasn't prepared for the seventh grade. Accordingly, she held him back a year for additional reading instruction.

The teacher's interest proved a turning point in the life of John Thompson. He moved on to surprising success, first as a schoolboy basketball star, then as a center at Providence College. But the real pleasure in his life wasn't directly related to athletics. He majored in economics at Providence and also worked with special-education classes in the Providence schools. In the spring of his senior year, the student congress at Providence voted him "The Outstanding Senior." What's more, Thompson was named to Who's Who in American Colleges and Universities.

After leaving Providence, Thompson went on to play two seasons with the Boston Celtics, for whom he served as a backup center to the great Bill Russell. Thompson could have extended his pro career —he was an expansion-draft choice of the Chicago Bulls in the spring of 1966—but he wanted to be a teacher. So he did something that few players have opted to do—he left pro basketball on his own. Without a job, he returned to Washington and eventually wound up as basketball coach at St. Anthony's, a small, underfinanced Catholic high school.

Thompson spent his spare time combing the Washington playgrounds for talent. His efforts paid off. He built St. Anthony's into a basketball powerhouse, winning 128 games and losing only 22 in six seasons.

His record for mixing strong academics and discipline with on-court success was solid enough to attract the attention of Georgetown officials in the spring of 1972 when they were looking for a young coach to turn their program around. The Hoyas had just finished a 3-23 season. Thompson, 30 years old, had turned down other offers, but he took this one. At Georgetown, he would have the opportunity to create the kind of successful program that he had established at St. Anthony's and, obviously, exhibit his coaching skills on a higher level.

It wasn't easy, but by the 1974-75 season Thompson had directed Georgetown into the NCAA Tournament. The appearance in the showcase event was only the second in history for the Hoyas. From that point, Thompson raised the level of competition a season at a time. Then, in the winter of 1980-81, he and his longtime friend, Georgetown assistant Bill Stein, landed prize recruit Patrick Ewing.

A 7-footer, Ewing had starred at a Boston-area high school, Rindge and Latin in Cambridge, after coming to the United States from Jamaica at age 12. Colleges across the country showed intense interest in him. Thompson's special mix of academic discipline and competitive basketball impressed Ewing and his mother, and Patrick signed with Georgetown.

The next season, 1981-82, with Ewing at center and Eric (Sleepy) Floyd standing out at guard, the Hoyas won 30 games and played for the national championship at the Superdome in New Orleans. With 15 seconds remaining and North Carolina ahead by one point in the NCAA tourney final, Georgetown put the ball into play. The Hoyas' hopes for setting up a possible game-winning shot were dashed, however, when sophomore guard Fred Brown threw the ball directly to Tar Heels star James Worthy.

After a rebuilding year—the Hoyas won 22 games in the 1982-83 campaign while reloading—Thompson's troops returned with a vengeance in 1983-84. It was quickly apparent that Thompson had put together some kind of juggernaut. He had the intimidating Ewing, a 240-pound junior center, and freshmen Reggie Williams and Michael Graham

along the front line, sophomore David Wingate as the shooting guard and second-year man Michael Jackson at the point. Actually, senior guard Brown drew regular starting assignments in Thompson's class-has-its-privileges approach, but swingman Williams found himself in the game before too many minutes had elapsed.

Additionally, junior frontcourt players Bill Martin and Ralph Dalton were key role players for this Georgetown club and senior guard Gene Smith was cast as the defensive specialist. Plus, Brown, back in action after missing nearly half of the 1982-83 season because of a knee injury, added a veteran's wisdom. If any of Thompson's players flagged in their desire to win the title, Brown's very presence would serve as a reminder of the task ahead.

From the fierceness of the team's full-court pressure to the intimidation of Ewing's shot-blocking, the Hoyas were a defensive team. Thompson's tenure with the Celtics had brought him close to Red Auerbach and, like the Celtics' great coach, he had come to believe in defense.

"Under adverse circumstances or real happy circumstances, you have to sustain a certain level of concentration," Thompson said of his philosophy. "You can go your lowest in certain situations, and you go your highest in other situations, but you have to maintain a certain level of concentration to win consistently. At Georgetown, we emphasize defense because I think that you can sustain a certain amount of consistency with defense that you might not be able to get with offense. It's easier to get five guys, year after year, to play consistent defense than it is to get guys who can shoot outside or run fast and make layups and those kinds of things."

Charged by this defensive intensity, the Hoyas bolted through the regular season with a 26-3 record and then dispatched Providence, St. John's and Syracuse in the Big East Tournament.

Quite often, Ewing was likened to Bill Russell, a comparison that Thompson sought to play down. But after the big center had dominated the action in the league tourney, even Thompson was moved to link the two. "He's the best I've seen at that (blocking shots) since Bill Russell," Thompson said of Ewing. "You don't teach that. It's just effort."

Just as important in the Georgetown mix were the first-year corner men. Williams, out of Dunbar High School in Baltimore, was a silky-smooth scorer and a startlingly effective rebounder despite his slight frame. Graham, on the other hand, became the Hoyas' controversial enforcer.

Thompson, not one to heap praise upon freshmen, couldn't contain himself when asked about the impact of the 6-7, 185-pound Williams.

"He's just so damn flexible," Thompson said. "He can play four positions out there for you. He handles the ball well, passes it well.... He's as versatile a player as we've ever had here." The coach's remarks

The powerful presence of Georgetown Coach John Thompson has always been reflected by his Hoyas on the basketball court.

had come five games into the season.

"He's going to score points, no matter where you play him," Thompson added. "You might not even notice that he's scoring a lot, but he is."

Bob Wade, Williams' high school mentor and later coach at Maryland, supported Thompson's viewpoint.

"When he (Williams) was in junior high school, he played pickup games with my friends and me, and he was the main scorer back then," Wade said. "He's always had a natural feel for the game."

Smith, the Hoyas' captain, said Williams "makes the game look easy. I have to work hard to get anything done. Reggie can just do it."

Graham, on the other hand, made the game look rough. He sported a shaved head and had a habit of woofing at opponents, a tactic that brought increasing criticism for Georgetown. Most of all, he played with arms flailing and a scowl on his face. Thompson wasn't concerned about Graham's on-court demeanor; instead, it was the 6-9 forward's inattention to classroom detail that worried the coach.

Soon, it was Southern Methodist's slowdown tactics that proved troublesome. Boasting 29 victories in 32 games, the Hoyas entered the NCAA Tournament's West Regional and immediately encountered an upset-bent SMU team. The Mustangs executed a delay game with considerable success, achieving a 34-34 tie in the late going. Georgetown's Smith, a mediocre foul shooter, was at the free-throw line with a one-and-one. In the huddle before the shot, Ewing told his teammates, "We're not going home, and that's it."

When Smith missed the free throw, Ewing muscled in for the rebound and follow-up field goal, giving Georgetown a 36-34 lead. After a Jackson foul shot and an SMU basket at the buzzer, the game ended, 37-36, Hoyas. Thompson's crew went on to oust Nevada-Las Vegas and Dayton and claimed a spot at the Final Four in Seattle.

After Houston slipped past Virginia in the first national semifinal game, a Kentucky team featuring the Twin Towers of Melvin Turpin and Sam Bowie bolted to a 27-15 lead against Georgetown. With Ewing on the bench after being whistled for three fouls in the first 11 minutes, the Hoyas jump-started their usually oppressive full-court press and narrowed the gap to 29-22 by halftime.

Unbelievably, Kentucky, which also had a stand-out frontcourt player in Kenny Walker, made only 9.1 percent of its second-half shots and scored a mere 11 points in the second 20 minutes of action. Georgetown's pressure defense had suffocated the Wildcats.

Bill Foster, longtime college coach who had just been named to take over a revived program at Miami (Fla.), spoke for the throng of coaches on hand for the Final Four. "No one had ever seen anything like it," Foster said. "Incredible."

Intimidating Patrick Ewing vaulted the Hoyas into the national spotlight in a four-year stretch that produced one national title and two near-misses.

Slick, silky-smooth Reggie Williams was a versatile performer who was equally adept as a passer, ballhandler or scorer.

Swingman David Wingate was an excellent shooter who finished second to Ewing on the team's 1983-84 and 1984-85 scoring charts.

Most stunned of all was Joe B. Hall, the Kentucky coach. "I can't explain it," he said afterward. "What happened is beyond me."

Kentucky failed to score on its first 14 possessions of the second half. For the half, the Wildcats made three of 33 field-goal attempts. Kentucky's starters missed all 21 floor shots they attempted after intermission.

"They took everything away from me," Turpin lamented after Georgetown had completed a 53-40 triumph. "Every time I turned around they were in my face."

Thompson, while saying that memories of 1982 helped ignite the Hoyas' comeback against Kentucky, acknowledged other factors. "Everybody had talked about Kentucky as one of the best teams ever assembled because of their size and talent," he said. "Our kids were just stubborn, and that might have been the most satisfying victory I've ever had in terms of execution and determination. Those kids were stubborn, and they worked and made a commitment and did the things that you wanted them to do."

On the heels of such an emotional victory, might the championship game against Houston seem anticlimactic for Georgetown? "That scared me," Thompson said. "I knew what those kids had accomplished in winning the Kentucky game. They played tremendous defense, they worked like hell, and really did the job. And then we lost Gene Smith (because of a leg injury) for the game with Houston. I said to myself, 'This is going to be tough.'"

Thompson identified with Smith and used his verve to inspire the team.

"Gene had been offered scholarships to Morgan State and to Georgetown," Thompson said. "I had to go in and talk to him (during recruiting) and tell him that he would never be a starter at Georgetown, that I wanted him for a special purpose. Then the kid worked his behind off, and he was the person who spearheaded our defense. He was just hard-nosed and tough. He was like the storybook kid who pulled himself up by his bootstraps among all the All-Americas.

"Here's a kid who by rights didn't belong in the Final Four, but who fought his way up, and I always respected him for that. But to be very honest, I'm not certain that, in a weird way, losing Gene might not have helped us more than it hurt us because it returned extra fear and caution. Had we not lost Gene, complacency might have been there a little bit more."

The Hoyas were anything but complacent for the championship match. Houston jumped to a 10-2 lead, all right, but Georgetown rebounded for a 40-30 halftime edge and rolled to an 84-75 victory. Williams, who finished with 19 points, provided critical scoring down the stretch. Four other Hoyas scored in double figures. Ewing, with 10 points and nine

Senior guard Gene Smith (left) came off the bench to work his defensive wizardry for the 1983-84 Hoyas, while Ewing (right) clogged up the middle like few centers before him.

Season Results

1983-84 (34-3)

71	At Hawaii-Hilo	42	87	Connecticut	62
97	At Hawaii-Hilo	35	78	Seton Hall	54
91	Morgan State	38	67	Brigham Young	51
84	St. Francis (Pa.)	61	59	At Villanova	46
82	St. Leo	50	59	At Providence	38
61	At DePaul	63	71	St. John's	75
97	South Carolina State	67	83	Boston Col. at Sp'f'ld, Mass.	70
80	American	62	71	Pittsburgh	52
53	Western Kentucky	41	88	Syracuse	71
82	Marshall at Las Vegas°	71	70	Providence at New York†	50
69	At Las Vegas° (OT)	67	79	St. John's at New York†	68
81	Connecticut at Hartford	69	82	Syracuse at New York†	71
74	At Seton Hall	63	37	SMU at Pullman, Wash.‡	36
74	Monmouth	54	62	UNLV at Los Angeles‡	48
63	Villanova (2 OT)	65	61	Dayton at Los Angeles‡	49
80	Providence	76	53	Kentucky at Seattle‡	40
83	At St. John's	61	84	Houston at Seattle‡	75
92	Boston College	83	°Las Vegas Classic		
63	At Pittsburgh	52	†Big East Conference Tournament		
80	At Syracuse	67	‡NCAA Tournament		

1984-85 (35-3)

81	At Hawaii-Hilo	47	71	Florida Southern	39
74	At Hawaii-Loa	45	78	At Boston College	68
80	S. Connecticut	46	57	Villanova	50
76	St. Leo	56	87	At Providence	73
82	Nevada-Las Vegas	46	70	Pittsburgh	46
86	American	64	68	Connecticut at Hartford	47
77	DePaul	57	85	At St. John's	69
89	Morgan State	62	90	Syracuse	63
69	At New Mexico	61	93	Connecticut at New York†	62
77	Tennessee at Puerto Rico°	64	74	Syracuse at New York†	65
61	N. C. A&T at Puerto Rico°	56	92	St. John's at New York†	80
73	Seton Hall	56	68	Lehigh at Hartford‡	43
82	Boston College (OT)	80	63	Temple at Hartford‡	46
90	At Seton Hall	70	65	Loyola (Md.) at Providence‡	53
52	At Villanova (OT)	50	60	Ga. Tech at Providence‡	54
85	Providence	44	77	St. John's at Lexington‡	59
65	At Pittsburgh	53	64	Villanova at Lexington‡	66
79	Connecticut	66	°Copa Navidad Tournament		
65	St. John's	66	†Big East Conference Tournament		
63	At Syracuse	65	‡NCAA Tournament		
56	Arkansas	39			

rebounds in the title game, was named the Most Outstanding Player.

Graham, who had scoring and rebounding averages of 4.5 and 3.9 entering the Final Four, totaled 22 points (on 11-of-15 shooting from the floor) and 11 rebounds against Kentucky and Houston. A starter 17 times in 1983-84, Graham did his damage in Seattle while coming off the bench in place of Dalton.

Thompson was happiest for senior Fred Brown.

"It was a real special feeling," the coach said of the championship, "because I always thought that his pass in the '82 final was taken out of perspective. I always felt bad that he would have to carry that with him. So it was like a tremendous relief when we won it. I grabbed him, and he and I just felt, you know, that it's over, that we had come back and won."

Houston's Olajuwon was impressed, that's for sure.

"They do everything a great team should do," Olajuwon said. "They don't care who takes the shots, who scores. That's the difference. They're not a selfish team."

One of the first people out of the stands to join the celebration was Thompson's old Celtics teammate, Russell.

"You know, I have always had a great deal of respect for Russ because I thought he was one of the most intelligent human beings I had ever been around in sports," Thompson said. "He combined

Point-guard duties were in the capable hands of Michael Jackson.

his ability with intelligence, and I thought that see-ing him right at the end was just the thing that topped it all off. Here's a guy who's coming over to congratulate me, and this was sort of like my little day.

"It was a tremendous compliment for me to see him make the effort to be there, because you know Russ runs away from crowds and fanfares. I knew that he had to be very happy for me if he would come out of the stands and get involved in all of that."

The sports media machine immediately began talking dynasty. "Georgetown has assembled the greatest amount of talent in college basketball since the Wooden era," wrote analyst Al McGuire, "and for the first time in years I think there is an odds-on chance for a repeat."

Over the summer, however, Thompson decided that Graham wasn't taking his studies seriously enough. He decided to sit down the power forward for the 1984-85 season so the young man could con-centrate on academics. Rather than do that, howev-er, Graham left the program. The loss of the intimi-dator was a blow.

Still, if a team was ever favored to win again, Georgetown was. The big reason, of course, was Ewing, who was winning rave reviews throughout the basketball community.

"The first thing I think about with Ewing is de-fense," said Joey Meyer, about to replace his father Ray as DePaul coach. "The second thing I think

Georgetown's enforcer in 1983-84 was Michael Graham, a powerful 6-9 forward with a menacing, no-nonsense look.

Two Georgetown seniors, Fred Brown (left, left photo) and Gene Smith, pose with the Hoyas' 1984 championship trophy. Forward Bill Martin (24) battles for a rebound in the '84 title game victory over Houston.

about is intimidation—not just defensively, but in his personality. He has that . . . never-smiling face. He makes sure you know he's all business out there."

North Carolina State Coach Jim Valvano said Ewing possessed "that mental toughness—he looks like he wants to beat your brains out."

Rod Thorn, then general manager of the Chicago Bulls of the National Basketball Association, said: "I just love his intensity. A lot of players with that kind of ability don't always play hard. Ewing never stops. He plays with a lot of heart."

While Ewing and company clearly were proving a handful on the court, they were proving equally difficult to deal with off the arena floor. Thompson by now had become a master of isolating his players from the media. He frequently kept his team in out-of-the-way hotels, restricted public access to his players and held practice sessions behind closed doors. Plus, in some people's minds, he did little to answer the charges of roughhouse tactics often leveled at his team. To many observers, Georgetown had developed a kind of "us-vs.-them" mentality that resulted in a public perception of what became known as "Hoya Paranoia."

Thompson, though, responded by saying that his players were merely young men playing a game and that they were subject to undue pressure exerted by adults.

And he had his supporters. Ewing was one of them.

"If I had gone (to school) somewhere else, I might have been exploited," said Ewing, who as a relative newcomer to this country had special academic needs upon entering college. "He (Thompson) is just like a father figure to me—more than just a coach. I think he understands me, and there is no question in my mind that he's the best coach in the world for me. . . ."

Tom McElroy, then communications director of the Big East Conference, saw reasons for Thompson's methods.

"I think John likes the mystique about him and his team," McElroy said. "I think he plays on it. I think he likes them being perceived as intimidating and he likes to keep you off guard."

Big East Commissioner Dave Gavitt was baffled by the criticism hurled at Thompson and the Georgetown program.

"Why don't people write about how John Thompson gets great high school players like Reggie Williams to come in and be so unselfish?" Gavitt wondered. "Or how he gets his team to play with such great intensity. That's the real story. Not where the team stays."

The Hoyas shrugged off all the barbs and rolled across the collegiate basketball landscape in 1984-85, finishing atop both major wire-service polls. They lost only two regular-season games—the first by one point (to St. John's) and, two days later, the second by two points (to Syracuse).

The fact that league rivals dealt Georgetown its lone two defeats gave strong evidence of the strength of the Big East; that three conference teams —Georgetown, St. John's and Villanova—won berths in the Final Four gave conclusive evidence of the league's stature. It marked the first time that three teams from one conference had reached the big event. Joining the Hoyas, Redmen and Wildcats in Lexington, Ky., were the Memphis State Tigers of the Metro Conference.

Thompson's cast was basically the same as it had been the previous season, with the only major change being the insertion of Martin into the lineup in place of Graham. With Smith and Brown having departed, freshman swingman Perry McDonald became a valuable addition off the bench and junior Horace Broadnax provided a lift in the backcourt for the second straight season.

Georgetown thrashed Lou Carnesecca's St. John's team in one semifinal, while Rollie Massimino's up-start Villanova club maneuvered past Memphis State in the other. Accordingly, the Hoyas seemed a good bet to repeat as NCAA champions; after all, Villanova had gone into the Final Four with 10 losses (two more than the other three teams combined). It was said that the Wildcats would have to play a perfect game—or close to it—to win.

Nearly perfect the Wildcats were. They made 78.6 percent of their field-goal attempts overall, an NCAA Tournament record, and sank 90 percent of their second-half floor attempts. It took that kind of an effort to upend Georgetown, and such an incredible performance was barely enough against the likes of the Hoyas. Villanova 66, Georgetown 64.

"I thought we would win it," Thompson said. "You know, I definitely thought we'd win it. But

1984 GEORGETOWN
Head Coach—John Thompson   Final Record—34-3

Player	Pos.	Hgt.	Wgt.	Cl.	G	FG	FGA	Pct.	FT	FTA	Pct.	Reb.	Pts.	Avg.
Patrick Ewing	C	7-0	240	Jr.	37	242	368	.658	124	189	.656	371	608	16.4
David Wingate	G-F	6-5	180	So.	37	161	370	.435	93	129	.721	135	415	11.2
Michael Jackson	G	6-1	172	So.	31	115	226	.509	84	103	.816	52	314	10.1
Reggie Williams	G-F	6-7	185	Fr.	37	130	300	.433	76	99	.768	131	336	9.1
Bill Martin	F	6-7	202	Jr.	37	118	232	.509	93	132	.705	219	329	8.9
Michael Graham	F	6-9	210	Fr.	35	69	123	.561	34	74	.459	139	172	4.9
Horace Broadnax	G	6-1	185	So.	35	69	159	.434	29	34	.853	49	167	4.8
Gene Smith	G	6-2	190	Sr.	36	45	88	.511	42	71	.592	74	132	3.7
Fred Brown	G	6-5	208	Sr.	36	36	74	.486	42	65	.646	93	114	3.2
Ralph Dalton	F-C	6-11	240	Jr.	36	37	65	.569	27	47	.574	79	101	2.8
Victor Morris	F	6-9	220	So.	16	10	26	.385	9	15	.600	21	29	1.8
Clifton Dairsow	F	6-7	225	Fr.	18	11	20	.550	9	19	.474	26	31	1.7
Team												92		
Georgetown					37	1043	2051	.509	662	977	.678	1481	2748	74.3
Opponents					37	799	2025	.395	545	821	.664	1129	2143	57.9

1985 GEORGETOWN
Head Coach—John Thompson   Final Record—35-3

Player	Pos.	Hgt.	Wgt.	Cl.	G	FG	FGA	Pct.	FT	FTA	Pct.	Reb.	Pts.	Avg.
Patrick Ewing	C	7-0	240	Sr.	37	220	352	.625	102	160	.638	341	542	14.6
David Wingate	G-F	6-5	185	Jr.	38	191	395	.484	91	132	.689	135	473	12.4
Bill Martin	F	6-7	215	Sr.	38	196	361	.543	76	117	.650	234	468	12.3
Reggie Williams	G-F	6-7	180	So.	35	168	332	.506	80	106	.755	200	416	11.9
Michael Jackson	G	6-2	180	Jr.	36	104	234	.444	55	75	.733	58	263	7.3
Horace Broadnax	G	6-1	190	Jr.	38	85	197	.431	29	44	.659	65	199	5.2
Perry McDonald	G-F	6-4	190	Fr.	38	64	158	.405	39	86	.453	97	167	4.4
Ralph Dalton	F-C	6-11	240	Sr.	36	39	64	.609	38	59	.644	95	116	3.2
Grady Mateen	C	6-10	210	Fr.	31	30	58	.517	24	40	.600	73	84	2.7
Ronnie Highsmith	F	6-8	225	Fr.	24	23	41	.561	9	22	.409	52	55	2.3
Kevin Floyd	G	6-4	185	Fr.	22	9	23	.391	14	21	.667	18	32	1.5
Tyrone Lockhart	G	5-10	155	So.	15	3	8	.375	3	4	.750	3	9	0.6
Team												133		
Georgetown					38	1132	2223	.509	560	866	.647	1504	2824	74.3
Opponents					38	833	2064	.404	512	733	.698	1160	2176	57.3

Thompson took his turn in the obligatory net-cutting ceremony that followed his team's 1984 NCAA championship-game victory.

the thing that irritated me most about it, and you know I don't say it in a negative sense but in an affectionate sense, is it's the damn Big East teams again. You're playing Louie, you're playing Rollie, and you're saying, 'Hey, I'd rather play anybody else.'

"You're happy that the league is doing well, but you don't want to get in the situation where you've played people two and three times and they keep coming back. I still feel that we had played them (the Wildcats) well; we played them three times and beat them twice. That was a great effort on their part. They shot the ball extremely well against a great defensive team and a confident team. But Villanova believed that it was good."

Thompson's teams featuring Patrick Ewing had won one national championship. They came close to winning three NCAA titles in four seasons. Despite any what-could-have-been reflections, the

Hoyas' greatness goes unquestioned. Sixty-nine victories over 75 games in the 1983-84 and 1984-85 seasons says it all.

Asked to provide a formula for success, Thompson said, "You have to have a system or a way of doing things that you believe is sound. You also have to have kids with ability, but ability alone is not enough. You have to have kids who have the cohesiveness and the willingness to believe in the system, who believe in the tradition that you've tried to establish, and who want to work toward your goals.

"You're not going to do it with kids who are just All-Americas, kids who have status but don't have togetherness. You need unity and a belief in what you're doing, and you've got to be a little stubborn."

Particularly when it comes to turning your disappointments into triumphs.

EIGHTEEN

Tar Heels Find Blue Heaven

NORTH CAROLINA

1981-82

In Chapel Hill, N.C., the ultimate state of mind is known as Blue Heaven. It takes hold whenever the North Carolina Tar Heels are bathed in that ineffable light of miracle known as the NCAA championship.

Blue Heaven first washed over the Carolina campus in 1957, when Frank McGuire coached the Tar Heels to a 32-0 record and their first national title. For the next 24 seasons, however, the otherwise blue Carolina skies slowly turned gray come NCAA Tournament time. The Heels advanced into the tournament 16 times, yet not once did they bask in that heavenly glow.

Like a good shepherd, McGuire had kept the program near the top following the Heels' 1957 title win, posting successive 19-7, 20-5, 18-6 and 19-4 records. Then came news that two of his players had been linked to college basketball's point-shaving scandal. McGuire departed after the 1960-61 season to coach in the National Basketball Association, and the Carolina program was left to the leadership of his 30-year-old assistant, Dean Smith.

Having played for Phog Allen's 1952 NCAA titlists at Kansas, Smith knew something about winning. He would guide North Carolina to more than 430 victories and six Final Four appearances in his first 20 seasons, through 1980-81.

But as fate would have it, the Tar Heels were destined to appear in four final series, and all came during the dynasty years of UCLA: in 1967, 1968 and 1969, when Lew Alcindor led the Bruin charges, and in 1972, the beginning of the Bill Walton era.

The frustration was extended in the 1977 title game, when Al McGuire worked his magic in his final game as Marquette's coach, and in 1981, when 19-year-old Isiah Thomas led Indiana to a convincing 63-50 victory over the Heels in the championship.

"I guess we can be like Penn State football," Smith mused following the Indiana setback. "Number 2 all the time."

Though he was once burned in effigy in his early years, Smith was genuinely idolized by the Carolina fans. He was a philosophical and innovative man, the father of the run-and-jump pressure defense and the Four Corners delay offense, which he described as "not a freeze, but a style which consumes time while drawing the opponent into defensive errors resulting in a score or foul shot."

His critics knocked the tactic as "stallball," but North Carolina was nevertheless a legitimate offensive power, averaging 82 points per game over Smith's first 20 seasons.

The Dean Smith system preached the team concept: passing, positioning and unselfishness ("the player with the good eight-foot shot *must* pass off to the player with the good five-foot shot," a former Tar Heel said, "and the player with the good five-foot shot *must* pass off to the player with the good two-foot shot"), but it was built on defense.

"The two questions we ask about every player who might come to Carolina," Smith once said, "are first, does he like to play defense, and second, is he quick enough to play defense?"

When Smith talked about his players, he most often mentioned the ones that played solid defense. And it was the players, or the school, he preferred to talk about, never himself. He despised the notion that he was obsessed with winning a national title.

In his 21st season as North Carolina coach, Dean Smith finally found Blue Heaven by winning the 1982 NCAA championship.

"We've never had the best team," he said. "I think if I'd thought we'd had the best team it would bother me, but that hasn't happened."

But with each missed opportunity, the pining among Carolina's supporters grew a bit louder. Sure, Smith could win games, but never the *right* ones. The Carolina faithful longed for Blue Heaven.

The 1981-82 season offered reason for hope. Despite the loss to graduation of Al Wood, their leading scorer and top outside shooter, the Tar Heels garnered the No. 1 ranking in both preseason wire-service polls. Carolina had relied heavily on forward James Worthy and two freshmen, center Sam Perkins and forward Matt Doherty, to advance to the 1981 championship game. All three were back, along with senior point guard Jimmy Black, who would be joined in the backcourt by a blue-chip recruit named Michael Jordan.

With these five starters, Carolina would carry Smith's team concept to near perfection. All five would average more than 35 minutes per game, and three—Worthy, Perkins and Jordan—would be future first-round NBA draft choices.

Jordan was still just a talented freshman guard, yet to soar into the realm of legend as perhaps the most electrifying player ever. He would be voted the Atlantic Coast Conference's Rookie of the Year, making an indelible impression with bursts of offensive improvisation and spectacular breakaway dunks, but he wasn't immune to growing pains.

"Mike could do more than he's doing offensively," Smith said at one point, "but he's sometimes afraid to invade Perkins' and Worthy's territory. He plays hard most of the time and is a good competitor, but occasionally he'll catch himself standing around out there."

It was Worthy and Perkins who made Carolina a force to be reckoned with inside, which was at the heart of the Dean Smith strategy. With the high-percentage shots located under the basket, the Heels had a pair of 6-foot-9 standouts who could soar and score.

Worthy was arguably the elite power forward on the college scene—an aggressive rebounder and outstanding ballhandler who parlayed his strength and mobility to become a devastating offensive force. A high school All-America from Gastonia, N.C., he would average 14.5 points and 7.4 rebounds per game in his Tar Heel career, passing up his final year of eligibility to become the first overall pick in the 1982 draft.

"Most people think Coach Smith put a leash on us and wouldn't let us just go out and play," Worthy said. "That's not true. He had a team-oriented system, but he didn't put any restraints on me. He took advantage of my individual talents."

Perkins was nearly Worthy's equal as an offensive weapon inside but excelled defensively, giving Smith his best scoring/rebounding/shot-blocking

James Worthy, an aggressive, mobile inside force, was a key figure in the Tar Heels' drive toward the 1982 national title.

center since Bob McAdoo. Indeed, Perkins still ranks as the Heels' leader in career rebounds and blocked shots, and is second only to Phil Ford in scoring.

Recruited out of New York, Perkins was playing only his fourth year of organized basketball when he was voted the 1981 ACC Rookie of the Year. At 6-9, he sometimes was lost in the shadow of such ACC giants as 7-4 Ralph Sampson at Virginia and 6-11 Thurl Bailey at North Carolina State. But when he stretched his 42-inch arms high into the air, his presence was unmistakable. "On defense, I might be standing 7-foot with my arms," he noted.

When opposing defenses tried to key on the two Carolina big men, the perimeter players spelled the

Lefthanded-shooting center Sam Perkins punctuated his solid offensive game with a strong defensive presence.

difference. Doherty, a good ballhandler and shooter, could work either inside or out as a swingman, and play aggressive defense at the other end.

"You can't ignore anyone on North Carolina's team," Alabama Coach Wimp Sanderson would say after his Tide succumbed to Carolina in the '82 NCAA Tournament. "We just did the best we could inside and gave up some shots on the perimeter. They just knocked them home."

As North Carolina stormed through its 1981-82 schedule, Smith conceded that this might be his best team ever. The Tar Heels fortunes dipped only slightly in midseason, when they were upset at home by a good Wake Forest team and lost to archrival Virginia on the road. Both Carolina and Sampson's Virginia finished 12-2 in the ACC standings, and the teams met in the conference tournament final, where Smith used the Four Corners stall to gain his ninth ACC title, 47-45.

As much as any single event, that game was a factor in the adoption of a shot clock in college basketball. The Tar Heels held the ball for the better part of the last 13 minutes and did not attempt a field goal in the final 7:31.

"You have that right—to make big people come out and chase you, and I think there's something to that," Smith said.

"We won. That's the bottom line," added Doherty. "We'd do anything to win. We wanted them to come out and play the ball."

Carolina relied on similar tactics to draw Villanova out of its zone in the NCAA regional finals. Quarterbacking the Tar Heel offense from the point, Black soon had Villanova on the run, breaking open a tight game and sending North Carolina to its seventh Final Four under Smith.

Black was the unsung playmaker for the Heels yet sometimes criticized as their weak link. Certainly, he was no scoring machine, averaging only 5.7 points per game over four seasons. But when he concluded his career, Black had played in more games at North Carolina than any other player and earned Smith's admiration for his defense, passing and leadership.

"Jimmy and I think a lot alike," Smith said. "It's like having a coach out there on the floor. I'll stand up and get ready to call something, and I'll look out there and Jimmy's already doing it."

Black didn't harbor any resentment over his low visibility. He made the most of his capabilities, leading the Heels in both assists and steals as a junior and senior, and finishing No. 2 on the career assist list behind Ford.

"My main job is simply to run the team," he said. "I want to get the ball to the other guys in certain positions so they can go to the basket. It's so important to get the ball in a spot where you can do something with it. Plus, I try to keep everybody moving on offense and defense."

Carolina's 1981-82 backcourt featured freshman Michael Jordan (left), who would soar into the national consciousness in succeeding years, and senior playmaker Jimmy Black.

182   College Basketball's 25 Greatest Teams

Though he often was lost in the shadow of other ACC big men, Perkins' mobility and constant improvement were keys to the Tar Heel success.

Season Results
1981-82 (32-2)

74	Kansas at Charlotte, N.C. 67	67	The Citadel at Char., N.C. 46
73	USC at Greensboro, N.C. 62	59	Maryland 56
78	Tulsa 70	66	Georgia at Greensboro, N.C. .. 57
75	South Florida 39	69	At Wake Forest 51
59	Rutgers at New York 36	55	At Clemson........................... 49
82	Kentucky at E. R'th'f'd, N.J. 69	77	Georgia Tech 54
56	Penn St. at S. Clara* (OT) ... 50	84	Duke 66
76	Santa Clara at Santa Clara* 57	55	Geo. Tech at G'boro, N.C.† ... 39
64	William & Mary 40	58	N.C. St. at G'boro, N.C.† 46
66	At Maryland........................... 50	47	Virginia at G'boro, N.C.† 45
65	Virginia 60	52	J. Madison at Char., N.C.‡ 50
61	At North Carolina State 41	74	Alabama at Raleigh, N.C.‡ 69
73	At Duke.................................. 63	70	Villanova at Raleigh, N.C.‡ 60
48	Wake Forest 55	68	Houston at New Orleans‡ 63
66	At Georgia Tech.................... 54	63	Georgetown at N. Orleans‡ .. 62
77	Clemson 72	*Cable Car Classic
58	North Carolina State............. 44	†ACC Conference Tournament
58	At Virginia............................. 74	‡NCAA Tournament
96	Furman at Charlotte, N.C. 69	

That Carolina was yet again flirting with that elusive national title was partly due to Black disrupting opposing offenses with defensive pressure on their point. Against Alabama, he tied up Ennis Whatley, who made only four of 13 shots from the field and committed six turnovers. He held Villanova's Stewart Granger to four points and forced four turnovers. And in the semifinal round of the Final Four Tournament, he held Houston standout Rob Williams scoreless from the floor in a 68-63 North Carolina victory.

Add, too, the impact of the Tar Heels' inside game (Perkins was nine of 11, Worthy seven of 10 from the floor) and Four Corners delay against Houston, and Carolina looked like a team that would not be denied, one quite worthy of its 31-2 record. The team concept was clicking, stifling the opposition on defense and controlling the offensive tempo with its poised, deliberate attack.

In the other semifinal matchup, meanwhile, Georgetown produced the most points and the most pressure in a collision of defensive-minded teams, downing Louisville, 50-46, to set up a sportswriter's dream for the NCAA title: Dean Smith vs. John Thompson. Two close friends. The 1976 U.S. Olympic team coach and his assistant, facing each other for the championship.

Both men played it down. They weren't competing, they said, their teams were. But it was the perfect backdrop for an NCAA title clash that is now regarded by many as the most dramatic ever. Veteran broadcaster Curt Gowdy believed it was this game, more than any other, that lifted the Final Four to the entertainment level of the World Series and Super Bowl.

Staged at the massive Louisiana Superdome in New Orleans, the championship game was a milestone of the largest proportions. Attendance records were shattered as 61,612 spectators filled every seat. More than 17 million homes watched on television.

"I had mixed emotions about playing against Dean because I have a great deal of respect and affection for him," Thompson said. "Dean was instrumental in helping me understand what the college game is about and helping me to structure my thoughts about what I had to do and how I could carry out the things I wanted to accomplish. And here, at the biggest moment of my career, I was playing against the guy who had as much to do with my thinking as anybody.

"I had to generate a little bit of competitiveness and stubbornness in order not to think of him as my friend. Because it was Dean, it caused me to be even more fired up."

For Smith, competition was also the key factor. "I was happy for John," he said. "But again, my job is with the young men, not the coaches. I want them to feel like they're champions. And so that part was

Forward Matt Doherty sank his teeth into this mission—the traditional cutting of the cords after North Carolina's 1982 victory over Virginia in the ACC Tournament final.

Worthy battles Houston big men Larry Micheaux and Akeem Olajuwon during action in the national semifinal game at New Orleans.

easy.

"A funny thing happened at halftime. You know Patrick Ewing took so long to shoot a foul shot. At halftime, I told Hank Nichols, the official, 'I'm serious, please don't call a technical foul on Patrick.' And I was serious as I could be. I thought that would mar the game. I didn't want to win that way.

"John thought I was trying to get Nichols to call the technical. John laughed—at least at the time he laughed. I said, 'No, I mean it.'"

There were other plums in the story line. Worthy and Georgetown guard Eric (Sleepy) Floyd were both consensus All-America selections, both from little Gastonia, N.C., both the catalysts of their teams. Ewing, Georgetown's 7-foot freshman center, had made his mark as perhaps the most intimidating player in college. With the big 19-year-old rejecting shots and muscling down rebounds, the Hoyas had strung up a 30-6 record and outscored opponents by an average margin of 14.2 points per game (second among Division I schools).

The pregame tension was thick in the cavernous dome, heavier than in any Final Four of recent memory. Ewing broke that somewhat in the early minutes by swatting away four Carolina shots, two by Worthy. All four blocks were ruled goaltending (as was another Ewing rejection on Worthy later in the half), giving North Carolina its first eight points without putting the ball through the hoop.

Some coaches might have worried that the blocked shots would have flattened Worthy's confidence, but not Smith. "I knew that didn't bother James in the least," he said. "Some guys hate to see their shots blocked, but James was so sky-high."

Worthy came alive with 18 first-half points. The lead became a pendulum. Georgetown held it at the half, 32-31, but the swinging continued through the final 20 minutes. With 2:37 left, Georgetown pulled to 61-60 when Ewing lofted a 13-foot field goal. When Carolina missed a key free throw on the ensuing possession, the Hoyas' center rebounded. Floyd scored on a short jump shot, and Georgetown had the lead, 62-61, with less than a minute remaining.

With 32 seconds left, Carolina called timeout.

"Usually, I don't like to take a timeout there," Smith said. "We should know what to do. But I called a timeout. I expected Georgetown to come back to the zone and jam it in. I said, 'Doherty, take a look for James or Sam, and Jimmy, the cross-court pass will be there to Michael.'

"As it turned out, Michael's whole side of the court was wide open because they were chasing James. If Michael had missed, Sam would have been the hero because he'd have had the rebound."

Black did, indeed, find Jordan wide open on the left wing with 15 seconds remaining. As a Tar Heel rookie, Jordan had adjusted well to Smith's coaching, ranking third on the team in both scoring (13.5

points) and rebounding (4.4), and loosening up the inside for Worthy and Perkins with his outside shooting. Whenever opposing defenses collapsed on the two big men—which the Hoyas did here on Worthy—Jordan's job was to pull the trigger.

From 16 feet out, his aim was true. The swish blew a heavenly blue breeze across Tar Heel land. It was the first big moment in the ever broadening fabric of the Jordan legend.

"We'd lost Al Wood, our best scorer," Smith said, "and Michael Jordan came in as a freshman. As you know, Michael was up and down his freshman year (he'd had a late-season slump), as any freshman would be. But his best game was the finals against Georgetown. If he hadn't made that shot, it would still have been the best game he played all year. Defensively, he played well (and led the club with nine rebounds)."

There was more to Carolina's victory than Jordan's shot, Thompson said. "We thought that Worthy hurt us more than anybody. You hear a lot about Michael Jordan's shot. That certainly broke our backs, but we were having a lot of difficulty with Worthy."

Flashing over and around Ewing, Worthy had scored 28 points and completely disrupted Georgetown's defense. "We did all we could on him," Hoyas forward Ed Spriggs said, "and then they started hitting from the outside in the second half, which made them doubly tough. Worthy is just so good."

Down 63-62 with 15 seconds left, Georgetown attacked immediately for a final shot. Guard Fred Brown worked the ball to the edge of the Carolina defense, where he thought he saw Floyd out of the corner of his eye. The shadowy form in white was Carolina's Worthy. Worthy was surprised, then

Doherty tries to get off a shot as Georgetown's Patrick Ewing blocks his path during the NCAA championship game.

1982 NORTH CAROLINA
Head Coach—Dean Smith   Final Record—32-2

Player	Pos.	Hgt.	Wgt.	Cl.	G	FG	FGA	Pct.	FT.	FTA	Pct.	Reb.	Pts.	Avg.
James Worthy	F	6-9	219	Jr.	34	203	354	.573	126	187	.674	215	532	15.6
Sam Perkins	C	6-9	224	So.	32	174	301	.578	109	142	.768	250	457	14.3
Michael Jordan	G	6-5	189	Fr.	34	191	358	.534	78	108	.722	149	460	13.5
Matt Doherty	F	6-8	210	So.	34	122	235	.519	71	92	.772	103	315	9.3
Jimmy Black	G	6-3	162	Sr.	34	100	195	.513	59	80	.738	59	259	7.6
Jim Braddock	G	6-2	171	Jr.	34	28	62	.452	10	12	.833	17	66	1.9
Chris Brust	F	6-9	231	Sr.	33	23	37	.622	10	22	.455	56	56	1.7
Buzz Peterson	G	6-3	165	Fr.	30	16	41	.390	3	7	.429	14	35	1.2
Cecil Exum	F	6-6	206	So.	17	8	21	.381	3	11	.273	17	19	1.1
Lynwood Robinson	G	6-1	176	Fr.	14	7	11	.636	1	5	.200	3	15	1.1
Jeb Barlow	F	6-8	206	Sr.	28	12	31	.387	4	9	.444	23	28	1.0
Warren Martin	C	6-11	220	Fr.	19	7	15	.467	0	5	.000	16	14	0.7
John Brownlee	F	6-10	215	Fr.	13	4	7	.571	1	5	.200	14	9	0.7
Timo Makkonen	C	6-11	202	So.	12	0	0	.000	2	4	.500	4	2	0.2
Team												59		
North Carolina					34	895	1668	.537	477	689	.692	999	2269	66.7
Opponents					34	811	1742	.466	263	407	.646	873	1885	55.4

(North Carolina totals include basket scored by opposing player.)

Blue Heaven: Worthy cutting the net after North Carolina's 63-62 victory over the Hoyas.

elated, to receive the ball and he headed downcourt, where he was fouled.

"To this day, I think that if Georgetown had been in their white uniforms they had worn all during the tournament instead of their dark uniforms, Brown would not have thrown the ball to James," Smith said. "James had gone for a steal on a fake moments earlier and was out of position. He shouldn't have been where he was on the court, and it fooled Brown, and James went for the steal."

Worthy missed two free throws with two seconds left but they were meaningless. Smith's team had finally found that pure blue nirvana. Worthy was voted the tournament's outstanding player. Perkins and Jordan were named to the all-tournament team, along with Georgetown's Floyd and Ewing.

Smith, of course, had reached the top. "I'm especially happy for coach," Black said. "Now I won't have to read any more articles from you sportswriters about how he chokes in the big games."

Yet Smith, a man who had been measured by his critics for what he had not achieved, took the victory in stride. "I don't think I'm a better coach now that we've won the national championship," he told reporters. "I'm still the same coach."

The only change being that ineffable aura of Blue Heaven around him.

The succeeding seasons have held their share of frustrations for Tar Heel fans. Carolina has won no fewer than 27 games each year (and lost no more than nine) but never returned to the Final Four. Perkins and Jordan would be named consensus All-Americas in both 1983 and 1984, their final season, when the Heels exited the NCAA Tournament in the regional semifinals, ending a 28-3 season.

The victory in 1982 was testament to the team concept at work. North Carolina had entered its season ranked No. 1 and, save for a few weeks, managed to maintain that status.

"I don't think that will happen again—to be the team that's shot at and then go through the whole year and still be sharp in the end," Smith said. "They were mad they weren't champions in 1981, and I was, too. I think that helped us. When you get that second crack with the same team, you usually respond.

"Worthy had a great (title) game, but he couldn't have done it without Jimmy Black (who dished out seven assists). He couldn't have done it without Matt Doherty's defensive work. Michael Jordan certainly helped. . . . Sam Perkins' effort will go unnoticed, but I think he did a great job."

And for one brief moment amid the championship celebration, Smith basked in the glow of Blue Heaven. "A great writer from Charlotte, N.C., once said that it was our system that kept us from winning the national championship," he said. "It's the most ridiculous comment ever made and I always wanted to say that."

NINETEEN

The Hurryin' Hoosiers

INDIANA

1952-53

You might call it the Big Mac Attack, 1953 style.

"Big Mac" was Indiana basketball Coach Branch McCracken, a silver-haired, bespectacled bear of a man. The "attack" part of the equation was his 1952-53 Hoosier squad. Quick. Aggressive. Deep. Most of the complimentary basketball adjectives applied to this bunch.

The Hoosiers had strength inside with 6-9 sophomore Don Schlundt at center. They had an outside threat in guard Bob (Slick) Leonard, a fiery floor general who laced the ball in from the perimeter. And they had indispensable specialists at forward, a gritty rebounder in Charley Kraak and a defensive hawk in Dick Farley.

Most of all, they had a system: McCracken's fast-breaking, up-tempo offense.

You can throw out the now-well-ingrained perception of Indiana University and deliberate, precision basketball. McCracken's teams were the "Hurryin' Hoosiers." That was the only way he wanted to approach the game. His philosophy was to get the ball off the defensive boards and head the other way—yesterday if not sooner. And to make sure his players had the wheels to go with the game plan, he ran them four miles a day, beginning with the first day of fall classes.

McCracken's penchant for the fast break may seem strange considering he played at Indiana for Everett Dean, a coach known for his methodical offense, full of patient passing and cutting plays. McCracken, a center, fit that system well enough to earn consensus All-America honors and lead the Big Ten Conference in scoring in 1930.

In his first year out of college, however,

McCracken went to coach at Ball State, where he developed his own ideas and, in turn, teams that were known for running and gunning. That system found its way to Bloomington before the 1938-39 season, when Dean left for Stanford and McCracken was hired as his replacement.

McCracken's first Hoosier team won 17 of 20 games. In just his second season, the "Big Bear" guided Indiana to the 1940 NCAA championship, defeating Kansas in the title game of only the second NCAA Tournament ever held.

"We always had a fast break," said Marv Huffman, a standout guard on those teams. "His contention was that you get down before them and you get back on defense before them, so we were fast-breaking both ways. We just ran like mad.

"I remember one of our first practices. I got a rebound and dribbled it a couple of times. Well, Branch blew his whistle and threw two balls up on the boards. I got one and dribbled it before I passed and he took the other one and just threw it downcourt. Then he looked at me and said, 'OK, now which one got there faster?'"

Entering the 1952-53 campaign, McCracken's Indiana teams had suffered only one losing season while posting a 173-59 record. Still, his Hurryin' Hoosiers had never won a Big Ten Conference championship, mostly because McCracken had trouble recruiting a big center to outmuscle league opponents. There may have been something about all that hustling that made the big Midwest farm boys think about playing elsewhere.

In the late 1940s, McCracken thought he had that big equalizer in a hulking Terre Haute kid named

Clyde Lovellette. The 6-9 prep star said he wanted to be a Hoosier, but a visit to the big, well-populated Indiana campus made him think he'd end up "a number." Lovellette enrolled at Kansas, where he led the nation in scoring and the Jayhawks to the NCAA championship in 1952. McCracken, meanwhile, made do with a 6-2 center and finished fourth in the Big Ten.

Ultimately, the coach's solution to the big-man problem was to grow one. When McCracken recruited Schlundt out of South Bend, the slender center stood 6-6. By his sophomore year in 1952-53, he had grown to 6-9 and his teammates had taken to calling him "Ox." McCracken's bushy eyebrows arched with his smile as he watched the blond giant laying in graceful bank shots with either hand.

Finally secure with an inside threat, McCracken was able to move the 6-3 Leonard from forward to guard, filling a vacancy left by Sammy Esposito, who had signed a professional baseball contract with the Chicago White Sox. Many believed Leonard's move into the backcourt was the key to the Hoosiers' season.

A veritable dynamo, Leonard was a natural for running the fast break yet equally dangerous when Indiana switched to a half-court attack. He had a smooth jump shot, both one- and two-handed, that was suited for a pick-and-screen offense. If Leonard didn't take the shot, the next move was to Schlundt.

"If the first pick or screen didn't work," Kraak recalled, "we looked for the big guy. He was always making his moves in the post. He could move pretty well. Once you hit him with the pass, he almost always got his shot off. He used the board a lot. He had a great touch. Anything he did around the basket was off the board. And if he was fouled trying to shoot, he was a good free-throw shooter."

At times, defenses would surround Schlundt, but Leonard's outside shooting was too much of a deterrent for that to last long. The one or two players left to defend against the big center often resorted to elbows and pushing and holding. Unwisely. Schlundt ranked seventh in the nation as a sophomore by sinking 80.3 percent of his free-throw opportunities. And though he was portrayed in one magazine story of the era as a gentle, slumbering giant, Schlundt taught his tormentors a painful lesson when pushed too far.

"In one of our games against Indiana," Michigan State Coach Pete Newell said, "we used three men to guard Schlundt at various times. All three came back to the bench with lumps on their heads big enough to hang their hats on. That Schlundt really had a lethal pair of elbows."

While Leonard and Schlundt received most of the publicity, Farley was the quiet backbone of the team—a fine passer, the leader in field-goal accuracy and the Hoosier who drew the toughest defensive assignments. He could play in the post, as well,

which became more of a factor when 6-11 backup center Lou Scott was ruled academically ineligible for the second semester.

Kraak was the rebounder of the bunch and did it the old-fashioned way, with positioning, quickness and leaping ability. "It's that little fraction of a second break that he has in reaction and movement that makes him so tough off the boards," McCracken said. Always looking for a stickback, Kraak averaged 10.3 rebounds per game to lead the team.

Guard Burke Scott rounded out the starting five and showed exceptional ballhandling skills for a sophomore, specializing in under-the-basket passes to Schlundt. The Hoosiers were a young team, without a senior on the squad, but they were also deep on the bench, with forward Dick White leading the reserves by averaging 5.6 points per game.

The 1952-53 season brought an explosion of offense to college basketball, partly due to more teams adopting fast-paced offensive schemes. But a revision in the foul-shooting rules also helped, in effect allowing players two-shots-to-make-one in the first 37 minutes of a 40-minute game. Scores soared with the change, increasing nearly 13 points per game (to an average of 140.2 points), as major scoring records fell. The Hoosiers would set no less than a dozen individual and team marks in the Big Ten.

Schlundt, though still a sophomore, established a conference mark for most points *in a career* and was voted the league's Most Valuable Player. He also shattered Indiana's single-season scoring mark, averaging 25.4 points per game. Yet Schlundt couldn't have done as much had he not been able to run in breakneck style with the rest of the team.

"Don has to run because we play a fast-breaking game," McCracken explained. "When the other club misses a shot and one of our boys takes it off the backboard, it's usually Schlundt who makes the recovery. Ordinarily our forwards fast break down the floor, Schlundt clears the ball to one of our guards along the sidelines and the guard tries to hit one of the forwards with a pass. But if the forwards are covered, the guards take the ball down while Schlundt runs extra hard to get to his offensive post near the circle. There, he keeps running and faking, moving from side to side and waiting for a chance to grab a pass. Playing center in our type of game is no job for a lazy man."

McCracken was confident his team had the tools to contend in the Big Ten, but Indiana lost two of its first three games, both at the buzzer, prior to the conference schedule. In South Bend, Notre Dame nipped the Hoosiers, 71-70, when Irish guard Junior Stephens drove the length of the floor and laid the ball in before time expired. The Hoosiers then traveled to Manhattan, Kan., where a Kansas State sub hit a last-second, 40-foot set shot to give the Wildcats an 82-80 victory.

Indiana Coach Branch McCracken with his 'Hurryin' Hoosiers' starting five (left to right): Charley Kraak, Bob Leonard, Don Schlundt, Dick Farley and Burke Scott.

Indiana came together quickly, however, when it returned to Bloomington and routed Michigan by 28 points to open Big Ten play. From there, the Hurryin' Hoosiers ripped off wins at an impressive clip. In mid-January, they pushed their conference record to 7-0 and took over sole possession of first place by defeating Illinois, the defending Big Ten champion, in double-overtime, 74-70.

Eager to keep the streak going, Big Mac kept wearing the same red necktie. His players followed suit, sporting their gravy-stained neckwear across the Midwest, from one Big Ten showdown to another. When they demolished Purdue, 113-78, shattering the Big Ten's single-game scoring record by 10 points, the Hoosiers stood atop the standings at 14-0.

Up next was a rematch with second-place Illinois, in Champaign. The Illini, already saddled with three conference losses, were in the game for only a half, however. Indiana pulled away to a 91-79 win, claiming the first outright Big Ten championship in school history. "It's a great basketball team," Illini Coach Harry Combes conceded afterward.

After finishing second seven times at Indiana,

McCracken took a championship ride from the floor on the shoulders of his players. "The boys did it," he told reporters. "They hustled all the way. They hustle in every game. Yes, in every practice."

Leonard had missed his first two shots, bringing calls from the Illinois crowd to "shoot," which he did, making seven long jumpers in the first half. He finished with 23 points.

"This is as good as we've played all season," he said afterward. "We had to play well to beat Illinois like we did. That's a good team, right through the eighth man, and I never expected we'd get so many points. But everything clicked."

McCracken interrupted to tell the writers that Leonard deserved all-star mention. "I see a lot of All-America picks," the coach said, "but they forget Leonard. I think he belongs on any all-star team."

Kraak, who had decided to attend Indiana over Illinois, seemed more pleased than anyone. "This is the greatest thing that has ever happened to me," he said. "I don't imagine Illinois can realize how badly we wanted this one. They've had so many."

Indiana won its 17th consecutive game two nights later by defeating Northwestern, 90-88, on a 40-foot

McCracken, affectionately known as the 'Big Bear,' was a staunch proponent of up-tempo basketball.

Season Results
1952-53 (23-3)

95	Valparaiso		56
70	At Notre Dame		71
80	At Kansas State		82
88	Michigan		60
91	At Iowa		72
91	At Michigan		88
69	At Michigan State		62
66	Minnesota		63
88	At Ohio State		68
74	Illinois		70
88	At Purdue		75
105	Butler		70
88	At Northwestern		84
66	Wisconsin		48
65	Michigan State		50
72	At Wisconsin		70
81	Ohio State		67
113	Purdue		78
91	At Illinois		79
90	Northwestern		88
63	At Minnesota		65
68	Iowa		61
82	DePaul at Chicago*		80
79	Notre Dame at Chicago*		66
80	LSU at Kansas City*		67
69	Kansas at Kansas City*		68

*NCAA Tournament

bucket by guard Paul Poff with four seconds remaining. The last-second antics swung the other way the next game, however, as Minnesota ruined the Hoosiers' perfect Big Ten season, 65-63, with a basket at the buzzer. By a total of five points, Indiana had lost three games on field goals scored with fewer than five seconds to play.

The Hoosiers closed the regular schedule with a 68-61 victory over Iowa and headed into the NCAA Tournament with a 19-3 record. They seemed in control against their first opponent, DePaul, leading by as many as 10 points in the fourth quarter, but were lucky to escape with an 82-80 victory in the face of the Blue Demons' frantic defense.

The Hoosiers atoned for that poor finish and one of their earlier last-second losses by defeating Notre Dame the next evening. Schlundt wound up with a career-high 41 points, eclipsing George Mikan's Chicago Stadium record, in a 79-66 victory. "Before you start thinking about beating Indiana," Notre Dame Coach John Jordan said, "you've got to figure out a way to stop that Schlundt. And nobody's been able to do it yet."

Louisiana State tried gamely—and paid the price—as the scene shifted to the Final Four in Kansas City's Municipal Auditorium. The Tigers opened the national semifinal game by swarming the big Hoosier center, limiting him to five shots in the first quarter. Leonard, meanwhile, fired away from long range, burying his first six attempts, until LSU spread out its clustered defense—thereby opening the middle for Schlundt. Leonard finished with 22 points and Schlundt, 29, to offset a 29-point game by LSU's Bob Pettit. Indiana advanced, 80-67.

"The Louisiana State game proved we were a well-balanced ball club," McCracken said.

Suddenly, the NCAA had a rematch of its 1940 championship game: McCracken's Hoosiers against Phog Allen's Kansas Jayhawks. Kansas had lost Lovellette from its 1952 title team, but 6-9 junior center B.H. Born had established his own identity as a scorer, leading the Jayhawk charges with 19 points per game. It was a team Allen himself called "half-scared and skinny-legged," with Born the only starter taller than 6-1. But Kansas played a relentless brand of pressure defense, proving as much with a 79-53 victory over Washington in the other semifinal matchup.

"After watching Kansas beat Washington, I was scared," Schlundt admitted. "I didn't see how we could beat them ... but I didn't say anything to anyone."

The championship clash developed as one of the tightest in tournament history, with the teams never more than six points apart. The tension was thick, sparking a variety of technical fouls and one heated controversy. Near the end of the third quarter, Born banged into Kraak and was whistled for the foul. The scoring official ruled the Jayhawk

The 6-foot-9 Schlundt (34) took his strength directly to the basket, unlike many of the hook-shooting big men of his day.

Leonard (left) helped steer Indiana's breakneck attack and also possessed a deadly outside shot. Farley (right) was the backbone of the team, a fine passer who always drew the tough defensive assignment.

player out of the game with five personals, but Allen protested, arguing that the Kansas book showed only four. The scorer rechecked, agreed with Allen and changed his decision. McCracken stormed off the bench.

"Your book shows five personals," McCracken shouted at the scorer. "Born should be out. We're your guest and you're robbing us." Born stayed in the game but fouled out midway through the final quarter.

Schlundt and Leonard, meanwhile, would both draw technicals for offensive remarks to the referees. Kraak picked up another when he slammed the ball onto the court after being whistled for his fifth foul.

"It got pretty heated," Kraak said. "I remember I got quite hot. I was fouled out, got a technical called on me and lost my cool, so to speak. I was probably more embarrassed about it than anything else. I was glad we won the game. If we had had to go back losers, it would have been quite unpleasant."

Kraak was the surprise of the final game, breaking loose for 17 points. But his fifth foul, a charging infraction, allowed Kansas to pull within two points when Hal Patterson sank one of the two free throws. And although the Jayhawks missed the technical shot, the ensuing possession helped them

tie the score at 68 on Dean Kelley's driving layup with 1:05 left.

Indiana set up to work for a final shot, but with 27 seconds left, Leonard was fouled under the Hoosier basket. "I wanted to make the shots as much as anything I've ever wanted in my life," he said later. "In fact, I had to make them."

Leonard missed his first attempt but the second was true, leaving the Hoosiers to play defense with a one-point lead. Kansas struggled to set up the perfect shot but managed only an off-balance attempt by substitute Jerry Alberts from the corner. It missed, and the celebration began in Bloomington when Indiana rebounded.

Schlundt had scored 30 points, but in a controversial vote, Born was named the tournament's outstanding player, the first time a player from a losing team would receive the award.

The Hoosiers didn't seem to mind. They had been playing for the team trophy. As the school's campus daily noted, "It was a case of the team from the state which made basketball famous showing the team from the school where the sport originated how to play the game."

Indeed, the Hurryin' Hoosiers played the game the way it was supposed to be played—the way Big Mac wanted it played.

The 1952-53 Hoosiers after sealing McCracken's first Big Ten Conference championship:
Front row (left to right)—Leonard, Kraak, Schlundt, Farley, Scott. Second
row—Manager Ron Fifer, Dick White, James DeaKyne, McCracken, Paul Poff, Phil
Byers, assistant coach Ernie Andres. Third row—Ron Taylor, James Schooley, Goethe
Chambers, Jack Wright.

1953 INDIANA

Head Coach—Branch McCracken   Final Record—23-3

Player	Pos.	Hgt.	Wgt.	Cl.	G	FG	FGA	Pct.	FT.	FTA	Pct.	Reb.	Pts.	Avg.
Don Schlundt	C	6-9	210	So.	26	206	477	.432	249	310	.803	...	661	25.4
Bob Leonard	G	6-3	185	Jr.	26	164	503	.326	96	144	.667	...	424	16.3
Dick Farley	F	6-3	183	Jr.	26	94	212	.443	75	108	.694	...	263	10.1
Burke Scott	G	6-1	165	So.	26	76	206	.369	55	85	.647	...	207	8.0
Lou Scott*	C	6-11	227	Jr.	10	28	83	.337	18	28	.643	...	74	7.4
Charles Kraak	F	6-5	180	Jr.	26	63	177	.356	60	102	.588	...	186	7.2
Dick White	F	6-1	170	So.	22	40	128	.313	43	58	.471	...	123	5.6
Paul Poff	G	6-1	181	So.	13	14	45	.311	12	19	.632	...	40	3.1
Phil Byers	G	5-11	165	So.	23	25	72	.347	13	24	.542	...	63	2.7
Jack Wright	F	5-10	168	Jr.	3	2	11	.182	4	4	1.000	...	8	2.7
James DeaKyne	G	6-3	190	Jr.	20	20	87	.230	5	12	.417	...	45	2.3
Goethe Chambers	F	6-2	175	So.	2	1	1	1.000	0	0	.000	...	2	1.0
Ron Taylor	F	6-3	185	Jr.	2	1	2	.500	0	0	.000	...	2	1.0
Don Henry	F	6-2	188	So.	2	0	1	.000	2	4	.500	...	2	1.0
James Schooley	F	6-5	188	Sr.	16	3	14	.214	6	12	.500	...	12	0.8
Indiana					26	737	2019	.365	638	910	.701	...	2112	81.2
Opponents					26	611	2041	.299	586	937	.625	...	1808	69.5

*Ineligible second semester.

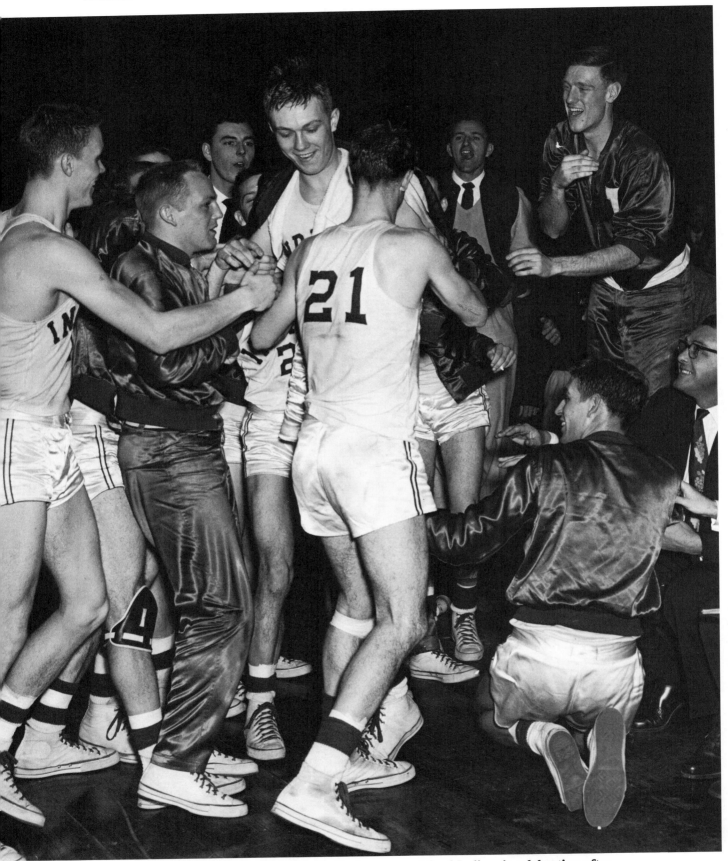

Leonard (21), Kraak (left) and Schlundt (facing camera) lead Indiana's celebration after the Hoosiers' title-game victory over Kansas in the 1953 NCAA Tournament.

TWENTY

Right On Schedule

LOUISVILLE

1985-86

In the old Hollywood westerns, the Indians had a saying, roughly translated, that to be great, a tribe had to have great enemies. At the University of Louisville, Coach Denny Crum reshaped that piece of celluloid wisdom into college basketball logic. To be a great team, Crum believed, you had to play a schedule filled with great opponents.

Crum's penchant for tough scheduling evolved from his association with John Wooden, as a UCLA player under Wooden in the late 1950s and as his top assistant when the Bruins won national titles in 1969, 1970 and 1971.

"I think it's something inherent in the system that I learned from Coach Wooden," Crum said. "His teaching process is a building process based on repetition. By year's end, the players are doing everything they can do to the best of their ability. Confidence is a crucial thing at tournament time, because it's a do-or-die situation, and the pressures are such that if you don't think you can win it, you probably can't.

"Our kids," Crum explained, "because we played everybody in the country by tournament time, knew we were competitive and that we had gotten better each week. We used to tell them: 'Get a little bit better each week. Learn something this week that you didn't know before.' By year's end, with the level of competition we played, our kids knew they were competitive and that they could win."

Shortly after recruiting Bill Walton for the Bruins, Crum left UCLA to become Louisville's head coach. In just his first season, he steered his club all the way to the 1972 Final Four, where Wooden and Walton dealt the Cardinals a 19-point

loss in the semifinals. Three seasons later, Crum brought Louisville back to the Final Four, only to lose once more in the semifinals to Wooden, whose Bruins rewarded him with his 10th NCAA title in his final year of coaching.

Because basketball is like a religion in Kentucky, the pressure on Crum to produce a national champion mounted each season until his 1979-80 team, led by Darrell Griffith, finished 33-3 and annexed the school's first-ever NCAA title.

"When we won our first championship at Louisville," Crum recalled, "I had a feeling of total relief. I wasn't really happy or joyous or excited. I was totally relieved that we had finally won one. . . . It was just too much pressure."

Just as Wooden felt a sense of relief at UCLA in 1964, that first Cardinal championship eased the strain on Crum. Life went on after losses in the Final Four semifinal games in both 1982 and 1983. Coaching was enjoyable, even in the face of his first real struggle in the 1984-85 campaign. Decimated by injuries, Louisville finished 19-18, breaking Crum's string of 13 consecutive seasons of 20 or more victories.

"Only diamonds are forever," Crum mused. "I enjoy this team. I really like the guys. Every team can't be 25-5."

What appeared to be terrible misfortune when senior guard Milt Wagner broke his foot two games into the season was, in retrospect, a blessing in disguise. Wagner became a medical redshirt, prolonging his career an additional season. And while he sat, the Cardinals' other starting guard, Jeff Hall, became the ballhandler he had never been regarded

Denny Crum, both a player and assistant coach under John Wooden at UCLA, built his own winning legacy at the University of Louisville.

as being. Always a fine perimeter shooter, Hall learned to set the table for the Cardinals, rounding out his game and the team's balance.

If this appeared to be a stroke of luck for Crum as he convened his 1985-86 squad, it would have mattered little had he not put together the talent to exploit the situation.

With 6-foot-7 forward Billy Thompson joining Wagner and Hall to form a senior trio, the Louisville lineup featured three players who would each score more than 1,200 career points. Thompson, Wagner's high school teammate in Camden, N.J., could play above the rim, just as Crum demanded of his inside men, and whip off a bullet pass without hesitation.

At the other forward position, 6-7 sophomore Herbert Crook was thin, quick and underrated, a superb offensive rebounder who was nearly impossible to box out. And when he peeled a rebound off the offensive board, Crook knew how to score.

Into this foundation of experience, Crum set his prize recruit out of Georgia, 6-9 freshman center Pervis Ellison, an exceptional shot-blocker and re-

bounder with long arms and excellent timing. Crum preferred quickness to size, and Ellison offered the ideal gifts—range, speed and anticipation —to take care of business that traditional, less mobile pivotmen often couldn't.

"We won our national championship with a 6-7 freshman (Rodney McCray) at center in 1980," Crum said in camp. "This group has as much potential as any we've ever brought in."

Although not as awesome, this team brought to mind Indiana's 1976 title team, inasmuch as the players were perfectly matched to the coach's system. They had the poise and physical tools to execute the Crum trademarks: a high-post offense, the fast break, a tough zone-press and man-to-man halfcourt defense, all of which Wooden had employed at UCLA.

"His style is almost identical to the one we played," Wooden said. "But Denny has refined things. He's added some things that are very good to the high-post offense. There have been changes in the game. His style is better."

None of which surprised Wooden, considering

The centerpiece of Crum's 1986 championship team was Pervis (Never Nervous) Ellison, a tall, talented freshman who stayed cool under the most trying circumstances.

Sophomore forward Herbert Crook was often overshadowed but played a major role as a workhorse rebounder and scorer.

Crum's quest for perfection as both a UCLA player and assistant coach.

"If possible, he was too competitive," Wooden said. "At times as a player, that took away from his efficiency instead of adding to it. I told him if he decided to go into coaching, he'd have to overcome his temperament.

"As a coach, he didn't always relate well with the players at first. They said, 'Get him off my back.' But he has learned, he has matured. And there was no question in my mind that he would."

Crum mellowed at Louisville, becoming in Wooden's eyes an "excellent, patient teacher." He exuded the calm of a laid-back Californian as he drilled his team, but there was no doubting that he expected steady growth and improvement. When discipline was required, Crum eschewed the show of strength and dealt with the situation on a case-by-case basis.

"Coach Wooden's basic philosophy, how to organize, how to do the things that help you be the best you can be at the end of the year, all of that is important," Crum said. "But the biggest thing is the ability to deal with and handle people.

"Every kid is different and you have to do different things to get the same things out of different players. People then say that everybody's not treated the same. Well, everybody is not the same and you can't treat them all the same. Some guys you have to jump all over, others you have to pat on the butt. . . .

"You don't treat everybody equal because everybody is not equal. The main thing is that you treat everybody fairly."

When substitutes Mark McSwain and Kevin Walls fumed over a lack of playing time early in the 1985-86 season, Crum, who had seen Wooden handle a traffic jam of talent at UCLA, smoothed over the matter, defining their roles as they pertained to the team's mission. As a result, Louisville moved on toward its destiny.

Other coaches might have wondered just what that held as the season unfolded. Crum had laid out his usual murderous schedule for the Cardinals, including a non-conference slate the NCAA rated as the toughest in the nation—for the second straight year. After opening the season with two victories in the Big Apple NIT, Louisville dropped its next two games in the tournament, to Kansas and St. John's, both Top 20 teams.

After four wins at home, the Cardinals returned to the road and lost to Kentucky, ranked No. 10 by UPI, in Lexington. Kentucky Coach Eddie Sutton was nevertheless impressed, especially with Ellison, who came away with 13 points, seven rebounds and four blocks in a battle with Wildcats center Kenny Walker, a consensus All-America selection in 1986.

"They have the type of squad, if they continue to improve and I think they will, that may very well be in Dallas (for the Final Four)," Sutton said.

From there, Louisville won two more at home before losing on the road by two points to fifth-ranked Memphis State. After two good road victories, the Cards beat No. 4 Syracuse in Louisville, led by Wagner's 24 points. "One thing about Milt," Syracuse guard Pearl Washington said afterward. "When he gets his points, they're honest. Just jumpers. Pure jumpers. For my money, he's the best shooter in the country."

Wagner's comeback hadn't been without some anxious moments. Physically, he was fit from the start, driving the basket with the same slippery moves he had prior to his injury. His field-goal shooting was initially lame, however, only a shade above 30 percent over Louisville's first seven games. That started to change in game No. 8, when he poured in 22 points in a thrilling 65-63 victory over Indiana. "I figured once a shooter, always a shooter," theorized the confident Cardinal known as "Ice."

Wagner would keep right on burning the cords, winding up second on the team in scoring—on the season and on Louisville's career list—and leading the team in assists. "Just my presence makes the team better," he would say matter-of-factly. "Me on the court makes a team better, it makes the team more confident."

Perhaps the Cardinals became too confident after downing Syracuse. Back-to-back losses followed immediately, to a mediocre Cincinnati team and to seventh-ranked Kansas, for the second time. Louisville's 11-6 record appeared very ordinary. Tough schedules, however, make appearances all the more deceiving.

"I told everyone at the start of the year," Crum said, "that this team would have its ups and downs and probably wouldn't have a great record, but that we had the potential to be an outstanding team by the end of the year. I still feel that way. We're not bad right now. Tell me who else has played five Top 10 teams. . . ."

Despite Crum's optimism, fan discontent remained high. Some of the home crowd had been booing Thompson, perhaps the nation's top recruit three years earlier who had struggled in his senior season. Crum was angered by the treatment. Thompson just said it hurt.

Thompson hadn't exactly been a model of consistency at Louisville, which he didn't deny. He averaged only 7.3 points per game as a freshman and only 9.2 as a sophomore. But as a junior, while shifting to guard to offset injuries there, Thompson led the Cardinals in scoring, rebounds and assists. And turnovers, too. That stuck in many people's minds. Never mind that Thompson was playing out of position. Crum stuck by his former recruiting prize for his "unselfishness."

Following the loss to Kansas, Louisville streaked

After missing the 1984-85 season with a broken foot, Milt Wagner returned as a fifth-year senior to provide scoring and leadership in the backcourt.

While Jeff Hall ran the offense from the point, Billy Thompson played his game above the rim. The two seniors were both playing the best basketball of their careers by NCAA Tournament time in 1986.

to four straight wins before suffering yet another road loss to another good team, North Carolina State. The irony was that Thompson played well with 21 points and nine rebounds, his second 20-point game in a string of four such efforts.

The Cardinals' fate changed dramatically from there. They ran off 11 straight victories and captured the Metro Conference's regular-season title and tournament championship. "We are capable of being a Final Four team," Wagner asserted. "We've got us a true center for the first time."

Without a doubt, Louisville was heading into the NCAA Tournament because Ellison had opened the door. Few freshman centers had ever made such an impact. Of the great first-year collegiate big men,

Ellison, averaging 13.1 points and 8.2 rebounds per game, outscored and outrebounded Patrick Ewing, Akeem Olajuwon, David Robinson, Sam Bowie, Kevin McHale, Joe Barry Carroll and Bill Cartwright.

Crum had recruited Ellison more for his quickness and agility than height ("He was my starter the first day he signed," Crum said), skills the slinky pivotman used to dominate the altitudes above and below the rim. Ellison always loomed as a shot-blocking threat, but it was his rebounding that earned him the early nickname "Windex." That, however, soon gave way to "Never Nervous" Pervis for the cool that belied his youth.

Indeed, with an automatic NCAA bid on the line

in the Metro Tournament final, Ellison scored 21 points and grabbed 13 rebounds, cinching the tourney's Most Valuable Player award in a scenario that would be repeated in the Final Four.

Pushing its winning streak to 15 games, Louisville rolled into Dallas for the big show by defeating Drexel, Bradley, North Carolina and Auburn. The Cardinals were devastating in the final four minutes of those four tournament games, outscoring the opposition by a combined total of 68-26. Against North Carolina, a team that featured Brad Daugherty, Kenny Smith, Joe Wolf and Jeff Lebo, Louisville held a 21-4 scoring advantage in the final 4½ minutes to win, 94-79.

"When the going gets tough for us, we're able to pull ahead," Crum said. "Early in the year, we didn't do things right at the end of the game. That has changed."

Louisville was peaking at the perfect time, getting production from all five starters. Because Crum believed in balance and versatility, all five regulars would wind up with double-figure scoring averages for the season, led by Thompson's 14.9 points per game and Wagner's 14.8-point average. Still a hawkish rebounder, Crook was coming into his own offensively, putting together back-to-back 20-point efforts against Carolina and Auburn, a mighty team led by Chuck Person and Chris Morris.

"Louisville is playing as well as any team in the country," Auburn Coach Sonny Smith said. "Denny has that team rolling. They're the loosest team I've ever seen. And I don't mean the laughing and joking kind of loose. I mean there's nobody out there who's afraid to take a tough shot at any time."

The trip to the big event would be Crum's sixth overall (only Wooden, with 12 Final Four appearances, and Smith, with seven, had more) and Louisville's fourth in seven years. Wagner now had played on three of those four teams. "I'm on a mission," he told reporters. "I've already been to the Final Four two times. Just getting here is not

The Cardinals' top scorer off the bench was forward Tony Kimbro, another freshman with poise and confidence.

Season Results
1985-86 (32-7)

81	Miami of Ohio at Cincinnati*	.65	
80	Tulsa at Cincinnati*	74	
78	Kansas at New York*	83	
79	St. John's at New York*	86	
77	Purdue	58	
88	Iona	75	
73	Western Kentucky	70	
65	Indiana	63	
64	At Kentucky	69	
94	Wyoming	62	
86	Eastern Kentucky	55	
71	At Memphis State	73	
59	At Southern Mississippi	54	
85	At Florida State	64	
83	Syracuse	73	
82	Cincinnati	84	
69	At Kansas	71	
72	La Salle	60	
91	UCLA	72	
74	South Carolina	72	
103	Virginia Tech	68	
64	At North Carolina State	76	
93	At Virginia Tech	83	
74	At Cincinnati	58	
72	At DePaul	53	
83	Southern Mississippi	74	
89	Florida State	67	
76	At Houston	59	
66	South Alabama	55	
65	At South Carolina	63	
70	Memphis State	69	
86	Cincinnati†	65	
88	Memphis State†	79	
93	Drexel at Ogden, Utah‡	73	
82	Bradley at Ogden, Utah‡	68	
94	North Carolina at Houston‡	79	
84	Auburn at Houston‡	76	
88	Louisiana State at Dallas‡	77	
72	Duke at Dallas‡	69	

*Big Apple NIT
†Metro Conference Tournament
‡NCAA Tournament

'Destination Dallas,' alluding to the site of the Final Four, was the battle cry of Louisville fans as the Cardinals advanced through the NCAA Tournament.

enough for me. My mission is not complete. This time I want to go out in style. I want to win this one."

Wagner did his share in the national semifinals, scoring 22 points, along with Thompson, to lead his teammates past Dale Brown's Louisiana State Tigers, 88-77. His mission might have been aborted, however, had it not been for Crum's pointed advice at halftime, when LSU led by eight. "He told me, 'You're my senior leader and you're playing like a freshman,' " explained Wagner, who had missed four of six shots and committed four turnovers. "We took his advice and took it to our knowledge."

In the other semifinal bracket, Duke squeezed past Kansas to set up a meeting between the Cardinals, once an 11-6 team but now 31-7, and the 37-2 Blue Devils, who already had won more games than any other team in NCAA history.

If the seniors had helped Louisville take the first big step in Dallas, the final push would be provided

by the freshman Ellison. Afterward, Duke senior forward Mark Alarie said his team was prepared for Ellison's shot-blocking, but none of the Blue Devils had expected the young center to possess so many athletic moves around the basket.

Early on, it was Duke guard Johnny Dawkins, a two-time consensus All-America, who flashed his quickness. Dawkins was nearly unstoppable on offense, scoring 22 points in the game's first 24½ minutes. He managed only two free throws thereafter, however, shut down by the tenacious one-on-one defense of Hall, who became the shadow after Wagner and freshman Kevin Walls faltered.

But it was Ellison who was in control when it mattered most. With 39 seconds left and Louisville clinging to a 66-65 lead, Ellison snared what looked like an air ball by Hall and laid the ball in. Seconds later, when Duke's David Henderson missed a driving layup, Ellison rebounded, drew a foul and sank both ends of a one-and-one, enhancing his "Never

Ellison blocks a shot by Duke's Mark Alarie during action in the NCAA title game.

1986 LOUISVILLE

Head Coach—Denny Crum   Final Record—32-7

Player	Pos.	Hgt.	Wgt.	Cl.	G	FG	FGA	Pct.	FT.	FTA	Pct.	Reb.	Pts.	Avg.
Billy Thompson	F	6-7	195	Sr.	39	221	384	.576	140	196	.714	304	582	14.9
Milt Wagner	G	6-5	185	Sr.	39	220	444	.495	137	159	.862	122	577	14.8
Pervis Ellison	F-C	6-9	195	Fr.	39	210	379	.554	90	132	.682	318	510	13.1
Herbert Crook	F	6-7	190	So.	39	171	324	.528	119	173	.688	252	461	11.8
Jeff Hall	G	6-4	180	Sr.	39	168	317	.530	65	73	.890	68	401	10.3
Tony Kimbro	F	6-7	190	Fr.	39	91	159	.572	26	44	.591	96	208	5.3
Mark McSwain	F	6-7	220	Jr.	28	32	57	.561	38	53	.717	80	102	3.6
Kenny Payne	F	6-7	195	Fr.	34	52	119	.437	17	22	.773	58	121	3.6
Kevin Walls	G	6-1	170	Fr.	27	16	36	.444	24	32	.750	12	56	2.1
Mike Abram	G-F	6-4	195	So.	17	12	23	.522	5	13	.385	19	29	1.7
Robbie Valentine	F	6-6	200	Sr.	16	9	17	.529	2	4	.500	9	20	1.3
Chris West	G	6-3	175	Jr.	22	6	12	.500	7	14	.500	9	19	0.9
Will Olliges	F	6-9	205	So.	12	2	5	.400	2	2	1.000	7	6	0.5
David Robinson	F	6-8	190	Fr.	5	1	3	.333	0	0	.000	6	2	0.4
Avery Marshall	F-C	6-7	220	Fr.	1	0	1	.000	0	0	.000	1	0	0.0
Team					1	1						89	2	
Louisville					39	1212	2281	.531	672	917	.733	1450	3096	79.4
Opponents					39	1067	2336	.457	560	823	.680	802	2694	69.1

Freshman Kevin Walls wears the victory net while Wagner signals No. 1 following Louisville's championship-game triumph over Duke.

Nervous" stature with a national title on the line.

"It's unbelievable that a freshman can handle that kind of pressure and play as well as he did," Crum said.

Ellison finished with 25 points, 11 rebounds and two blocks to earn the tournament's outstanding player award, only the second freshman to do so, next to Utah's Arnie Ferrin in 1944. Louisville, in turn, earned a 72-69 victory and its second national championship of the 1980s.

From there, all the weight of the Final Four hype descended on Ellison. "I'm pretty sure I get nervous at times," the freshman told reporters who asked. At the right time, however, he was all cool.

"Ellison was terrific," Duke Coach Mike Krzyzewski said. "He played a sensational game. He was a true force inside, both offensively and defensively. He does the same things as (Navy's David) Robinson but he has better personnel around him."

Most notably, someone like Thompson, who redeemed himself after a streaky regular season by averaging a team-high 18.3 points during the tournament while pulling down nearly eight rebounds per game.

Looking back, Crum relished the fact that Louisville had won two national titles with freshman centers. "In '80," Crum said, "Rodney McCray took his brother Scooter McCray's place when Scooter got hurt. In the championship game against UCLA in Indianapolis, he had 11 rebounds and played super. Then in '86, Pervis played great in the championship game.

"But the teams were a lot different. The '80 team had three sophomores, a freshman and Darrell Griffith. So it was an exceptionally young team but they had Darrell, a superstar who could carry you through all the tough spots. The '86 team had Milt Wagner, but he had been injured the year before, and it took him half the season to get into the swing of things. As he started playing better, our team got better and better. Coming into the tournament, we were really playing well."

Asked if the championships were a triumph of the system he learned from Wooden, Crum said: "I don't think there is any one system that is better than any other. You have to do what you do best. You can't teach what you don't know. The little things make the difference when something is working or not working, and they can only be learned over the years by trial and error.

"Something I think is very important is to play the toughest competition that you can play. Because you have to win six in a row in the tournament, you can't have an off night. And the only way you can learn to play your best every night is to play your best throughout the year."

It's the same old trick espoused by those Hollywood Indians—and perfected by those Louisville Cardinals.

TWENTY ONE

Jayhawks Take A Giant Step

KANSAS

1956-57

For years, Kansas Coach Forrest (Phog) Allen had bemoaned the presence of the big man in college basketball, going so far as to call 7-foot center Bob Kurland of Oklahoma A&M a "glandular goon."

In fact, the legendary coach wanted the height of the basket raised from 10 to 12 feet because he couldn't stand the notion that one player might dominate the game simply because of height.

Finally, in his fourth decade of coaching, Allen moderated his views—to the point that a 6-9 recruit from Terre Haute, Ind., looked mighty good to him. That prospect, Clyde Lovellette, went on to power Kansas to the 1952 NCAA championship.

Yet, even then, Allen resented the dominance of taller players.

"Dr. Allen objected to big men playing over the heads of everyone else," recalled Dick Harp, who served as Allen's assistant before succeeding the grand old man as the Jayhawks' coach. "He continued to believe that until his death (in 1974)."

Allen, however, didn't let those feelings get in the way in 1955 when he recruited the ultimate big man, a Philadelphia schoolboy of unique skills named Wilt (The Stilt) Chamberlain.

Chamberlain was the kind of player who made a coach stop and reconsider his basic beliefs about the game. Unlike most of the giants who had come before him, Chamberlain was not a plodding hulk. He showed marvelous coordination and the athletic skills of men much shorter.

Since his ninth-grade days, Chamberlain had been the darling of Eastern basketball. Scouts from college and professional teams followed his every move. As a 6-11 sophomore, Wilt led powerful Overbrook High School to the finals of the city championship against a veteran team from West Catholic High.

The scenario that developed would become miserably familiar to Chamberlain over the years. West Catholic packed four players around him inside, and Wilt's teammates couldn't make the open shots. Overbrook lost.

By Chamberlain's junior and senior years, he and Overbrook were dominant. He scored 90 points in one game. Over three varsity seasons, Chamberlain averaged 36.9 points and his teams won 58 games and lost just three.

In the spring of 1955, the basketball world was at Chamberlain's doorstep—literally. Colleges across the country, even some in the segregated South, sent recruiters. Word of Wilt's prowess had spread, to be sure. A friend in the National Basketball Association's public-relations office had gotten Chamberlain a job at Kutsher's in the Catskills, and Wilt demonstrated his basketball skills in summer-league competition at the New York resort. While still in high school, he played against the best talent that pro and college basketball had to offer.

He humbled Philadelphia Warriors center Neil Johnston in one game. When he did the same to B.H. Born, the leading scorer on Kansas' national runner-up team of 1953, Born relayed the news to Allen in Lawrence, Kan., about just how good Chamberlain was.

Allen promptly entered the recruiting fray. And whereas many coaches seemed to ooze ego and con-

Legendary Kansas Coach Phog Allen was forced to retire and never got to coach Wilt Chamberlain, his prize recruit, on the varsity level.

descension in those days, Allen was kind and courteous. He also took the time to talk about academics and played up the Jayhawks' great basketball tradition dating to Dr. James Naismith, founder of the game itself and Kansas' first coach.

In the mid-1950s, Philadelphia's big-time college basketball programs—La Salle, St. Joseph's, Temple, Pennsylvania and Villanova—were flourishing. La Salle, in fact, had won the NCAA championship in 1954 and wound up second in 1955. However, city kid Chamberlain was turning his attention elsewhere. Wilt had heard that the Midwest was playing the best brand of basketball; plus, he always had harbored a fascination of sorts with rural life.

Chamberlain finally narrowed his choices to Kansas, Indiana, Dayton and Michigan. According to the budding superstar, all of the contending schools offered incredible inducements. Nothing was documented in that regard, however.

Kansas finally won out, thanks in large measure to an Allen-led campaign that enlisted the help of influential blacks—including a businessman, a journalist and an entertainer—and various education leaders, all of whom had ties to the university or the state of Kansas. Needless to say, leading

alumni pitched in, too.

On Allen's 70th birthday, November 18, 1955, Chamberlain made his long-awaited basketball debut in Lawrence. With 14,000 fans on hand at the Jayhawks' eight-month-old Allen Fieldhouse (named for the venerable coach), freshman Wilt scored 42 points in an eye-popping performance as the Kansas yearlings spilled Allen's varsity, 81-71.

Allen, having reached the mandatory step-down age during Wilt's freshman season, had hoped to get the university to waive the retirement rule so he could coach his prize recruit for at least one varsity season. The request was denied.

So, after 39 seasons as Kansas' coach, Allen was out. The 38-year-old Harp, a Kansas assistant for eight seasons, was in.

"He and I talked often after that, but seldom about basketball and never at great length," Harp said of Allen more than three decades later. "He went on with his life."

Harp, a guard on Allen's 1940 Jayhawk team that finished second in the NCAA Tournament and a man whose only head-coaching experience at the collegiate level had been at William Jewell in Liberty, Mo., assumed control of a team that was heavily favored to win the national title. "I knew the situation would be difficult in terms of what people might do or think," he said. "But I wasn't overwhelmed with the pressure of it."

Nor was Chamberlain. The Philadelphia product took a full academic load and found time to hone his track-and-field skills (a talented triple-jump and shot-put performer, he was particularly gifted as a high jumper).

Chamberlain did encounter problems, though— off the court and away from the classroom. Accustomed to a relatively discrimination-free environment in Philadelphia, Wilt encountered various forms of segregation upon his arrival in the Lawrence/Kansas City, Mo., area. Society hadn't come to terms with its racial problems in the mid-'50s—not even in middle America. Chamberlain was enough of a presence, though, to integrate many eating establishments around Lawrence. It didn't happen overnight, and it wasn't easy. While change, in part, may have come for the wrong reasons, Chamberlain's talent clearly was forcing people to reconsider their positions.

Unlike Lew Alcindor, who a decade later would enter a UCLA program brimming with talented players, Chamberlain had come to a Kansas team not quite skilled enough to maximize his talents.

Many of the Jayhawk players were, naturally, Kansas and Missouri products, with Kansas City (35 miles from Lawrence) proving a major recruiting spot. Other than Chamberlain, the only highly recruited outsider was 6-4 sophomore forward Ron Loneski, out of Indiana.

Loneski and the other starting forward, 6-3 Gene Elstun, were fine rebounders. They combined with Chamberlain, who would average almost 19 rebounds in the 1956-57 season, to make the Jayhawks an excellent team on the backboards.

The Jayhawks had to be good on the boards. "We were not a great outside-shooting team," Harp said. And that was the flaw that would keep them from achieving everything they set out to do.

Kansas' offense, understandably, focused on Chamberlain inside. Which meant that opposing defenses did the same. "That was always the problem when Wilt was playing with us," Harp said. "The defense was always going to concentrate on him. Teams would rig zone defenses around him with three and four men, making it impossible for him to move, particularly around the basket.

"That, as you can imagine, was quite frustrating, then as now, for big men."

Since Kansas couldn't shoot well from outside, the zones stayed packed around Chamberlain. Defenders became markedly physical with him, beginning a tradition of rough play in the pivot that—as Harp and many traditional coaches see it—has become somewhat of a curse on the modern game.

"It was difficult for the officials to be objective

When Allen retired, the Kansas coaching reins were passed to Dick Harp, the Jayhawks' 38-year-old assistant.

about Wilt," Harp said. "There were numerous opportunities for officials to call defensive fouls. But most of the time, they didn't."

When officials did attempt to confront the problem, they found themselves constantly blowing the whistle, a course of action that can create another set of woes for a referee.

As might be imagined, the circumstances frustrated Chamberlain greatly, but the sophomore kept his composure, Harp said. And even with the defenses he faced, he powered through opponents. But, as Chamberlain himself has acknowledged, his frustrations led to errors in his method.

When he rebounded, Chamberlain liked to take the ball in one hand and slam it against the other, making a gunshot of a sound that startled players around him. What he should have been doing was whipping a quick outlet pass downcourt.

And when he blocked shots, Wilt enjoyed smacking the ball loudly and violently—and usually out of play. As a result, opponents retained the ball and another chance to score. This habit would prove particularly detrimental in pro ball when he went up against Bill Russell, the great Boston Celtics center, who had developed a technique of brush-blocking the ball and thus keeping it in play. By forcing a turnover, Russell also created a real opportunity for his team.

While Chamberlain has claimed that none of his coaches ever changed his bad habits, Harp said he sought to take advantage of Chamberlain's full range of athleticism. The young center's unique ability to run and jump combined with his size made him an awesome factor in any game, regardless of the defenses.

"Wilt understood the game of basketball," Harp said. "He had an opinion about the game and was bright about it. He wanted to use his size in close proximity to the basket. But he didn't develop his skills beyond that. If he wanted to, he could have been a significant playmaker (which he became in the pros). Wilt had demonstrated he could have shot the ball and been an effective passer."

The Kansas coaching staff spent some time trying to broaden Chamberlain's game. "But Wilt believed his most effective role was shooting the percentage shot," Harp recalled. "Wilt had strong opinions. He was a bright guy. But it's unfair to say he was difficult to work with. It wasn't easy for me. But from what he's written, it wasn't always easy for him to deal with me, either."

Over the years, Chamberlain has contended that Harp was too nice to coach a basketball team, that he continued to play struggling players because he didn't want to hurt their feelings.

The differences of opinion between the star player and his coach have never really changed. But even with their fundamental disagreements, the 1956-57 Jayhawks came within a pass of winning the national championship. And, as a unit, the Jayhawks would still be extremely competitive today. Chamberlain, of course, was the major factor, but he had plenty of help.

Backcourt veteran Maurice King, the only other black player on the team, played a strong defensive game and had something of a perimeter shot (he was more of a scorer than a shooter). He possessed the size and the ability to go on to a brief career in pro basketball. As a junior in 1955-56, King had led Kansas in scoring with a 14-point average.

Chamberlain's primary help in the frontcourt

Desperate coaches and defenders tried everything they could think of to negate Chamberlain's superior size and ability.

Season Results
1956-57 (24-3)

87	Northwestern 69	62 Oklahoma State..................... 52	
78	Marquette............................. 61	91 At Missouri........................... 58	
77	At Washington...................... 63	76 Oklahoma 56	
92	At Washington...................... 78	54 At Oklahoma State 56	
66	At California 56	87 Nebraska.............................. 60	
83	Wisconsin 62	68 At Colorado 57	
58	Iowa State at Kansas City*.57	64 At Kansas City..................... 57	
74	Oklahoma at Kansas City*....56	78 Colorado................................ 63	
80	Colorado at Kansas City*......54	73 SMU at Dallas† 65	
92	Missouri................................ 79	81 Oklahoma City at Dallas†......61	
59	At Oklahoma 51	80 San Fran. at Kansas City†....56	
51	Kansas City 45	53 N. Carolina at Kansas City†..54	
37	At Iowa State....................... 39	*Big Eight Tournament	
75	Iowa State 64	†NCAA Tournament	
69	At Nebraska 54		

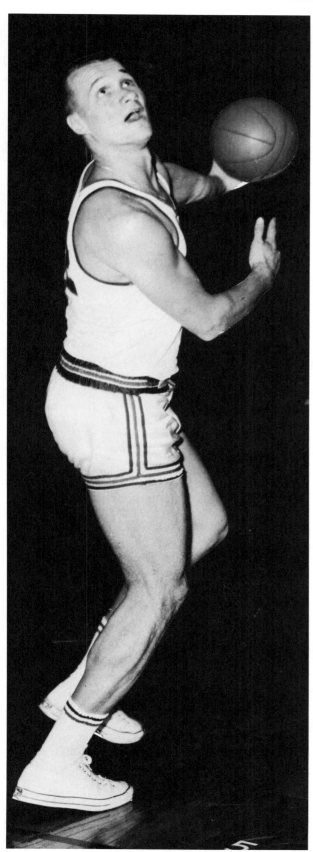

Ron Loneski, a 210-pound forward, was an excellent rebounder who did most of his shooting while close to the basket.

came from senior Elstun. Not much of a leaper, Elstun had a knack for offensive rebounding and playing position defense. Plus, he had some range on his jump shot, a scarce commodity for the Jayhawks. The other corner position was manned by Loneski, a 210-pounder who was an effective rebounder and used his position to score. Loneski's shooting range didn't go much beyond 12 feet.

The third senior in the starting lineup was point guard John Parker. A good athlete, he had played quarterback in high school and was an accomplished javelin thrower for Kansas. However, he had little speed or real quickness.

Parker's deficiencies in terms of movement mirrored that of the Kansas squad. Because the Jayhawks had little quickness, they didn't press much on defense. They played good man-to-man defense, though, made opponents work for their shots and sealed off the defensive boards. Most of all, they had Chamberlain in the middle, which was enough to make anybody stop and think before attacking the basket.

On offense, the Jayhawks used a controlled break and, of course, went to Wilt. "We didn't have great speed," Harp explained, "but we could get up and down the floor when we had the opportunity."

With that crew, Kansas went unbeaten for the first six weeks of the 1956-57 season and impressed virtually everyone. Opposing coaches stayed up nights trying to figure out a defense to contain Chamberlain. The Jayhawks faced triangle-and-twos and 1-3-1 zones and numerous "junk" alignments.

Chamberlain had opened the season—and his varsity career—in spine-tingling fashion. Playing before an Allen Fieldhouse capacity crowd of 17,000 fans, he burned Northwestern for a school-record 52 points as the Jayhawks frolicked, 87-69. Not only did Wilt go on a scoring binge, he picked off 31 rebounds—also a Kansas mark.

Victimized in the incredible outburst was Wildcats center Joe Ruklick, a much-ballyhooed sophomore in his own right. Ruklick tossed in 22 points, but was left shaking his head.

"It's ridiculous," said Ruklick, alluding to Chamberlain's talent level. "I've seen guys who could move better, guys who could do other things better. But this Chamberlain. He made me feel like a 6-year-old kid."

In his second varsity contest, Wilt ravaged Marquette. He scored 39 points, garnered 22 rebounds and blocked 14 shots. The damage came against another touted sophomore, Mike Moran. While the Warriors' Moran went on to post a 20.4 season scoring average, he was limited to four points (and one field goal) by Chamberlain. Kansas coasted, 78-61, despite the absence of Loneski, who had suffered a foot fracture against Northwestern.

Wilt and Kansas then took their show on the

Jayhawk guard Maurice King (8) failed to stop this shot (left) by North Carolina's Lennie Rosenbluth in the 1957 NCAA Tournament title game. B.H. Born (right), a Kansas star in the early '50s, wound up playing a recruiting role in the quest for Chamberlain's services.

road for the first time. They scored two 14-point victories against the Washington Huskies in Seattle, then moved down the coast to play California. Coach Pete Newell's Golden Bears seized an eight-point halftime edge and inched ahead by 10 points on two occasions in the second half, but front-line players Lew Johnson and Ronnie Johnston fueled a Kansas comeback that netted a 66-56 triumph.

Overcoming a mix of sagging defenses in the weeks ahead, Kansas ran its record to 12-0 on January 12 by beating archrival Kansas State by six points at Allen Field House. The game marked the return to action of Loneski.

Opponents' zone contraptions finally achieved the desired result in the 13th game when Iowa State played slowdown ball, held Chamberlain to 17 points and hit a shot at the final buzzer for a 39-37 triumph at Ames.

Cyclones Coach Bill Strannigan clearly was demonstrating that there were ways to deal with Kansas' mighty force. In the Big Seven Conference's preseason tournament 2½ weeks earlier, he had devised a strategy in which Wilt was held to 12 points. The implementation of a 1-3-1 zone, with 6-8 Don Medsker positioned behind Wilt, a forward deployed in front of the Kansas center and a guard sagging back, built a three-man fence around Chamberlain and helped limit him to three field goals (and six free throws); on the other hand, the strategy had enabled other Jayhawks to get easy shots, and Kansas managed a one-point victory on Elstun's 20-foot jump shot in the last six seconds.

This time, Strannigan stationed Medsker (who made the game-winning field goal) in front of Wilt and had Iowa State's forwards providing protection — on an alternating basis — from the rear.

"Actually, it was a 2-3 zone, with the forwards dropping off in a more normal way," the Iowa State coach explained. "The weak-side forward in the zone would go behind Wilt to block his path. The guards didn't drop back this time. They stayed out front to contain the other shooters."

Whatever the game plan, Strannigan's team offered hope to every other team. Chamberlain and Kansas could be beaten.

Kansas won its next five games, then dropped another buzzer-beater. Playing at Oklahoma State, the Jayhawks got 14 field goals and 32 points from Chamberlain — as always, Cowboys Coach Hank Iba insisted on using a man-for-man defense — but received more than one field goal from only one other player. Mel Wright's 20-foot jump shot with two seconds remaining produced a 56-54 victory for Oklahoma State, which benefited from 18 points by forward Eddie Sutton, who later would make his mark in the collegiate coaching ranks.

Kansas finished the regular season with a three-game bulge in the Big Seven standings and a 21-2 record overall. By reigning as conference champions, the Jayhawks moved into NCAA Tournament play and drew Southern Methodist in the first round.

Harp's team stayed 30 miles out of Dallas, site of the Midwest Regional and home of SMU, but someone still burned a cross in the yard across from the Jayhawks' quarters. And fans at the Jayhawks-Mustangs game on the SMU campus punctuated the event with racial epithets. Chamberlain answered them with 36 points and 22 rebounds, but Kansas had to go to overtime to win, 73-65.

Against Oklahoma City in the regional final, there were more racial comments and rough play. It got so bad that Oklahoma City standout Hub Reed apologized to Chamberlain for his teammates' behavior. Chamberlain later said he appreciated Reed's comments, and the fact that Kansas overwhelmed the Chiefs, 81-61, provided additional salve.

In the Final Four, held in Kansas City, the second-ranked Jayhawks appeared before what basically was a home crowd and played like it, blowing out defending national champion San Francisco (minus Bill Russell and K.C. Jones) in one semifinal, 80-56.

The players from undefeated and top-ranked North Carolina, having survived a three-overtime struggle against Michigan State in the first semifinal, watched the destruction. But while most observers figured that the scenario—particularly the Kansas-oriented crowd and Wilt's presence—favored the Jayhawks in the championship match, North Carolina wasn't about to let Chamberlain dictate the course of events.

Carolina Coach Frank McGuire opened the game with a psychological ploy—he had 5-11 guard Tommy Kearns jump center against Chamberlain, figuring that Wilt would win the jump regardless of his opponent and that the maneuver just might unnerve the big guy.

The comedic move disconcerted the Kansas center, and North Carolina followed up by surrounding Wilt with a stifling zone. In response, Kansas shot terribly. The Tar Heels ended the first half with a 29-22 lead. But in the second 20 minutes, Chamberlain shook loose from the zone and the Jayhawks moved into position to claim the national championship. With one minute, 45 seconds, left on the clock, Chamberlain whipped a pass to Elstun, who not only boosted Kansas into a three-point lead (44-41) by cashing a field goal but also drew a foul from North Carolina All-America Lennie Rosenbluth. It was Rosenbluth's fifth foul of the game.

Elstun proceeded to miss the foul shot, though, and North Carolina scrambled back for a 46-46 tie at the end of regulation. The first overtime produced a single basket by each team, and the second extra session was scoreless.

As Kansas guarded a 53-52 lead with time ticking down in the third overtime of this stem-winder, Tar Heels center Joe Quigg found himself with the ball near the top of the key and maneuvered for a shot. King, hustling over to lend help defensively, fouled the 6-9 Quigg, a 71.9 percent free-throw shooter for the season. Quigg sank both foul shots.

1957 KANSAS
Head Coach—Dick Harp　　　Final Record—24-3

Player	Pos.	Hgt.	Wgt.	Cl.	G	FG	FGA	Pct.	FT.	FTA	Pct.	Reb.	Pts.	Avg.
Wilt Chamberlain	C	7-0	214	So.	27	275	588	.468	250	399	.627	510	800	29.6
Gene Elstun	F	6-3	175	Sr.	26	110	259	.425	73	112	.652	189	293	11.3
Maurice King	G	6-2	190	Sr.	27	101	278	.363	61	88	.693	122	263	9.7
Ron Loneski	F	6-4	210	So.	17	51	155	.329	61	87	.701	115	163	9.6
John Parker	G	6-0	173	Sr.	27	60	132	.455	28	39	.718	53	148	5.5
Ron Johnston	F	6-1	180	Sr.	12	17	50	.340	17	25	.680	41	51	4.3
Lew Johnson	C-F	6-6	198	Sr.	26	31	102	.304	15	29	.517	101	77	3.0
Bob Billings	G	5-11	173	So.	22	10	34	.294	28	35	.800	19	48	2.2
John Cleland	G	6-3	170	Jr.	6	4	5	.800	4	5	.800	4	12	2.0
Larry Kelley	G	5-11	155	So.	1	1	2	.500	0	0	.000	2	2	2.0
Eddie Dater	G	6-2	195	Sr.	15	11	29	.379	2	2	1.000	10	24	1.6
Harry Jett	F	6-3	166	Sr.	8	3	10	.300	4	4	1.000	4	10	1.3
Blaine Hollinger	G	5-10	159	Sr.	18	8	26	.308	5	12	.417	14	21	1.2
Monte Johnson	F	6-5	168	So.	11	4	19	.211	4	5	.800	16	12	1.1
Lee Green	F	6-5	190	Sr.	10	5	12	.417	0	2	.000	14	10	1.0
Gary Thompson	F	6-4	207	Jr.	7	3	5	.600	1	4	.250	10	7	1.0
Lynn Kindred	G	6-2	156	So.	16	1	14	.071	2	5	.400	14	4	0.3
Joe Ensley	G	6-1	167	So.	1	0	0	.000	0	0	.000	2	0	0.0
Team												59		
Kansas					27	695	1720	.404	555	853	.651	1299	1945	72.0
Opponents					27	586	1688	.347	411	648	.634	949	1583	58.6

Kansas' last-ditch hopes for victory were dashed when Loneski, driving the middle, failed to make connections on a pass intended for Chamberlain. North Carolina, for the second straight night, had prevailed in triple overtime. This triumph, 54-53, meant the national championship for the Tar Heels.

For Kansas, the defeat meant anguish. After showering, dressing and summing up his reaction to the defeat with a terse, "We lost, that's all, we lost," Chamberlain left Municipal Auditorium and walked back to the team's nearby hotel. There was a slight drizzle, and a small boy from North Carolina chided the Kansas center the whole way: "We wilted the Stilt."

Chamberlain, the title game's top scorer (23 points) and leading board man (14 rebounds) and voted the No. 1 player in the Final Four, said nothing. As long as he played basketball, he would be considered something less than a champion. In pro basketball, where his teams time and again fell short of the Russell-led Celtics, the 1957 NCAA title game would be cited as the first piece of evidence that Chamberlain simply couldn't deliver in the clutch.

"It was a tragic time," Harp recalled, "because we all thought at the end of the game that we had it won. Defeat always bothered me. And that game bothered me for a long, long time, principally because of the young men who played for us."

Harp also has been disturbed by the criticism directed Chamberlain's way.

"Wilt Chamberlain is the dominant player in the history of the game as far as shooting and rebounding," Harp contended. "Wilt has never received his due."

Chamberlain subsequently eased the pain of the title-game loss, at least to some extent, by turning his attention to his track-and-field specialties. Plus, he zeroed in on his other major interests—cars and music. "I beat it out...I'm a real cat," Wilt responded in the jargon of the day when asked about his preference for rhythm and blues.

By now, Chamberlain had even gotten used to the gawkers. Asked if he hated all the "How's-the-weather-up-there?" queries, he said: "Why should I? It (his height) is getting me an education and the things I want. It's not too bad having people know me."

Fans and opponents would get to know Wilt even more in 1957-58.

Of the top seven scorers for the national runner-up Jayhawks, five were seniors. Elstun, with an 11.3 scoring average, and King, at 9.7, would be the principal losses as Harp looked ahead to the '57-'58 campaign. Chamberlain and Loneski, 29.6 and 9.6 scorers as sophomores, would carry the load.

A groin injury during the '57-'58 season kept Wilt out of two conference games, however, and the Jayhawks lost both of those contests. Those

Chamberlain left Kansas after his junior season and joined the Harlem Globetrotters, owned and founded by Abe Saperstein (left).

defeats put the Jayhawks behind Kansas State in the regular-season standings, and although they routed the Wildcats in their regular-season finale, Harp's charges came up short in the Big Seven race (they tied for second with Iowa State, two games behind Kansas State). In those days of a restricted NCAA Tournament, Kansas' season was over.

Frustrated by the slowdown style of play he had encountered in collegiate basketball, Chamberlain left Kansas after his junior season and joined the Harlem Globetrotters for a year's duty before entering the NBA.

While Chamberlain's image may have been flawed in the minds of some members of the press and among a segment of fans as well, it seldom was tarnished for those who competed against him.

"People cannot imagine the impact that man had on us all at the time," Quigg said a quarter-of-a-century later. "Wilt was just a colossus."

And, because of the presence of one Wilt Chamberlain, the 1956-57 Kansas basketball team ranks as a giant among the college game's best all-time units.

TWENTY TWO

Big Man On Campus

OKLAHOMA A&M

1944-45 1945-46

When Bob Kurland arrived at Oklahoma A&M in 1942, he was a tall, thin, awkward redhead who walked with a pronounced stoop, as if he was trying to shrug his body into a smaller frame. The youngster was fast approaching 7-foot tall and there was nowhere to hide, not even on a basketball court.

Seven-footers were unheard of in this era of basketball innocence, so Kurland's self-consciousness was understandable. He was considered something of a freak and was treated as such by taunting fans. Phog Allen, Kansas' legendary coach, even went so far as to call him "a glandular goon."

That remark may seem cruel, but "goon" was the buzzword for exceptionally tall players in those formative years. Basketball was still considered a sport for smaller men, and "goons" were thought to be unathletic giants who survived only by virtue of their height.

Bob Kurland helped change that perception. Through determination and excessive hours of hard work, he honed his skills, learned to intimidate opponents and silenced the critics. He combined with 6-10 DePaul center George Mikan, the other dominant big man of the era, to redirect the course of basketball history.

"We opened the door to the idea that the big man could play the game," Kurland recalled with pride, "which in our day was, by Eastern standards, played by guys 5-10, 5-11, who were quick, took the set shot and so forth. We opened the door for what the game is today, played by magnificent athletes who are just performing geniuses."

That breakthrough might well have been left to others had it not been for the coaching genius of one Henry Iba. Known for his slow, deliberate style of play, Iba took a chance on this young giant and helped him grow from a skinny, uncoordinated kid into a solid, dominating basketball player. Slowly but surely, under the patient tutelage of Iba, the "glandular goon" was transformed into "Foothills," the man mountain who would lead the Aggies to back-to-back NCAA championships.

The pairing of Kurland and Iba was perfect. By the 1940s, Iba was well known for his incredible patience, not only in game strategy, but in his teaching methods. And Kurland would stretch those qualities to the limit.

But Iba was up to the challenge, just as he had been as a youngster in Easton, Mo. Raised on a farm and apparently doomed to a life of rural naivete, Iba parlayed an avid interest in sports into a college education. He starred in basketball, baseball and football at Westminster College in Fulton, Mo., before playing minor league baseball briefly in the St. Louis Cardinals chain. When he finally turned to the coaching—and teaching—profession, he became an immediate success.

He turned out a state championship team at an Oklahoma City high school before carving out a 101-14 mark as coach at Maryville Teachers College (later called Northwest Missouri State). After a year at Colorado, the 30-year-old Iba took the Oklahoma A&M (later to be called Oklahoma State) job in 1934.

It was there that he refined a system that would come to epitomize ball control and discipline. His style was not always appreciated by critical Eastern

Oklahoma A&M Coach Henry Iba (center) with key members of his 1945-46 championship team: (left to right) Bob Kurland, Blake Williams, Weldon Kern, J.L. Parks, A.L. Bennett and Sam Aubrey.

coaches, who preferred a faster-paced game. But it was difficult to argue with success. And the unyielding Iba, who would compile 767 coaching victories (third on the all-time list) before his retirement in 1970, had plenty of that.

Kurland remembers his old coach as demanding, but not unrealistic.

"One thing Iba told us early in the scheme of things—and this was the great thing about him—he said, 'You guys are going to have all the wins. I'm going to take all the losses, but we'll do it my way,'" Kurland said.

"Old Iba was known for being a volatile man with a loud voice on the bench. At halftime he was anything but that. It was cold calculated logic in terms of our strategy. We had guys who kept shot charts, but we didn't have 14 advisors and assistant coaches and all that. Henry would come in at halftime after standing in the hall and thinking about it and would say, 'Here's your problems.'

"We had complete confidence in what he told us. There was never a deviation from the strategy and the style and the tactics that he developed. We were good mechanics, not great athletes. We knew the game, we knew where everyone was on the floor at all times, we knew the tempo of the game and what the strategy was."

Both Iba's patience and his strategy suited the times. Today, training methods and the development of athletes seem to follow an ever-spiraling sophistication. In the 1940s, the times were more innocent, the methods less aggressive.

"Iba played what he called 'the percentages,'" Kurland said. "He took his abilities, his players and what he taught, and he maximized the things he had to work with. Again it comes back to the fact

that he was a teacher. He was a terrible recruiter. He would not recruit. He was a mentor, and he expected people to come to him because he was a teacher."

Kurland, despite the general resentment toward big men, was contacted by coaches from across the country when he played his high school ball in a St. Louis suburb. But his fate was sealed when Iba brought his Aggie team to St. Louis for a Missouri Valley Conference game and invited the youngster, then a high school senior, to eat a steak dinner with the team. Afterward, Iba arranged for Kurland to ride a bus to Stillwater for a tryout.

"We had just come through the Depression," Kurland recalled. "I was in St. Louis, and I wanted to be an engineer. Oklahoma A&M had a good engineering school. Henry Iba was a man whose reputation and integrity had been established.

"I remember sitting in Henry Iba's office. He said, 'I don't know if you can play college-level basketball or not. But I'll make you this promise: If you'll go to school, if you'll practice every day, I will see that you will get room, board, tuition, books and an education.' And that was our deal."

Iba had faced many basketball challenges, but the development of a big man was a new concept in 1942.

"You have to remember that Iba had never had —there were almost no coaches who'd ever had— people as tall as I was," Kurland said. "So the early coaches really were pioneers in discovering skills that were required in playing a post type of game. Iba helped me develop physically by jumping rope and teaching me to move, particularly on defense, which I took great pride in."

As with the rest of society, the course of college basketball was altered by World War II. Every-

Kurland, once described as 'a glandular goon' by Kansas Coach Phog Allen, used his 7-foot frame to help open the door for big men in college basketball.

where, the atmosphere was heavy with uncertainty.

"It was very difficult," Kurland recalled. "I started school in '42 when college athletics was still organized. But many schools had decided to discontinue their athletic programs."

With his patience, his discipline and his ability to teach, Iba was just the coach to thrive amid the chaos of war.

"When I was a freshman at Oklahoma A&M, there were 132 guys who came out for basketball," Kurland said. "Henry Iba never cut a guy off the team. He never said, 'You can't play.' But after two weeks or three weeks they kind of weeded themselves out after four-hour practice sessions every day. And those that stayed, played."

Even something as tragic as war can provide a silver lining. For Kurland, this came in the form of his offensive development, which was helped along his sophomore season by a man who, under normal circumstances, already would have graduated from college.

"I think I learned as much from a man named Floyd Burdette, who happened to be in the Air Corps training program, as anybody," Kurland said. "He had re-enrolled at Oklahoma State in 1943 and was on the team. Floyd was 28 and about 6-6. He taught me how to hook a guy inside with your elbow, put your elbow on your defender's hip, to roll on him and to really develop my shot, a quick little jump-push shot."

Kurland's real strength, however, was his defense. His presence around the basket was so intimidating that Iba devised a revolutionary strategy that would prompt outcries from a distraught coaching fraternity. It was called goaltending.

Under the rules of 1944, it was perfectly legal for a player to knock away shots that were on their downward flight. The defender was not allowed to interfere with balls once they were in the cylinder, but with Kurland's superior height, many would-be baskets didn't make it that far.

"There were other people who could goaltend," Kurland explained, "but we were the first team to sit down and deliberately devise a strategy and to play a defense that included goaltending as its central theme. I first tried it against Oklahoma University when I was a freshman (1942-43). Oklahoma had beaten us down at Norman. They had a good team. . . . We had no way to beat them except by coming up with something unique.

"I had jumped rope that whole year and by this time I could put part of my arm well above the rim. We had only practiced three days on this defense. Coach Bruce Drake and the Oklahoma team came into Stillwater, which is a madhouse to play in, and they took the first shot. I knocked it down. They took the second shot and I knocked it down. Allie Paine and Gerald Tucker (Oklahoma stars), God, they went crazy. They called a timeout, and they didn't know what the heck to do. That was the last game of the season (a 40-28 A&M victory).

"Iba thought about it," Kurland said, "and we started off the next year with a rinky-dink team because most of the guys had gone to war. We had a pickup team, and we had to find something that was different. So we developed a technique where it was literally a zone defense with me knocking the ball down. We were very effective at it. People in many cases would beat themselves psychologically, and that was a bad thing for the game. But it was a way of winning, and it was within the rules."

Even without a great supporting cast, Kurland and his goaltending defense carried the 1943-44 Aggies to a 27-6 record and a berth in the National Invitation Tournament in New York. A&M, which had led the nation by limiting opponents to 28.8 points per game, fell in the second round to DePaul, 41-38.

After the season, the NCAA acceded to pressure and changed its goaltending rule. No longer were players allowed to knock away shots when the ball was on its downward arc to the basket. To balance that measure, the rules committee also decided that players should be allowed five fouls, instead of four, before fouling out.

Those who thought the goaltending change would diminish Kurland's effectiveness were sadly mistaken. The Aggie big man, more mature and confident, was just getting started. The final two

Season Results
1944-45 (27-4)

46	At Phillips	37	58	Liberal AAF ... 35
57	Glennan Hospital	34	46	At DePaul ... 48
44	Westminster (Pa.) at Buff.	33	41	NATTS Skyjackets ... 29
44	At New York University	41	58	Will Rogers AAF ... 29
44	At Temple	46	23	Oklahoma ... 17
63	Baylor at Oklahoma City*	16	60	Texas Christian at O.C. ... 26
42	Rice at Oklahoma City*	28	46	At Tulsa ... 23
43	Arkansas at Oklahoma City*	34	73	NAS Zoomers ... 42
31	At NATTS Skyjackets	34	84	Tinker Field ... 30
38	At Arkansas	41	78	Tulsa ... 27
49	Arkansas at El Dorado	40	62	Utah at Kansas City† ... 37
66	Frederick AAF	37	68	Arkansas at Kansas City† ... 41
89	Phillips	28	49	New York University† ... 45
86	Pentathlon Military (Mex.)	27	52	DePaul at New York‡ ... 44
45	At Oklahoma	31		*All-College Tournament
53	Wyoming at Wichita	28		†NCAA Tournament
39	Wyoming at Oklahoma City	31		‡Red Cross Benefit Game

1945-46 (31-2)

56	Tinker Field	17	38	At Tulsa ... 16
42	DePaul	46	53	Arkansas ... 29
45	Westminster (Pa.) at Buff.	23	46	Arkansas at Oklahoma City ... 31
49	At Long Island	33	71	Washington (Mo.) at Tulsa ... 26
38	At Temple	36	86	St. Louis ... 33
69	Texas at Oklahoma City*	34	35	At Wichita ... 24
46	Kansas at Oklahoma City*	28	51	Drake ... 34
65	Baylor at Oklahoma City*	46	47	Oklahoma ... 41
53	Creighton at Oklahoma City*	34	65	At Drake ... 25
52	Wichita	41	45	At Creighton ... 24
64	Ft. Riley	43	50	At Oklahoma ... 34
34	Wyoming at Oklahoma City	24	49	Kansas at Kansas City† ... 38
40	Wyoming at Wichita	24	44	Baylor at Kansas City† ... 29
53	Tulsa	22	52	California at Kansas City† ... 35
39	At St. Louis	27	43	N. Carolina at New York† ... 40
60	At Washington (Mo.)	35		*All-College Tournament
46	At DePaul	38		†NCAA Tournament
37	Bowling Green at Chicago	48		

years of his college career became a study in domination.

With Kurland showing the world that he could play defense with his feet as well as his long arms, the Aggies rolled to 23 victories in 27 games during the 1944-45 regular season. Iba's team, as was the case with most college teams that season, was boosted substantially by a flood of veterans returning from the war.

"They were good basketball players," Kurland said of his 1944-45 teammates. "Cecil Hankins was a great athlete. He could dunk the ball and was only 6-1. Dunking in those days was exceptional.

"John Wylie (a reserve guard) was slow. Doyle Parrack was excitable. J.L. Parks (a reserve forward) was the toughest kid I ever saw. He didn't have fingers, he had fists when he dribbled the ball. He was the quickest starter and he could break faster then any kid I ever saw.

"Blake Williams had a bad heart. And this is a fact: There were times in major games when we'd have to break and call timeout and his heart would fibrillate, and he'd have to lay down before his heart would come back into rhythm."

Finally, Iba had the athletes to run his control game to near perfection. The starting unit of Kurland at center, Hankins and 5-10 Weldon Kern at the forward positions and Parrack and Williams at the guard spots frustrated opponent after opponent with its deliberate, mistake-free passing precision—the product of long, grueling, repetitive practice sessions. Kurland and Hankins did most of the scoring. Everybody played defense.

"We became good mechanics of the game," Kurland said. "All of us could play every position on the court. Despite the fact that I was 7-foot tall, we had an offense where I rotated to the guard position. All of us knew exactly where everyone was on the floor at all times.

"We had three or four offenses against the man-to-man defense. We had a tight man-to-man and three zone defenses, and each one required personal discipline as to the position you played on the court."

In terms of entertainment, the 1944-45 basketball season was a jewel. The game's two dominating big men, Mikan and Kurland, were the marquee performers. Both had matured fast and were eager to prove that tall boys could play the game—if not with grace, at least with guile and power. The center stage for both would be Madison Square Garden, the hotspot of Eastern basketball. The reward for Kurland and Iba, of course, would be the NCAA championship. Mikan and DePaul would reign supreme in the NIT.

The NCAA Tournament was in its seventh year in 1945 and featured eight teams—four from the West, four from the East. The Aggies' first-round opponent in the West Regional was defending-

Iba, a firm believer in the slow and deliberate style of play, guided his Aggies to consecutive national championships.

champion Utah. The Utes had lost stars Arnie Ferrin and Fred Sheffield to service duty after their final regular-season game and fell meekly to the powerful Aggies, 62-37. Kurland served notice by scoring 28 points.

Their next opponent was a good Arkansas team that had handed A&M one of its four regular-season losses (in three meetings). But there was no stopping the Aggies and Iba's control game on this day. A&M prevailed, 68-41, with Hankins scoring 22 points, Parrack 16 and Kurland 15.

That set up a title showdown that had New Yorkers drooling. Howard Cann's New York University team had dropped a 44-41 early-season decision to the Aggies, but the Violets had since added freshman sensation Dolph Schayes to their roster.

Kurland looks for a pass during action in the 1946 NCAA Tournament title game against North Carolina.

With high-scoring forward Sid Tanenbaum teaming with the 6-6 freshman center, hopes were high that the New Yorkers could derail the Kurland-Iba express.

This anticipated matchup almost was ruined in a semifinal game by Ohio State. With 18,500 noisy fans, the first capacity crowd in NCAA Tournament history, looking on, the Buckeyes built a 10-point lead and appeared headed for victory with only two minutes remaining. But Cann directed his players to foul and Ohio State, with the choice of shooting free throws or taking the ball out of bounds, chose the former. The Buckeyes missed, the Violets didn't miss and a set shot by New York's Don Forman in the closing moments tied the score at 62, sending the game into overtime. The Violets controlled the extra session and escaped with a 70-65 victory.

For the first time, the NCAA had a final in Madison Square Garden featuring a New York team. Iba's Aggies had to overcome NYU's homecourt advantage while controlling a Violet offense that thrived on quickness and ball movement.

"They were tough neighborhood kids who usually played on the playground," Kurland recalled of the NYU team, "and they would run right through you. They were great at driving, and we were disciplined by Coach Iba to expect that. We had a strategy laid out for the Eastern style of playing. It consisted of driving in the middle and knocking them down."

Cann's Violets played A&M tight in a contest that became a classic of possession basketball. With each

1945 OKLAHOMA A&M

Head Coach—Henry Iba   Final Record—27-4

Player	Pos.	Hgt.	Wgt.	Cl.	G	FG	FGA	Pct.	FT.	FTA	Pct.	Reb.	Pts.	Avg.
Bob Kurland	C	7-0	215	Jr.	31	214	...	....	101	176	.574	....	529	17.1
Cecil Hankins	F	6-1	175	...	23	127	...	....	53	102	.520	....	307	13.3
Weldon Kern	F	5-10	145	Jr.	31	114	...	....	77	136	.566	....	305	9.8
Doyle Parrack	G	6-0	165	..	19	62	...	....	20	31	.645	....	144	7.6
J.L. Parks	F	6-0	160	Fr.	31	47	...	....	30	51	.588	....	124	4.0
Blake Williams	G	6-1	188	Fr.	31	52	...	....	14	26	.538	....	118	3.8
Gentry Warren	G	6-1	190	Jr.	10	12	...	....	4	7	.571	....	28	2.8
Jack Lyon	G	5-10	135	Fr.	10	10	...	....	5	9	.556	....	25	2.5
Harry Fenimore	F	5-10	148	Fr.	2	2	...	....	0	0	.000	....	4	2.0
Auddie Hall	G	6-2	192	Fr.	2	2	...	....	0	0	.000	....	4	2.0
John Wylie	G	6-0	165	Fr.	28	20	...	....	10	17	.588	....	50	1.8
Bill Johnson	G	...	...	...	7	3	...	....	2	7	.286	....	8	1.1
Dick Caldwell	..	...	...	...	2	1	...	....	0	0	.000	....	2	1.0
D.W. Jones	G	5-10	145	Fr.	12	4	...	....	3	5	.600	....	11	0.9
Bill York	G	5-9	160	Fr.	8	1	...	....	4	5	.800	....	6	0.8
Joe Halbert	C	6-7	200	Fr.	20	5	...	....	1	1	1.000	....	11	0.6
Carl Alexander	F	6-1	168	Fr.	3	0	...	....	1	2	.500	....	1	0.3
Art Rigg	F	5-11	130	So.	1	0	...	....	0	0	.000	....	0	0.0
Charles Crook	G	6-0	160	Sr.	5	0	...	....	0	0	.000	....	0	0.0
Oklahoma A&M					31	676	...	....	325	575	.565	....	1677	54.1
Opponents					31	368	...	....	302	508	.594	....	1038	33.5

team afraid to take a bad shot, the score stayed close. In the end, Kurland made the difference. Scoring 22 points and limiting Schayes to six, Kurland chalked one up for the big men. Oklahoma A&M prevailed, 49-45, and Iba heaped praise on the Aggie players who patiently, and unselfishly, had worked the ball inside to their big center.

With the NCAA championship in their back pockets, the Aggies had one more battle to fight. By virtue of their title, A&M would play in the third, and last, of the Red Cross benefit games. Their opponent would be NIT champ DePaul. Finally, Kurland versus Mikan.

It was billed as the "Game of the Century," but the much-ballyhooed battle of the big men turned out to be a disappointment. Kurland, taller and more agile, outscored Mikan, stronger and a more dangerous offensive threat, 14-9, primarily because the DePaul center fouled out 14 minutes into the game. Kurland also was plagued by foul trouble in a contest won by A&M, 52-44.

Hankins and Parrack were gone when the 1945-46 season opened, but Oklahoma A&M still had Kurland and it added newcomer Sam Aubrey, a war veteran who had been wounded in Italy and would go on to earn all-league selection in the Missouri Valley Conference. The Aggies, needless to say, were considered one of the nation's dominant

powers and they did nothing to dissuade their supporters.

Iba's grand defensive machine was working on all cylinders as it ripped through its regular-season schedule, losing only twice while piling up 28 victories. The highlight of the season for Kurland came in his hometown of St. Louis, when Iba turned him loose offensively and he responded with a 58-point effort against the Billikens. The big center went on to lead the nation in total points (he finished with a 19.5 average), though Mikan captured his second straight scoring title.

It seems ironic in retrospect that the 28-2 Aggies were not even awarded an automatic berth in the NCAA Tournament. Kansas, a member of the same district in which Oklahoma A&M competed, had won 19 of 20 decisions and lobbied hard for inclusion in the field. A pre-tournament playoff game was set up in Kansas City and the Aggies and Jayhawks met for the right to continue postseason play.

It was no contest. Kurland scored 28 points and Phog Allen watched the "glandular goon" intimidate his team defensively in a 49-38 A&M victory. With that matter settled, Iba prepared his team for a run at its second straight NCAA title. No team had managed two titles, consecutive or otherwise, in the short history of the event.

1946 OKLAHOMA A&M
Head Coach—Henry Iba   **Final Record—31-2**

Player	Pos.	Hgt.	Wgt.	Cl.	G	FG	FGA	Pct.	FT.	FTA	Pct.	Reb.	Pts.	Avg.
Bob Kurland	C	7-0	212	Sr.	33	257	...	.....	129	223	.578	.....	643	19.5
Weldon Kern	F	5-10	145	Jr.	25	71	...	.....	64	103	.621	.....	206	8.2
J.L. Parks	G	6-0	165	So.	33	70	...	.....	47	80	.588	.....	187	5.7
Blake Williams	G	6-2	190	So.	33	57	...	.....	34	58	.586	.....	148	4.5
A.L. Bennett	F	6-2	175	So.	22	34	...	.....	15	24	.625	.....	83	3.8
Joe Bradley	G	6-2	165	Fr.	30	42	...	.....	17	29	.586	.....	101	3.4
Sam Aubrey	F	6-4	195	Sr.	33	42	...	.....	24	32	.750	.....	108	3.3
James Moore	C	6-10	205	Fr.	5	4	...	.....	2	4	.500	.....	10	2.0
Clarence Parker	G	6-4	180	Fr.	3	3	...	.....	0	0	.000	.....	6	2.0
Joe Pitts	F	5-10	155	Fr.	25	18	...	.....	11	16	.688	.....	47	1.9
Gene Bell	G	...	...	...	16	9	...	.....	13	14	.929	.....	31	1.9
Joe Halbert	C	6-7	210	So.	27	15	...	.....	7	12	.583	.....	37	1.4
Bill Crowe	F	6-3	165	Sr.	11	6	...	.....	2	3	.667	.....	14	1.3
Paul Geymann	F	6-1	170	Jr.	21	9	...	.....	4	8	.500	.....	22	1.0
Martin Loper	F	6-2	200	Fr.	2	1	...	.....	0	0	.000	.....	2	1.0
Wayne Boles	F	6-0	170	Fr.	8	3	...	.....	1	3	.333	.....	7	0.9
Larry Hayes	F	6-1	175	Fr.	3	0	...	.....	2	2	1.000	.....	2	0.7
Ted Hughes	G	6-0	185	Fr.	3	1	...	.....	0	0	.000	.....	2	0.7
Lou Steinmeier	C	6-5	195	Sr.	12	2	...	.....	2	2	1.000	.....	6	0.5
Ollie Helderle	F	6-4	185	Fr.	2	0	...	.....	1	3	.333	.....	1	0.5
Bill Long	F	...	...	...	2	0	...	.....	0	0	.000	.....	0	0.0
James Stroup	F	6-0	170	Fr.	2	0	...	.....	0	0	.000	.....	0	0.0
Jack Meredith	C	6-4	180	Fr.	1	0	...	.....	0	0	.000	.....	0	0.0
Bill Cooper	G	6-2	170	Fr.	1	0	...	.....	0	0	.000	.....	0	0.0
Don Slocum	C	6-6	165	Fr.	1	0	...	.....	0	0	.000	.....	0	0.0
Charles Darr	F	6-2	170	Fr.	1	0	...	.....	0	0	.000	.....	0	0.0
Totals					33	644			375	616	.609	.....	1663	50.4
Opponents					33	358			342	559	.612	.....	1058	32.1

Oklahoma A&M's 1944-45 championship team: Front row (left to right) — Assistant coach Herman Millikan, Cecil Hankins, John Wylie, Carl Alexander, Bill York, Kern, Art Rigg, Parks, Don Bentley, assistant coach Jack Hopkins. Second row — Publicity director Otis Wile, Dick Caldwell, Bill Johnson, Gentry Warren, Joe Halbert, Kurland, Williams, Charles Crook, Sidney Wilson, Doyle Parrack, Iba.

Did the Aggies feel any pressure as they began their quest?

"In '45 and '46, we had guys that were in the war and had been shot at," Kurland said. "Some of them had been in Iwo Jima and Italy, and these were not boys. These were guys that didn't rattle. These were men playing a boy's game."

Kurland scored 20 points in the first-round game as A&M overpowered Baylor, 44-29. He followed that with a 29-point effort as the Aggies scored an easy 52-35 victory over California. There was no denying that it would take an outstanding performance if anybody was to defeat Oklahoma A&M in the championship game.

New Yorkers were denied a replay of the 1945 title-game matchup when New York University fell to North Carolina, 57-49, in a first-round game. The Tar Heels then dispatched Ohio State in an overtime thriller to reach the finals. North Carolina would pin its hopes for an upset of A&M on the shooting of forward John Dillon and the post play of a skinny, talkative, 27-year-old former serviceman named Horace (Bones) McKinney.

With the 6-6 McKinney playing tough defense on Kurland and Dillon throwing in hook shots, the Tar Heels almost scratched Iba's masterpiece. McKinney managed only five points before fouling out early in the second half, and Kurland subsequently took control of the game. Still, it came down to a frantic final moment, when the Aggies, ahead 41-40, had to inbound the ball against the pressing Carolina defense. A&M was successful and scored to claim a second championship, 43-40.

Kurland finished the championship game with 23 points and was given the tournament's Most Outstanding Player Award for the second consecutive year. Not bad for a self-proclaimed "freak" who had listened to his coach tell him three years earlier that he wasn't sure if he could play college-level

basketball. Bob Kurland had traveled a long, tough road to success and the respect he earned along the way was punctuated by the numerous professional offers that came his way after graduation.

Kurland turned down those offers, choosing instead to go to work for Phillips Petroleum while playing for the company's Amateur Athletic Union team. He also represented the United States on the 1948 and '52 Olympic teams. Mikan went on to star in the National Basketball Association, leading the Minneapolis Lakers to five titles in six years in a career that earned him election to the Naismith Memorial Basketball Hall of Fame.

Asked how his Aggies would fare in the modern version of the NCAA Tournament, Kurland said, "I think that they wouldn't get past the first round. The reason is that the game has changed so much. Today you have men my size who at 11 or 12 years of age go into programs that discipline them for the next seven years. We didn't have a weight room. When the semester was over, I got back on the bus, went back to St. Louis, and started looking for a job. I didn't pick up a basketball until the next September. We were not physically prepared.

"But I'll say this. From the standpoint of the mechanics of the game, we executed, lost the ball fewer times, had a better percentage of shooting than many of the teams do today. If I take pride in anything, it is first that I have great admiration for men like Henry Iba and Ray Meyer (former DePaul coach), who were brave enough to take odd people or strange giants like myself and had the courage to put their careers on the line in trying to teach us how to play. You can't measure our performance to today's performance or tomorrow's performance. That's foolish.

"But the other thing I take pride in is that we opened the door for the big man and caused people to think."

TWENTY THREE

The Phi Slama Jamas

HOUSTON

1982-83

Phi Slama Jama.

The name alone immediately calls to mind the dunk-dealing fraternity of flight on the University of Houston campus, rushing toward the Final Four with acrobatic slams and atomic jams.

The 1982-83 Houston Cougars took that identity to heart and made it their mission. "We figure the team with the most dunks will win," one Cougar explained. Theirs were the stuffs of which legends are made.

Certainly, Houston sportswriter Thomas Bonk hit upon something when he christened the Cougars basketball's first dunking fraternity after watching them indulge in a routine jamarama blowout. The name was manifest of the tremendous athleticism of the Houston players and the style of Coach Guy Lewis, who was so enamored of the dunk that he made it a part of the team's statistics.

Yet, perhaps unfairly, the Phi Slama Jama tag suggests the Cougars trafficked solely in run-and-gun playground theatrics. Stuff it, the Phi Slams would say. While they weren't a perfect team, the Cougars definitely were a balanced team. They were fierce defensively. Positively overwhelming offensively. And determined enough to overcome gaps of inexperience. The imperfections, for the most part, were circumstantial, but the talent and chemistry were very real.

The chink most talked about was the inexperience at point guard. The Cougars had reached the Final Four in 1982 behind the brilliant play of junior point man Rob Williams, their leader in scoring and assists in each of his three seasons. But after a 68-63 loss to eventual NCAA champion North Carolina in the national semifinals, Williams declared hardship status and turned pro.

"There's no doubt in my mind," Lewis contends, "that if Rob Williams had stayed in school, no one would have stopped us the next year."

The turn of events left Lewis scrambling to find a point guard that fall of 1982. He tried junior-college transfer Derek Giles, sophomore Eric Dickens and freshman Alvin Franklin, the No. 4 man on the depth chart. Yet after Houston demolished his Lamar team in November, Cardinal Coach Pat Foster was convinced the Cougars "could win with a nun at point guard." It made for a nice quote, but Guy Lewis knew that few teams had ever won a championship without a proven ballhandler and floor leader.

Fortunately for Houston, Franklin was a determined worker. A shooting guard in high school, he made steady progress learning the point as a backup through midseason. At that point, Lewis decided he could wait no longer. Franklin broke in as a starter on January 17 at home against Texas Tech but played only 15 minutes. Yet the following game, against undefeated Arkansas on national cable television, Franklin was in the starting lineup.

With the Razorbacks sporting a pair of high-pressure guards in Darrell Walker and Alvin Robertson, Lewis knew the game would be a major test for the freshman. When Arkansas opened with the press, Franklin broke it—and scored. His confidence set, he finished with 10 points and three assists, and the Cougars won by 15.

Through the rest of the season, Franklin made

few mistakes. He would commit only 25 turnovers in 30 games, including just five in five NCAA Tournament contests. Even so, one of the most telling statistics for Houston was that sixth-man Reid Gettys, a 6-foot-7 sophomore guard, led the team in assists. To his credit, Gettys was an outstanding passer, good enough to set the Cougars' all-time assist record. "He gets the ball where we want it—to the post, to the studs," Lewis said.

But in the clutch moments of the season, the Cougars lacked the backcourt leadership of a veteran. That, of course, was no fault of Franklin's. He played far beyond what could be expected of a freshman.

What made this team a force was its strength in the frontcourt. There, the leadership came from two players: senior Larry Micheaux, a 6-9 power forward, and junior Clyde Drexler, a 6-7 small forward. Both were products of Houston's public school system, along with guard Michael Young, Dickens and Gettys.

Drexler was one of the nation's best two-way players, a tremendous leaper whose glissading moves brought him notoriety as "The Glide." Typical of Lewis' teams, Phi Slama Jama employed a variety of presses. Zone presses. Man presses. Drexler figured prominently in all of them.

"He was a super defensive player," Lewis said. "He had great quickness, good hands and great anticipation. He set a team record that year for the most steals in a season, 113, and had 11 in a game against Syracuse."

Drexler was the core of Houston's transition game and is remembered by Lewis as a scorer rather than a pure shooter. "He had always said he could shoot," Lewis joked, "but he never proved it here." Yet Drexler averaged just under 16 points over the season and scored and rebounded in double figures in the same game 45 times over his career. When he swooped toward the rim, he executed the most stylish of dunks, always keeping in mind the Slama Jama objective: "Once we get ahead, we keep putting it to 'em."

Angels of mercy they weren't. Particularly Micheaux, who, in the words of one writer, "was good for one smile a night, and only then in the last minute of a 15-point win."

"Micheaux was a tough, tough guy," Lewis said. "A good leader. No foolishness on the floor. And strong. He was our enforcer. They nicknamed him 'Mr. Mean,' and he liked that."

Micheaux had started at center the previous three seasons but slid back to his natural position at power forward with the emergence of 7-foot sophomore center Akeem Olajuwon. That move allowed Micheaux to "really go wild," he said, "because I know Akeem is back there." And it gave Lewis the option of switching to a double low-post offense on the rare occasions the Cougars played a half-court

Players, coach, fans and even the Cougar mascot were caught up in the Phi Slama Jama craze that swept the Houston campus.

game.

Interestingly, when Ralph Sampson was asked who the better player was, Sam Perkins or Patrick Ewing, he answered: "Neither. That guy Micheaux is."

And Micheaux, according to Lewis, had been a raw recruit who "came to the program with no post moves whatsoever. But he really worked to learn the drop step and spin moves."

Olajuwon struggled to learn those same moves. A native of Lagos, Nigeria, he had played plenty of soccer but little basketball while growing up in Africa, though a stint with the Nigerian national team convinced his family that basketball could help him achieve a college education in the United States.

"An old friend of mine, Christopher Pond, called me and told me about Akeem," Lewis said. "Chris worked for the State Department and coached a Central Africa Republic team, and he had about six or seven schools for Akeem to visit. His first visit was here, and he liked it so much (particularly the Southern climate) he decided to stay."

Olajuwon had received a good education in Africa and spoke English, French and four Nigerian dialects. Basketball, Lewis said, was one of his few deficiencies. "I don't mind telling you, when I first saw him play, I wasn't sure he could do it," he re-called. "He was 6-11. He could run and he could jump. But he knew absolutely nothing about bas-ketball. And he couldn't shoot."

Olajuwon started only six games as a freshman during the 1981-82 season and averaged 8.3 points per game. He remained, in essence, an unpolished reserve who got most of his playing time in practice. He described a typical game experience this way: "I go in, I get my five fouls and I go back to the bench. Coach Lewis keeps yelling at me, 'Akeem, stay on the floor.' Basketball wasn't fun."

The neophyte center entered the 1982-83 season still unsure of his capabilities. Lewis remembered having a good laugh when he heard a TV an-nouncer explain that Olajuwon had learned his post moves by playing soccer in Africa. Soccer cer-tainly helped him develop excellent footwork, but the intricacies of playing the post were another matter.

"We really spent time working with all our post people," Lewis said. "Having played the post myself, I have always emphasized its importance. But after a year of working with Olajuwon, it still wasn't there yet."

On raw talent, Olajuwon managed some big games early in his sophomore season, scoring 30 points against Utah in December and grabbing 22 rebounds against Southern Methodist on January 8, both career-high totals. The turning point, howev-er, came after he totaled two points and one re-bound in a 54-51 victory over Texas Christian on January 12.

"I sarcastically told him he had won the game for us," Lewis said. "I told him he had gotten more publicity and done less than any player in the his-tory of Houston basketball. From that point, he seemed determined to show me. He just became dominating in practice."

Not to mention one of the most feared centers in the nation. Akeem's specialty on offense was, of course, the jam (he topped the Cougar dunk list that

The headmaster of the Cougars' dunking fraternity was Guy Lewis, a vocal advocate of the spectacle of the dunk and coach of five Final Four teams at Houston.

Season Results
1982-83 (31-3)

104	Arizona*	63	86	At Texas A&M	66
106	Lamar*	72	85	At Southern Methodist	68
74	Mississippi State	65	74	Texas Christian	66
78	At Biscayne	59	106	Texas	63
77	Auburn	65	84	At Texas Tech	75
87	At Syracuse	92	86	Rice	52
63	Virginia at Tokyo†	72	74	At Arkansas	66
82	Utah at Tokyo†	57	93	At Baylor	64
93	At Pepperdine	92	75	So. Methodist at Dallas‡	59
112	Pacific	58	62	Texas Christian at Dallas‡	59
84	Texas A&M	61	60	Maryland at Houston§	50
105	Southern Methodist	71	70	Memphis St. at Kan. City§	63
79	Southwestern Louisiana	78	89	Villanova at Kansas City§	71
54	At Texas Christian	51	94	Louisville at Albuquerque§	81
77	At Texas	52	52	N.C. State at Albuquerque§	54
98	Texas Tech	73			
75	Arkansas	60			
76	At Rice	40			
86	Baylor	69			

*Kettle Classic
†Suntory Classic
‡SWC Postseason Classic
§NCAA Tournament

Midway through his sophomore season, center Akeem Olajuwon began harnessing the skills that would fulfill his billing as 'The Dream.'

season with 68 slams), but he also possessed a nifty jump hook he had picked up at a local recreation center. But it was on defense that he made his biggest impact, leading the Cougars in blocked shots and intimidation.

"Houston is a good team," Arkansas Coach Eddie Sutton said, "but Olajuwon makes them a great team. He gives them the one thing they haven't had since Elvin Hayes: the big guy who stands in there and blocks shots."

Olajuwon would finish his sophomore season with a school-record 175 blocks (an average of 5.1 per game) and break the mark the following year with 207 rejections (the number Navy's David Robinson totaled to establish the NCAA standard when the statistic became official in 1986). Most important, with Olajuwon looming near the basket, his Cougar teammates had the confidence to go for steals and play more aggressively on defense. Led by Drexler, Houston would average 11.4 steals per game.

"No question, this is their best defense since Hayes and (Don) Chaney in 1968," Texas A&M Coach Shelby Metcalf said. "It's unbelievable the way Akeem has improved. Elvin played in a 1-3-1 and guarded the baseline. Now they play a 2-3 and Akeem takes care of the middle. You think more of brute force with Olajuwon and more of finesse with Elvin."

Such comparisons were inevitable as Olajuwon took command of his game. And while Lewis still maintains that Hayes was the superior shot-blocker, the "Big E" offered a surprising opinion.

"I really couldn't compare with Akeem," he told a reporter, "but I don't know of anyone else who could. As a forward, I got mine coming at an angle from the blind side. Akeem plays right there in the middle of the defense, right under the basket. The shots he blocks are from guys coming directly at him. Those are the hardest in the game.

"I still don't understand how he does it so consistently. He's got the quickest jump of any 7-footer I have ever seen."

The Cougars themselves only gained momentum after back-to-back losses to Syracuse and Virginia in mid-December dropped their record to 5-2. As Franklin gained confidence at the point and Olajuwon found his footing in the post, Phi Slama Jama took on the look of a Final Four team. Most opposing coaches said as much.

Leading the scoring was 6-6 junior guard Michael Young, another Houston native with a gift for shooting. To prevent a constant sag on the Cougars' inside strength, Young polished a deadly 15-foot jumper that led him to double-figure outings in 31 of 34 games and a 17.3-point scoring average.

"I kind of gave him a free hand to shoot it whenever he wanted to," Lewis said. "A great shooter needs to have that confidence. And with his size he

Power forward Larry Micheaux (left), Houston's enforcer, was known to teammates as 'Mr. Mean.' Freshman Alvin Franklin (right) took over Houston's point-guard duties and kept his poise during the Final Four run.

could rebound, too."

Formerly a forward, Young was too physical for most guards to stop, stronger even than Mr. Mean Micheaux. "He shoots through people," noted assistant coach Donnie Schverak. "He's so strong that he gets fouled and doesn't know it."

As the Cougars slammed and jammed their way through the Southwest Conference, their offense made headlines across the country. Lewis was unabashedly tickled by the Phi Slama Jama phenomenon. "I enjoyed it," he said. "I think it added something to our team. I don't think there's a coach in the world who liked the stuff like I did. It's the most exciting part of the game of basketball. You can tell that simply by how the crowd reacts."

Yet, at the same time, Lewis said he was irritated by insinuations that Houston played a lower grade of hoops. "People would write about us," he said, "how all we ever did was throw the ball out on the floor and let them play."

If anything, Lewis had the sense to allow his players to do what they did best, rather than have them fall into formation like soldiers as he shouted out

plays from the bench. The Cougars' victims attested to the fact they were more than a one-dimensional team. The defense disrupted even the best-shooting teams, helping Houston outshoot its opponents by nearly 10 full percentage points, 53.1 percent to 43.4 percent, and outscore them by an average of 17.4 points per game (best among Division I schools).

"You go in the paint on them and they'll mess up your digestive tract," Metcalf said. "Akeem alone can have you passing leather for a week."

Metcalf would know. The Phi Slams routed his Aggies by 23 and 20 points on their way to a perfect sweep through the Southwest Conference schedule. But even as they dismembered one opponent after another, the Cougars never considered themselves untouchable. They were confident, but not careless. Mr. Mean, the lone senior among the starters, saw to that. "I don't stand for no shucking and jiving when I get into the game," he said.

Hardly the attitude of a playground team.

"This is the best team I've ever had at getting ready for people," Lewis acknowledged. "I'm not sure I can coach a frame of mind, but I can dang

Clyde (The Glide) Drexler (left) was one of the best two-way players in college basketball. Houston's top shooter was Michael Young (right) who, at 6-foot-6, could dominate opposing guards.

sure try.

"The one thing about this team is that we very seldom have a bad game. We may have a bad first half or a bad second half, but we don't have bad games."

No one was prepared to dispute that as the Cougars rode into the NCAA Tournament with a 22-game winning streak and the No. 1 ranking in the polls. Maryland Coach Lefty Driesell, however, had an idea about slowing down Houston with a "tease offense" in the Cougars' tourney opener. Simply put, his Terps held the ball.

"A stall," Drexler said, "is the worst thing in the world that can happen to us. But we can deal with it . . . no matter what happens, we can deal with it."

When Maryland went to the locker room at half-time trailing by only a basket, 26-24, Driesell pumped his fist in exultation. Houston answered in the second half with a slowdown of its own and a batch of jumpers from Olajuwon and Young, and Driesell's hopes eventually expired, 60-50.

"I don't blame him at all," Lewis said of Lefty's tactics. "And I don't blame me for a 10-point victory."

Driesell said he wished his players had fouled more (two fouled out, two others had four fouls), given Houston's 14-for-29 mark at the free-throw line (and 62 percent success rate during the season). It was a thought that would occur to other coaches as the tournament progressed.

But for at least one game, Houston's weakness turned out to be its strength. In a 70-63 victory over Memphis State, the Cougars sank 16 of 20 foul shots as Olajuwon and Young again sparked the offense. Akeem the Dream was brilliant, hitting 10 of 14 field-goal attempts; Tiger All-America Keith Lee was not, missing nine of 15.

"We had a little trouble keeping them off the boards," Memphis State Coach Dana Kirk said. "We gave up too many second shots. They are a great rebounding team."

That was painfully apparent to Villanova in the regional championship. The one-two inside punch of Akeem and Mr. Mean combined for 25 rebounds, 50 points and 14 blocks, but it was Villanova's preoccupation with the Cougar backcourt that ultimately led to its undoing. The Wildcats had intended to put Houston's young guards in a dither with a furious press to open the second half. They wound up playing right into Phi Slama's hands—and losing, 89-71.

"Our philosophy," Lewis explained, "is that if you press us, we'll try to stuff it to you at the other end." Which is what they did, passing the ball over the press to set up a series of unstoppable breaks and an insurmountable lead.

"It was a matter of athletic ability," Drexler suggested. "It was talent versus talent, and we overshadowed them."

Overshadowed, yes, but not overwhelmed. That distinction was made explicitly clear in the national semifinals against the second-ranked Louisville Cardinals.

In the rarefied air of Albuquerque, Phi Slama Jama bounded to a new plane on the wing of the most electrifying comeback ever staged in college basketball's big event. Trailing 57-49 in the second half, the Cougars outscored Louisville 21-1 with a 5½-minute dunking exhibition that left the Cardinals dumbstruck and eventually defeated, 94-81.

"At sea level, maybe we'd get beat by 30," Cardinal Coach Denny Crum speculated.

Of Slama Jama's season-high 13 dunks, 11 came in the second half. Three were thrown down by backup Benny Anders, known in the Cougar camp as "Instant Offense," who took over when Micheaux fouled out early in the second half.

"I told them to quit pussyfooting around, to take it to the basket and slam," Lewis said. "I was afraid Tommy Bonk was gonna kick us out of the fraternity."

"The explosiveness of Houston is just incredible," noted one spectator—one Jim Valvano of North Carolina State.

Valvano's Wolfpack had defeated Georgia in the other semifinal game and was riding a crazy voodoo that had begun in the Atlantic Coast Conference Tournament. There, the Wolfpack upset North Carolina and Virginia to gain a berth in the NCAAs with a 20-10 record. The Pack worked a miraculous comeback to defeat Pepperdine in double-overtime in the opening round, edged past Nevada-Las Vegas with a tip-in at the buzzer, blew out Utah, then squeezed by Virginia again with two free throws in the waning moments.

"If we get the opening tip, we won't take a shot till Tuesday morning," Valvano joked in a press conference before the final against Houston.

Instead, the Pack played almost arrogantly in the first half, opening with a dunk and scoring frequently. Down by eight points at halftime, Lewis reminded his players of their credo: The team with the most dunks wins.

His prophesy was fulfilled—by the Wolfpack, that is, which won the dunking derby, 2-1. The decisive stuff decided the game, as well, as Lorenzo Charles slammed home an air ball at the buzzer for a 54-52 N.C. State victory.

The Cougars had looked as if they'd dash off to the championship with a 15-2 flurry to open the second half. But with 10 minutes left, Lewis opted to slow the pace. "I went in it for a couple of minutes trying to rest my team," he explained. "The altitude in Albuquerque left us gasping."

Lewis, meanwhile, held his breath every time a Cougar walked to the free-throw line. He had hoped the spread offense would pull N.C. State out of its tightly packed zone and open up the back door.

Houston's top two reserves were Benny Anders (left), alias 'Instant Offense,' and Reid Gettys (right), the team leader in assists.

That didn't happen. If a Cougar strayed too close, the Pack put him on the line. Houston missed nine of its 19 free-throw opportunities, the last by Franklin on the front end of a one-and-one with 1:05 left and the score tied at 52.

"People said all year that the free throws would hurt us," said Young, who missed all of his four chances. "I have to admit that it hurt us in the end."

Olajuwon did little wrong and was named the Final Four's Outstanding Player, totaling 41 points, 40 rebounds and 19 blocks in the two games.

Years later, the loss still plays on the minds of Houston fans. "I run into people all the time, I'm talking about total strangers, who tell me, 'I almost cried for you in that game.' " Lewis said. "I run into that all over the United States."

No, there is no national championship listed in the record books for the 1982-83 Houston Cougars. Even the next season, with a good part of the dunking fraternity still intact, the Cougars would fall again in the title game, this time to the Georgetown Hoyas. Yet the members of Phi Slama Jama were winners nonetheless, champions of another sort. They never made excuses for playing run-and-gun basketball—fun basketball—and anyone who ever saw them is glad for that.

"This team had so many strong points ... but people still didn't believe in us," said reserve guard David Rose, one of the co-captains. "All season long people tried to put negative things in our minds. . . .

"Well, now we have put some things in their minds."

The towel got a workout as Lewis sweated his way through the 1983 NCAA Tournament.

1983 HOUSTON

Head Coach—Guy Lewis   Final Record—31-3

Player	Pos.	Hgt.	Wgt.	Cl.	G	FG	FGA	Pct.	FT.	FTA	Pct.	Reb.	Pts.	Avg.
Michael Young	F-G	6-6	220	Jr.	34	266	519	.513	56	88	.636	195	588	17.3
Clyde Drexler	F	6-7	210	Jr.	34	236	440	.536	70	95	.737	298	542	15.9
Akeem Olajuwon	C	7-0	240	So.	34	192	314	.611	88	148	.595	388	472	13.9
Larry Micheaux	F	6-9	220	Sr.	34	193	328	.588	82	146	.562	232	468	13.8
Benny Anders	F-G	6-5	188	So.	30	75	150	.500	28	45	.622	48	178	5.9
Alvin Franklin	G	6-2	185	Fr.	30	58	136	.426	28	45	.622	22	144	4.8
David Rose	G	6-3	185	Sr.	31	46	87	.529	18	31	.581	22	110	3.5
Reid Gettys	G	6-7	190	So.	34	46	84	.548	24	34	.706	42	116	3.4
Eric Dickens	G	6-4	170	So.	27	32	84	.381	6	14	.429	10	70	2.6
Derek Giles	G	6-3	175	Jr.	25	14	33	.424	9	19	.474	16	37	1.5
Renaldo Thomas	G	6-4	215	Fr.	13	6	12	.500	6	10	.600	6	18	1.4
Bryan Williams	F	6-7	215	Sr.	23	12	22	.545	3	14	.214	32	27	1.2
David Bunce	C	6-11	225	Sr.	15	6	14	.429	5	7	.714	11	17	1.1
Dan Bunce	C	7-0	235	So.	3	1	2	.500	1	2	.500	4	3	1.0
Gary Orsak	F	6-7	200	So.	11	3	7	.429	4	5	.800	9	10	0.9
Team												78		
Houston					34	1186	2232	.531	428	703	.609	1413	2800	82.4
Opponents					34	883	2037	.433	441	677	.651	1136	2207	64.9

Olajuwon reaches high to block the shot of N.C. State's Lorenzo Charles—the man who dashed Houston's championship dream with a last-second basket in the NCAA final.

TWENTY FOUR

Pirates Put Up Their Dukes

SETON HALL

1952-53

There was nothing pretty about the 1952-53 Seton Hall Pirates, a bruising band of basketball buccaneers who ravaged the college ranks en route to a National Invitation Tournament championship. They featured a multi-talented All-America in 7-foot Walter Dukes, a ballhawk of a guard in Richie Regan and a host of bang-it-out role players —hungry athletes right out of Brooklyn and Jersey who would fight for rebounds like they were $10 bills lying on a sidewalk.

But there also was a sweet side to these Pirates. They had a "honey" of a coach—John David (Honey) Russell—who would lead them, by both word and example, to a 31-2 record and national prestige.

Nobody will ever know for sure whether the Pirates were the best team in college basketball in 1952-53 because they never played Indiana, a 23-3 team that won the NCAA Tournament and finished No. 1 in both major polls.But there's no doubt that they were an experienced, polished group of winners who reflected the intense dedication and well-honed philosophies of their battle-tested coach.

That, of course, was Russell, a basketball junkie in the truest sense. Russell, in fact, was a man for all seasons who worked stints as a professional football player (two seasons with the Chicago Bears), a professional baseball scout (with the Boston and Milwaukee Braves, the Montreal Expos and the Chicago White Sox) and a college basketball coach around his grueling 28-season career as a professional basketball star.

He also moonlighted as an insurance adjuster and served as the first coach in the history of the Boston

Celtics (the team began play in the National Basketball Association in 1946), a two-season job that filled the void between his two stints as Seton Hall coach (1936-43 and 1949-60).

Russell actually was playing professional basketball before his graduation from Brooklyn's Alexander Hamilton High School in 1919. He was known for his toughness and unrelenting defense, attributes he later would work to instill in his players. Though he never was known for his scoring, Russell earned enough respect to be one of the first five players elected to the Naismith Memorial Basketball Hall of Fame.

His toughness and tenacity were well documented by the time Regan arrived at the South Orange, N.J., campus. The youngster received a first-hand sampling when Russell, nearing age 50, would get out on the court and compete against his players in tough practice sessions. He physically intimidated his students while refusing to give quarter.

Regan also recalled a 1953 game against Louisville in which a brawl broke out and a dozen Seton Hall players found themselves facing a horde of angry Cardinal fans.

"Honey was right in the middle of the fight with all of us," Regan said. "In the locker room after the game, we were trembling we were so frightened, because there were 8,000 people in the place and only 12 of us.

"A minute or two later, Honey came walking down. He was all disheveled, but he was cool as a cucumber. He always had his wits about him. He told us, 'Don't worry about this. I've been through hundreds of these things.' "

And he had. With the Cleveland Rosenblums.

Honey Russell was a Hall of Fame-caliber professional player in a long basketball career that also included two stints as Seton Hall coach.

The Rochester Centrals. The Brooklyn Visitations. The Brooklyn-New York Jewels. The Chicago Bruins. Just about anywhere they had played pro basketball in the early days, Russell had mixed it up. At an age when most guys began their retirement, he was still humping it up and down the floor as a player/coach.

"He was a rough, tough, gruff Brooklyn guy, a hard-nosed guy," Regan said. "He was an old two-

fisted pro. Honey could sit down at a bar and drink everybody under the table, but you'd never know he'd had a drop."

During his years as a professional player/coach, Russell found time to coach the Pirates while earning a degree from the university. That was in the late 1930s and early '40s, a span in which his teams compiled six straight winning seasons. His 1939-40, 1940-41 and 1941-42 teams featuring Naismith Hall of Famer Bob Davies finished 19-0, 20-2 and 16-3. But the turmoil of World War II interrupted Russell's coaching tenure at the Hall (the school dropped basketball from 1943-46), and he didn't return until 1949.

After he was replaced in Boston by Alvin (Doggie) Julian in 1948 (he had compiled a 42-64 record with the Celtics), Russell served a brief coaching stint with the club's Schenectady farm team in the Eastern League. It had been a tough year, and Russell moved into the Seton Hall job with a burst of enthusiasm. Even before he set up office on campus, he began using his considerable eye for talent to round up some of the best high school players in the East.

But the pick of the recruiting crop had already been signed, sealed and delivered. Walter Dukes was a big, gangling 7-foot youngster who had been spotted two years earlier playing high school ball in Rochester by Davies, who was then playing professional ball with the Rochester Royals. Dukes was a serious student, concerned that his growing athletic reputation was beginning to take too much of a toll on his studies. That worked to Seton Hall's advantage.

Davies arranged to have Dukes transfer to Seton Hall Prep, where the youngster believed he could better prepare for university life. The one negative to this arrangement was that Prep's high school competition got word of the 7-footer and refused to play if he was in the lineup. So Dukes sat out, spending his last year of high school playing for athletic clubs that, in retrospect, probably gave him a better level of competition.

What Russell saw upon his arrival at Seton Hall was an unrefined basketball player who was athletically gifted beyond his peers. Basketball fundamentals could be taught. Athletic ability couldn't.

"Walter was one of the finest-conditioned athletes I've ever seen," Regan said. "His stamina was unending. He could go a whole game and be hardly breathing when it was over. Our track coach, John Gibson, said Walter, if he wanted to, could have been an Olympic quarter miler."

Dukes did, in fact, run track his freshman year. He ran a 1:58 in the half mile and anchored the Seton Hall mile relay team that set a record in the Penn Relays. "I tried high jumping, too," Dukes told a reporter at the time, "but I kept landing on my back. Besides, the basketball coach didn't think it was a good idea."

Russell discouraged his track pursuits and Dukes readily agreed, preferring instead to concentrate on his pre-law studies while refining his basketball skills. Intelligent and conscientious, Dukes would go on to earn his degree and later become a practicing attorney. His running needs were fulfilled on the basketball court, a result of the fast-break style that Russell brought to Seton Hall.

The always-intense Russell barks instructions to a Seton Hall player during a Pirates game in the mid-1950s.

"Dukes was the perfect center for the up-tempo game," Regan said. "Walter would get the rebound, throw it out and still be the first person down the court on the break."

And there were plenty of rebounds. Long legs would bend, the body would soar high above the rim and long arms would extend and pull loose balls away from shorter opponents. By his sophomore season, Dukes already was a terror on the boards. Two years later, the 1952-53 campaign, he would set an NCAA record by grabbing 734 rebounds (22.2 per game), a mark that still stands.

His offensive game, however, did not come so naturally. But Russell worked diligently with Dukes and he soon began to emerge into an offensive force. Working in low while also displaying a smooth hook shot and a turnaround jumper, the youngster compiled a 26.1 scoring average in his senior campaign.

Dukes was not without his weakness, however. When he began varsity play, his free-throw shooting was atrocious.

"He couldn't shoot a foul to save his soul," Russell told a writer for Sport magazine in 1952. "He'd stand up there and miss and the fans would get on him. And so it would go and it was affecting the rest of his game. He was afraid to step to the foul line, so his way of solving it was to keep from being fouled.

"I tried all sorts of things with him, but none worked. Finally, I brought in (5-4 exhibition performer) Bunny Levitt, who's the best foul-shooter in the world. He's supposed to have the record for

The premier player on Seton Hall's 31-2 NIT championship team was 7-foot center Walter Dukes (left). Dukes was spotted and recruited for the Pirates by Bob Davies (right), a former Seton Hall star who went on to fame in professional basketball.

consecutive fouls—something like 499 in a row. He never misses and he shoots them all the same way—two hands, underhand.

"But Dukes was kind of stubborn and I couldn't sell him on two hands, underhand. Well, Bunny came in and you should have seen the show he put on. He must have dropped in 75 without a miss. That convinced Dukes, so now he's shooting his fouls all the same way, two hands, underhand—and making them.

"That was all he needed to make him the best center in the country."

With Dukes' maneuverability in the post, the fouls came in bunches. During his senior season, Dukes made 317 free throws while shooting 74.6 percent—a clear endorsement for Levitt's teaching ability.

Off the court, Dukes was shy but personable. Around campus he could be seen driving his old Dodge coupe, with the front seat pushed back to where the rear seat should have been to accommodate his long legs. At a glance, it would appear that no one was driving the car, Regan recalled. "He was the invisible driver."

There was nothing invisible about his game, however. To complement this great talent, Russell brought in a dozen freshmen his first season. And although some of them transferred at the end of the year because there wasn't enough playing time to go around, the cream of the crop remained.

The best of the supporting cast was Regan, a playmaker and shooter out of Newark. His offensive forte was the old two-handed set shot, featuring the step fake. Regan was a self-described hotshot until he spent a summer session at Kutsher's, a New York resort in the Catskills that attracted top basketball talent from around the East. That's where he encountered Red Auerbach, who soon would begin his legendary coaching career with the Boston Celtics.

"I was an 18-year-old snot-nosed kid out of Newark," Regan said. "I thought I could beat anybody in the world."

But Auerbach straightened him out and Regan arrived at Seton Hall with a new attitude. He became the perfect guard to run Russell's break and, when it came time to slow things down, he was the kind of player who could put the finishing touches on a victory.

Regan and Dukes provided the senior leadership for a team that also included juniors Harry Brooks, Henry Cooper and Mickey Hannon and sophomores Arnie Ring and Ronnie Nathanic.

Brooks, a 5-10 guard who worked opposite Regan, played his high school ball at Union City, N.J., where he once score 60 points in a game. But the youngster, known to his teammates as "Happy" because of his unsmiling countenance, had problems early adjusting to Russell's break-neck defensive style. When he showed big improvement in 1952-53, he became a starter and finished the season as the team's third-leading scorer at 12.2.

Cooper, a forward, was Seton Hall's defensive specialist. His role was well defined—guard the opposing team's center and allow Dukes to guard a weaker player, thus freeing the big man to better protect the basket. It wasn't a zone, but it was the next best thing.

The addition of Nathanic and Ring in the 1952-53 campaign put the Pirates over the top. Both were 6-3 forwards and both were graduates of the school of hard knocks. They could dish it out as well as take it.

"He (Nathanic) could run and was a great guy on the end of the fast break," Regan said. Nathanic also played good position defense and knew how to rebound.

Ring missed the first half of the season because of academic problems, but returned to provide a big boost during Seton Hall's postseason run. "He could do it all," Regan said. "He had a one-handed set shot, he was a great rebounder and a good defender."

He also was a zoot suiter. Tight pants. The whole works. "He came out of Brooklyn like a hood," Regan said of Ring, who today is a bank vice president in New York. "Today he looks like he just stepped out of Harvard Business School. He was a battler. Whenever the other team had somebody tough, Honey would put Arnie on 'em."

Hannon was a valuable player off the Pirate bench. The 6-2 swingman came to Seton Hall as a multi-talented athlete who could do just about anything on a basketball court. But a pair of knee operations in his first two seasons limited Hannon's playing time and mobility and reduced him to a role player.

Given this cast of characters, Seton Hall's 1952-53 success was not all that surprising. With Dukes and Regan performing their magic, the 1950-51 Pirates had compiled a 24-7 record while battling to the

Season Results
1952-53 (31-2)

84	Arnold College	61	103	Memphis	71
77	At St. Francis (N.Y.)	61	82	Albright	52
79	Loyola (Md.)	67	84	At Villanova	76
69	West Texas St. at N.Y.	46	74	St. Bonaventure at N.Y.	67
97	Kings	51	62	Siena	49
77	Louisville	66	88	At Muhlenberg	75
89	John Carroll	77	83	Villanova	68
77	W. Kentucky at New York	74	52	At Loyola of Chicago	49
67	St. Peter's	66	83	Baldwin-Wallace	75
67	Iona	54	65	At Dayton	70
87	Loyola of Louisiana	60	67	At Louisville	73
75	Wittenberg	60	109	At John Carroll	82
75	LeMoyne	52	79	Niagara at New York*	74
64	At Scranton	57	74	Manhattan at New York*	56
86	Xavier (O.)	78	58	St. John's at New York*	46
69	At Fordham	62			
82	Dayton	74	*NIT		
92	Boston College	71			

Dukes (left) and guard Richie Regan, the one-two punch of Seton Hall's 1952-53 powerhouse.

semifinals of the NIT before losing to eventual champion Brigham Young. The 1951-52 Pirates had finished 25-3 after losing to eventual champion La Salle in the NIT's opening round.

So the foundation had been poured and Russell was working hard to provide chemistry as the new season neared. He drilled his players hard, particularly on defense, while keeping them loose with jokes and tales of his basketball conquests. But there was another side to the likable coach.

"Honey could also give a speech where we were deathly afraid of him," Regan said. "Physically, Honey was a very tough guy. He used to play with us and Honey was a knocker."

He expected the same from his players. His defensive focus was half-court, "mostly nose-to-nose," Regan said. "And if your man got by you, there was the 7-footer behind us to knock his shot down."

Dukes' presence covered a multitude of sins and erased the need for desperate fouls. As a team, the 1952-53 Pirates averaged 15.9 fouls per game, a neat little factor in the days of the hack.

With Dukes leading the way, the Pirates embarked on a trail of destruction that would result in a then NCAA-record 27 straight victories and a final team scoring average of 78.2. The closest call for the No. 1-ranked Pirates came in their eighth game, when unbeaten Western Kentucky rolled to a seven-point halftime lead before finally succumbing, 77-74.

Seton Hall appeared to be headed for a 30-0 regular season as the Pirates left New Jersey for a two-game Western swing that would take them to Dayton and Louisville. They had recorded early-season home victories over both opponents, beating the Flyers by eight points and the Cardinals by 11. But suddenly their best-laid plans went awry.

Dayton, led by Jimmy Paxson, the father of current National Basketball Association stars John and Jim Paxson, put the first dent in Seton Hall's armour. Playing inspired basketball, the Flyers rallied behind Paxson's 23-point effort to record a 70-65 upset. Both Dukes and Regan fouled out with six minutes left, but that wasn't why Seton Hall lost. "They just played a great game against us, no excuses," Regan said.

He wasn't so generous, however, in his praise of Louisville—the team that would hand Seton Hall its second straight loss (73-67) the following night. That's the game that ended in a full-scale donnybrook, which Regan blames on Louisville's roughhouse tactics.

The fight, he said, broke out between Brooks and Al Russak, a Brooklyn kid who played for the Cardinals. Brooks ended up needing 40 stitches in his lip.

"Brooks hit (Cardinal) Corky Cox with an elbow as the game ended," Louisville's Chet Beam told reporters. "I walked over to Brooks to shake hands. I told him, 'The game is over, let's not have any trouble.' I started to walk away, and as I turned I saw a fist coming. I ducked and it grazed me. The next thing I knew, Chuck Noble charged at Brooks and knocked him to the floor. Then everybody rushed out on the floor."

Brooks later acknowledged taking the shot at Beam, but said he did so only after Russak swung at him. As authorities were restoring order, a fan hit Hannon, knocking him cold. He and Brooks were treated at a local hospital.

Russell laid the blame on the two officials whom, he said, could have avoided the incident. "They let the game get out of hand in the first half," he said. "The Louisville players were tackling, tripping and throwing elbows at us all through the game."

That late-season double whammy dropped the Pirates out of the top spot in the polls and probably

Other key contributors to the Pirates' NIT title run were (left to right) Henry Cooper, Ronnie Nathanic, Harry Brooks, Mickey Hannon and Arnie Ring.

1953 SETON HALL

Head Coach—John (Honey) Russell   Final Record—31-2

Player	Pos.	Hgt.	Wgt.	Cl.	G	FG	FGA	Pct.	FT.	FTA	Pct.	Reb.	Pts.	Avg.
Walter Dukes	C	6-11	220	Sr.	33	272	574	.474	317	425	.746	734	861	26.1
Richie Regan	G	6-2	190	Sr.	33	193	469	.412	83	122	.680	155	469	14.2
Harry Brooks	G-F	5-10	175	Jr.	32	139	290	.479	113	146	.774	122	391	12.2
Arnie Ring	F	6-3	195	So.	13	44	89	.494	29	52	.558	118	117	9.0
Ronnie Nathanic	F	6-3	185	So.	33	111	222	.500	50	88	.568	116	272	8.2
Henry Cooper	F-G	6-2	197	Jr.	32	27	75	.360	86	110	.782	106	140	4.4
Bill Hammersley	F-G	6-5	215	Sr.	10	16	45	.356	9	19	.474	23	41	4.1
Mickey Hannon	G-F	6-2	190	Jr.	31	45	127	.354	10	18	.556	48	100	3.2
Charles Travers	G-F	5-10	165	So.	18	17	41	.415	17	23	.739	23	51	2.8
Joe O'Hare	G-F	5-10	165	Sr.	21	16	49	.327	12	21	.571	13	44	2.1
Ronnie Marra	G-F	....	...	...	15	9	21	.429	6	13	.462	6	24	1.6
Dick Brownley	F-G	6-3	190	Sr.	10	3	6	.500	9	19	.474	8	15	1.5
Jack Milani	C	6-6	195	Jr.	12	8	18	.444	1	4	.250	6	17	1.4
Hank Bockrath	F-G	6-4	190	Jr.	16	6	24	.250	5	15	.333	17	17	1.1
Bill Loeffler	C-F	6-7	185	So.	6	3	4	.750	0	0	.000	2	6	1.0
Gus Eppinger	F-G	...	...	...	7	3	6	.500	0	0	.000	8	6	0.9
Lee Straub	G-F	...	...	...	9	2	7	.286	3	7	.429	2	7	0.8
Cappy Trowbridge	F-C	6-5	205	...	11	2	8	.250	0	0	.000	8	4	0.4
Team												191		
Totals					33	916	2075	.441	750	1082	.693	1706	2582	78.2
Opponents					33	818	2619	.312	503	811	.620	1139	2139	64.8

This future star is taken aback by the size and reach of Dukes, one of basketball's early 7-footers. The basket in the photo is only 8-foot tall.

cost them a final No. 1 ranking. They recovered nicely, however, against John Carroll in their season finale (109-82) and began peparation for NIT play. The Associated Press ranked the Pirates No. 2 in its final poll, United Press International No. 4. Both polls were finalized before tournament play.

Ironically, the Pirates could have accepted an at-large bid to the NCAA Tournament, which was growing in stature over the once-dominant NIT. But they voted to turn it down. Russell was still irritated that the NCAA had not extended a bid to his 25-2 team the previous season.

First on the NIT agenda was Niagara, which boasted such stars as Eddie Fleming, Larry Costello and Charlie Hoxie. Costello and Fleming went on to careers in professional basketball, and Costello later coached the Milwaukee Bucks to the 1971 NBA championship.

Niagara gave Seton Hall its toughest test of the tournament. The game went down to the wire before the Pirates could seal their 79-74 victory. The game was decided on Seton Hall's late free-throw shooting.

Two nights later, the Pirates were matched against Manhattan College, the second of three New York-based schools that Seton Hall would face in the tournament. Manhattan managed to stay close through the early going, but Dukes and Co. finally pulled away for a 74-56 victory.

The championship game against St. John's was only a mild test. The Redmen fell, 58-46, as Dukes scored 21 points to seal tournament Most Valuable Player honors.

When Indiana went on to capture the NCAA Tournament with a one-point victory over Kansas, fans were left to wonder which team was actually the best—Indiana or Seton Hall? The ideal close to the season would have been a game against the Hoosiers, Regan said 36 years later.

"I'm sure they felt the same as we did," he said. "They would have liked to play head to head to settle who was the best."

Dukes finished his college career as a consensus All-America. Earlier in the season, a reporter had asked him about playing in the pros.

"I came to college to get an education," Dukes replied. "I may pass up pro ball to go to law school."

He did, in fact, do both, signing a contract with the Harlem Globetrotters, then playing eight seasons in the NBA while still finding time to fit law school into his schedule.

Russell went on to coach Seton Hall for seven more seasons before devoting full time to his baseball scouting career. He died in 1973.

But the legacy he brought to the little Catholic university of South Orange lives on. And the question of what team really *was* No. 1 in 1953 will do likewise.

TWENTY FIVE

The Terrapins Come Up Short

MARYLAND

1973-74

It was college basketball's version of a Texas Death Match. Only this winner-take-all battle was fought in Greensboro, N.C., deep in the heart of Atlantic Coast Conference country. Maryland versus North Carolina State. Goliath versus Goliath.

To say that basketball was thriving in the ACC during the 1973-74 season is a massive understatement. State finished its regular season as the nation's No. 1-ranked team in both major polls, Maryland was only a few notches back and North Carolina, the "weak sister" of the three, was but a few spots below the Terrapins. So, much was at stake when the ACC opened its postseason tournament—the selection process that would determine the conference's one and *only* representative to the NCAA Tournament.

History shows that State passed this survival-of-the-fittest test and went on to claim the national championship. Maryland went home. But it took every ounce of fortitude the Wolfpack could muster to turn back the Terps in the tournament final, a 103-100 overtime thriller that ranks as one of the all-time great games in ACC history. The thought of that near-miss still rings hollow in the hearts of Maryland fans, who fondly remember the 1973-74 Terps as the greatest team in school history, one of the greatest of all-time. It was a team with a dream that never quite materialized.

The dream was created and nurtured by Charles (Lefty) Driesell, who replaced Frank Fellows as coach in 1969 and boldly promised to build Maryland's sagging program into "the UCLA of the East." That statement drew a lot of attention and Driesell's immediate recruiting success, indeed,

seemed to bode well for the future.

It was enough to make victory-starved Terrapin fans believe. As Lefty's recruiting successes mounted, those fans began flocking back to Cole Field House. Basketball games became a "happening" on the College Park campus and the colorful Driesell became something of a hero.

Even as his first two teams struggled to 13-13 and 14-12 records, the excitement continued to build. Each home game would begin in the same pulsating manner with Driesell's courtside entry into the packed arena. The applause would swell until Lefty would look up and thrust his arms skyward, his fingers forming a V-for-victory sign. The crowd would go wild as the Maryland pep band would break out with a stirring rendition of "Hail to the Chief."

And Driesell soon began complementing his theatrics with on-court success. His 1971-72 Terrapins further enhanced visions of grandeur when they won 27 games and captured the National Invitation Tournament championship. When Maryland's 1972-73 season ended with a second-round loss to Providence in the NCAA Tournament, longing eyes were cast toward the 1973-74 campaign, in which the talented and now experienced Terps would make their UCLA-like run at national honors.

Maryland's frontcourt was big, deep and talented. Seniors Tom McMillen, a 6-foot-11 forward, and Len Elmore, a 6-10 center, formed a formidable double-post combination. Both went on to professional careers and later academic distinction, McMillen becoming a Rhodes Scholar and Elmore graduating from Harvard Law School. The other

Colorful Lefty Driesell arrived at College Park in 1969 with the promise that he would turn the Maryland program into 'the UCLA of the East.'

forward spot was filled by a pair of 6-9 alternates—Tom Roy and Owen Brown. Roy also backed up Elmore in the pivot when needed.

Maryland's backcourt featured sophomore John Lucas, a talented playmaker who would go on to a distinguished professional career, and Moe Howard, a hard-working off-guard.

"That was a great, great basketball team," said former N.C. State Coach Norm Sloan.

And the reason it was great was Lefty Driesell, a former encyclopedia salesman who used personality and salesmanship to lure great players to the Maryland campus. Having driven little Davidson College to six 20-victory seasons and four Top 10 rankings in the 1960s, the outspoken, flamboyant and ambitious Driesell was pegged as just the right man to breathe life into a stagnant Maryland program. Athletic department officials recognized those qualities and worked hard to interest him in the Terrapin job.

It just so happened that the Terrapins also were hot on the trail of McMillen, a talented prep star who would average 47.7 points per game the next season as a senior at little Mansfield (Pa.) High. They used McMillen as bait.

While trying to persuade Driesell to take the job, the enterprising Maryland officials arranged a lunch meeting with McMillen's brother Jay, a former Terrapin star (1965-67) who ranked as the school's second all-time leading scorer. The hope was that they could snag two birds with one meal.

"I said we (the Terrapins) would be the UCLA of the East for one reason, to get Tom McMillen," Driesell recalled 20 years later. "Jay McMillen is the one who gave me the idea for that line. When I went to lunch with Jay he said, 'We want you to come here.' He said, 'I really think that Maryland could be the UCLA of the East. They are very similar schools. UCLA is in Los Angeles, which is a very big city, and Maryland is located in Washington, D.C., which is the nation's capital. They're a commuter school. They don't have very many kids living on campus. Maryland's a commuter school.'

"And he said, 'You know, this could be the UCLA of the East.' I told him, 'I'll come here if you'll get your brother to come here.' He said, 'I'll do everything I can, but I can't promise you anything.' Truthfully, that UCLA statement probably helped us."

Driesell took the Maryland job, but the signing of McMillen was anything but automatic. As decision time neared, the three-time high school All-America, one of the most highly recruited prep stars ever, was leaning toward North Carolina. His mother wanted him to go to the University of Virginia, where Bill Gibson, an old family friend, was head coach. And brother Jay and McMillen's father wanted him to become a Terp.

The ensuing tug-of-war brought more than a few

Driesell's biggest recruiting success was 6-foot-11 Tom McMillen, who helped turn the Terrapins into a national power.

Season Results
1973-74 (23-5)

64	At UCLA	65	101	Duke	83
106	Eastern Kentucky	57	88	At Virginia	81
115	Georgetown	83	92	At George Washington	71
78	At San Francisco*	60	91	North Carolina	80
53	Santa Clara at San Fran.*	32	56	At Clemson	54
102	Holy Cross†	75	98	Duquesne	72
58	Boston College†	37	64	At Duke	61
96	At Richmond	60	77	Wake Forest	68
89	Clemson	60	110	Virginia	75
72	At Wake Forest	59	85	Duke at Greensboro, N.C.‡	66
74	At North Carolina State	80	105	N. Carolina at G'boro, N.C.‡	85
112	Fordham	73	100	N.C. St. at Gr., N.C. (OT)‡	103
72	Navy at Baltimore	50		*Cable Car Classic	
86	Canisius	73		†Maryland Invitational	
73	At North Carolina	82		‡ACC Tournament	
80	North Carolina State	86			

Big Len Elmore was an excellent rebounder and an intimidating, shot-blocking center.

tense moments. McMillen recalled one involving North Carolina Coach Dean Smith, who also was hot on the trail of 7-4 high school phenom Tom Burleson. Smith, it seems, had grand illusions of pairing McMillen in the same frontcourt with Burleson and encouraged McMillen to call Burleson and talk it over. When McMillen's father heard the conversation, he threw Smith out of his house.

"There was a little animosity," McMillen said. "Dean took the brunt of that. He is a fabulous college coach and a great guy. But my parents felt Dean was steering their son away against their wishes. And my father liked Lefty."

As it turned out, Driesell didn't get his man until the very last instant, the final day for registration at Maryland. Jay McMillen phoned the coach and told him Tom would be at the campus that afternoon to register. "We had to get him a room real quick because all the basketball rooms were taken," Driesell said. "We had to put him in a football dorm."

Driesell claims now that that was the only time in his 17 seasons at Maryland that he ever beat out North Carolina for a major recruit. Smith suffered a double blow that year when Burleson opted for North Carolina State.

McMillen, now a U.S. Congressman out of Maryland, went on to become the high-scoring, versatile forward that Maryland fans and Driesell had envisioned. He possessed a smooth lefthanded outside shot and a nice hook from in close. His finesse game was a perfect complement to Elmore's rugged inside game.

Elmore had been a star center at New York's Power Memorial Academy, the same school that had produced Lew Alcindor a few years earlier. Elmore did not score a lot in high school, but his rebounding and shot-blocking abilities were excellent. He knew how to play the game. He seriously considered going to Georgetown or to an Ivy League school where he could enhance his academic pursuits, but Driesell ultimately won him over.

"There was a great camaraderie between Len and myself," McMillen said. "I was outside, Len was inside rebounding and blocking shots. We were a great double-post tandem."

Driesell would post up McMillen and tell his guards to get the ball to Elmore when the defense sagged off. And when it didn't, McMillen would shoot and Elmore would be in position for the offensive rebound.

The other major offensive factor was Lucas, the son of a Durham, N.C., high school principal. Lucas' basketball skills were not as refined during his prep days as those of McMillen and he relied mostly on his amazing quickness and keen court sense. He actually was more highly recruited as a tennis player and went on to earn All-America honors with his racket at Maryland. But his first love remained basketball.

When an old friend called Driesell and suggested the Maryland coach sign Lucas, Lefty sent then-assistant George Raveling down to scout the youngster. "George said he was no good," Driesell recalled. But the old friend was persistent, so Lefty sent his other assistant, Joe Harrington, down for a look. Harrington came back with rave reviews. Driesell and the fun-loving Lucas hit it off immediately and the youngster chose Maryland over several other ACC schools.

Despite some obvious limitations—Lucas never learned to shoot a jump shot and he did not possess great leaping ability—he became an immediate starter in 1972-73, his freshman campaign. He was a beneficiary of the new NCAA ruling that allowed 1972 incoming freshmen to play varsity ball. By his sophomore campaign, Lucas was an excellent passer and defensive player who could generate points, lots of points, with his quickness and deadly one-hand push shot. He also was the team's leader, both on the court and in the locker room.

"Lucas had the flair, class and charisma," McMillen said. "He was our glue player."

Howard, the other starting guard, was a Philadelphia product with a good outside shot and a quick first step. He also was adept at getting out and filling the lane when the Terps ran their fast break.

Jap Trimble and Billy Hahn provided relief help at the guard positions, although Hahn's contributions probably were more noticeable in the locker room. "He was a pepper pot," Driesell said. "He'd cuss guys out in the locker room if they weren't doing well."

On offense, Maryland often ran a double post featuring the two big men. But they also ran a "special" with McMillen and Lucas stacked on one side, and a free-lance play where Driesell would allow Lucas to work his one-on-one magic. That often resulted in two points for the 6-4 guard or an easy basket for one of his teammates under the hoop.

On defense, the Terps played a half-court man-to-man, and they played it tight. Driesell disdained zones and he had shot-blocking wizard Elmore ready in the middle when opposing players would drive the lane. Roy, Brown and McMillen were all good at boxing out and rebounding, so there were few holes fundamentally.

"We were a good defensive team, played great team defense," Driesell said. "We were physical inside and quick at the guards."

The team's one major shortcoming was its lack of an athletic middle-sized player who could match up defensively against North Carolina State's David Thompson. The Wolfpack's 6-4 forward possessed tremendous quickness and leaping ability that allowed him to run circles around Maryland's big frontcourt.

Driesell thought he had solved his problem in 1973 when he came close to signing Adrian Dantley,

McMillen was a good outside shooter who could move inside when necessary.

then a big high school star at DeMatha in a Maryland suburb of Washington. But Dantley decided to attend Notre Dame, leaving Maryland to enter the season with that spot unfilled.

"The secret was Adrian Dantley," Driesell said. "He could have guarded David Thompson. He was more his size. We were guarding Thompson with taller players and that gave us a match-up problem. We probably over-recruited Adrian because we wanted him so bad."

The Terrapins' championship resolve was tested early in the 1973-74 campaign. As fate would have it, Maryland was scheduled to open its season in Los Angeles. UCLA East vs. UCLA West. As the Terps made the long flight to the West Coast, there was plenty of time to contemplate the unenviable task that lay before them. UCLA, winner of the last *seven* national championships, was riding a 75-game winning streak. Bruins center Bill Walton was the most dominating big man in college basketball. John Wooden was the sport's best coach. Pauley Pavilion was a virtual snakepit for opposing teams.

The timing couldn't have been worse for McMillen, whose father was extremely ill (he would die less than a month later, just a few days after learning of his son's selection as a Rhodes Scholar). It was the first of two West Coast road trips in December, "a tough month for a college kid," McMillen recalled.

The Terps surprised UCLA that day—and maybe even themselves. They jumped to a good first-half lead, only to watch the Bruins pull close late. At the end, UCLA took a 65-64 lead and had the ball. The Terps fouled UCLA's Richard Washington with seconds left, and he missed the free throw. Suddenly, Maryland had a chance to end the Bruin streak.

The Terps ran their "special," with Lucas and McMillen on one side. Lucas controlled the ball and McMillen broke open in close. But the Bruins double-teamed Lucas in the corner and he couldn't make the pass. He tried a desperation shot but had the ball stripped away, leaving Maryland a point short of a major upset.

"It was unfortunate," McMillen recalled. "We got bottled up in the corner. Walton was a great player, and they were very good. But I think we could have won it, had we played on a neutral court. They were surprised, I think. They didn't know how good we were."

Some coaches might have feared losing a big game like that to open the season. But not Driesell. "I think it helped us," he said. "It was a great game for us and a big confidence builder."

That appeared to be the case as the Terps rolled past their next nine opponents (nobody came closer than 13 points) before the first of three meetings with powerful N.C. State. The Wolfpack, featuring Burleson and Thompson, had gone undefeated in 1972-73 and had defeated Maryland in the cham-

pionship game of the ACC Tournament. But because N.C. State was on probation for recruiting violations, Maryland, as the tournament runnerup, was awarded the conference's NCAA Tournament berth.

The Wolfpack, believing that it could have won a national title the previous season, was hungry. It didn't help that State had been humbled by UCLA on a neutral floor in the third game of the season. When Maryland arrived in Raleigh, emotions were high and the Wolfpack rode that incentive to an 80-74 victory.

The Terps posted three more victories before traveling to Durham for a game against North Carolina. The Tar Heels pounded out an 82-73 victory before their home fans and N.C. State followed that up by recording another six-point win over Maryland (86-80) at College Park.

The Terrapins' record now stood at 12-4, all of their losses coming to national powers, three on the opponents' home court. A nine-game winning streak, which included a 91-80 home victory over the Tar Heels, closed out the regular season and Maryland entered the conference tournament with a 21-4 ledger and high hopes.

North Carolina State had two key advantages as the teams prepared to open play in the ACC's postseason classic. First, the Wolfpack, by virtue of its conference championship, had a first-round bye, meaning that it would only have to win games on consecutive nights to win the title. The other finalist would have to win three straight days. Second, the event was to be played in Greensboro, giving N.C. State and the Tar Heels a distinct home-crowd advantage.

Maryland opened tournament play against Duke and literally blew the Blue Devils away, 85-65. But their second-round path was blocked by North Carolina. The Tar Heels, featuring Walter Davis, Bobby Jones, Mitch Kupchak and Tommy LaGarde, were in much the same predicament as the Terps. They had lost only four games, three to N.C. State and one to Maryland.

A large Carolina Blue cheering section wouldn't make any difference on this day. The Terps came out with fire in their eyes and opened up an early lead. When the final buzzer sounded, Maryland owned a 105-85 victory and a spot in the tournament finals.

Like Maryland, the Wolfpack had no trouble advancing, thrashing Virginia, 87-66, in the other semifinal match. N.C. State, better rested and hungry after its 1972-73 probationary snub, was ready to defend its ACC Tournament championship and make a run at a bigger prize.

But Maryland would have something to say about that, and the Terps looked unbeatable in a remarkable first half that produced a 55-50 lead. They shot 63.4 percent, committed only four turn-

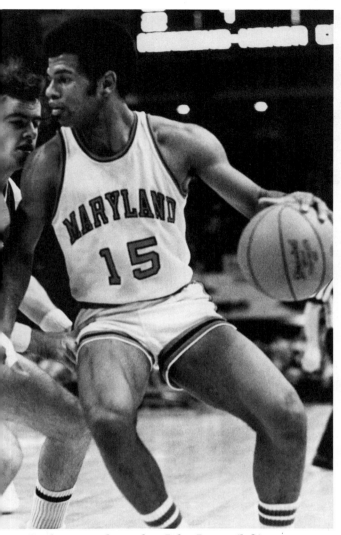
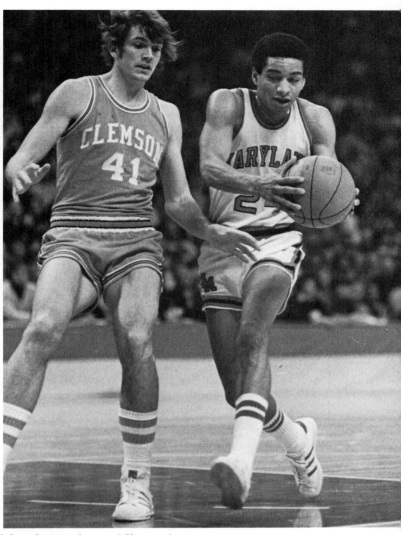

Sophomore playmaker John Lucas (left) was a super-quick point producer. Off-guard Moe Howard (right) had a quick first step and was able to fill the open lane on Maryland's fast break.

1974 MARYLAND

Head Coach—Charles (Lefty) Driesell   Final Record—23-5

Player	Pos.	Hgt.	Wgt.	Cl.	G	FG	FGA	Pct.	FT.	FTA	Pct.	Reb.	Pts.	Avg.
John Lucas	G	6-4	175	So.	28	253	495	.511	58	77	.753	82	564	20.1
Tom McMillen	F	6-11	215	Sr.	27	214	404	.530	96	126	.762	269	524	19.4
Len Elmore	C	6-9	230	Sr.	28	170	324	.525	69	91	.758	412	409	14.6
Maurice Howard	G	6-2	170	So.	26	136	246	.553	44	56	.786	81	316	12.2
Wilson Washington	C	6-8	205	Fr.	1	5	9	.556	0	2	.000	8	10	10.0
Owen Brown	F	6-9	205	Jr.	28	99	207	.478	37	55	.673	142	235	8.4
Jap Trimble	G	6-3	180	Jr.	23	51	111	.459	36	43	.837	50	138	6.0
Tom Roy	C-F	6-9	210	Jr.	28	50	114	.439	27	42	.643	152	127	4.5
Rich Porac	G	6-0	180	Sr.	16	14	32	.438	3	5	.600	6	31	1.9
Billy Hahn	G	5-10	155	Jr.	20	12	23	.522	4	5	.800	9	28	1.4
Stan Swetnam	G	6-3	175	Jr.	12	7	13	.538	2	2	1.000	6	16	1.3
John Boyle	F	6-7	195	So.	13	1	5	.200	0	0	.000	9	2	0.2
Team												89		
Dead Ball												43		
Totals					28	1012	1983	.510	376	504	.746	1358	2400	85.7
Opponents					28	798	1993	.400	335	475	.705	1066	1931	69.0

**McMillen was the presiding hero in 1972 when Maryland captured the National
Invitation Tournament championship.**

overs and played a sticky defense that was causing problems for the Wolfpack. But N.C. State remained close behind the shooting of Burleson and, like the Terps, committed only four turnovers.

Then the Wolfpack went on a 16-6 run in the first six minutes of the second half, grabbing a 66-61 lead. The momentum swung back to Maryland, however, as Lucas and Howard made several key steals and layups. Midway through the half, Maryland owned a 77-72 lead.

It was a real dogfight the rest of the way. The Wolfpack finally caught Maryland at 89-89 with about five minutes remaining and built a 97-93 lead with 2:12 left. But baskets by Roy and Elmore forced another tie and that's the way it stayed through regulation, with Lucas missing a desperation shot that could have won the game.

Maryland owned a 100-99 lead with 2:16 remaining in overtime, but that's when the bottom fell out. Lucas, a 75.3 percent foul shooter for the season, stood at the line for a one-and-one, physically exhausted. He missed and State took the lead on a layup by Phil Spence. Two Monte Towe free throws in the final minute sealed State's victory.

Maryland had shot 61 percent for the game and lost. State hit 55 percent of its shots and Burleson enjoyed an incredible performance, making 18 of 25 field-goal attempts while scoring 38 points and grabbing 13 rebounds. McMillen and Howard both scored 22 points for the Terps, with Lucas and Elmore getting 18 apiece. Thompson scored 29 for the Wolfpack, despite missing 14 of 24 shots.

In terms of intensity and outstanding play, it had been a classic. Sloan expressed compassion for Driesell and went so far as to call the Terps the second-best team in the country.

"His team shot near 60 percent, they scored 100 points, they had few turnovers and they still lost," Sloan said. "Maryland didn't get to go to the NCAA Tournament. They were one of the best teams of the decade, one of the best ever."

Sloan said that he knew Driesell was driving home alone after the game, and that he was worried about the Maryland coach, that he might have a wreck or some kind of trouble. Driesell said that he doesn't remember how he got home afterward, but he does remember getting on the N.C. State bus and wishing Sloan's team good luck the rest of the way.

Driesell said he wasn't upset, simply because he thought his team had played well, the best it could. "They (the Wolfpack) had a bye in the first round," he said. "It was our third game in three days. That was the difference. We had a big lead in the first half, and a big lead at halftime. But David Thompson had a great game. He was a great, great player."

McMillen agreed: "We played a great game. It was very difficult. We were tired, and we had to play in a hostile environment. They weren't Maryland fans in Greensboro. They were State fans."

Elmore, Maryland's inside enforcer, pulls down a rebound during one of the Terps' 1972-73 games.

The biggest thorn in the side of the 1973-74 Terrapins was North Carolina State star David Thompson, who is pictured (above) pulling down a rebound.

In the locker room afterward, the Maryland players were offered a chance to play in the NIT, a tournament they had won two years earlier. The coaches and players unanimously decided to turn down the invitation.

"Looking back on it, I wish we could have gone," Driesell said.

But McMillen, who had averaged 19.4 points for the season (just behind Lucas' 20.1-point average), disagreed. He said he had come to Maryland with the expressed purpose of winning a national championship, the one goal that came up short. McMillen's other goals—winning a Rhode's Scholarship, leading his team in scoring (he did in 1971-72 and 1972-73) and of earning a pre-med degree—all were reached.

"It was expectations," he said of the Maryland team that fell short. "People always said we never reached our expectations. I don't view it as a horrible thing, as some people represent it. It would have been wonderful to have won it. The climax for us was the great game against State in the ACC Tournament. And that's not bad."

The irony of this story is that the NCAA expanded its tournament field to 32 teams (adding seven) prior to the next season, opening its doors to more than one representative from the same conference for the first time. Maryland, now playing without McMillen and Elmore, won two games before falling to Louisville in a regional final, while North Carolina was a second-round loser to Syracuse.

But it was too little, too late for the Terrapins of 1973-74—one of the all-time great teams that could finish no better than second in its conference.